**BTEC** Nation

# Business

## Book 2

David Dooley

Phil Guy

John Goymer

Catherine Richards

Neil Richards

**www.heinemann.co.uk**
✓ Free online support
✓ Useful weblinks
✓ 24 hour online ordering

**01865 888058**

Heinemann Educational Publishers
Halley Court, Jordan Hill, Oxford OX2 8EJ
Part of Harcourt Education

Heinemann is the registered trademark of
Harcourt Education Limited

© David Dooley, John Goymer, Phil Guy, Cathy Richards, Neil Richards
2006

First published 2006

09 08 07 06
10 9 8 7 6 5 4 3 2 1

British Library Cataloguing in Publication Data is available
from the British Library on request.

10-digit ISBN: 0435 462350
13-digit ISBN: 978 0435 46235 2

Edited by Jan Doorly
Typeset and illustrated by ⟋ Tek-Art, Croydon, Surrey

Original illustrations © Harcourt Education Limited, 2006

Cover design by Peter Stratton
Printed in the UK by Thomson Litho
Cover photo: © Getty Images

**Websites**
Please note that the examples of websites suggested in this book were up
to date at the time of writing. It is essential for tutors to preview each site
before using it to ensure that the URL is still accurate and the content is
appropriate. We suggest that tutors bookmark useful sites and consider
enabling students to access them through the school or college intranet.

# Contents

# Acknowledgements

The authors and publisher would like to thank the following for permission to reproduce copyright material:

123 Publishers Ltd, Unit 36 Harbour's Deck, The New Harbours, Gibraltar, pages 106 and 107
*Amazon.co.uk*, page 116
B&Q Direct (a trading division of B&Q), page 103
Body Shop International plc, page 171
*Fightback.com*, page 120
InternetCamerasDirect, page 101
*Management Today*, Haymarket Publishing, page 59
*Marketing Week*, Centaur Communications, page 59
*Supply Management*, Personnel Publications Ltd, page 59
The Fairtrade Foundation, page 191
UNISON, page 147
*Verticalnet.com*, page 118

Crown copyright material is reproduced under Class License No. C01W0000141 with the permission of the Controller of HMSO and the Queen's Printer in Scotland

Every effort has been made to contact copyright holders of material published in this book. We would be glad to hear from any unacknowledged sources at the first opportunity. Any omissions will be rectified in subsequent printings if notice is given to the publishers.

The authors and publisher would like to thank the following for permission to reproduce photographs:

Adesse Images/Channel Island Pictures/Alamy, page 179
Bicester Village, page 280
Boris Horvat/AFP/Getty Images, page 187
Carphone Warehouse, pages 303, 309
Corbis, pages 192, 195
Gateshead Shopping Centre, page 293
Getty Images/Photodisc, pages 4, 111
GREENPEACE/Shailendra Yashwant , page 172
Harcourt Education/Gareth Boden, page 137
Homer Sykes/Alamy, page 23
James Lange/PYMCA, page 244
London Fire Brigade, page 140
London Stock Exchange, page 169
Max Nash/AFP/Getty Images, page 231
Mike Hill/Alamy, page 272
Network Rail, page 180
Royal Mail, page 142
Sainsbury's, page 33
Selfridges Birmingham, page 220
Susi Paz, page 229
Tesco, page 124
Tibbett & Britten, page 26

# Introduction

The fact that you are reading this book suggests that you are already succeeding on your BTEC National course, so congratulations on getting this far! One of the best aspects of this course is that it offers real breadth to business students. You can choose to do a programme that gives you a sound knowledge in many business areas or you can specialise in those areas in which you are strong or that you would like to pursue in a professional career later.

The units that you find in this book are a range of Specialist Units from the BTEC National Specification. If you are doing the National Diploma then you will need to successfully complete twelve of these during your course, for the National Certificate you will need to complete five and for the National Award you will need to complete two. It is important that you consult with your tutor about the units you are doing to ensure that you complete an appropriate combination of Compulsory and Specialist Units for your chosen course.

Four of these Specialist Units were also covered in the first book in this series, 'BTEC National Business'. For this new book we have tried to select a range of units that you will find both interesting to study and useful in your future career. We very much hope that you find studying these units both stimulating and enjoyable.

## *About this book*

The format of this book is very similar to that of the first book in the series, so you should be familiar with the style. The 8 units covered in the book are:

Unit 10 Final Accounts

Unit 12 Marketing and Research

Unit 14 E-Business and Internet Marketing

Unit 18 Human Resource Management

Unit 26 Business Ethics

Unit 27 Contracts and Legislation

Unit 29 Business and Markets

Unit 33 Effective Retailing

## What's in a unit?

Each chapter contains all the information you should need to achieve a particular unit of your BTEC National course. Close reference has been made to the course specification throughout the book, and key terms are clearly explained.

### *Introduction*

Each chapter begins with an introduction to the unit, breaking it down into the relevant areas that feature in the specification (syllabus). This gives you an overall view of the unit.

### *Thinking Point activities*

There are a number of Thinking Point activities in each unit. These are designed to help you reflect and build on your skills. Completing these exercises should help you to do better in your assessed coursework. Some may involve thinking about what you have read, or discussing issues in small groups. All these thinking activities will help you to broaden your knowledge and improve your abilities in business.

### *Practice Point activities*

Practice Point activities are practical tasks. They may involve producing a poster, writing a letter or working out calculations. They allow you to develop your skills and practise the concepts you are learning.

### *Case studies*

Throughout the book, case studies and 'Real Lives' features have been selected to enable you to keep up to date and aware of what is happening in the business world. These are followed by questions or points to consider, to help you gain a wider understanding of modern business life.

## Outcome activities

Outcome activities relate directly to the unit performance criteria, and are included at the end of each section of each unit. These activities will help you to produce coursework that can be assessed for your BTEC National qualification.

You will need to work with your assessor to select the right outcome activities for you. Each outcome activity has been divided into areas according to whether you are working towards a Pass, Merit or Distinction.

To achieve a Pass in a unit, you will need to complete all the Pass outcome activities in that chapter to a satisfactory standard. There will be different numbers of activities depending on the size and type of each unit you are studying.

To achieve a Merit in a unit, you will need to achieve all the Pass *and* Merit activities. To achieve a Distinction, you will need to achieve all the Pass *and* Merit *and* Distinction activities.

All the outcome activities have been designed to build on your developing skills. The work you will complete at Pass level allows you to show different skills and knowledge. Merit and Distinction work needs you to add more detail and thought, and to make connections between relevant points. You shouldn't need to work with new material at Merit and Distinction level, but you do need to add analysis (explore how and why things happen) and evaluation (examine all the relevant points of view and give a judgement). The Merit and Distinction work should build on the Pass activities, not be done separately.

## Key terms

Within the text, important terms are shown in **bold type**. These are included in the Glossary at the end of the book and in the key terms at the end of each unit, listed in alphabetical order with clear explanations. Use the key terms list at the end of each unit to check that you have understood the important terms for that unit.

## End-of-unit tests

At the end of each chapter a unit test has been provided to help you assess your learning. You may choose to complete the unit test before you start work on the outcome activities, in order to check your understanding.

## Resources

A list of useful resources such as books, magazines, journals and websites is given at the end of each unit. This provides you with the opportunity to do further research and gain deeper understanding of the area you are studying. This is particularly useful if you are aiming for a Merit or Distinction.

## Glossary

At the end of the book is a comprehensive glossary of terms. This contains all the key terms you will need to understand. Many are used in more than one unit, so the Glossary is intended to enable you to access their meanings quickly and easily at any point in your work.

# Using this book

This book can be used in many different ways. You may wish to use it as a classroom-based resource by completing activities in class and sharing your ideas with your fellow students. You may also wish to use it on your own to help you stay focused on your learning.

The activities will help you practise your skills in all the key areas. It is important for you to make maximum use of all the materials you are provided with in order to achieve success in your BTEC National Business course.

We wish you good luck with your course, and hope you enjoy it. Welcome to the world of Advanced Level Business!

**Q** When does someone decide to become an accountant?

**A** When they realise they don't have the charisma to become an undertaker!

Is that your impression of accountants? Dry, dreary and dull? Or maybe you're the sort of person who runs a mile when accounts are mentioned. If I had a pound for every time a student said to me 'I don't like accounts – I've never been good at maths', I'd need an accountant to add up all my pounds!

Accounts and accountants always seem to suffer from a bad press, but much of it is undeserved. First, accounts are a vital function of businesses; without a good accounting system a businessperson would never be able to assess the true performance of the business. Second, students often exaggerate the importance of maths to accounting. If you can add, take away, multiply and divide you can do most of the maths an accountant requires.

So don't be afraid of accounts – they are really not so daunting. When you get your final accounts to balance, be content in the knowledge that such skills will help businesses to measure their success accurately and to expand prudently.

Unit 10 is divided into four main areas:

● 10.1 Profit and loss accounts

● 10.2 Assets, liabilities and balance sheets

● 10.3 Fixed and working capital

● 10.4 Reviewing business performance using ratio analysis.

## *Profit and loss accounts*

'Business without profit is not business any more than a pickle is candy.' So said Charles F. Abbott, the famous American lawyer, and he was right – a business without profit really is no business at all, although the directors of Eurotunnel might wish to argue that point.

*Profit and loss*

One of the fundamental questions for any business to ask is 'How profitable is the business?' Many factors need to be taken into account in determining this. The profit and loss account is the first of the legally required financial statements for a business, and it contains much vital information for the owners or shareholders of the business. In essence the profit and loss account simply calculates the total income for the firm and deducts its expenses to give a total profit figure. It is important that these documents are always prepared using the same layout and conventions, so that a company's performance can be accurately assessed and compared with other businesses.

## Trial balance

If you have previously studied Unit 9: Introduction to Accounting, you will already be familiar with the **trial balance**, but if you are new to this accounting document, read on.

### What is the trial balance?

Before compiling a full set of final accounts, the accountant will wish to check the accuracy of the figures presented by the company's bookkeepers. This is a simple process to understand (although it is somewhat harder to do). The accountant will draw up a document with all the credit entries for the company on one side and the debit entries on the other; as long as they equal each other it is safe to proceed. The trial balance is the act of totalling all the debit balances and all credit balances to confirm that total debits equal total credits. This confirms that the final set of accounts should balance once constructed.

For the purposes of this unit you will not need to construct a trial balance, but you will need to be familiar with them as they are the documents used to prepare final accounts. For this unit we will use the accounts of a sole trader called Jon Anderson who runs a business making wooden toys. Here is Jon's trial balance for the financial year ending 31 March 2006. We will refer to this throughout this unit.

**Jon Anderson**
**Trial balance 31.3.06**

|  | Dr £ | Cr £ |
|---|---|---|
| Capital |  | 65,000 |
| Buildings | 0 |  |
| Equipment | 85,000 |  |
| Motor vehicle | 9,500 |  |
| Opening stock | 1,750 |  |
| Cash | 275 |  |
| Bank overdraft |  | 2,920 |
| Money in bank | 0 |  |
| Bank loan (long term) |  | 28,000 |
| Purchases | 155,250 |  |
| Sales |  | 248,150 |
| Creditors |  | 6,250 |
| Debtors | 3,450 |  |
| Wages | 43,500 |  |
| Drawings | 24,950 |  |
| Purchase returns |  | 1,960 |
| Sales returns | 2,575 |  |
| Non-operating receipts |  | 5,000 |
| Rent and rates | 26,845 |  |
| Advertising | 1,560 |  |
| Sundry expenses | 45 |  |
| Motor expenses | 1,950 |  |
| Telephone and postage | 630 |  |
|  | 357,280 | 357,280 |

**Additional information**

| Closing stock | 2,350 |
|---|---|

Depreciation on straight-line basis

| Equipment | 15% on cost |
|---|---|
| Motor vehicle | 20% on cost |
| Buildings | 0% on cost |

Note that these two figures are the same, therefore the trial balance balances!

## Common entries in a trial balance

Here is an explanation of each of the entries in the trial balance.

| | |
|---|---|
| **Capital** | Money put into the business to get it started or to buy equipment. |
| **Capital items purchased** | The original values of capital items (also known as the **fixed assets** of the firm) bought for the business. In Jon's case this includes equipment and a motor vehicle, but it could include buildings if these were owned by the firm. |
| **Opening stock** | The value of stocks of finished products, work in progress (partially completed products) and raw materials held in the business at the start of the year. |
| **Cash** | Cash held on company premises. |
| **Bank overdraft** | Money owed by the firm to the bank. An overdraft occurs when the firm draws more money out of its account than it has available. |
| **Money in bank** | Money held in a bank account. |
| **Long-term bank loans** | Loans that do not need to be repaid in the next 12 months. |
| **Purchases** | For a manufacturing company this is the value of raw materials purchased. For a service business it would be the cost of items bought to sell to customers or used to provide a service to customers. |
| **Sales (or turnover)** | The total amount of money received in sales for the year. |
| **Creditors** | People and organisations who are owed money by the business. These are normally suppliers who have supplied goods or services on credit and who will be paid later. |
| **Debtors** | People and organisations who owe money to the business. These are normally customers who have bought on credit and will pay later. |
| **Wages and salaries** | Paid to employees. |
| **Drawings** | Money drawn out of the business by the owners, in this case Jon, for their own use. |
| **Purchase returns** | Money paid back to the company by suppliers when the firm returns items, for whatever reason. |
| **Sales returns** | Money paid back to customers when they return items, for whatever reason. |
| **Non-operating receipts** | Some businesses may receive extra income other than normal sales income; this could include rent received or commission received. |
| **Expenses** | All businesses have many general expenses; for Jon's business they are rent and rates, advertising, motor expenses, telephone and postage. |
| **Sundry expenses** | A variety of small purchases such as stationery items. |

### Additional information required for drawing up accounts

At the bottom of Jon's trial balance you can see a short table of additional items that will be required for completion of a full set of final accounts. These are closing stock and depreciation, each of which is explained in detail later (see pages 4 and 6).

## Trading account

Trading is the basic process of business. Manufacturing companies, for example, buy in raw materials and use them to make products for sale, whereas retail companies buy in finished goods for sale at a higher price; this is the basis of their trade.

The **trading account** for either of these types of business shows how much profit the firm makes by this basic business process, ignoring other expenses the company may incur. It simply looks at how profitably the firm makes goods or processes them for sale to customers. The profit earned by this process is known as the **gross profit**.

### Components of the trading account

Most of the components we have seen before. These are sales (or turnover), sales returns, opening stock, purchases and purchase returns. But there are two additional items that need explaining:

● **closing stock** is the value of stocks of finished products, work in progress (partially completed products) and raw materials held in the business at the end of the year

● **gross profit** is the difference between the company's total revenue and how much it cost to make the product or buy products in.

*Manufacturing companies buy in raw materials and use them to make products for sale*

## Calculating the gross profit using the trading account

The trading account is always laid out in the same way, and gross profit is calculated using this pattern:

|        | Sales/turnover     |
|--------|--------------------|
| minus  | sales returns      |
| equals | net sales          |
| minus  | cost of goods sold |
| equals | gross profit       |

Cost of goods sold is calculated as follows:

|        | Opening stock      |
|--------|--------------------|
| plus   | purchases          |
| minus  | purchase returns   |
| minus  | closing stock      |
| equals | cost of goods sold |

It is easier to see this in action, so here is the full trading account for Jon's business:

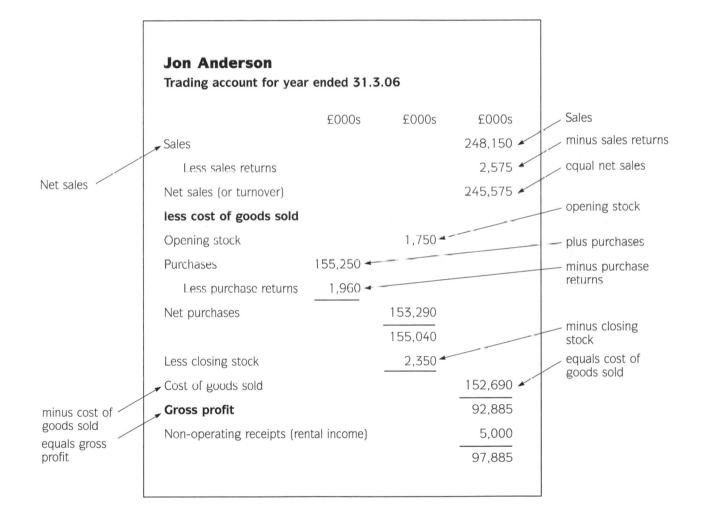

**Jon Anderson**
**Trading account for year ended 31.3.06**

|                                        | £000s   | £000s   | £000s   |
|----------------------------------------|---------|---------|---------|
| Sales                                  |         |         | 248,150 |
| Less sales returns                     |         |         | 2,575   |
| Net sales (or turnover)                |         |         | 245,575 |
| **less cost of goods sold**            |         |         |         |
| Opening stock                          |         | 1,750   |         |
| Purchases                              | 155,250 |         |         |
| Less purchase returns                  | 1,960   |         |         |
| Net purchases                          |         | 153,290 |         |
|                                        |         | 155,040 |         |
| Less closing stock                     |         | 2,350   |         |
| Cost of goods sold                     |         |         | 152,690 |
| **Gross profit**                       |         |         | 92,885  |
| Non-operating receipts (rental income) |         |         | 5,000   |
|                                        |         |         | 97,885  |

Labels (left): Net sales; minus cost of goods sold; equals gross profit.

Labels (right): Sales; minus sales returns; equal net sales; opening stock; plus purchases; minus purchase returns; minus closing stock; equals cost of goods sold.

Study this trading account.

- Look back to the trial balance to see where each of these figures comes from.

- Check all of the calculations to make sure that you can see how the totals are arrived at.

## Practice point

Gurditta Khan runs a hardware shop. Here is his trial balance for the year ended 31 March 2006:

### Gurditta Khan
**Trial balance     31.3.03**

|  | Dr £ | Cr £ |
|---|---|---|
| Capital |  | 45,000 |
| Buildings | 50,000 |  |
| Equipment | 5,000 |  |
| Motor vehicle | 8,000 |  |
| Opening stock | 3,500 |  |
| Cash | 25 |  |
| Bank overdraft |  | 300 |
| Money in bank | 0 |  |
| Bank loan (long term) |  | 10,000 |
| Purchases | 21,630 |  |
| Sales |  | 84,080 |
| Creditors |  | 550 |
| Debtors | 0 |  |
| Wages | 15,000 |  |
| Drawings | 29,575 |  |
| Purchase returns |  | 240 |
| Sales returns | 0 |  |
| Non-operating receipts |  | 0 |
| Rent and rates | 6,050 |  |
| Advertising | 100 |  |
| Sundry expenses | 90 |  |
| Motor expenses | 1,000 |  |
| Telephone and postage | 200 |  |
|  | 140,170 | 140,170 |

**Additional information**

| Closing stock | 3,600 |  |
|---|---|---|

Depreciation on straight-line basis

| Equipment | 20% on cost |
|---|---|
| Motor vehicle | 20% on cost |
| Buildings | 0% on cost |

Using the figures above, prepare the trading account for Gurditta.

## Profit and loss account

Although the trading account shows us what the firm has made from its basic line of business, it does not reveal the true profit of the firm as it does not take into account any of the general expenses of the business. The profit and loss account takes the gross profit of the firm and deducts all the expenses to find the final profit for the year, known as the net profit.

● **Expenses** – Amounts that the firm has had to pay out, such as rent, wages, petrol and many others. Note that drawings (sums that the owner takes from the business for his or her personal use) and the cost of fixed assets are not classed as an expense and do **not** appear in the profit and loss account. They will appear later in the balance sheet.

● **Depreciation** – Most of a firm's capital assets do not retain their value. Motor vehicles, for example, lose value each year. This reduction is known as depreciation. It is important to show this reduction in value in the firm's accounts, otherwise the final accounts will overstate the value of the business. Depreciation is an expense to the firm (even though no money actually changes hands) and so it appears in the profit and loss account. There are two main methods of accounting for depreciation; either may be used.

### Straight-line depreciation

A fixed percentage of the original cost of the asset is taken off each year. This means that the amount of depreciation on a particular asset will be the same each year.

For example, a machine that cost £80,000 to buy could be depreciating by 20% per year on a straight-line basis. The amount per year is:

£80,000 × 20% = £16,000 per year for each of five years.

The number of years used will be based on the firm's estimate of the useful working life of the asset. In the above example the firm must consider that after five years the asset will be valueless and will probably need replacement.

However, most assets will have some value left at the end of their useful lives (known as the residual value of the asset), so the best way to calculate straight-line depreciation is to use the following formula:

$$\frac{\text{Cost of asset} - \text{residual value}}{\text{Number of years of expected useful life}}$$

Using the previous example, if we assumed that after five years the asset would be worth £5,000 to the company, the new calculation would be as follows:

$$\text{Depreciation} = \frac{£80,000 - £5,000}{5}$$

Depreciation = £15,000 each year.

### Reducing balance depreciation

If the firm chooses to use this method a consistent percentage figure is used, but it is applied to the reduced balance each year. Using the same example, a machine costing £80,000 to buy and depreciated by 20% per year, using the reducing balance method the depreciation would be as follows:

Original cost £80,000

Year 1 depreciation (£80,000 × 20%) = £16,000

Value at end of Year 1 (£80,000 – £16,000) = £64,000

In Year 2 it will be as follows:

Value at end of Year 1 £64,000

Year 2 depreciation (£64,000 × 20%) = £12,800

Value at end of Year 2 (£64,000 – £12,800) = £51,200

In Year 3 it will be as follows:

Value at end of Year 2 £51,200

Year 3 depreciation (£51,200 × 20%) = £10,240

Value at end of Year 3 (£51,200 – £10,240) = £40,960

You can see that with this method the amount of depreciation reduces each year.

**Practice point**

Stephanie Howe is a sole trader. She buys a machine worth £200,000 for her business. She expects depreciation on this asset to be 10% per year. Complete the following table showing the balance at the end of each subsequent year using the two different methods:

|  | Straight-line | Reducing balance |
|---|---|---|
| **Initial cost** | £200,000 | £200,000 |
| **Value end Year 1** | | |
| **Value end Year 2** | | |
| **Value end Year 3** | | |
| **Value end Year 4** | | |
| **Value end Year 5** | | |

1 What is the residual value after five years using each of the methods?

2 What do you notice about the rate of depreciation using the two methods?

3 We should ensure that the asset depreciates to the same residual value whichever method is chosen. What does this tell you about:
   - the relative percentage rates required using each method to achieve the same residual value?
   - Stephanie's method of deciding how much to charge for depreciation on this asset?

### Calculating net profit using the profit and loss account

The profit and loss account follows on from the trading account and simply deducts all the firm's expenses from the gross profit. The resulting figure is the net profit.

Continuing the example of Jon Anderson, here is his trading and profit and loss account for the year ending 31 March 2006.

**Jon Anderson**
Profit and loss account for year ended 31.3.06

|  | £000s | £000s | £000s |
|---|---|---|---|
| Sales |  |  | 248,150 |
| Less sales returns |  |  | 2,575 |
| Net sales (or turnover) |  |  | 245,575 |
| **less cost of goods sold** |  |  |  |
| Opening stock |  | 1,750 |  |
| Purchases | 155,250 |  |  |
| Less purchase returns | 1,960 |  |  |
| Net purchases |  | 153,290 |  |
|  |  | 155,040 |  |
| Less closing stock |  | 2,350 |  |
| Cost of goods sold |  |  | 152,690 |
| **Gross profit** |  |  | 92,005 |
| Non-operating receipts (rental income) |  |  | 5,000 |
|  |  |  | 97,885 |
| **Less expenses** |  |  |  |
| Administration |  |  |  |
| Rent and rates |  | 26,845 |  |
| Wages and salaries |  | 43,500 |  |
| Telephone and postage |  | 630 |  |
| Motor expenses |  | 1,950 |  |
| Advertising |  | 1,560 |  |
| Sundry expenses |  | 45 |  |
| Depreciation |  |  |  |
| Buildings |  | 0 |  |
| Equipment |  | 12,750 |  |
| Motor vehicles |  | 1,900 | 89,180 |
| **Net profit** |  |  | 8,705 |

This top section is the trading account (you should notice that this is the same as the one we looked at previously)

Look back at Jon's trial balance to see where each of these expense items comes from

This bottom section is the profit and loss account and it includes all of the expenses of the firm

Each of the expense items comes from the trial balance, except the items for depreciation. Here is how they are calculated.

At the bottom of the trial balance you will see the following details:

**Additional information**

| Closing stock | 2,350 |
|---|---|

Depreciation on straight-line basis

| Equipment | 15% on cost |
|---|---|
| Motor vehicle | 20% on cost |
| Buildings | 0% on cost |

Don't worry about the closing stock item; we will use that later.

Towards the top of the trial balance you will see the following entries, showing the original values of the capital items bought by the firm:

| Buildings | 0 |
|---|---|
| Equipment | 85,000 |
| Motor vehicle | 9,500 |

Depreciation is calculated as follows:
Equipment: £85,000 × 15% = £12,750
Motor vehicle: £9,500 × 20% = £1,900

These are the figures included at the bottom of the profit and loss account.

Go back and check all the figures in the profit and loss account so that you are clear where each of them comes from.

Now practise what you have learned by completing the following two Practice Points. The first is a less complex task, and the second is more challenging.

---

**Practice point**

Sean McGrath has set up a small business buying and selling second-hand CDs and DVDs which he runs in his spare time. Here is his trial balance. Compile trading and profit and loss accounts for Sean.

### Sean McGrath
**Trial balance 31.3.06**

|  | Dr £ | Cr £ |
|---|---|---|
| Capital |  | 5,000 |
| Equipment | 3,700 |  |
| Opening stock | 1,500 |  |
| Cash | 900 |  |
| Purchases | 9,600 |  |
| Sales |  | 21,700 |
| Expenses | 8,000 |  |
| Drawings | 3,000 |  |
|  | 26,700 | 26,700 |

**Additional information**

| Closing stock | 1,750 |
|---|---|
| Depreciation on straight-line basis | |
| Equipment 20% on cost | |

---

**Practice point**

Using the trial balance and trading account that you compiled for Gurditta Khan in the task on page 6, compile his trading and profit and loss account for the year ending 31 March 2006.

---

## Appropriation account

Final accounts for a sole trader do not require an appropriation account. When we are compiling final accounts for a sole trader there is nothing further to do for the profit and loss account, since the net profit is simply available for the owner to use as he or she sees fit.

However, in the case of a partnership or a limited company decisions have to be made about how to distribute the net profit. The appropriation account is the statement of how net profit is distributed to the partners or shareholders.

## Components of a partnership appropriation account

The details of how net profit is to be distributed to each partner will be recorded in the original partnership agreement, drawn up when the partnership commenced. It may contain details about the following methods of distribution.

### Salaries

Salaries for individual partners may be specified, for example, the agreement may state that Partner 1 is entitled to a salary of £10,000 each year and Partner 2 to £15,000 per year. The size of the salaries may represent the amount of contribution each partner makes to the running of the company. Note that salaries to staff will appear in the profit and loss account, but partners' salaries will always appear in the appropriation account.

### Interest on partners' capital

The partnership agreement may also allow for interest to be paid on the capital that each of the partners introduced into the business. The agreement will state the rate of interest that will be paid.

### Share of remaining profits

The agreement will state how remaining profits are to be split between the partners. For example, it may say that they are to be split in the ratio of 40% to Partner 1 and 60% to Partner 2. Thus if the net profit (after salaries and interest) is £30,000, the partners will receive the following amounts:

Partner 1: £30,000 × 40% = £12,000
Partner 2: £30,000 × 60% = £18,000.

Here is an example of the appropriation account

for a partnership between Singh and Smith. In this case the partnership agreement allows for salaries of £4,000 for Singh and £1,000 for Smith, and for remaining profits to be split 65:35 in favour of Singh.

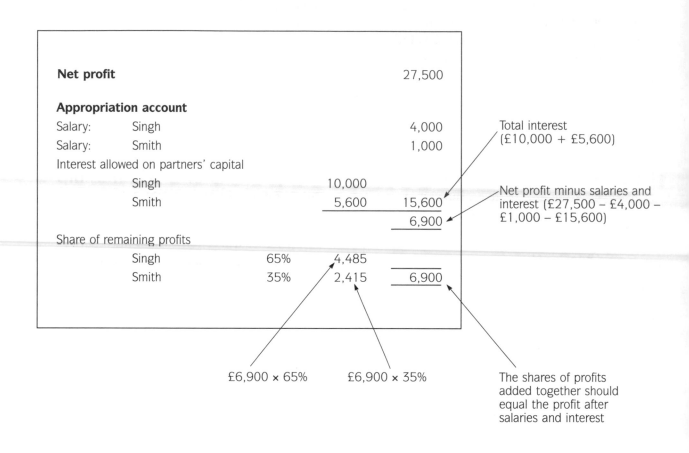

| Net profit | | | 27,500 |
|---|---|---|---|
| **Appropriation account** | | | |
| Salary: Singh | | | 4,000 |
| Salary: Smith | | | 1,000 |
| Interest allowed on partners' capital | | | |
| Singh | | 10,000 | |
| Smith | | 5,600 | 15,600 |
| | | | 6,900 |
| Share of remaining profits | | | |
| Singh | 65% | 4,485 | |
| Smith | 35% | 2,415 | 6,900 |

Total interest (£10,000 + £5,600)

Net profit minus salaries and interest (£27,500 − £4,000 − £1,000 − £15,600)

£6,900 × 65%  £6,900 × 35%

The shares of profits added together should equal the profit after salaries and interest

Page and Plant are a partnership. Their net profit this year was £100,000. Capital introduced by each partner is as follows:

Page: £50,000
Plant: £40,000

Interest at 8% is allowable on this capital.

Remaining profits are to be shared as Page 40% and Plant 60%.

Page is entitled to a salary of £15,000 and Plant £25,000.

Draw up the appropriation account for Page and Plant.

## Components of a limited company appropriation account

For a limited company the appropriation account is constructed differently and may include the following entries.

### Corporation tax

**Corporation tax** is a tax on business profits and is accounted for first in the appropriation account.

### Interim dividends

**Interim dividends** are dividends that are paid part-way through a company's financial year before final profits are calculated.

## Proposed dividends

Dividends paid by the company at the end of the financial year, after profits have been calculated, are called **proposed dividends**.

## Reserves

Limited companies will often retain some profit in the company rather than distribute it all to shareholders; retained profits are called **reserves**. Various reserves accounts may be set up for different purposes. For example, some reserves may be put on one side to pay for the replacement of a capital asset, such as a machine, at a later date.

## Retained profit

Any profit left over after transfers to reserves is also retained for future use, and is called **retained profit**.

Here is an example of an appropriation account for a limited company. Makem Limited is a manufacturing company:

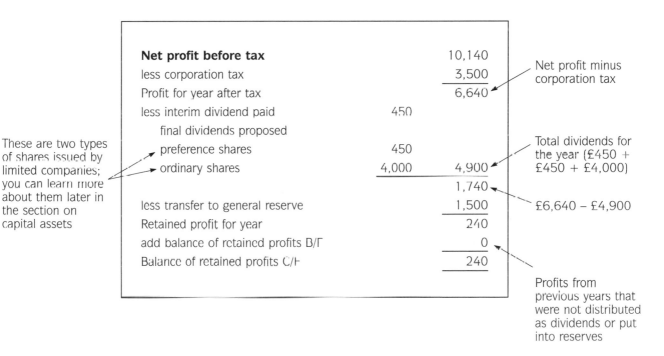

| | | |
|---|---|---|
| **Net profit before tax** | | 10,140 |
| less corporation tax | | 3,500 |
| Profit for year after tax | | 6,640 |
| less interim dividend paid | 450 | |
| final dividends proposed | | |
| preference shares | 450 | |
| ordinary shares | 4,000 | 4,900 |
| | | 1,740 |
| less transfer to general reserve | | 1,500 |
| Retained profit for year | | 240 |
| add balance of retained profits B/F | | 0 |
| Balance of retained profits C/F | | 240 |

*Net profit minus corporation tax*

*These are two types of shares issued by limited companies; you can learn more about them later in the section on capital assets*

*Total dividends for the year (£450 + £450 + £4,000)*

*£6,640 – £4,900*

*Profits from previous years that were not distributed as dividends or put into reserves*

---

### Outcome activity 10.1

For the purposes of this assignment, assume you are working as an accounts clerk for a firm of accountants known as Mason, Wright and Partners.

#### Pass

You have been approached today by one of your clients, Mr Kong Han, who has a shop selling collector's items of science fiction memorabilia. You have the following trial balance that has been prepared by one of your assistants. Your tasks are to do the following.

○ Calculate the depreciation of the fixed assets of Mr Han's business, on a straight-line basis at the rate of 15% per year on equipment and 20% per year on the motor vehicle.

○ Prepare the trading and profit and loss accounts for Mr Han for the year ending 31 March 2006.

## Kong Han
### Trial balance    31.3.06

| | Dr £ | Cr £ |
|---|---|---|
| Capital | | 16,000 |
| Equipment | 15,500 | |
| Motor vehicle | 3,000 | |
| Opening stock | 7,700 | |
| Cash | 250 | |
| Money in bank | 560 | |
| Bank loan (long term) | | 10,000 |
| Purchases | 35,700 | |
| Sales | | 63,850 |
| Creditors | | 1,610 |
| Debtors | 150 | |
| Wages | 3,920 | |
| Drawings | 15,000 | |
| Sales returns | 250 | |
| Rent and rates | 6,000 | |
| Advertising | 1,500 | |
| Sundry expenses | 240 | |
| Motor expenses | 1,500 | |
| Telephone and postage | 190 | |
| | 91,460 | 91,460 |

### Additional information

| | |
|---|---|
| Closing stock | 7,400 |
| Depreciation on straight-line basis | |
| Equipment   15%  on cost | |
| Motor vehicle   20%  on cost | |

One of your assistants, Greta Harman, has recently started working on final accounts for limited companies and consequently she has never seen appropriation accounts before. You decide that you will prepare a booklet that will help trainee accountants understand the workings of limited company accounts, including appropriation accounts. The booklet will be in three sections and the first part of the booklet will simply describe the components of a limited company's trading, profit and loss account and show how such a set of accounts is laid out. Produce the first section of your booklet.

### Merit

Continuing the booklet you began for the previous task, explain the components of a limited company's trading, profit and loss account. You should explain in detail what each of the entries means.

While producing this section of your booklet, it will be helpful to refer to a set of final accounts for a limited company so that you can explain and give examples. To do this you can either use a published set of final accounts from a company, or alternatively use the following trading, profit and loss account for Waters and Gilmour Limited, a firm manufacturing components for the motor industry.

## Waters and Gilmour Limited
**Profit and loss account for year ended 31.3.06**

| | £000s | £000s | £000s |
|---|---|---|---|
| Sales | | | 453,000 |
| Less sales returns | | | 10,000 |
| Net sales (or turnover) | | | 443,000 |
| **less cost of goods sold** | | | |
| Opening stock | | 30,500 | |
| Purchases | 271,000 | | |
| Less purchase returns | 3,000 | | |
| Net purchases | | 268,000 | |
| | | 298,500 | |
| Less closing stock | | 30,000 | |
| Cost of goods sold | | | 268,500 |
| **Gross profit** | | | 174,500 |
| Rent received | | | 2,500 |
| | | | 177,000 |
| **Less expenses** | | | |
| Administration | | | |
| Rent and rates | | 34,000 | |
| Wages and salaries | | 79,000 | |
| Insurance | | 3,500 | |
| Motor expenses | | 3,500 | |
| Debenture interest | | 6,000 | |
| Depreciation | | | |
| Buildings | | 0 | |
| Equipment | | 5,000 | |
| Motor vehicles | | 4,000 | 135,000 |
| **Net profit before tax** | | | 42,000 |
| Less corporation tax | | | 20,000 |
| Profit for year after tax | | | 22,000 |
| less interim dividend paid | | 0 | |
| final dividends proposed | | | |
| preference shares | | 0 | |
| ordinary shares | | 10,000 | 10,000 |
| | | | 12,000 |
| Less transfer to general reserve | | | 3,000 |
| Retained profit for year | | | 9,000 |
| Add balance of retained profits B/F | | | 23,000 |
| Balance of retained profits C/F | | | 32,000 |

## Distinction
Complete your booklet by analysing the appropriation account of the organisation that you used in the previous question.

# Assets, liabilities and balance sheets

The true value or worth of a firm is tied up in many things, such as the things that it has bought, the things it has made, the regular customers it has and even the reputation of the company or its brand.

While the trading and profit and loss account shows the profit that a firm has earned in a particular year, the **balance sheet** shows what the firm is truly worth and what makes up its value.

It starts with a comparison of the items of value within the firm (its **assets**) and the money that it owes (its **liabilities**). The balance sheet is

*The balance between assets and liabilities is vital*

the last document in a set of final accounts and can be defined as an overview of a company's financial position on a particular date, showing the total assets and liabilities of the firm.

## Assets and liabilities

### Fixed assets

The first section on a balance sheet details the fixed assets of the firm. These comprise the capital items of value that the firm has bought and will use for an extended period of time, such as buildings, machinery, equipment and vehicles. These are often referred to as tangible fixed assets (tangible means you can touch them). The fixed assets section of the balance sheet will show the original prices paid for these assets, the amounts by which their value has depreciated, and the net current value of each of them (original price minus depreciation).

Occasionally you will see an item in this section entitled 'goodwill'. This is an example of an intangible fixed asset (intangible means that it is something you cannot touch). Goodwill does not represent an item of value but arises when a new owner pays above the book value of the firm to

compensate the previous owner for the good reputation of the business.

### Current assets

The second section in the balance sheet contains assets that are readily available in the company for paying debts, called **current assets**. This generally includes stocks, debtors, money in the bank and cash held on the premises.

### Current liabilities

The third section in the balance sheet contains amounts that are owed to suppliers or lenders that are due to be repaid fairly shortly (normally within one year). These are known as **current liabilities**. This section will typically contain creditors, bank overdrafts, VAT and loans that are due to be repaid in less than one year. For limited companies, this section may also include corporation tax and dividends.

In the final accounts for a PLC, current liabilities are usually called 'Creditors: amounts falling due within one year'.

### Long-term liabilities

Section 4 of the balance sheet contains those debts that have to be paid for in more than one year's time, such as a mortgage on company property, **debentures** or a long-term bank loan.

In the final accounts for a PLC, **long-term liabilities** are usually called 'Creditors: amounts falling due in more than one year'.

### Financed by

The final section of the balance sheet shows us where the money came from to run the business. In the final accounts for a sole trader this will typically be capital introduced by the owner and retained profits from previous years of trading. This section will also show the amount that the owner has taken from the business for his or her own use, known as drawings.

Note that there is further detail on the contents of the balance sheet in the 'Fixed and working capital' section of this unit, on page 21, and you would do well to read that as well for further explanation of some of the entries in the balance sheets.

You will know if the accounts balance by comparing the net assets figure with the final figure in the 'Financed by' section – if they are the same, the accounts balance. If not, you need to go back and check your working, because something must have gone wrong!

# Balance sheet

## Balance sheet for a sole trader

This follows the example of Jon Anderson, whose business we examined earlier in this unit.

Look back at the trial balance and the trading, profit and loss account for Jon (pages 2 and 8) to refresh your memory. Jon's balance sheet is shown below.

Study this example carefully so that you are sure where each of the entries comes from and how all the calculations are done.

Then practise what you have learned by completing the following two Practice Points. The first is a less complex task, and the second is more challenging.

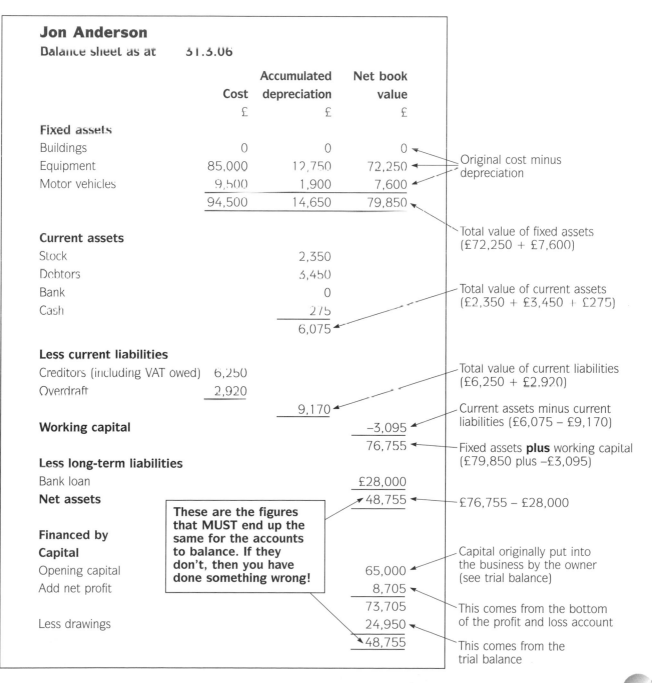

**Jon Anderson**
Balance sheet as at 31.3.06

|  | Cost £ | Accumulated depreciation £ | Net book value £ |
|---|---|---|---|
| **Fixed assets** | | | |
| Buildings | 0 | 0 | 0 |
| Equipment | 85,000 | 12,750 | 72,250 |
| Motor vehicles | 9,500 | 1,900 | 7,600 |
| | 94,500 | 14,650 | 79,850 |
| **Current assets** | | | |
| Stock | | 2,350 | |
| Debtors | | 3,450 | |
| Bank | | 0 | |
| Cash | | 275 | |
| | | 6,075 | |
| **Less current liabilities** | | | |
| Creditors (including VAT owed) | 6,250 | | |
| Overdraft | 2,920 | | |
| | | 9,170 | |
| **Working capital** | | | −3,095 |
| | | | 76,755 |
| **Less long-term liabilities** | | | |
| Bank loan | | | £28,000 |
| **Net assets** | | | 48,755 |
| **Financed by** | | | |
| **Capital** | | | |
| Opening capital | | | 65,000 |
| Add net profit | | | 8,705 |
| | | | 73,705 |
| Less drawings | | | 24,950 |
| | | | 48,755 |

Original cost minus depreciation

Total value of fixed assets (£72,250 + £7,600)

Total value of current assets (£2,350 + £3,450 + £275)

Total value of current liabilities (£6,250 + £2,920)

Current assets minus current liabilities (£6,075 − £9,170)

Fixed assets **plus** working capital (£79,850 plus −£3,095)

£76,755 − £28,000

Capital originally put into the business by the owner (see trial balance)

This comes from the bottom of the profit and loss account

This comes from the trial balance

> These are the figures that MUST end up the same for the accounts to balance. If they don't, then you have done something wrong!

**Practice point**

Using the trial balance and trading and profit and loss account that you compiled for Sean McGrath in the previous section (page 9), compile his balance sheet for the year ending 31 March 2006.

**Practice point**

Using the trial balance and trading and profit and loss account that you compiled for Gurditta Khan in the previous section (page 9) compile his balance sheet for the year ending 31 March 2006.

## Final accounts for a partnership

Partnership balance sheets are constructed slightly differently. Here is the full set of final accounts for Singh and Smith, whom we met briefly on page 10.

**Partnership: Singh & Smith**
**Profit and loss account for year ended 31.3.06**

|  | £000s | £000s | £000s |
|---|---|---|---|
| Sales |  |  | 55,250 |
| Less sales returns |  |  | 3,500 |
| Net sales (or turnover) |  |  | 51,750 |
| **less cost of goods sold** |  |  |  |
| Opening stock |  | 13,500 |  |
| Purchases | 11,000 |  |  |
| Less purchase returns | 500 |  |  |
| Net purchases |  | 10,500 |  |
|  |  | 24,000 |  |
| Less closing stock |  | 13,000 |  |
| Cost of goods sold |  |  | 11,000 |
| **Gross profit** |  |  | 40,750 |
| Non-operating receipts |  |  | 1,000 |
|  |  |  | 41,750 |
| **Less expenses** |  |  |  |
| Administration |  |  |  |
| Rent and rates |  | 3,000 |  |
| Wages |  | 1,750 |  |
| Telephone and postage |  | 100 |  |
| Motor expenses |  | 1,640 |  |
| Advertising |  | 300 |  |
| Sundry expenses |  | 60 |  |
| Depreciation |  |  |  |
| Equipment |  | 6,100 |  |
| Motor vehicles |  | 1,300 | 14,250 |
| **Net profit** |  |  | 27,500 |
| **Appropriation account** |  |  |  |
| Salary: Singh |  |  | 4,000 |
| Salary: Smith |  |  | 1,000 |
| Interest allowed on partners' capital |  |  |  |
| Singh |  | 10,000 |  |
| Smith |  | 5,600 | 15,600 |
|  |  |  | 6,900 |
| Share of remaining profits |  |  |  |
| Singh | 65% | 4,485 |  |
| Smith | 35% | 2,415 | 6,900 |

## Partnership: Singh & Smith
Balance sheet as at 31.3.06

| | Cost £ | Accumulated depreciation £ | Net book value £ |
|---|---|---|---|
| **Fixed assets** | | | |
| Equipment | 72,500 | 6,100 | 66,400 |
| Motor vehicles | 18,100 | 1,300 | 16,800 |
| | 90,600 | 7,400 | 83,200 |
| **Current assets** | | | |
| Stock | | 13,000 | |
| Debtors | | 23,425 | |
| Bank | | 13,585 | |
| Cash | | 2,120 | |
| | | 52,130 | |
| **Less current liabilities** | | | |
| Creditors | 8,300 | | |
| Overdraft | 0 | | |
| | | 8,300 | |
| **Working capital** | | | 43,830 |
| **Net assets** | | | 127,030 |
| **Financed by** | | | |
| **Capital accounts** | | | |
| Singh | | 79,000 | |
| Smith | | 46,000 | 125,000 |

| **Current accounts** | Singh | Smith | |
|---|---|---|---|
| Opening balance | 1,500 | 1,160 | |
| Add salary | 4,000 | 1,000 | |
| Interest on capital | 10,000 | 5,600 | |
| Share of profit | 4,485 | 2,415 | |
| | 19,985 | 10,175 | |
| Less drawings | 17,190 | 10,940 | |
| | 2,795 | −765 | 2,030 |
| | | | 127,030 |

- Original capital put in by each partner
- Balances left over from last year
- The same figures as in the appropriation account
- From trial balance
- £2,795 plus −£765
- £125,000 plus £2,030

Sub-totals

These figures will be carried forward as opening balances next year. Note that Smith has drawn out more than he earned!

You can tell that the accounts balance because the net assets figure equals that at the end of the 'Financed by' section: £127,030.

## Final accounts for a limited company

Limited company balance sheets are also constructed slightly differently. Here is the full set of final accounts for Makem Limited, the company we were introduced to on page 11.

### Makem Limited
**Profit and loss account for year ended 31.3.06**

|  | £000s | £000s | £000s |
|---|---:|---:|---:|
| Sales |  |  | 232,759 |
| Less sales returns |  |  | 1,700 |
| Net sales (or turnover) |  |  | 231,059 |
| **Less cost of goods sold** |  |  |  |
| Opening stock |  | 26,820 |  |
| Purchases | 167,194 |  |  |
| Less purchase returns | 2,325 |  |  |
| Net purchases |  | 164,869 |  |
|  |  | 191,689 |  |
| Less closing stock |  | 29,072 |  |
| Cost of goods sold |  |  | 162,617 |
| **Gross profit** |  |  | 68,442 |
| Rent received |  |  | 3,730 |
|  |  |  | 72,172 |
| **Less expenses** |  |  |  |
| Administration |  |  |  |
| Rent and rates |  | 10,995 |  |
| Wages and salaries |  | 23,075 |  |
| Insurance |  | 3,422 |  |
| Motor expenses |  | 2,980 |  |
| Debenture interest |  | 900 |  |
| Director's fees |  | 15,500 |  |
| Depreciation |  |  |  |
| Buildings |  | 0 |  |
| Equipment |  | 4,000 |  |
| Motor vehicles |  | 1,160 | 62,032 |
| **Net profit before tax** |  |  | 10,140 |
| Less corporation tax |  |  | 3,500 |
| Profit for tear after tax |  |  | 6,640 |
| Less   interim dividend paid |  | 450 |  |
| final dividends proposed |  |  |  |
| preference shares |  | 450 |  |
| ordinary shares |  | 4,000 | 4,900 |
|  |  |  | 1,740 |
| Less transfer to general reserve |  |  | 1,500 |
| Retained profit for year |  |  | 240 |
| Add balance of retained profits B/F |  |  | 0 |
| Balance of retained profits C/F |  |  | 240 |

## Makem Limited
### Balance sheet as at 31.3.06

| | Cost | Accumulated depreciation | Net book value |
|---|---|---|---|
| | £ | £ | £ |
| **Fixed assets** | | | |
| Buildings | 0 | 0 | 0 |
| Equipment | 13,615 | 4,000 | 9,615 |
| Motor vehicles | 10,250 | 1,160 | 9,090 |
| | 23,865 | 5,160 | 18,705 |
| | | | |
| **Current assets** | | | |
| Stock | | 29,072 | |
| Debtors | 32,483 | | |
| less provision for bad debts | 0 | | |
| | | 32,483 | |
| Bank | | 14,275 | |
| Cash | | 1,135 | |
| | | 76,965 | |
| **Less current liabilities** | | | |
| Creditors | 18,980 | | |
| Overdraft | 0 | | |
| Proposed dividends | | | |
| preference shares | 450 | | |
| ordinary shares | 4,000 | | |
| Corporation tax | 3,500 | | |
| | | 26,930 | |
| **Working capital** | | | 50,035 |
| | | | 68,740 |
| | | | |
| Less long-term liabilities | | | |
| 10% debentures | | | 9,000 |
| **Net assets** | | | 59,740 |
| | | | |
| **Financed by** | | | |
| **Authorised share capital** | | | |
| 50,000 ordinary shares of £1 each | | | 65,000 |
| 10,000 8% preference shares of £1 each | | | 12,500 |
| | | | 77,500 |
| | | | |
| **Issued share capital** | | | |
| 100,000 ordinary shares of 50p each | | | 50,000 |
| 16,000 9% preference shares of 50p each | | | 8,000 |
| | | | 58,000 |
| | | | |
| **Revenue reserves** | | | |
| General reserve | | 1,500 | |
| Profit and loss account | | 240 | 1,740 |
| | | | 59,740 |

**Authorised share capital** shows the maximum amount of share capital the firm would be allowed to issue if it chose to

**Issued share capital** shows the actual amount of share capital the firm has raised

These figures are for information only, they are not added in to the final balance

These come from the profit and loss account

Issued share capital (£58,000) plus revenue reserves (£1,740)

Once again, you can tell that the accounts balance because the net assets figure equals that at the end of the 'Financed by' section: £59,740.

### Outcome activity 10.2

You are still working as an accounts clerk for a firm of accountants known as Mason, Wright and Partners as in Outcome Activity 10.1 on page 11.

**Pass**

1 Using the details from Outcome Activity 10.1, prepare a balance sheet for Kong Han, not forgetting to adjust fixed assets for depreciation.

2 You are pleased with the success of the booklet you prepared in Outcome Activity 10.1 and you decide to prepare a further booklet to cover limited company balance sheets. This booklet will also be in three parts. Prepare the first part describing the components of a limited company's balance sheet.

**Merit**

Continuing the booklet you began for the previous task, explain the components of a limited company's balance sheet. You should explain in detail what each of the entries means.

While producing this section of your booklet, it will be helpful to refer to a set of final accounts for a limited company so that you can explain and give examples. To do this you can either use the published set of final accounts you used for the first booklet, or alternatively use the following balance for Waters and Gilmour Limited, the company you were introduced to in Outcome Activity 10.1.

### Waters and Gilmour Limited
#### Balance sheet as at 31.3.06

|  | Cost | Accumulated depreciation | Net book value |
|---|---|---|---|
|  | £ | £ | £ |
| **Fixed assets** | | | |
| Buildings | 160,000 | 0 | 160,000 |
| Equipment | 50,000 | 10,000 | 40,000 |
| Motor vehicles | 20,000 | 14,000 | 6,000 |
|  | 230,000 | 24,000 | 206,000 |
| **Current assets** | | | |
| Stock | | 30,000 | |
| Debtors | 70,000 | | |
|  | | 70,000 | |
| Bank | | 7,000 | |
| Cash | | 15,000 | |
|  | | 122,000 | |
| **Less current liabilities** | | | |
| Creditors | 23,000 | | |
| Overdraft | 0 | | |
| Proposed dividends | | | |
| Preference shares | 0 | | |
| Ordinary shares | 10,000 | | |
| Corporation tax | 20,000 | | |
|  | | 53,000 | |
| **Working capital** | | | 69,000 |
|  | | | 275,000 |
| Less long-term liabilities | | | |
| 10% debentures | | | 60,000 |
| **Net assets** | | | 215,000 |

| Financed by | | |
|---|---|---|
| **Authorised share capital** | | |
| 300,000 ordinary shares of £1 each | | 300,000 |
| | | 300,000 |
| **Issued share capital** | | |
| 180,000 ordinary shares of £1 each | | 180,000 |
| | | 0 |
| | | 180,000 |
| **Revenue reserves** | | |
| General reserve | 3,000 | |
| Profit and loss account | 32,000 | 35,000 |
| | | 215,000 |

**Distinction**

Complete your booklet by analysing the components of the limited company's balance sheet that you used in the previous question.

# Fixed and working capital

In essence, the **fixed capital** is the money put into the business by the owners, and the **working capital** is the ready money that is available to pay bills; both are essential. If a business were compared to a motor car, you might think of the fixed capital as the engine of the car and the working capital as the oil that keeps the parts moving. Both are vital to the smooth running of the vehicle. The engine gets you going, but the oil keeps you moving; thus the fixed capital of the firm is essential to getting a business up and running, but the working capital is equally important.

If you let your car run out of oil the engine will seize up and the car will break down, regardless of how good its engine is. So fixed and working capital work together to ensure a smoothly functioning business. It is true to say that many businesses fail because the owners or managers pay insufficient attention to working capital needs.

## Fixed capital

Fixed capital is money or value contributed by the owner(s) of a business. For a sole trader there is just one owner, but limited companies may have many shareholders. The figure for fixed capital may increase each year if profits are retained. Additional capital can also be raised through

*Keeping the engine of business running*

share issues for a limited company, or with a sole trader by introducing additional money to the business.

At the bottom of a completed set of accounts you will have seen a section headed 'Financed by' – it sometimes carries the heading 'Capital and reserves'. This section shows all the fixed capital that has been introduced into the company by the owners, and also any profit that has been retained in the business. The entries in this section comprise the different types of shares and reserves for the company. Here are some of the main ones you are likely to come across.

### Share capital

In the case of a limited company, the fixed capital comes mainly from shareholders, and there are a number of different types of shares that may be held.

- **Ordinary shares** are the most common form of share, and are often referred to as equity capital. Holders of ordinary shares become part owners of the company and because of this they are able to vote at general meetings of the firm. Ordinary shareholders are entitled to receive dividends, which are a share of the company profits each year. Since profits will vary from year to year, ordinary share dividends may rise and fall annually.

- **Preference shares** offer the holder a specific dividend, usually expressed as a percentage return. This is a fixed rate of return that will not change even if the company makes very high profits. Although preference shareholders are part owners of the company, they are not allowed to vote at meetings in the same way as ordinary shareholders can.

- **Deferred shares** are the same as ordinary shares except that they only receive dividends in certain circumstances, such as specific levels of profit being earned, or a particular date being reached. Sometimes the conditions of a deferred share require that dividends are only paid after certain amounts are paid out to ordinary shareholders.

**Case study    Share capital**

Examine the published accounts of some limited companies and identify how many of the different types of shares they have issued. You may be able to find copies of such accounts in your school or college library, or you could visit the website *www.carol.co.uk*, which is an on-line database of company accounts in the UK.

What do you think are the advantages or disadvantages to a company of:

- ordinary shares
- preference shares
- deferred shares?

### Partnership/sole trader capital

Partnerships and sole traders do not issue shares, so you will not find any of the above forms of fixed capital in their accounts. Instead, the 'Financed by' or 'Capital and reserves' section of the balance sheet of a sole trader will simply contain an entry indicating the amount of money he or she has put into the business, either initially or later on during the life of the company. This is normally entitled 'Capital' or 'Capital Introduced'. Drawings (the amount the sole trader has paid himself or herself) will also be deducted at this point.

Partnerships are dealt with in a similar fashion, except that a separate capital account is required for each of the partners in the balance sheet. You will also see current accounts for each of the partners. The capital accounts are fixed and will alter only if the partner introduces additional capital to the business, or takes some out. The current account changes annually as shares in company profits and interest on partners' capital are added and each partner's drawings are deducted.

You can see full examples of each of these in the 'Profit and loss accounts' and 'Assets, liabilities and balance sheets' sections of this unit.

*Shareholders expect dividends, but they also want the value of their shares to rise*

### Retained profit

There is an amount left in the profit and loss account of the business after all the expenses have been paid and this is used in two ways. Some is allocated to dividends (see below) and the rest stays in the business as retained profits. Although strictly speaking this retained profit is the owed to the ordinary shareholders, it is retained in the business for future use.

Over the years retained profits may become a very significant part of the 'Capital and reserves' or 'Financed by' section of the balance sheet for a limited company. However, these profits will gradually be used by the company to buy new fixed assets such as machinery and buildings so that the firm can expand.

The directors of the company have to maintain a careful balance between paying dividends and retaining profit in the business. Paying all of the profits out in dividends might please the shareholders initially, but in the long term it will hinder the growth potential of the company and this is likely to reduce the value of the shares on the stock market, so eventually the shareholders

might see the value of their shares fall. Therefore both paying good dividends and retaining sufficient profit for expansion are important to the shareholders of the company.

> **Thinking point**
>
> Identify the advantages to a firm of using retained profits to finance the purchase of fixed assets instead of using:
> - bank loans
> - debentures
> - share issue.

### Dividends

When investors buy shares in a company they expect to receive something back for their investment, just as they are paid interest on investments in a bank or building society. Dividends are what the shareholders receive – they are a share in the profits of the company over a six-month or yearly period. Dividends will normally only be paid if the company makes a profit, but sometimes the company will draw on reserves from past profits to pay dividends.

Note that dividends do not appear in the 'Capital and reserves' or 'Financed by' section of a firm's balance sheet; they are an expense to the company and therefore they only appear in the profit and loss account (see the 'Profit and loss accounts' and 'Assets, liabilities and balance sheets' sections of this unit for examples).

# Working capital

Working capital (also known as net current assets or current capital) measures how much a company has available to pay bills. Working capital is calculated by deducting current liabilities (those debts that must be paid shortly) from current assets (money that is readily available in the company). This should be a positive figure, otherwise the business may find it hard to meet its debts. You will find the figure for working capital at the heart of the balance sheet (see the 'Profit and loss accounts' and 'Assets, liabilities and balance sheets' sections of this unit for examples).

Note that in the final accounts for a PLC, working capital is usually called 'net current assets'.

## Current assets

A firm's current assets typically comprise the following items:

*Keeping the business liquid can be a full-time job*

- stock – the total value of raw materials that will be made into goods for sale, partly manufactured items, and also items that have been completely made or bought in by the firm and are available for sale to customers

- debtors – the total of all monies owed to the company, which is likely to be made up of customers who have received goods but have not yet paid for them

- bank – the total amount of money held in the company's bank account(s)

- cash – the total amount of cash held in the tills or cash boxes on the company's premises.

## Current liabilities

Note that in the final accounts for a PLC, current liabilities are usually called 'Creditors: amounts falling due within one year'.

A firm's current liabilities typically comprise the following items.

- Creditors – the total of sums owed to suppliers that have offered the company credit. When a firm has a good relationship with its suppliers, it is common practice for the supplier to offer credit terms. So the firm may buy raw materials but will be asked to pay for them in, say, 28 days' time. The supplier is therefore a creditor of the firm, as it is owed money that will need to be repaid soon. The figure for creditors may also include corporation tax that is shortly to be paid.
  Sums that have to be paid for in more than one year's time are referred to as long-term liabilities, and these are not included in the current liabilities of the firm. Examples of these might be a mortgage on company property or a long-term bank loan. These will still appear in the balance sheet but are accounted for separately from the current liabilities.

- Bank overdraft – if the company has drawn out more than it has in its bank account, it will be running an overdraft. This will need to be repaid and therefore appears as a current liability.

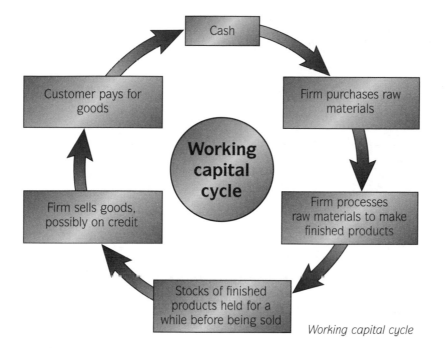

*Working capital cycle*

## Managing working capital using the working capital cycle

The **working capital cycle** monitors the movement of cash within the business, and careful management of the cycle can help a company improve its working capital position. In general terms, the firm's cash becomes tied up once raw materials are purchased and it only becomes available again once the finished product is sold. Reducing the period between these two events can relieve any working capital problems. The cycle for a manufacturing company is shown above.

It is possible to calculate a firm's working capital cycle using the following formula:

Stock turnover *(the number of days goods are held in stock)*

plus    debtor collection period *(number of days it takes debtors to pay)*

minus  creditor payment period *(number of days' credit from suppliers)*

equals  working capital cycle

It may be that you do not have the information for such calculations to hand, in which case the periods can be calculated from the company's final accounts. In the next section (page 28) you will find ratios that will help you to calculate these.

Example:

| | |
|---|---|
| Stock turnover | 30 days |
| + Debtor collection period | 21 days |
| – Creditor payment period | 28 days |
| Working capital cycle = | 23 days |

This shows that this firm has its cash tied up for 23 days on average. It is difficult to tell whether this is good or bad – the firm should compare this figure with those of similar companies to see whether it is better or worse, and also compare it with the same figure for previous years to see whether there is a developing trend.

The higher the figure in days, the longer the firm's cash is tied up. To improve its working capital position the company should try to reduce this figure. There are a number of ways this could be achieved:

● reduce stocks held, which will speed up stock turnover

● encourage debtors to pay more quickly, possibly by offering shorter credit periods to customers

● negotiate longer credit periods from suppliers, giving the firm longer to pay for raw materials purchased.

### Thinking point

1 Calculate the working capital cycles for the following four firms.

|  | Firm 1 (days) | Firm 2 (days) | Firm 3 (days) | Firm 4 (days) |
|---|---|---|---|---|
| Stock turnover | 30 | 3 | 14 | 40 |
| Debtor collection period | 21 | 28 | 0 | 40 |
| Creditor payment period | 28 | 28 | 28 | 7 |
| Working capital cycle |  |  |  |  |

2 What conclusions can you draw about each of the firms?

3 What recommendations would you make to the managers of each of the firms?

## Managing working capital using stock control

As we have seen, improving **stock control** and reducing the stock turnover period can help in improving a firm's working capital position. What can a firm do to achieve this? This depends to a certain extent on the stock control method used by the firm.

- **The minimum stock level method** is where a firm identifies the minimum stock that it requires to satisfy potential customer demand and reorders once that level is received. To improve stock turnover a firm could review these levels to see whether they can be adjusted downwards without compromising customer service.

- **The stock review (maximum stock level) method** is where a firm reviews stock periodically and places orders on each review to bring stock levels back up to a maximum level. In this case the firm might review whether it is possible to reduce the maximum level used and increase the regularity of the reviews.

*Under the JIT system, ordering and delivery of stocks must be timed precisely*

- **The just-in-time method (JIT)** is an excellent method for keeping stocks to a minimum and is often used by supermarkets that have good computerised stock control systems. A JIT system helps the firm keep stocks at a barest minimum level. The computer system generates an order to the suppliers when stocks are about to run out. The timing of the order is crucial, as the idea is for the new stock to arrive just as the old stock runs out. This is the best method for keeping stocks as low as possible, but the firm needs very reliable systems and suppliers to make it work. Such a system reduces stocks to help working capital.

## Managing working capital by managing debtors

Debtors will not manage themselves, and a company that does not actively manage its debtors runs the risk of failure when the expected money does not arrive quickly enough. Here are a few simple rules that a company may adopt to manage debtors more effectively.

- **If in doubt only take cash** – unless you are confident of prompt payment from a customer, insist on cash. Then you have no worries about prompt payment.

- **Check creditworthiness of customers** – before you offer credit it is a good idea to check whether the customer you are selling to has been a good payer in the past with other companies. This could be done by taking references from the customer's bank, inquiring with other firms who have advanced the customer credit, or even making inquiries with credit reference agencies.

- **Start with a small credit limit** – this can be increased later when the customer has proved to be a good payer.

- **Keep in regular contact with the customer** – customers are then less likely to forget to pay you!

- **Send out invoices promptly** – this seems obvious, but is overlooked by too many firms. In addition, outstanding debts should be chased up promptly and referred to debt collection when doubt begins.

- **Don't supply more to a customer if he or she has bills overdue for payment** – make sure systems are in place to identify such customers so that sales staff do not process further orders until the original debts are cleared.

- **Offer incentives for prompt payment** – many firms offer discounts, thus encouraging debtors to pay quickly.

- **Penalise late payers** – a firm may choose to add interest to overdue payments. Such details will be included on the original invoice.

- **Do not be afraid to take legal action if necessary** – often a simple letter from the company solicitor may be enough to prompt a debtor into paying, but it is important that further action is taken if this does not provoke a response. Remember that you do not want to appear to be a 'soft touch' for your debtors. Napoleon once said 'You have to shoot a general every now and then to encourage the others' – and this is not a bad motto for debt collection!

- **Manage your cash flow** – forecasting cash flow and monitoring those forecasts will also help the firm to manage its working capital better. You can learn more about this in *BTEC National Business*, in the units 'Business Enterprise' (see pages 197–205) and 'Finance, Cash Flow and Insolvency' (see pages 266–281).

## Outcome activity 10.3

You are still working as an accounts clerk for a firm of accountants known as Mason, Wright and Partners as in Outcome Activities 10.1 and 10.2.

### Pass

Your manager is very pleased with the booklets that you produced in the previous two tasks. She has noticed that clerks in the company often get confused between fixed capital and working capital, so she asks you to produce a third booklet outlining what these are. Once again the booklet will have three sections.

Using the accounts for Kong Han and Waters and Gilmour Limited from the previous outcome activities, identify and describe fixed and working capital in the case of these two business organisations.

### Merit

Continuing the booklet begun in the previous task, you now need to do the following.

1 Explain the differences between fixed capital for a sole trader/partnership and for a limited company, making references to the accounts of Kong Han and Waters and Gilmour Limited.

2 Explain the importance of working capital to these organisations.

### Distinction

Conclude your booklet by explaining how an organisation should manage its fixed and working capital and the implications of failing to do so effectively. You may make reference to the accounts of Kong Han and Waters and Gilmour Limited when preparing this section.

# Reviewing business performance using ratio analysis

You now know how to compile a set of accounts, but what do they really tell us about the company? The accounts contain many messages for those who choose to read them, but the messages are not all obvious when we first look at them.

When we visit a foreign country we need a phrase book to help us interpret other languages; we also need some tools to help us interpret the messages in a set of accounts.

Some messages are very straightforward. For example, you should easily be able to identify the total profit made in a year by a firm. But what if you wanted to know how good an investment a firm was for its shareholders? Or how efficient it is in chasing customers who owe money? Or whether it keeps costs under control? Or whether its position is improving or deteriorating?

All of this information is available if you know where to look and how to interpret it.

**Ratio analysis** is the accountant's phrase book. Armed with a number of simple tools we can make accurate judgements about the company's performance. This section describes some of the most important ratios that you can use. Ratio analysis is used by many of a firm's stakeholders, such as:

- **owners** – to inform them when they are making decisions about the future of the firm

- **investors** – to check that their investment is doing well and providing a fair return on their money

- **suppliers** – if they are owed money by the firm, they will want to know how likely it is that they will get their money back, and if they are asked to supply on credit they can use the accounts of the firm to decide whether it is worthy of credit

*Making sense of accounts*

- **employees** – individual employees or trade unions may check the firm's accounts to monitor how profitable the firm is and therefore whether they can request pay rises or improvements in their working conditions

- **customers** – to check that the firm is likely to stay in business and therefore be able to keep supplying them

- **tax authorities** – to check that the firm is paying the correct amounts of tax

- **creditors** – such as the bank, which may check that the firm is still in a position to make repayments on loans it has advanced.

## Profitability ratios

One of the facts that is most important to a company's stakeholders is its profitability. The following ratios help us to monitor the company's profit performance.

### Return on capital employed (ROCE)

For a sole trader, return on capital employed is calculated using the following formula:

$$\frac{\text{Net profit}}{\text{Average capital employed}} \times 100 = \text{Percentage return}$$

Average capital employed would be calculated by adding together the opening stock and closing stock figures and dividing by two.

For a limited company, the formula would be slightly more complicated, as follows:

$$\frac{\text{Net profit for year before interest and tax}}{\text{Capital employed}} \times 100 = \text{Percentage return}$$

The phrase 'capital employed' here covers ordinary share capital + preference share capital + reserves + debentures/long-term loans.

### What does ROCE show?

This shows us the percentage return that the investors have received on the capital they invested. It is like the interest rate that you would receive on a building society account, and investors will often compare the return on capital employed to the current rates of interest being offered at building societies, to see whether they are getting a better or worse deal.

## Practice point

The ROCE for a number of companies is as follows:

| | |
|---|---|
| Crowther PLC | 6% |
| Chatterjee PLC | 4% |
| Turner PLC | 2% |
| Griffiths Limited | 19% |

Using the Internet, check the current interest rates offered at two major building societies for accounts requiring a maximum of four weeks' notice.

1 Which of the above firms are offering attractive deals to their investors?

2 What other factors would be important when deciding whether to invest in a building society or shares in a limited company?

3 What problems might an investor encounter in trying to invest in Griffiths Limited?

## Return on net assets

Return on net assets is calculated using the following formula:

$$\frac{\text{Net profit for year}}{\text{Net assets}} \times 100 = \begin{array}{l}\text{Percentage return} \\ \text{on net assets}\end{array}$$

Net assets here is defined as fixed assets + current assets – current liabilities.

## What does return on net assets show?

This is very similar to the ROCE ratio above and is used in the same way. It shows how well a firm is using its assets to generate profit. Once again a percentage figure is produced, which shows how much profit has been earned per pound of assets. A return on net assets of 15% shows that 15p has been earned for every £1 worth of assets.

## Gross profit percentage

Gross profit percentage is calculated using the following formula:

$$\frac{\text{Gross profit for year}}{\text{Sales for year}} \times 100$$

## What does gross profit percentage show?

This ratio shows how much gross profit is being made compared with the amount of sales made. For example, a gross profit percentage of 15% means that £1.50 of gross profit is made from every £10 of sales.

It is usual to compare these figures from one year to the next, and ideally the percentage will stay relatively stable, showing that the company is remaining stable in its trading. If it changes, especially if the percentage falls, this should be investigated and the reasons determined. A deteriorating percentage could mean, for example, that purchase costs are increasing or that sales are falling.

## Net profit percentage

Net profit percentage is calculated using the following formula:

$$\frac{\text{Net profit for year}}{\text{Sales for year}} \times 100$$

In the case of a limited company, for the purposes of this ratio, net profit for the year is profit before the deduction of tax and dividends.

## What does net profit percentage show?

This ratio is similar to the gross profit percentage but this time shows how much net profit is being made compared with the amount of sales made. For example, a net profit percentage of 5% means that 50p net profit is made from every £10 of sales made by the firm.

It is useful to compare the gross profit percentage with the net profit percentage as this shows how much of gross profit is being taken up by the expenses of the firm, such as running vehicles and paying wages and salaries. Ideally the gap between the two should decrease over the years as this would show that the company was working well on controlling expenses.

A fall in net profit percentage would indicate that expenses were increasing, and this should be examined to see where the problem lies and what steps can be taken to rectify it.

## Case study — Gross profit and net profit

The gross profit percentage and net profit percentage for organisations in different industries will not be the same, so we should take care about comparing the results. However looking at the results of two firms in the same industry can be revealing. Consider the following extracts from the accounts of two companies for 2006:

| 2006 | Gross profit | Net profit | Sales |
|---|---|---|---|
| Walker Brothers Limited | 450 | 100 | 4,000 |
| Wahid & Co Limited | 900 | 150 | 12,000 |

**1** Calculate the gross profit percentage and net profit percentage for each of the firms.
**2** What conclusions can you draw from your results?

Here are the results for the same companies for the previous year:

| 2005 | Gross profit % | Net profit % |
|---|---|---|
| Walker Brothers Limited | 14% | 4% |
| Wahid & Co Limited | 7.4% | 1.3% |

**3** What further conclusions can you draw when comparing the 2006 figures with the 2005 figures?

## Gearing ratios

The **gearing** ratio is calculated using the following two formulae.

For a sole trader or partnership, the formula is as follows:

$$\frac{\text{Long-term loans}}{\text{Capital}} \times 100$$

For a limited company, the formula is as follows:

$$\frac{\text{Preference share capital} + \text{Long-term loans and debentures}}{\text{Ordinary share capital} + \text{reserves}} \times 100$$

## What do gearing ratios show?

Gearing ratios show how much borrowing the business has in comparison to the amount of capital invested by the owners. A gearing ratio of 50%, for example, shows that the firm has borrowed £1 for every £2 invested by the owners.

In a limited company this is of interest to the shareholders, as the lenders are likely to have a preferential claim before the ordinary shareholders on the company's assets if the business should fail. It therefore gives a measurement of the risk being borne by the shareholders.

The gearing ratio will also be of interest to the company's bankers if they are approached for more lending, as it shows the degree of risk being borne by the shareholders or owners compared to the bank. Banks are cautious and do not like to bear more risk than the shareholders or owners, so this may be significant in deciding whether to lend more money to a company.

### Thinking point

Genesis PLC has a gearing ratio of 75% today compared with 50% this time last year.

**1** What factors might have caused this change?
**2** Consider each of the stakeholders of the company. Are there any reasons for concern for them?

## Price/earnings ratio

The price/earnings ratio is calculated using the following formula:

$$\frac{\text{Market price of ordinary share (in pence)}}{\text{Earnings per ordinary share (in pence)}}$$

The market price of ordinary shares needs to be obtained from a publication or website that quotes current market prices for quoted shares, such as the *Financial Times* or *www.londonstockexchange.com.*

## What does the price/earnings ratio show?

This ratio compares the price charged for buying the share with the amount earned by investors in dividends from each share. The result of the formula shows the number of years it would take to repay the investment. For example, with a market price of £1.50 and earnings per share of 10p, the result would be:

$$\frac{150}{10} = 15$$

This result of 15 means that it would take 15 years to repay the investment, assuming that earnings per share do not change. Investors will use this ratio to compare the value of different potential investments.

## Dividend cover

Dividend cover is calculated using the following formula:

$$\frac{\text{Net profit after tax and preference share dividends}}{\text{Ordinary dividends (interim and final)}}$$

## What does dividend cover show?

This ratio compares the profits earned by the company with the amount of dividend it is paying, and it shows how easy it will be for a company to make those dividend payments to shareholders – it indicates to investors how safe their dividend payments are.

Since dividends will only be paid to ordinary shareholders if profits allow, a high level of dividend cover indicates that profits would have to fall a long way before the dividends were threatened. If the result is less than 1, this indicates that the company will have to use retained profits from previous years to pay dividends, and if this were to continue it is unlikely that the company would be able to carry on making dividend payments. A higher result indicates a safer dividend – a result of 4, for example, tells the investor that profits are four times the size of dividend payments, and therefore would have to fall a long way before the company would be unable to pay dividends.

## Case study    Dividend cover

Consider the following extract from three companies' accounts:

|  | ABC PLC | MNO PLC | XYZ PLC |
|---|---|---|---|
| **Market price of ordinary share (in pence)** | 150 | 600 | 15 |
| **Earnings per ordinary share (in pence)** | 20 | 50 | 10 |
| **Net profit** | £125,000 | £725,000 | £80,000 |
| **Ordinary dividends** | £20,000 | £500,000 | £100,000 |
| **PE ratio** |  |  |  |
| **Dividend cover** |  |  |  |

1  Complete the table by calculating the price/earnings (PE) ratios and dividend covers for each of the companies.
2  Compare the three companies as possible investments. Comment on each of the ratios – compare and contrast them for each of the companies.

# Productivity ratios

**Productivity** looks at how efficiently a company is using its factors of production to produce products or services, and profit. The following ratios give us an indication of that efficiency.

## Stock turnover

Stock turnover is calculated using the following formula:

$$\frac{\text{Average stock}}{\text{Cost of goods sold}} \times 365 = \text{Stock turnover in days}$$

Average stock is calculated by adding opening stock to closing stock and dividing by two.

## What does stock turnover show?

This ratio shows the number of days that an average item of stock is held at the company, in other words how long it takes to sell the item. It is difficult to decide what is a good rate of stock turnover for a business, as the situation is different for firms in different industries. For example, a manufacturer of electrical goods may hold stock for several weeks before it leaves for a retailer, but a supermarket would expect a much shorter turnover as food items perish quickly. In general terms, however, businesses will be looking to reduce the number of stock days wherever possible. The important things to consider are as follows.

- How does the company's ratio compare with those of similar businesses in the same industry?

- How does the ratio compare with this time last year? A shorter period than last year indicates that the company is becoming more efficient; a longer one implies that the firm needs to determine why this is happening and correct the trend.

## Asset turnover

Asset turnover is calculated using the following formula:

$$\frac{\text{Sales}}{\text{Net assets}} : 1$$

Net assets here is defined as fixed assets + current assets – current liabilities.

## What does asset turnover show?

This ratio gives us a measurement of how efficiently the assets of the company are being used to generate sales for the company. The ratio should also be compared year on year, and an increasing ratio would indicate that the company is working more efficiently. A declining ratio might suggest that the firm's efficiency is declining, but look at such a result carefully as it could easily be caused by the recent purchase or revaluation of fixed assets.

*Supermarkets expect a quick turnover of fresh food items*

## Practice point

Consider the following extract from a company's accounts:

|  | 2004 | 2005 | 2006 |
|---|---|---|---|
| Sales | 1,002,500 | 1,052,625 | 1,042,556 |
| Opening stock | 150,000 | 180,000 | 189,000 |
| Closing stock | 180,000 | 189,000 | 196,560 |
| Net assets | 1,262,500 | 1,262,500 | 1,450,000 |
| Cost of goods sold | 880,000 | 914,000 | 950,560 |
| Stock turnover |  |  |  |
| Asset turnover |  |  |  |

1  Complete the table by calculating the stock turnover and asset turnover for the company for each of the three years.

2  Comment on how the company's position might be improving or declining as indicated by your calculations.

### Debtor collection period

The debtor collection period is calculated using the following formula:

$$\frac{\text{Debtors}}{\text{Credit sales for year}} \times 365 = \frac{\text{Debtor collection}}{\text{period in days}}$$

If it is not clear how many sales were on credit, the sales figure from the profit and loss account should be used.

### What does the debtor collection period show?

It shows how long it takes on average for debtors to pay for goods bought on credit. This will be different for businesses in different industries, as some sell on credit more than others. Shops, for example, do not sell on credit nearly as much as trade suppliers.

You should compare this figure with that of previous years to make any sense of the result. If the number of days is increasing, then the company's procedures for chasing debtors ought to be examined, as this is likely to be having an adverse effect on the company's cash flow. If the figure is stable, this suggests that debt collection is under control. It is also interesting to compare

this ratio with the following one, the creditor payment period.

### Creditor payment period

The creditor payment period is calculated using the following formula:

$$\frac{\text{Creditors}}{\text{Credit purchases for year}} \times 365 = \frac{\text{Creditor payment}}{\text{period in days}}$$

If it is not clear how many purchases were on credit, the purchases figure from the profit and loss account should be used.

### What does the creditor payment period show?

This ratio reveals how long the firm is taking to pay for goods it has bought. If this period is increasing, this implies that either the firm is negotiating better terms from its suppliers or it is having difficulty paying its bills. You may like to compare the creditor payment period with the debtor payment period.

If the creditor payment period is greater than the debtor payment period, the company is getting better terms for buying on credit than it is giving to its customers. This will clearly help cash flow

Consider the following extract from a company's accounts:

| | 2004 | 2005 | 2006 |
|---|---|---|---|
| Debtors | 15,750 | 17,325 | 19,058 |
| Creditors | 13,650 | 14,332 | 15,049 |
| Credit sales for the year | 143,000 | 150,150 | 157,658 |
| Credit purchases for the year | 100,000 | 110,000 | 121,000 |
| Debtor collection period | | | |
| Creditor collection period | | | |

1 Complete the table by calculating the debtor collection period and the creditor collection period for the company for each of the three years.

2 Comment on what your results show, and how the company's position might be improving or declining.

as money will be received from purchases before bills have to be paid for supplies.

If the debtor payment period is greater than the creditor payment period, the situation is not so good as the firm is allowing longer periods for its customers buying on credit than it is receiving from its suppliers. This will clearly hinder cash flow as bills for supplies will need to be paid before money is received from sales.

## Solvency ratios

As we saw previously, working capital is vital to the health of a company. The following ratios are commonly used to measure how **solvent** the firm is – how easily it can pay its debts.

### Current ratio (also known as the working capital ratio)

The current ratio is calculated using the following formula:

$$\frac{\text{Current assets}}{\text{Current liabilities}}$$

### What does the current ratio show?

This shows the proportion of current assets to current liabilities – how easily the company can raise enough money to pay the debts it has to pay in the near future.

If a company had a ratio of 2:1, this would simply mean that it has £2 worth of current assets for every £1 of current liabilities. A result of 2:1 is usually considered to be adequate **liquidity** for most organisations, although a company dealing mainly in cash may well be able to survive with a lower ratio.

If the ratio is 3:1 or more, the company should query whether it is managing its current assets well enough. Such a ratio implies that the firm is holding too much in current assets, so the components of this should be examined. Perhaps it is holding too much stock, or has large sums of cash sitting idle in the business. In the latter case the firm should consider finding a productive use for this cash, rather than letting it sit in the bank account producing no revenue.

### Acid test ratio

The acid test ratio is calculated using the following formula:

$$\frac{\text{Current assets} - \text{stock}}{\text{Current liabilities}}$$

### What does the acid test ratio show?

This ratio is very similar to the current ratio, except that the stock figure is omitted. The reason for this is that sometimes it is difficult to sell stock quickly and for the anticipated price if the money is needed straight away. Consequently it is perhaps unrealistic to rely on stocks to pay the firm's debts as they become due. This ratio therefore shows the readily available assets the company could rely on if a creditor insisted on immediate payment.

If a company had a ratio of 1:1 this would simply mean that the firm has £1 worth of current assets for every £1 of current liabilities. A result of 1:1 indicates that the company should not have a problem paying bills as they become due,

but if it falls below 1:1, such as 0.9:1, the company has fewer **liquid assets** and this could cause problems. The lower the ratio, the more illiquid the firm is and the closer it is to insolvency. If a firm has a healthy current ratio but a poor acid test ratio, this suggests that it is holding too much stock.

## Analysis of ratios

It is important to remember that ratios on their own are relatively meaningless. It is only when they are put into the context of the organisation that they make any sense. Very often you will need to do some comparison of ratios to draw any meaningful conclusions, and this may involve:

● comparing one business year on year

● comparing the ratio with those of similar businesses.

Let us now look at a fully worked example for a manufacturing company, Makem Limited.

---

**Practice point**

Consider the following extract from a company's accounts:

|  | 2004 | 2005 | 2006 |
|---|---|---|---|
| **Current assets** | 61,425 | 67,568 | 74,325 |
| **Current liabilities** | 29,580 | 33,538 | 37,227 |
| **Stock** | 28,080 | 32,292 | 37,489 |
| **Current ratio** |  |  |  |
| **Acid test ratio** |  |  |  |

1 Complete the table by calculating the current ratio and acid test ratio for the company for each of the three years.

2 Comment on what your results show and on how the company's position might be improving or declining.

## Makem Limited

**Profit and loss account for year ended 31.3.06**

|  | £000s | £000s | £000s |
|---|---|---|---|
| Sales |  |  | 232,759 |
| Less sales returns |  |  | 1,700 |
| Net sales (or turnover) |  |  | 231,059 |
| **Less cost of goods sold** |  |  |  |
| Opening stock |  | 26,820 |  |
| Purchases | 167,194 |  |  |
| Less purchase returns | 2,325 |  |  |
| Net purchases |  | 164,869 |  |
|  |  | 191,689 |  |
| Less closing stock |  | 29,072 |  |
| Cost of goods sold |  |  | 162,617 |
| **Gross profit** |  |  | 68,442 |
| Rent received |  |  | 3,730 |
|  |  |  | 72,172 |
| **Less expenses** |  |  |  |
| Administration |  |  |  |
| Rent and rates |  | 10,995 |  |
| Wages and salaries |  | 23,075 |  |
| Insurance |  | 3,422 |  |
| Motor expenses |  | 2,980 |  |
| Debenture interest |  | 900 |  |
| Director's fees |  | 15,500 |  |
| Depreciation |  |  |  |
| Buildings |  | 0 |  |
| Equipment |  | 4,000 |  |
| Motor vehicles |  | 1,160 | 62,032 |
| **Net profit before tax** |  |  | 10,140 |
| Less corporation tax |  |  | 3,500 |
| Profit for tear after tax |  |  | 6,640 |
| Less   interim dividend paid | 450 |  |  |
| final dividends proposed |  |  |  |
| preference shares |  | 450 |  |
| ordinary shares |  | 4,000 | 4,900 |
|  |  |  | 1,740 |
| Less transfer to general reserve |  |  | 1,500 |
| Retained profit for year |  |  | 240 |
| Add balance of retained profits B/F |  |  | 0 |
| Balance of retained profits C/F |  |  | 240 |

## Makem Limited
Balance sheet as at 31.3.06

|  | Cost £ | Accumulated depreciation £ | Net book value £ |
|---|---|---|---|
| **Fixed assets** |  |  |  |
| Buildings | 0 | 0 | 0 |
| Equipment | 13,615 | 4,000 | 9,615 |
| Motor vehicles | 10,250 | 1,160 | 9,090 |
|  | 23,865 | 5,160 | 18,705 |
|  |  |  |  |
| **Current assets** |  |  |  |
| Stock |  | 29,072 |  |
| Debtors | 32,483 |  |  |
| Less provision for bad debts | 0 |  |  |
|  |  | 32,483 |  |
| Bank |  | 14,275 |  |
| Cash |  | 1,135 |  |
|  |  | 76,965 |  |
| **Less current liabilities** |  |  |  |
| Creditors | 18,980 |  |  |
| Overdraft | 0 |  |  |
| Proposed dividends |  |  |  |
| preference shares | 450 |  |  |
| ordinary shares | 4,000 |  |  |
| Corporation tax | 3,500 |  |  |
|  |  | 26,930 |  |
| Working capital |  |  | 50,035 |
|  |  |  | 68,740 |
| Less long-term liabilities |  |  |  |
| 10% debentures |  |  | 9,000 |
| **Net assets** |  |  | 59,740 |
|  |  |  |  |
| **Financed by** |  |  |  |
| **Authorised share capital** |  |  |  |
| 50,000 ordinary shares of £1 each |  |  | 65,000 |
| 10,000 8% preference shares of £1 each |  |  | 12,500 |
|  |  |  | 77,500 |
| **Issued share capital** |  |  |  |
| 100,000 ordinary shares of 50p each |  |  | 50,000 |
| 16,000 9% preference shares of 50p each |  |  | 8,000 |
|  |  |  | 58,000 |
| **Revenue reserves** |  |  |  |
| General reserve |  | 1,500 |  |
| Profit and loss account |  | 240 | 1,740 |
|  |  |  | 59,740 |

We can now calculate the ratios for the firm and comment on them.

## Makem Limited

**Ratio analysis year ending 31.3.06**

**Return on capital employed** $= \dfrac{£10,140}{£59,740 + £9,000} \times 100 =$ **14.75%**

A return of almost 15% compares very favourably with most other investments, so this suggests the company is a good investment.

**Return on net assets**      **14.75%**

Details are the same as for return on capital employed.

**Gross profit percentage** $= \dfrac{68,442}{231,059} \times 100 =$ **29.62%**

A result of over 29% looks very healthy, £29 being earned for every £100 of sales made. However, this should be compared with previous years to check that it is not deteriorating.

**Net profit percentage** $= \dfrac{10,140}{231,059} \times 100 =$ **4.39%**

This result seems rather low, only £4.39 of net profit from every £100 of sales. However, this should be compared with previous years and with similar businesses. There does, though, appear to be a large gap between gross and net profit percentages, which could indicate that the company's expenses are rather high.

**Gearing ratio** $= \dfrac{£8,000 + £9,000}{£50,000 + £1,740} \times 100 =$ **32.86%**

Debt is only 33% of capital invested which does not seem too high. If the percentage were closer to 100% an investor might be worried about the safety of his or her investment should the loans have to be repaid, but in this case there would seem little to worry about.

**Price/earnings ratio**

This cannot be calculated unless we have a figure for the company's share price. This is not reported in the company accounts.

**Dividend cover** $= \dfrac{6,640 - 450 - 450}{4,000} =$ **1.44**

A figure of 1.44 does not give high dividend cover – it suggests that profits will not have to fall by a long way before dividends could be under threat. This would be a warning sign for the investor.

**Stock turnover** $= \dfrac{(26,820+29,072)/2}{162,617} \times 365 =$ **62.73 days**

Almost 63 days to sell stock seems quite a long time, but this is a manufacturing company and lengthy stock turnover periods are not rare. It would be helpful to compare this with previous years to check that the situation is not deteriorating.

**Asset turnover** $= \dfrac{231,059}{68,740} =$ **3.36:1**

This is a fairly low figure, but that is to be expected from a manufacturing company which uses a lot of fixed assets. Again we should compare this figure with previous years to check whether the situation is changing.

**Debtor collection period** $= \dfrac{32,483}{231,059} \times 365 =$ **51.31 days**

Debtors are taking a long time to pay their bills – almost two months on average – so we might conclude that the company is either offering long periods of credit or is not managing its debt collection as well as it might. This is made worse when we look at the creditor payment period below.

**Creditor payment period** $= \dfrac{18,980}{167,194} \times 365 = $ **41.44** days

An average of 41 days to pay bills suggests that the company has either negotiated good credit terms with suppliers or is struggling to pay its bills. The company is also having to pay bills 10 days, on average, before it is paid by debtors. This suggests possible cash flow problems.

**Current ratio** $= \dfrac{76,965}{26,930} = $ **2.86:1**

The current ratio looks reasonably healthy; current assets are nearly three times as much as current liabilities, so the firm should not find too much difficulty meeting debts that need to be paid in the near future.

**Acid test** $= \dfrac{76,965 - 29,072}{26,930} = $ **1.78:1**

The acid test also shows a good picture. Even with stocks taken out of the current assets the firm still has sufficient liquid assets to cover its bills, so it seems to be in a liquid position.

It should be noted here that there are significant limitations to the value of the analysis above. The ratios give an accurate picture, but only of the company at one specific moment in time. Although we can draw some conclusions from the results, it would be helpful to put the results into context. For example, how do the ratio results compare with other companies in the same line of business? A ratio might look good, but comparison across the industry could reveal that the firm is underperforming.

Equally, it would be useful to compare the results with those for the same company but from previous years. The acid test result of 1.78:1, for example, looks healthy, but how does this compare with last year? Is it improving or worsening? If the situation were worsening, this would put a very different light on the result.

## Outcome activity 10.4

You are still working as an accounts clerk for a firm of accountants known as Mason, Wright and Partners as in Outcome Activities 10.1, 10.2 and 10.3 previously.

### Pass
Having completed his set of final accounts, Kong Han asks you to make an analysis of them to identify any strengths and weaknesses of his business. Therefore, using the final accounts that you prepared in Outcome Activities 10.1 and 10.2 and using appropriate ratios, analyse his trading account, profit and loss account and balance sheet.

### Merit
Comment on each of the ratios that you calculate, explaining what it shows and identifying the strengths and weaknesses of the business. Your answer to this task should be presented in the form of a letter addressed to Mr Han at Kong's Collectibles, 95 Front Street, Sheffield S2 5PJ.

### Distinction
Conclude your letter by identifying and explaining the limitations of your ratio analysis to Mr Han. You should do the following.

1 Examine each of the ratios you have calculated and critically examine the result that it gives.
2 Explain how reliable you believe the results of each of the ratios are.
3 Explain what Mr Han should do or what other information he would need, to make sure that the messages he gets from the ratio analysis are sufficiently reliable for him to base significant business decisions on them.

## Key terms

**Assets**
items of value held by an organisation including money owed to the firm (debtors)

**Balance sheet**
an overview of a company's financial position on a particular date, showing its total assets and liabilities

**Capital**
money put into the business by the owner(s) to get it started or to buy equipment

**Closing stock**
the value of stocks of finished products held in the business at the end of the year

**Company reports and accounts**
documents produced annually by each public company giving details of its financial position and a summary of the past year's trading

**Corporation tax**
tax on business profits

**Creditors**
the total of sums owed to suppliers who have offered the company credit

**Current assets**
money that is readily available in the company for paying debts

**Current liabilities**
amounts that are owed to suppliers or lenders that are due to be repaid fairly shortly (normally within one year)

**Debenture**
a method for a company to borrow money; a bond that pays a fixed rate of interest and is usually secured on the assets of the company

**Debtors**
the total of all monies owed to the company

**Deferred shares**
similar to ordinary shares except that dividends are only paid in certain circumstances, such as at a certain level of profit; they appear in the 'Capital and reserves' or 'Financed by' section of the balance sheet

**Depreciation**
the loss in value of the assets of the firm over time, due mainly to wear and tear

**Dividend**
a share of company profits received by shareholders every six months or annually; they appear in the appropriations section of the profit and loss account

**Drawings**
money taken from the business by the owner or a partner for his or her own use

**Fixed assets**
capital items of value that the firm has bought and will use for an extended period of time, such as buildings, machinery, equipment and vehicles

**Fixed capital**
money or value contributed by the owner(s) of a business; often used to buy fixed assets for the business

**Gearing**
how much borrowing the business has in comparison to the amount of capital invested by the owners

**Gross profit**
the profit figure at the end of the trading account; the difference between a company's total revenue and how much it cost to make the product or buy products in – not including the general expenses of the firm

**Interim dividends**
dividends that are paid part way through a company's financial year before final profits are calculated

## Key terms

**Just-in-time (JIT)**
a stock control system where an order is generated for new supplies when stocks are about to run out and is timed so that the new stock arrives just as supplies run out

**Liabilities**
monies that the firm owes

**Liquid assets/liquidity**
monies immediately available to a company for business use

**Long-term liabilities**
sums that have to be paid for in more than one year's time, such as a mortgage on company property or a long-term bank loan

**Opening stock**
the value of stocks of finished products held in the business at the start of the year

**Ordinary shares**
the most common form of share ownership – holders become part owners of the company and may vote at general meetings of the firm; ordinary shares appear in the 'Capital and reserves' or 'Financed by' section of the balance sheet

**Preference shares**
shares that offer the holder a fixed percentage dividend; they appear in the 'Capital and reserves' or 'Financed by' section of the balance sheet

**Productivity**
how efficiently a company uses its factors of production to produce products/services and profit

**Proposed dividends**
dividends paid by the company at the end of the financial year, after profits have been calculated

**Purchases**
for a manufacturing company, the value of raw materials purchased; for a service business, the cost of items bought to sell to customers or used to provide a service to customers

**Purchase returns**
money paid back to the company by suppliers when it returns items, for whatever reason

**Ratio analysis**
mathematical tools used to judge the financial condition and performance of a company

**Reserves**
profit that is not distributed to shareholders but is put on one side and may be used for replacement of capital assets in the future

**Retained profit**
profits that have not been distributed to the shareholders but are saved to finance future expansion of the business; they appear in the appropriations section of the profit and loss account

**Sales (or turnover)**
the total amount of money received in sales for the year

**Sales returns**
money paid back to customers when they return items, for whatever reason

**Solvency**
how easily a firm can pay its debts

**Stock**
the total value of raw materials that will be made into goods for sale, partly manufactured items, and also items that have been completely made or bought in by the firm and are available for sale to customers

**Stock control**
ensuring that there is always enough stock to meet demand from customers but never too much, as that ties up money that could be used for other purposes in the business

**Trading account**
the first of the set of final accounts, showing how profitably the firm makes goods or processes them for sale to customers; it calculates the gross profit earned

## Key terms

**Trial balance**
the act of totalling all the debit balances and all the credit balances to confirm that total debits equal total credits

**Working capital**
money needed for the day-to-day running of the business, calculated by current assets minus current liabilities

**Working capital cycle**
the movement of cash within the business from when it is paid out to buy raw materials to the time it comes back in when goods are sold

# End-of-unit test

1 What is a trial balance and what is it used for?

2 What is a trading account and how is it constructed?

3 What is the difference between gross profit and net profit? Where would you find each of these figures in a set of final accounts?

4 State the two main methods used to depreciate the fixed assets of a company, and using examples explain how each of them works.

5 When would you draw up an appropriation account and what will it contain?

6 What are reserves, and how are they used?

7 Where does corporation tax appear in a set of limited company final accounts?

8 What is the difference between a firm's assets and its liabilities? Give examples of each.

9 Explain the difference between a firm's fixed assets and its current assets.

10 How can you tell if a balance sheet balances?

11 What entries appear in the balance sheet of a limited company that we would not see in those of a sole trader?

12 Explain the difference between authorised share capital and issued share capital.

13 What is fixed capital and what is working capital?

14 Name and describe the different types of share capital that a firm may issue.

15 What are dividends, and where will they appear in a limited company balance sheet?

16 What are liquid assets? Give examples of them.

17 What does 'current liabilities' mean? Give some typical examples of current liabilities.

18 What is the working capital cycle of a firm, and how can it be calculated?

19 Explain five methods for managing the working capital cycle through good management of debtors.

20 State the formulae for five accounting ratios and explain their uses.

# *Resources*

## Texts

Bendrey, Hussey and West: *Accounting and Finance in Business 4th Edition*, DP Publications, 1996

Cox, D: *Business Accounts*, Osborne Books, 1999

Glew, Watts, Surridge and Merrills: *Advanced Vocational Business*, Harper Collins Publishers, 2000

Melville, A: *Financial Accounting 2nd Edition*, Pearson Education, 1999

St John Price, A: *Understand Your Accounts 4th Edition*, Kogan Page Limited, 1999

## Websites

*www.statistics.gov.uk* The Office for National Statistics

*www.telegraph.co.uk* The *Daily Telegraph*

*http://www.bbc.co.uk/schools/gcsebitesize/business/finance/accountsrev2.shtml* BBC Bitesize accounts revision

*http://www.bized.ac.uk/learn/business/accounting/busaccounts/notes/pl.htm* Bized, a databank of knowledge for business students

*www.londonstockexchange.com* The London Stock Exchange

*www.carol.co.uk* Company Annual Reports On-Line; a great source for on-line sets of final accounts for UK companies

*http://www.bizhelp24.com* UK business and finance information source

*http://www.businesslink.gov.uk* Business Link, a government initiative to support small business

# Unit 12    Marketing Research

This unit explores how marketing research should be organised and highlights the topics that can be investigated. It builds on the work in Unit 11: Introduction to Marketing. You will be invited to research why Tesco has been so successful in spite of fierce competition from Asda, Sainsbury's and Morrisons.

The unit then reviews the methods that can be used to gather the information required, and the stages to be followed to ensure success. Lyons Tetley's approach to researching the concept of the round teabag will be examined.

The third section of the unit considers how to implement the research plan including deciding who to interview and how to design an effective questionnaire. For example, how do organisations choose the people for their marketing research projects?

The final part examines how to analyse and present the information – what is the best way to give colleagues a visual representation of the way the length of checkout queues affects the level of customer satisfaction? The section concludes with a reminder that research does have its limitations.

Unit 12 is therefore divided into four main sections:

- 12.1 Principles of marketing research
- 12.2 Plan research
- 12.3 Implement research
- 12.4 Research findings.

## Principles of marketing research

### Purpose

The purpose of **marketing research** is to help organisations make effective decisions by providing information on consumers, competitors and the market. It can help in the development of marketing strategies and marketing activities. The outstandingly successful Twenty/20 cricket competition was developed in response to marketing research findings.

The potential contribution of marketing research to successful marketing strategies is summarised on the next page.

*Data collected for sales purposes cannot be described as marketing research*

45

| Marketing strategy | Aim of strategy | Contribution of marketing research |
|---|---|---|
| Market penetration | To sell more of an existing product to established markets | Marketing research can test whether a sales promotion will encourage greater usage of a product. |
| Product penetration | To improve and modify existing products so they will have more appeal to existing consumers | Marketing research can check whether the modifications made to a product will provide the benefits consumers are seeking. |
| Market development | To expand into new markets with existing products | Marketing research can survey a number of new geographical markets (e.g. new countries joining the European Union) to ascertain which might buy the product. |
| Diversification | To develop new products for completely new markets | Marketing research can investigate the competitors in the market. |

Marketing activities are the tasks that have to be undertaken to achieve the objectives of the marketing team.

| Marketing activity | Marketing research contribution |
|---|---|
| Contemplating product improvements | Show new product concepts to consumers to learn their reaction |
| Implementing a price increase | Ascertain whether new prices still represent 'value for money' for the consumer |
| Designing a new advertising campaign | Check that the new advertising is conveying the intended consumer message |
| Offering products directly to consumers over the Internet | Investigate the effectiveness of the proposed website with potential consumers |

Some organisations claim to be undertaking marketing research when they are in fact gathering information that they intend to use for selling purposes. The use of questionnaires and other data-collection methods to gather information for selling purposes cannot be described as marketing research. Marketing research never needs to collect personal details; if a researcher asks for personal details such as a telephone number, that is a strong indicator that the data is being collected for selling purposes.

# Research stages

Professionally organised marketing research projects follow a number of stages. For a project to be successful, the following stages are necessary.

Define objectives

Write a research brief

Write a research proposal

Plan and forecast

Collect data

Analyse and evaluate data

Present research findings and recommendations

Re-evaluate marketing activities

## 1 Define objectives

A vast number of marketing research objectives are possible. Defining them accurately is a very important step because organisations must guard against collecting inappropriate data. For example, a company may be experiencing falling sales but fail to notice there is a general fall in demand for the product, and that this is the important issue. Instead, it may believe that competitor activity is to blame, and consequently make an investigation of the competition the objective of its marketing research. What it should have explored were the reasons for the overall market decline, and how the company could improve its products or introduce new products to stop the decline.

The research may be concerned with the types of strategic aims and objectives you have considered in Unit 1: Introduction to Business.

| Strategic aims and objectives | Possible research objectives |
| --- | --- |
| Service provision | Identifying service level targets (e.g. waiting times for appointments) for primary health trusts, through consultation with patients |
| Profit maximisation | Investigating the potential sales of a service (e.g. catering), to a market at a profit |
| Growth | Considering how the market size or the organisation's market share will grow in the long term |
| Ethics | Identifying the concerns of key stakeholders, such as the local community or staff |

## 2 Write a research brief

Once the marketing research objectives have been correctly determined, a **research brief** should be written. A written brief:

- provides a check that the data is genuinely needed
- ensures that the information collected will be useful for the decisions being considered
- checks that the results of the project will be available when the key decisions have to be made.

During this stage an investigation should be undertaken to check whether the information is already available in the organisation. It often seems more exciting and interesting to develop new information than to delve through old files and reports.

The format of a typical brief is illustrated on the next page.

**Research brief**

1. Background to organisation

● Its products and its markets

2. The project

● The reason for the project being required (e.g. a need to revitalise a product range)

● Decisions to be influenced by project results (e.g. to select a number of potential new products for further development)

3. Objectives

● The precise information required (e.g. possible prices for new products, best ways to promote these products, stores that should stock them and key product benefits to consumers)

● Outline of the approach to be taken (i.e. whether to have a qualitative focus on a small number of people, or a quantitative focus on a large number of people)

4. Possible research methods

● For example, whether a **secondary research** project, such as reading existing research reports, should be undertaken before deciding to authorise more expensive **primary research** such as telephone interviews

● The sampling options that could be used to ensure reliable and valid data will be collected; sampling (discussed in more detail on page 69) is concerned with how to select the people involved in the research project, not simply a case of interviewing people as they come along

5. Reporting and presentation requirements

● Whether written or verbal reports are needed, and if any progress meetings are required during the project

6. Timing

● The timescales for submission of the proposal and completion of the research

The budget available for the project is rarely included within the brief. This is to ensure that the research is designed to meet the information needs of the organisation rather than the size of the budget available. However, it is probably sensible to indicate a maximum budget that the researcher should keep in mind when designing the research.

### 3 Write a research proposal

The research manager should produce a **research proposal** to respond to the research brief. A fully completed proposal appears on page 67.

### 4 Plan and forecast

Several management tools can be used for planning and forecasting the research project. The most popular methods are Gantt charts and the critical path method (CPM). CPM is an approach that involves dividing the research project into parts and forecasting the time required to complete each activity. A Gantt chart is a type of flow chart that provides a diagrammatic representation of the project across time.

| Task | Week 1 | Week 2 | Week 3 | Week 4 | Week 5 | Week 6 |
|---|---|---|---|---|---|---|
| Plan project | ▓ | | | | | |
| Recruit 'consumers' to be interviewed in their homes | | ▓ | ▓ | | | |
| Undertake interviews | | | ▓ | ▓ | | |
| Analyse data | | | | | ▓ | |
| Present information | | | | | | ▓ |

*A Gantt chart used for planning and forecasting purposes*

## 5 Collect data

Research projects generally collect both primary and secondary research. Secondary data is information that has already been gathered for some purpose other than the current research project.

There are two sources of secondary data. **Internal data** is information available within the organisation (such as sales team reports). **External data** is information available from published and electronic sources outside the organisation (such as government reports). Secondary data is used in many studies because it can be obtained quickly at low cost.

Primary research has two approaches to collecting new data. **Qualitative research** uses small groups of carefully selected consumers to produce non-statistical insights into behaviour, motivations and attitudes. For example, do people see sugar-free products as important to a healthy lifestyle? **Quantitative research** asks a large number of consumers questions that produce statistical insights into behaviour, motivations and attitudes. For example, it could find the percentage of buyers who use credit cards when they buy petrol.

## 6 Analyse and evaluate data

The analysis of qualitative data is conveyed typically through consumer comments and the conclusions of the researcher, in a written or verbal report. It should not be presented in a statistical format.

Quantitative data produces statistics to describe trends and factors such as competition, market structure and consumer habits. It is normally presented using tables, charts and graphs, produced using software such as Microsoft Excel.

### Practice point

*Social Trends* 1970 to 2005 covers 35 years of social change. The following statistics were sourced from *www.statistics.gov.uk/horizons*.

- Since 1970 the number of people in the UK has grown by 3.6 million, to 59.6 million in 2003.
- A retired teacher recently said, 'I feel that our links with Europe have grown stronger since 1970'.
- The population is getting older. There were 9.5 million people aged 65 and over in the UK in 2003, a 28% increase since 1970.
- A secondary school student recently commented, 'modern films are more exciting than the ones made around 1970'.
- A commuter remarked, 'I believe that the service provided by public transport has declined considerably over the past 35 years'.
- The number of children under 16 (11.7 million in 2003) has fallen by 18% since 1970.

Look at these various marketing research findings and decide which are quantitative and which are qualitative results. Review the findings and comment on which of the trends identified may not continue into the future.

| Research finding | Current activity | Revised activity |
|---|---|---|
| Promotional effectiveness could be improved | Using newspapers such as *The Times* | Use magazines such as *FHM* |
| Product looking old-fashioned | Offering brown only | Include grey colour option |
| Prices are too high | £1.25 each | Offer a special deal such as three for the price of two |
| Products are not widely available | Availability in local shops | Make available in supermarkets |

*Re-evaluating marketing activities*

### 7 Present research findings and recommendations

Most projects involve an oral presentation and written report. The quality of these is crucial as it is difficult for the organisation benefiting from the research to take the findings seriously if they are confusing, inaccurate or lack relevance to the key marketing decisions. A format for the written report is presented on page 88.

### 8 Re-evaluate marketing activities

In the light of findings, the organisation benefiting from the research should re-evaluate the marketing activity it is currently undertaking and make considered changes.

## Types of research

### Strategic research

Strategic research delivers the knowledge needed to guide decisions that are likely to have long-term implications for the organisation.

### Technical research

Technical research is designed to help an organisation undertake its current marketing more effectively – for example, improving the effectiveness of advertising activities.

### Databank research

Databank research involves the collection and updating of all relevant market information stored by an organisation.

### Ad hoc research

Ad hoc, otherwise called 'one-off' research, meets information needs that cannot be identified far in advance. For example, a new opportunity may present itself to the organisation or some specific problem may need to be explored.

### Continuous research

Any type of research may be organised so as to produce a continuous stream of data. The advantage of doing this is that it indicates trends and measures performance over time. This is particularly valuable in enabling an organisation to spot changes in the market before they become serious problems.

| | Strategic research | Technical research | Databank research |
|---|---|---|---|
| **Continuous** | Assessing new geographical markets | Monitoring the effectiveness of advertising | Updating figures for market size and market share |
| **Ad hoc** | Assessing the potential of a new product idea | Testing the impact of new advertising | Reporting on a newly emerging competitor |

*Types of research – the options matrix*

# Research objects

Marketing research can cover a wide number of objects, from trying to understand customer behaviour to looking at the activities of competitors. The table below gives a list of possible marketing research objects and the possible content of the research.

| Research object | Research content |
|---|---|
| Customer behaviour | What factors influence customers' product selection?<br>How do they gain product information?<br>Where do they expect to buy the product? |
| Buying patterns | How are sales spread over the year?<br>How sensitive is buying to advertising activity?<br>Which are the most popular price points? |
| Consumer preferences | Which colours do consumers prefer?<br>Which stores do consumers use most?<br>Which information sources do consumers use extensively? |
| Customer satisfaction | How well do products provide the benefits consumers want?<br>Do consumers receive satisfactory customer service?<br>Is the promotional activity delivering the information the consumer requires? |
| Sales trends | Which products are experiencing rising sales?<br>Which stores are recording falling consumer sales?<br>How have products been selling in international markets? |
| Marketing mix changes | What has been the impact of introducing a deluxe product option?<br>Have sales reacted to a special price offer?<br>What is the potential for making sales directly over the Internet? |
| Brand awareness | Do consumers know the brand without prompting?<br>What characteristics does the brand have in the consumer's mind?<br>Do product prices reflect the image of the brand? |
| Advertising awareness | Are consumers aware of the products available?<br>Do consumers understand the key benefits of a product?<br>Is the power of the advertising message likely to encourage consumers to switch brands? |
| Product development success | Which new products have been the most successful?<br>What new products have competitors launched successfully?<br>How well have the new products been accepted in international markets? |
| New product opportunities | How could present products be modified to ensure they appeal to important international markets?<br>Would some further pack size options increase overall sales?<br>What new consumer tastes are emerging which might require new products? |

| Research object | Research content |
|---|---|
| Changes in the market | How could a product be modified to take account of changing consumer tastes? |
| | Should prices be raised to reinforce the quality image the product has acquired in recent years? |
| | How acceptable would it be to send text messages to promote a product? |
| Emergence of new markets | What products are likely to have appeal in this new market? |
| | Where would consumers expect to buy this type of product? |
| | How might awareness of the product be raised? |
| PESTLE analysis (see Unit 11: Introduction to Marketing) | **P**olitical factors – what government ideas might affect the organisation or its market (e.g. further enlargement of the European Union)? |
| | **E**conomic factors – will the economy continue to flourish, maintaining demand for a firm's products (e.g. new houses)? |
| | **S**ocial factors – might changing social factors boost or suppress demand for a business' service (e.g. with an ageing population)? |
| | **T**echnological factors – how might technology (e.g. mobile phones) be used to promote a company's products? |
| | **L**egal factors – what might be the impact of possible new laws (e.g. new gambling laws)? |
| | **E**nvironmental factors – what is the attitude of consumers to current packaging styles (e.g. replacing polystyrene cartons with recycled cardboard cartons)? |

**Practice point**

Think about the data you could try to collect about competitors. Key words that might help direct your analysis might be finance, products, marketing activity, and features of the organisation. In groups, conduct reviews for Asda, Morrisons, Tesco and Sainsbury's. What has made Tesco so successful recently?

## Thinking point

Complete the mind map below to help your learning about marketing research objects. Start with local, national and global companies, and then add branches for their products before identifying marketing research objects that you might want to investigate in respect of those products. Try to add further branches by highlighting the information you might like to collect about those objects. Information on how to produce a mind map can be found on the website *www.mind-map.com*.

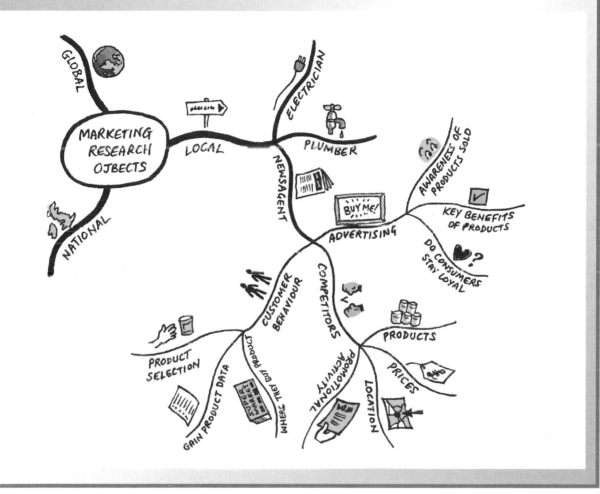

## Outcome activity 12.1

You work for CJG Electronics PLC in its marketing department. CJG has been producing successful electronic products for the past 30 years, including PCs, hi-fis, radios, DVD players and personal stereo systems. At a recent board meeting it was decided that the company should look into the possibility of producing a rival to the Apple iPod. The board members feel that the future of personal portable music probably lies in this direction. They need more market information to help them make their decisions.

### Pass

Explain how the principles of marketing research might be applied to the market development of CJG Electronics PLC's new products.

Comment on the overall purpose of any marketing research undertaken, describe the stages the research should follow, identify the type(s) of research which could be undertaken, and note the research objects that might be beneficial to CJG Electronics PLC.

# Plan research

## Secondary research

Secondary research makes use of research already carried out by somebody else for some other marketing research project. An example would be the statistics published by the government. Secondary research is useful because it:

● may answer some of the organisation's research needs quickly and inexpensively – for example, identifying trends in the market

● could assist in the design of a research project – for example, finding out where to conduct research interviews

● should enable researchers to interpret primary research data better, allowing them to truly understand the broader picture

● could provide a source of comparative data to help check results

● may provide data that cannot be collected in any other way, such as information on government spending.

## Internal sources of secondary research

Internal data is information held inside the organisation conducting the research. The sources of internal data are discussed below in the order of their importance, with the most important first.

### EPOS (electronic point of sale)

EPOS systems are mainly used by businesses that have large numbers of regular sales, such as retail stores and hotels.

An EPOS terminal linked to a back-office computer handles payments quickly, updates stock lists and provides instant information.

EPOS software can provide a business with data about individual store sales, product sales by region, product sales by department or by product category, such as gardening.

It can also reveal changing consumer buying behaviour, such as a move towards credit card transactions or changing shopping patterns.

### Loyalty schemes

Loyalty cards, such as the Advantage card offered by Boots, records details of every individual purchase made by a cardholder. Consequently the card issuers have details on:

● the frequency with which they visit stores

● the range of products they purchase

● the consistency with which they buy particular brands

● the extent to which they will try new products

● whether advertising influences their purchasing patterns.

The fact that organisations such as Tesco with its Clubcard, Sainsbury's with the Nectar card and Boots are willing to invest a lot of money in these schemes shows how much they value the information gathered.

### Sales records

Organisations generally have a lot of sales data at their fingertips. It needs to be reported in an efficient manner so it can become important marketing research data. This normally involves summarising the sales from individual customers into useful categories. The example below shows the same sales data summarised and presented in two entirely different ways for SuperClean Vacuum Cleaners.

## Case study  SuperClean Vacuum Cleaners

| Product description | Invoice price (£) | Unit sales | Total Revenue (£) |
|---|---|---|---|
| Superclean 50 | 100 | 9,500 | 950,000 |
| Superclean 100 | 125 | 7,500 | 937,500 |
| Superclean 150 | 150 | 5,000 | 750,000 |
| Superclean 200 | 175 | 2,000 | 350,000 |
| Superclean Deluxe | 200 | 750 | 150,000 |
| Category total | | 24,750 | 3,137,500 |

*Sales by product category, UK, January to March*

| Channel of distribution | Unit sales |
|---|---|
| Hardware stores | 12,500 |
| DIY warehouses | 2,250 |
| Builder's merchants | 6,500 |
| Others | 3,500 |
| Total | 24,750 |

*Sales by channel of distribution, UK, January to March*

1 How might the sales team wish to see this information presented?
2 What other information could transform this information into even more useful marketing research data?
3 How might the information be used by the organisation?

## Website monitoring

It is possible for web-based traders to monitor the number of times different pages on their sites are accessed, what search engines brought people to the site, and the peak times at which most people access the site. A web trader can identify when users revisit the site and the sections of the site that they visit.

For example, an organisation such as Amazon (*www.amazon.co.uk*) can monitor the types of book that particular customers are interested in and whether the customers spend time reading the reviews or considering alternatives. Web-based traders have an advantage over traditional retailers as they can obtain information on browsers (the equivalent of window shoppers) as well as customers.

## E-transactions

Web-based traders can use sophisticated software products to keep a database of customers, which can be used to e-mail information about special products and offers tailored to their past store-browsing patterns. For example, when a consumer enters *www.amazon.com*, he or she receives a personalised greeting and some product recommendations based on previous purchases.

| Information | Uses of information |
|---|---|
| Geographical location of customers | Ask the sales team to seek new customers in areas where few customers are located |
| Which products are purchased | Devise a sales promotion to boost the sale of products that should be selling better |
| When products are bought | Advertise best-selling products when demand peaks |
| When the product was last bought | Send a direct mail letter suggesting customers consider upgrading to the latest model |
| Average order value | Revise the discount scheme to encourage customers to increase their order value |

## Data records

Organisations hold all kinds of data records, some of which might contain valuable market research data. A good example would be the records held in the sales office.

## Accounting records and production records

An indication of a product's popularity may be its production output figures. However, products may simply have been transferred into the warehouse, so it is sales to consumers that are the important figures for the sales office.

The accounts department will also have records that may be of interest to a researcher. They may know the payment method customers are using – credit or debit card, cheque with banker's card, loan arrangements or simply cash. This sort of information contributes to building a comprehensive picture of the organisation's customers.

## Sales personnel

The management of many organisations is dependent on their sales personnel for marketing information. Sales people commonly discover information on the following.

- Promotional activity by competitors. Competitors are likely to be actively offering special deals. The impact of a particular idea, such as offering a free handbag with a purchase of a fragrance, can be useful information.

- Price offers that may indicate a competitor is struggling to meet sales targets or holding too much stock. It might be a signal for the replacement of a range and the imminent launch of new products.

- Competition data, such as the announcement of a national advertising campaign, changes in delivery arrangements and improvements in after-sales service.

- Market trends, such as a shift to healthy foods or a shift to a new holiday destination.

Sales personnel might gain this data from speaking to consumers, reading the sales brochures of competitors, speaking to contacts in the industry or attending exhibitions and conferences.

## Delphi technique

The Delphi method can be used with experts from within the organisation, to help develop a picture of how the future might unfold for the business.

A panel of experts is recruited, but they never meet, to remove the possibility that panel members might influence each other. The method works as follows.

- Each member of the panel gives an opinion without consulting other panel members.

- A nominated person gathers together all the opinions. At this stage any extreme views are discarded and the general view of the panel is established.

- This view is then described to each panel member for further thought. The members will have the opportunity to amend their views.

- Over time, a general agreement emerges about the future from the experts.

A Delphi panel might be as follows.

| Delphi panel members | Topics for potential discussion |
|---|---|
| Marketing director<br>Research and development manager<br>International sales manager<br>Customer care co-ordinator | The impact of the Internet on selling methods.<br>What will the High Street look like by 2020?<br>How will lifestyles develop in the next 15 years? |

The conclusions from this type of activity are normally used to develop future plans for the organisation. In other words a number of 'futures' are considered. Regardless of which one proves the most accurate, at least the organisation will have spent some time considering the implications.

## External sources of secondary data

External data is that which is available outside the organisation conducting the research. The sources described below are listed in general order of importance.

### Internet

A large amount of secondary data is now available in electronic format. Even if the information is unavailable electronically, the sources of data can frequently be identified by electronic means. It is becoming a very useful and important source of marketing research information.

If you do not know the location of the information you are seeking from the Internet, you can use a search engine. They allow you to enter one or more key words relating to a product, market, country or company and in response the search engine displays a list of sites that has information relating to those key words.

**Thinking point**

Consider the options in the table below and think about where in the organisation the following marketing research data may be found.

| Internal research sources | Which department? |
|---|---|
| Sales personnel market reports | Marketing/production/sales office |
| E-transaction data | Finance/IT/libraries |
| Production records | Newspapers/production/human resources |
| Website monitoring information | Distribution/quality/IT |
| Delphi techniques commentaries | Design/marketing/government |
| Accounting records | Internet/sales/finance |

| Search engine | Web address | Features |
|---|---|---|
| Ask Jeeves | www.ask.com | Simply input a question |
| Google | www.google.com | Examines over two billion web pages |
| Yahoo! | www.yahoo.com | Has local country-based versions |

There are many more useful business sites. Listed here are some that students have often found useful.

http://education.ntu.ac.uk/resources/BusEd.html – links to business-related sites

http://www.bized.ac.uk – lots of business information

http://europa.eu.int/comm/index_en.htm – the European Commission home page.

### Government statistics

The government regularly analyses business activity and publishes the results in reference books that are often available in college or university learning centres. Increasingly this information is available through government reports that can be downloaded from the Internet. Many such reports can be found at www.statistics.gov.uk.

- *Social Trends* draws together social and economic data from a wide range of government departments and other organisations. It paints a broad picture of Britain and how it is changing.

- *Monthly Digest of Statistics* summarises information on monthly economic trends.

- *Expenditure and Food Survey* provides information on spending patterns in these key areas.

- *Regional Trends* includes economic regional profiles, details of households, labour market facts and indicators of living standards.

- *Labour Market Trends* has, among other facts, detailed statistics showing employment in different industries, levels of unemployment and wage rates.

- *Annual Abstract of Statistics* covers population, social conditions, production prices and employment.

### Practice point

Go to www.statistics.gov.uk and double click on the 'Neighbourhood' icon at the top of the screen. Type either your postcode or your area's name into the search engine in the 'Neighbourhood profile' box, and click on 'Search'. A summary of useful statistics on that area should then be available.

1 What is the population total for your area?

2 What percentage of people in your area are between the ages of 16 and 19?

3 What percentage of people in your area are employed?

4 How might this site be useful if you were thinking of starting a business?

### Libraries

Libraries generally contain the following sources of information:

- business information from a comprehensive collection of sources, including UK and international telephone directories

- foreign newspapers and company reports

- financial and statistical company information

- market research reports

- company databases with contact names and addresses

- reference books on business topics.

### Universities

Universities, apart from holding the resources found in most libraries, have journals which provide a much richer source of information, because the journal articles are themselves pieces of research. The university will also publish the research work of its own academic staff. For example, Nottingham University researches issues important to the insurance industry, so consequently companies in that industry may be especially interested to view the research work of the university.

### Company reports

Company reports are useful when compiling a competitor analysis report, since they contain information such as sales and profit figures. This information may be provided for the past five years. Some contain statements from key directors about the previous trading period and the prospects for the future.

It is possible to order company reports over the Internet from *www.hemscott.net* or *www.ftannualreports.com*. Companies are obliged to send their accounts annually to Companies House, which can provide copies of the accounts. Use *www.companieshouse.gov.uk* to review the complete range of services offered to the researcher.

### Reports by specialist agencies

Market research companies produce reports on markets and products and then offer them to organisations with an interest in that particular market – producers, retailers and suppliers. These reports are expensive to buy.

Mintel produces a wide variety of reports covering market size, market segments, levels of advertising, factors determining market growth and future forecasts.

Thomson Financial produces Datastream, a valuable source of current financial data including stock market share prices, historical economic data, economic forecasts and interest rate and exchange rate information.

Dun & Bradstreet publishes comprehensive financial reports on companies and on the trading prospects in a particular industry.

Economic forecasts and changes in market information can be obtained from the *Investors Chronicle*, *www.investorschronicle.co.uk* or *www.bloomberg.com*.

### Trade journals

Trade journals contain invaluable information. They discuss key trends and developments in an industry, and are published by people who work in the industry. They provide information on new products and services. They often carry profiles of successful companies and examine the prospects for important product categories. A list of trade journals can be found on Yahoo at Directory>Business and economy>Business-to-business>News and media>Magazines>Trade magazines.

*Trade journals provide valuable information and discuss key trends*

## Criteria for selection

Just because data has been found that appears relevant to the questions being investigated by the research project, that does not mean it is accurate, reliable and useful. The flow chart below describes how to decide whether the source is appropriate.

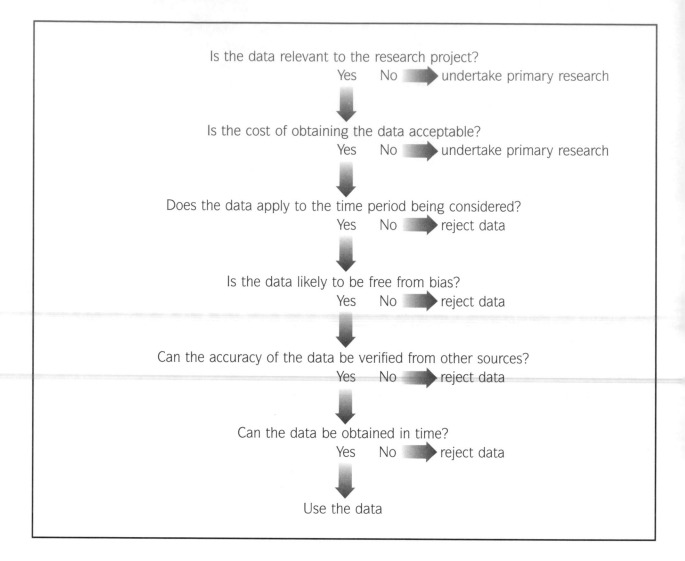

Is the data relevant to the research project?
Yes      No  ━━▶ undertake primary research

Is the cost of obtaining the data acceptable?
Yes      No  ━━▶ undertake primary research

Does the data apply to the time period being considered?
Yes      No  ━━▶ reject data

Is the data likely to be free from bias?
Yes      No  ━━▶ reject data

Can the accuracy of the data be verified from other sources?
Yes      No  ━━▶ reject data

Can the data be obtained in time?
Yes      No  ━━▶ reject data

Use the data

## Use of IT applications

Before the widespread use of computers, when surveys involved relatively small numbers of questionnaires, data processing was carried out by hand. Simple counts were made of the answers given to questions, and numbers and percentages for each response were calculated. Apart from being time-consuming, however, manual analysis also prevented any complex interpretation of the data.

The introduction of data processing as a tool for storing, organising, retrieving and reporting data has been a major advance. Once the data has been fed into the computer it is possible to carry out many checks on the data and to analyse it in all kinds of ways that would not be possible using manual procedures. In addition to giving far greater scope for data analysis, computers also reduce the cost of carrying it out.

## Primary research methods

Primary research is used for collecting new information required for a marketing research project – information that has never previously been collected. A variety of methods are used.

### Observation

Observation is a data-gathering approach that involves collecting information without any questions being asked. The researcher is the witness of behaviour and events. Observation cannot explain the underlying reasons for the behaviour it records, so for this reason observation methods are often combined with other research methods. The following are examples of information gathered by observation.

| Observation in a store | Observation in the home |
|---|---|
| Arrival time in the store | TV viewing – what do people watch and for how long? |
| Shopper movement once in the store | How do children play with a new toy? |
| Time spent queuing | How do people use a cleaning product? |
| Interaction with customer-care personnel | |

The major advantage of observation research is that the data collected does not contain distortions or inaccuracies as a result of memory error or the giving of socially desirable answers. In other words, the research process itself does not influence the behaviour of the individual. For behaviour that the individual feels reflects badly on them, such as smoking or drinking, properly conducted observation may give a more accurate picture than personal interviewing. Doctors believe that patients underestimate their drinking and smoking by 100%. Observation data records the actual behaviour that takes place.

Retailers send out employees, called mystery shoppers, to visit their own and competitors' stores. They are required to observe fixture layouts, displays, store traffic and special promotions. Some organisations even send out specially trained staff to pose as customers. They are generally concerned with the standard of customer service.

## Experimentation

Experimental research allows the researcher to change one aspect of an offer (such as price) and observe the impact on another aspect of the same offer (such as sales). All the other aspects of the offer remain the same – product, promotion, packaging, and shelf display. For example Lyons Tetley, when launching the round teabag, experimented by analysing purchasing behaviour while altering the shape of the teabag; all other aspects of the offer were kept constant.

## Case study    Tetley and the round teabag

Lyons Tetley found itself losing market share to supermarket own-brand teabags. The company developed a round teabag to counter this trend. It chose experimentation as the method to research the idea.

It recruited 240 heavy buyers of tea, people who used at least 80 teabags in a fortnight and bought one of the leading national brands – Tetley, Typhoo, Quick Brew and PG Tips.

The panel members were visited each week by a researcher who had an illustrated brochure of tea brands and packaging options along with the lowest prices being offered by the local supermarkets. Tetley's round bags was one of the brands included in the brochure. To induce trial, the round bag was offered at a promotional price over the first two weeks.

In the panel, 46% of participants tried round teabags and made at least one repeat purchase. People preferred the product because of their perception of its improved flavour, even though the tea was the same as in the square bag; only the shape differed.

It was originally planned for the panel to operate for 12 weeks, by which time stable repeat purchasing rates had emerged. But Lyons Tetley was still concerned about the novelty value wearing off, so it ran the panel for a further eight weeks. There was no perceptible erosion of the repeat purchase rate, however, even after over four months of exposure to the brand.

Analysing the purchasing patterns in detail and using the results to forecast potential sales, Lyons Tetley decided to launch the round teabag onto the market. In spite of considerable competitive activity at the time of the launch, the product was a major success.

1 Outline the marketing research method used by Lyons Tetley.
2 Describe an alternative marketing research method it could have considered.
3 What secondary marketing research sources might have been used?

## Surveys

Surveys are used to collect marketing research data from a carefully chosen group of consumers. Those who take part are called **respondents**. There are several different methods of conducting surveys, which are outlined below.

## Face-to-face surveys

Personal interviews involve the respondent and researcher speaking face-to-face. At one time it was a very popular way of conducting surveys, particularly in home interviews for consumer products such as televisions, furniture and food. However, face-to-face interviews are expensive and generate low response rates unless a great deal of time is spent in revisiting people. Nowadays fewer people are at home when interviewers are most likely to want to call, and personal interviews are largely conducted in shopping centres. Personal interviews are also conducted at businesses and other types of organisations.

## Telephone surveys

Telephone interviews are used for business-to-business and consumer research. This is an ideal method when a national, regional or even international survey is required.

Telephone interviews are generally computer controlled. Each question appears on the interviewer's screen and he or she reads the question exactly as it appears. Generally questions are short-answer questions, where responses are limited to a choice of possibilities. Answers are immediately entered into the computer for analysis.

| Advantages of face-to-face interviews | Limitations of face-to-face interviews |
| --- | --- |
| Little of the researcher's time is wasted | People in a hurry are difficult to question |
| Possible to use illustrative materials during interview (e.g. new packaging) | Interviews have to be done in clusters (e.g. in the city centre) to keep costs under control |
| Possible to motivate respondent to take part | Sometimes difficult to control interviewer bias – interviewers may pick friendly looking people, and those who appear not to be in a hurry |
| Possible to check respondent is of the type being sought before the interview is conducted | Interview cost is the highest of any method |
| Respondent can be convinced that the researcher and research are genuine | Refusal rates are high, between 5% and 30% |

| Advantages of telephone interviews | Limitations of telephone interviews |
| --- | --- |
| People feel a compulsion to answer the telephone | The telephone number list can be outdated |
| Good coverage is gained as 95% of UK households have telephones – including people normally difficult to contact | A telephone interview can generally be no longer than 15 minutes |
| Very high response rate | There is no way to use visual aids |
| No travel is involved – saving time and costs | Sometimes interviews are used to disguise a selling approach |
| Question order can be changed by the computer to eliminate the bias of last and first responses being favoured choices | It is not possible to ask complex questions |
| Data can be analysed almost immediately | Telephone ownership is not widespread in some developing nations |

## Thinking point

Research Computer-Assisted Telephone Interviewing (**CATI**) and Completely Automated Telephone Interviews (**CATS**). What are the advantages and limitations of this type of marketing research technology?

## Postal surveys

In postal surveys, questionnaires are mailed to pre-selected respondents along with a return envelope, a covering letter and possibly an incentive. The respondents complete and return the questionnaire. Although postal surveys have been around for many years, their importance has grown as a result of the availability of customer databases and the need to measure customer satisfaction.

Postal surveys can look an attractive proposition because they have low costs, but unfortunately they tend also to have low response rates. It is not uncommon for surveys to experience response rates as low as 20%.

| Advantages of postal surveys | Limitations of postal surveys |
|---|---|
| National and international areas can be covered | Low response rate |
| Data can be obtained from people who are normally difficult to interview (e.g. carers) | Questionnaires are often not fully completed |
| Responses can be obtained on sensitive issues such as personal hygiene and income | They may not be completed by the right person |
| They are low cost – telephone surveys can be three times more expensive, and face-to-face interviews nine times | Those who respond may not be representative of the people mailed – just people with time on their hands |
| They can be completed when it is convenient for the respondent | They are only suitable for tick-box questions |
| | The return of questionnaires can be spread over several weeks |

## E-mail surveys

E-mail surveys involve delivering a questionnaire through desk-based PCs but also through digital television and WAP-enabled mobile phones. They are essentially postal surveys delivered electronically.

This type of research tends to be cheaper and faster to implement than postal surveys. Respondents may also give more detailed responses to open-ended questions than is the case with postal surveys as they have a keyboard in front of them and are used to producing short responses using e-mail.

The amount of junk mail 'spam' being sent to computer users is growing, which may make it more difficult to succeed with e-mail surveys. It is considered a good idea to ask people to participate rather than simply to send them an unexpected questionnaire. Some respondents may be concerned about confidentiality as the returned questionnaire will have the respondent's e-mail address attached.

### E-marketing research

Web surveys generally appear in two forms, the standard questionnaire format and the interactive questionnaire. The standard questionnaire format appears as it would on paper. The respondent scrolls down the page, answering each question. The interactive questionnaire has questions appearing on the screen one at a time. The respondent submits an answer and then the computer selects a new question according to the answers to previous questions.

Web surveys are currently useful for monitoring web usage and attitudes towards websites, as well as feedback on computers and technology in general. It can be anticipated that in the future web-based surveys will replace a significant number of postal surveys.

### Focus groups

Focus groups are in-depth interviews undertaken with a group comprising eight to twelve people. They involve interaction between the participants. The aim of focus group research is to learn and understand what people think about a topic at length and in detail.

Focus groups provide a rich and detailed source of information. The purpose is to discover how people feel about a product, concept, idea or organisation. The views of one person may become the stimulus for another's ideas or may start a useful discussion. People tend to be encouraged to talk when they realise that others have similar experiences and attitudes.

### Panels

A panel is a form of survey that collects data from people over an extended period of time. They provide a measurement of change over time. Panels can consist of households, organisations and individuals. They are useful for a variety of purposes, such as:

- identifying broad trends in a market, for example are consumers buying more sugar-free products?
- investigating consumer behaviour, for example how often do consumers switch brands?
- discovering customer attitudes or reactions to a product – for example a new model barbecue.

Information may be gathered by questionnaire, telephone interview, diaries (booklets where respondents record their behaviour and purchases over a period such as a month) or through the Internet. The best-known examples of panel research are the consumer purchase panels monitoring individual or household buyer behaviour in the areas of food and drink.

### Organisational issues with panel surveys

The following organisational issues are important when using panel surveys.

- It can be quite difficult to retain the panel members for the entire task.
- For consistency, there is a need to replace people who leave with similar people.
- There is the need to check that panellists are completing recording procedures correctly.
- It is difficult to obtain a representative group of people, as the only people who participate may be those who have a deep interest in the product.
- There is a need to ensure that people do not change their behaviour because they know their actions are being recorded, such as starting to clean their teeth regularly.

### Field trials and piloting

Some products need to be tested over a period of time, such as refrigerators in the home, cycles on the road and chairs in the office. This process is called field trial testing.

Pilot testing involves administering a questionnaire to a limited number of potential respondents in order to identify and correct design flaws.

| Technique | Appropriateness | Limitations |
|---|---|---|
| Field trials | When the consumer has to undertake some preparation or installation<br><br>When a long period of consumer use is required to fully appreciate a product's strengths and weaknesses<br><br>The method has been used by confectionery and food companies (e.g. Cadbury's Wispa) prior to a national launch | Expensive to organise and supervise<br><br>Needs the 'final' product for testing, consequently substantial investment in productive capacity takes place ahead of consumer testing<br><br>Testers drop out because they get bored or lose interest in the product |
| Piloting | Used with a questionnaire when there are concerns over the format of questions, the time needed to complete the questionnaire and how respondents may react to certain questions, especially ones of a personal nature | Pilot and full surveys must be conducted with same type of respondents<br><br>Pilots must be undertaken with a relatively small number of people who reflect the views of the whole group |

ARE YOU SURE THIS IS WHAT THE MARKETING MANAGER MEANT WHEN SHE SAID TO ORGANISE SOME FIELD TRIALS ?!

# Appropriateness of each method

The different primary research methods can be summarised as follows.

| | Observation | Experimentation | Surveys | Focus groups | Field trials |
|---|---|---|---|---|---|
| Fitness for purpose | Useful for quantitative data | Provides quantitative data | Provides both qualitative and quantitative data | Provides detailed, qualitative data | Provides both qualitative and quantitative data |
| Cost | Low, once technology is bought and installed (e.g. CCTV in store) | High – time consuming, and needs careful monitoring and analysis | Low – although face-to-face can be expensive | High – it may be necessary to conduct several groups before common views emerge | High – recruitment of participants is costly, and there is a need to check records are being kept properly |
| Accuracy | Good – records exactly what happens | May be difficult to identify the factors (i.e. price, product features or promotional activity) that are really influencing consumer reactions | Depends on the quality of the sample; the sample determines whether appropriate people participate | The group may follow the views of the most vocal participant; members may give socially acceptable answers | Behaviour might change because records are being kept; people may act in a socially acceptable manner |
| Time | May require a considerable amount of time to organise project and complete observation; may need to review tapes several times to ascertain behaviour | If a number of factors are being investigated it may take a considerable length of time | Can take a long time for all face-to-face interviews to be completed or for postal surveys to be returned | Takes time to recruit, organise the group discussion and analyse comments | This method is designed for long-term projects |
| Validity | Sees what is happening – but interpretation may be wrong | A false situation, so people start acting differently | Can produce invalid answers because people have poor memories or do not understand the questions | Good – moderator can explain and explore issues | Excellent if recording is done properly – it records what is happening |
| Response | Not an issue – people may not even realise they are participating | May be difficult to recruit participants and retain them for the period of the experiment | Generally poor, especially for postal surveys | Once recruited, members tend to talk freely in the group | Fine once people have agreed to be panel members |

# Stages of research

A full explanation of the various marketing research stages can be found earlier in this unit on page 47–50. Below is a fully completed research proposal that illustrates those stages.

---

**Research proposal: Franji Drinks – An approach to entering the UK soft drinks market**

### 1  Background to organisation

Franji is a soft drinks manufacturer contemplating developing some products for launch in the UK market. It does not have any production units of its own, but instead uses contract producers to make products it feels would have market appeal. This provides the company with the ability to satisfy consumer tastes and preferences, whatever they might turn out to be.

### 2  The project

Franji wants to gain a thorough understanding of the current trends in the UK soft drinks market and the strengths and weaknesses of the competition. It also needs a clear idea of what new products to consider introducing.

### 3  Target audience

Everybody drinks soft drinks and therefore every group in the population should be included in the audience for this project.

### 4  Objectives and data to be collected

- Provide market size data for the past five years in terms of both litres drunk and value of consumption.
- Provide market share data for past three years showing and explaining shifting patterns.
- Provide figure for the value of sales by category in recent years, including a forecast of likely consumption patterns.
- Identify main competitors and provide an analysis of their approach to the **marketing mix** – product, price, place and promotion.
- Provide a list of possible new drinks that would have appeal to UK consumers.

### 5  Research methods and timing

- Undertake secondary, quantitative, external research to ascertain market size, market share, category sales and competition profiles by referring to company reports and soft drink information Internet sites such as *www.britvic.co.uk*.
- Undertake secondary, qualitative, external research to ascertain consumer opinions on current drinks by consulting market reports from organisations such as Mintel.
- Explore further consumer tastes (such as in flavours) and preferences (such as for screw-top bottles) through qualitative primary research using focus groups and face-to-face interviews.
- Respondents to be selected using the judgement sampling technique.

## 6 Reporting and presentation requirements

- Progress meeting 10.30 am on 7 January at Franji Drinks' head office.
- Preliminary results to be presented verbally 9.30 am on 4 February at Rapid Research Ltd, 45 Dovecote Lane, Beeston, Nottingham NG9 1HR.
- Written report (six copies) to be delivered to Franji Drinks by 18 February.

## 7 Fees

- Face-to-face interviews – 12 at £450 each.
- Focus groups – two at £1,250 each.
- Mintel report purchase – Soft Drinks – £4,500
- Internet searches – four hours at £120 per hour.
- Company report appraisal – four hours at £120 per hour.
- Other expenses including hotel accommodation and travel £1,640.
- Total budget requirement £15,000.

## 8 Researchers

- Ellie Strickson – has worked for Rapid Research for six years and has been involved in work for Mars confectionery and Dulux paints.
- Carlos Perreira – has worked for Rapid Research for 10 years, completing research for organisations such as Ford and David Lloyd Leisure Centres.

## 9 Contract terms and other points

- Payment seven days after receipt of written reports.
- Research team to discuss content or findings of project only with Franji.

### Outcome activity 12.2

Continue the assignment concerning CJG Electronics from Outcome Activity 12.1.

You have selected a marketing research company called Rapid Research to help you complete the project.

**Pass**

Select an appropriate method of data collection and plan research for a selected product or service.

You will need to write a research brief and then a research proposal that responds to the brief. (CJG's marketing manager would write the research brief while a researcher at Rapid Research would produce the research proposal.)

It is possible that you could conduct the research in a group, although interpretation and analysis must be done on an individual basis.

# Implement research

This section explains how you can carry out some marketing research.

## Census or sample?

Research involving everybody in a particular population is called a census. This is seldom possible because of the expense involved; they are used only when a market is very small, which can be a characteristic of some industrial markets. Consequently, samples are usually used when researching. In marketing terms, a sample means a small number of individuals who can give an insight into the views of a whole group.

### Choosing the sample

There are several ways of selecting a sample. Sampling methods can be grouped under two headings: **probability sampling** and **non-probability sampling**. A respondent is a person who is asked to participate in a marketing research project.

### Probability sampling

This method systematically selects people; the chances of somebody being selected could be expressed as a mathematical probability.

- **Random sampling** means all members of a population have a known and equal chance of being included in the sample. For example, the names of every household in a community could be written on slips of paper and the slips deposited in a box. The box could then be shaken so that the slips of paper become thoroughly mixed. Someone drawing out successive slips of paper would be taking a random sample of the households in that community.

  This technique works well for small groups, but for larger ones the method is not appropriate, since it is difficult to obtain a list of all the members of the group.

- **Systematic sampling** produces samples that are almost identical to those generated by simple random sampling. However, it is considered easier to implement, as it does not need to identify every member of the population individually. A random starting point may be generated, possibly by computer, and after that people are selected at regular intervals, say, every twenty-fifth person in the population. This method does require a full listing of the population in an appropriate random order, such as an alphabetic list.

  If the number of students in a class is 30 in total and it is decided to select every fifth student starting from the random number of 5, then students 5, 10, 15, 20, 25 and 30 would be selected for the sample.

- **Stratified sampling** takes into account the fact that some customers are more important than others. It weights the sample on the basis of the importance of each group of customers in the market.

  If an organisation has 10,000 small users of products accounting for sales of £1 million, 8,000 medium users accounting for £1 million and 1,000 large users accounting for £2 million in sales, a random sample of 200 would not be representative of the whole market. To make the sample representative, the large users should be allocated half of the sample because they make up half of the sales. A quarter of the sample should be allocated to each of the medium and small user groups. The stratified random sample would have 100 large users, 50 medium users and 50 small users all randomly chosen from their respective categories.

- **Cluster sampling** involves dividing the total population into separate groups that represent the population in microcosm; in other words, the cluster has the same characteristics as the total population. This means each cluster group is the same, which is different from stratified groups where each group is very different. Once the clusters have been identified they are sampled in a random manner. Area sampling is a common technique; areas are selected that represent perhaps a region. The results would be expected to mirror the views of the whole nation.

**Multi-stage sampling** is used to reduce the cost of random sampling without losing the element of randomness. In the case of sampling UK households, at the first stage of the process a simple random sample may be taken of all parliamentary constituencies in the UK. For the constituencies selected, a list of wards is compiled and a simple random sample selected from wards within each constituency. At the third stage each ward could be divided into groups of streets known as polling areas, and a simple random sample taken from these streets.

There is no need to have a complete list of everybody in the population. Another advantage of this method is that the interviewing generally takes place in a confined geographical area. This reduces administration and travelling costs when the fieldwork is undertaken.

## Non-probability sampling

Although probability sampling, if properly conducted, produces the best results, it can be costly and time consuming and in some situations it is difficult to identify a random sample. Under these circumstances non-probability sampling is used.

Non-probability sampling uses subjective methods to select people, meaning it is impossible to know the probability of somebody being selected.

**Quota sampling** ensures that the proportions in a sample reflect the whole market. Quotas are identified on the basis of known features of the market under investigation. Dividing a market into age groups is a popular way to ensure that the characteristics of the sample reflect the features of the whole group. This prevents particular groups, such as older or younger people, from dominating a sample.

Because quotas can be selected from a relatively small geographical area they are cost-effective in gathering data. Anyone who refuses to participate can be replaced by someone else who fits the quota characteristics.

**Judgement sampling** involves researchers selecting the sample based on who they think will most likely reflect the views of the group to be interviewed. This method is used in industrial research where a few large companies dominate a market. All the major companies in a sector might be included, plus a sample of the smaller ones. The purpose is to weight the results with the views of the important members of the sample. For example, the pharmaceutical giants GlaxoSmithKline and Pzifer, plus a selection of all the smaller companies, would be appropriate in that industrial sector.

**Convenience sampling** uses no sample design. For example, when an interviewer questions people met on the street, choice is left entirely to the interviewer. The sample is chosen on the basis of who can be contacted easily.

Another example might be a company producing a prototype washing machine and asking some of its employees to test it in their own homes. Such a sample provides useful information as long as the sample seems to be reasonably representative of the likely customer. For example, asking students about their reading habits would not shed light on the reading habits of the nation.

*Be careful about telling interviewers they can speak to anyone they can contact conveniently and easily*

| Probability sampling | Non-probability sampling |
|---|---|
| Results can be projected to represent the total population.<br><br>Results are definitive rather than indicative.<br><br>Researchers can be sure of obtaining information from a relatively representative group of the population being investigated.<br><br>Respondent selection and sample design significantly increase the research/interviewer cost and time. | Cost is significantly lower than probability sampling.<br><br>Sample sizes tend to be smaller.<br><br>Researchers can target most important respondents.<br><br>The results reveal likely views rather than definitive views.<br><br>Researchers do not know how representative the sample is of the population being investigated. |

*Comparing sampling methods*

## Cost and accuracy of information

The different sampling methods may be summarised as follows regarding their accuracy and cost.

**Thinking point**

Your school or college has decided to undertake a research project. It wants all the groups that make up the student community to be involved. Suggest three sampling methods that could be used, and make a recommendation with a justification.

| Sample selection method | Cost | Accuracy | Comments |
|---|---|---|---|
| Probability – random | very high | excellent | |
| Systematic random | high | excellent | |
| Stratified | high | good | |
| Multi-stage | lower | good | cost effective |
| Cluster | lower | good | cost effective |
| Quota | lower | good | very popular method |
| Judgement | lower | reasonable | appropriate for some markets |
| Convenience | low | open to question | |

## Sample size

There are three ways of determining sample size: by the budget available, by choosing the sample sizes used in previous studies, or by using a statistical method.

Frequently the sample size is determined by the amount of money that is available for the project. A marketing manager may declare that £17,500 is available to investigate a particular issue. After deducting the costs for such tasks as questionnaire design and analysing the data, an amount would remain that could be spent on interviews. This is perhaps how a large number of research projects determine their sample sizes.

Many researchers will rely on past experience to determine an appropriate sample size. Previous studies investigating similar research objectives may guide the researcher.

The final method of determining sample size is to use a statistical technique. Statistical methods are only used to calculate sample sizes for probability sampling methods. Statistical methods allow researchers to have confidence in the fact that results from a randomly selected sample are truly representative of the population being studied. The researcher can calculate the degree of confidence that can be applied to the results, and the accuracy of the results can be expressed as a likely deviation from the final figure. For example, the researcher might have a high degree of confidence (such as 99%) in a result that showed the average young person drinks 18 cans of soft drinks a week, with an accuracy of plus or minus four cans.

The degree of confidence required from a sample and the level of accuracy thought appropriate can all be decided prior to the research commencing and the required sample size being calculated.

# Questionnaires

Questionnaires are used in a variety of contexts in marketing research. They can be the format used for conducting surveys including mail surveys, telephone interviews and formal, structured personal interviews. Irrespective of the context in which the survey research is being conducted, the ways in which the questionnaire is constructed are broadly similar.

A questionnaire is a data-collecting device. It formally sets out the way research questions should be asked.

## Design

Even the most simple questionnaires need careful wording and organisation to produce accurate information. Consideration needs to be given to the content, the phrasing of questions, the type of questions to be used, the layout and the sequence. Questionnaires should be tested – this is called piloting – before they are used.

Effective questionnaires generally have the following design characteristics:

- they start with a statement about the reason for the survey, to put respondents at ease and reassure people this is not a selling activity

- they provide example questions and answers at the beginning to show how the questionnaire should be completed

- they avoid the use of jargon (such as 'cookie'), acronyms (such as 'BTEC') or complex language

- questions are phrased precisely

- questions do not ask for information outside the objectives of the research project.

## Questions to be asked

Three types of information can be gathered using questionnaires – facts, opinions and motives.

- *Factual* data is for example about age, gender or geographical location.

- *Opinion* data can be very useful to decision-makers. It provides them with information about beliefs, attitudes, feelings and knowledge but the answers have to be treated with some caution as they will not be as reliable as factual data.

- Knowing people's *motives* for a particular action can be important to those wishing to influence them, such as advertisers. Analysis is inevitably **subjective** and can only deliver an impression rather than certainty about people's real motives.

## Sequencing

The **sequencing** of questions is important. The early questions should attempt to create interest, so that the respondent will continue. The questions should follow a logical order. Overall the questions should move from the general to the more detailed, and there should be a logical flow from question to question and from topic to topic. All questions relating to a particular topic should be asked before moving on to another topic. Questionnaires should be easy to use and encourage the user to answer the questions posed. Any potentially embarrassing or personal questions should be left until late in the questionnaire.

## Dichotomous questions

Dichotomous questions are the simplest form of closed question as the respondent is limited to two fixed alternatives, as in the example below:

Have you shopped at Asda before?        Yes/No

These types of questions do not provide much detail but are useful as screening questions to determine whether a respondent should be asked further questions on a particular subject.

## Multiple-choice questions

Multiple-choice questions provide respondents with a choice of potential responses. The respondents are normally asked to tick one alternative that best matches their views. Such questions are difficult to design because the designer needs to know all the potential answers; however, other options can be accommodated by inserting 'Others (please specify)' as one of the options.

## Scaled questions

It is sometimes necessary to judge the strength of feeling about a topic. This requires the use of a rating or response scale question. There are various types; Likert scales, for example, show how strongly a respondent agrees or disagrees with a statement.

Semantic differential scales, as illustrated in Question 3 of the sample questionnaire on page 74, use two key words describing the opposite ends of a scale, with a series of points highlighted between. The respondents are asked where on the scale their opinion lies.

## Open-ended questions

Open questions invite respondents to offer their opinions and allow them to express themselves freely, possibly at length. This can lead to a wide variety of replies and can therefore be difficult to interpret. Such questions are simple to design and are often used when the researcher is not sure what the likely responses are. An example of an open-ended question is:

*What do you think of the BTEC National Diploma in Business?*

_____

_____

## TELL US ABOUT YOUR PROGRAMME AND COLLEGE

This questionnaire will only take a few moments to complete

**BC**
**BUSINESS COLLEGE**

**Return to Student Services, Business College, Cardiff**

1  Please tick which compulsory unit is your favourite on the BTEC National Business programme:

Business Enterprise            ☐

Creative Product Promotion     ☐

Introduction to Business       ☐

Presenting Business Information ☐

Business On-line               ☐

Business and Management        ☐

2  We would like to know your opinions on the following topics.

|  | Strongly agree | Agree | Neither agree nor disagree | Disagree | Strongly disagree |
|---|---|---|---|---|---|
| This course has prepared me well for work | | | | | |
| Teachers prepared interesting lessons | | | | | |
| I was well prepared for my assignments | | | | | |
| The refectory food is good | | | | | |

3  Finally, tell us a little more about the refectory food. Place a cross on the scale below to express your views on the food in the refectory.

| Good value | 1 | 2 | 3 | 4 | 5 | Poor value |
| Tasty | 1 | 2 | 3 | 4 | 5 | Tasteless |
| Plenty of choice | 1 | 2 | 3 | 4 | 5 | Limited choice |
| Satisfying | 1 | 2 | 3 | 4 | 5 | Unsatisfying |

## Length of questionnaire

If the topic being investigated is of genuine interest to the respondent, he or she may well be prepared to complete a lengthy questionnaire. Postal surveys, where there is no one present to encourage completion, have to cover less ground. Good sequencing and easy-to-follow instructions will help.

Questionnaires should be no longer than 40 questions, but should be as short as practically possible. Questions towards the end of a long survey may provoke hasty answers, producing inaccurate information. The use of **skip questioning**, where respondents are asked to skip certain question on the basis of previous answers, can reduce the length of the questionnaire as it ensures people are asked only relevant questions.

---

**Case study** — **Students are important customers**

Students are nowadays asked about their learning experience and environment so it can be improved. Using the questionnaire on page 74, pilot it with eight to ten students.

1 Review the questionnaire and recommend any improvements based on the pilot.
2 Pick a question and rewrite it using another question method.
3 Can you suggest any additional questions that you feel should have been included?

---

## Bias

**Bias** is defined as the difference between the answer obtained from respondents and the truth. The ordering of potential responses in a multiple-choice question is important as it can influence a respondent's choice, especially when he or she is slightly unsure of the answer. Research has shown that respondents are more likely to choose answers at the beginning or end of a list rather than in the middle. To reduce the impact of this, interviewers are asked to frequently rotate the sequence of questions.

Questions that may reveal the respondent in a poor light should be avoided, as many people will give an answer that they think will gain approval rather than the truthful answer. Questions that require an explanation also run the risk of introducing bias into the survey.

## Relevance

It is important that respondents are asked only questions that are relevant to them. Early questions may use the **skip questions** technique, determining which questions need to be answered by a respondent further into the questionnaire. If a customer shops only at Asda, skip questions can prevent him or her being asked about Tesco or Sainsbury's. On completion of a skip question, respondents will typically be directed, for example: 'If you answered NO go to Question 6. If you answered YES go to Question 7'.

## Encouraging response

**Response rate** is the number who participated in a research project compared with the total number of people approached. Answering a questionnaire requires a respondent to give time, attention and thought to a subject that, though it is of interest to the researcher, may not be of much interest to the respondent. The length should be kept to a minimum, although some topics will maintain the respondent's interest longer than others.

Questions should be as easy for the respondent to understand and answer as possible: an uncertain respondent is more likely to terminate the interview. Explanations should be included to bridge any changes of question topic. A respondent who feels the overall content makes no sense is again more likely to cease co-operating. As much as possible, the format and type of question used should be made varied and interesting for the respondent.

A covering letter introducing and explaining the purpose of the questionnaire can influence the rate of response to postal surveys. Reminder letters to non-respondents can also gain more responses. Small incentives such as free entry to a prize draw often improve response rates.

## Pilot stage

If time and costs allow, questionnaires should be piloted with some test respondents. Using the questionnaires with ten or twelve respondents should reveal any major problems. A pilot will help identify errors in the order of questions or the questions themselves. It will also indicate whether the questionnaire will meet the research objectives.

### Practice point

Design a questionnaire that your college or school could use to investigate what students think of the organisation. Use a variety of questions while also making sure it will be easy to analyse the answers. You could use it in conjunction with the sampling method you recommended in the Thinking Point on page 71. Remember to pilot the questionnaire with a few students first.

### Outcome activity 12.3

Continue the assignment concerning CJG Electronics from Outcome Activities 12.1 and 12.2. You have been asked to gather the necessary information and present it verbally to the board.

#### Pass

Conduct both primary and secondary research using the sampling method mentioned in the research proposal.

You will need to design a questionnaire if you are undertaking surveys such as telephone, postal and face-to-face interviews. Remember to pilot the questionnaire before using it with the sample outlined in your research proposal.

#### Merit

Analyse the effectiveness of primary and secondary research, including appropriate data collection and sampling methods.

You will need to look at all the various marketing research methods available to the researcher, looking at their advantages and limitations. A tabular format might be an ideal method of presentation. Then look at the various probability and non-probability sampling techniques that could be employed by the marketing researcher.

#### Distinction

Evaluate the application of selected research methods and make recommendations for improvement.

Comment on the effectiveness of the techniques that you chose to use for your marketing research project. You need to make recommendations – in other words, what would you do differently if you had to organise a similar project again? Justify your recommendations by discussing the impact of the proposed improvements. Include a section about the sampling technique you used and whether it helped you collect reliable and valid data.

# Research findings

The communication of research findings in the form of a written report or a verbal presentation is the culmination of the research project. This step is particularly important, as the clarity and the relevance of the findings are critical to the client's final satisfaction with the marketing research project. A manager may question the overall value and accuracy of the research if it is presented in a confusing or hesitant manner.

## Statistical procedures

A variety of statistical procedures are available to help researchers draw conclusions from the findings of the research they have undertaken.

## Arithmetic mean

It is often useful to talk about an average, such as the average number of customers served in a day or the average distanced travelled to deliver a product. The mean is the most commonly used average. To find the mean of a set of numbers, add them together and divide by the number of values in the set.

*Example:*

The demand for a product on each of 20 days was as follows (in units):

3 12 7 17 3 14 9 6 11 10 1 4 19 7 15 6 9 12 12 8

$$\frac{\text{Sum of demand}}{\text{Number of days}} = \frac{185}{20} = 9.25$$

The mean daily demand is for 9.25 units.

## Median

The median is the middle value in a set of numbers. To find the median, place the numbers in order and find the middle value. This average has the advantage of not being affected by extreme numbers at either end of a set of numbers. It may be a more appropriate measure of an average where a few extreme values may impact adversely on the calculation of an arithmetic mean.

*Example:*

To find the median of the following values:

8 6 9 12 15 6 3 20 11

First put the values in order:

3 6 6 8 9 11 12 15 20.

Now select the middle value, in this case the fifth value. The median is 9.

## Mode

The mode is the value that occurs most frequently in a set of numbers. The mode has one unique characteristic for an average in that there can be any number of modes. If the prices of a range of products are being examined, it is perfectly possible for a number of price points to be very popular with customers, such as £1.99, £3.99

and £9.99. The mode would highlight these important prices, which both the mean and the median may fail to reveal.

*Example:*

The daily demand (in units) for a product in a 10-day period is as follows.

| Demand | Number of days |
|--------|----------------|
| 6 | 3 |
| 7 | 6 |
| 8 | 1 |
| | <u>10</u> |

The mode is 7 units, because it is the value that occurs most frequently.

## Range

It is sometimes useful to examine the spread of a set of numbers. Identifying the range is probably the simplest measure, and it is found by calculating the difference between the largest and smallest values in a range of numbers.

The extreme numbers in a set directly affect the range. This method could, for example, help to establish the price difference between the basic product and the super deluxe option – the difference between the basic Ford Focus and the Ford Focus Ghia, for instance.

### Practice point

Find the mean, median, mode and range of the following numbers: 2, 4, 7, 7, 9, 12, 14, 16, 41.

## Interquartile range

The interquartile range reduces the impact of any extreme values. It divides the data into quarters and disregards the lowest and the highest quartiles. Therefore it only looks at the two central quartiles, which account for 50% of the values being analysed.

This can be shown by plotting a cumulative frequency distribution chart on a graph. The curve will always be 'S' shaped. The data is divided into quarters before calculating the interquartile range. This technique might be useful to analyse the delivery distances consumers request, when deciding at which distance to introduce a charge.

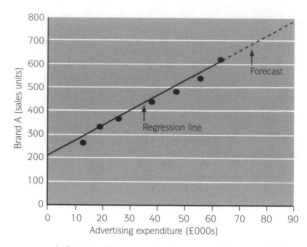

1 Scatter diagram showing a positive correlation between advertising and brand sales

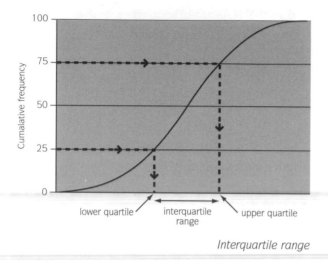

Interquartile range

## Scatter diagrams

Scatter diagrams plot the dependent variable (such as sales) on the horizontal 'y' axis and the independent variable (such as advertising) on the vertical 'x' axis.

Correlation refers to situations in which there is an association between the behaviour of two variables. When both variables are moving consistently in the same direction – for example, sales increase when advertising increases, or consumption increases as income increases – there is a positive correlation.

When one variable moves consistently in the opposite direction from the other variable, so that one falls as the other rises, there is said to be a negative correlation. For example, the more supermarket checkouts are open, the lower the queuing time.

When there is no pattern to the relationship between two variables, there is said to be no correlation. This might occur, for example, if complaints were plotted against the number of sales assistants on duty.

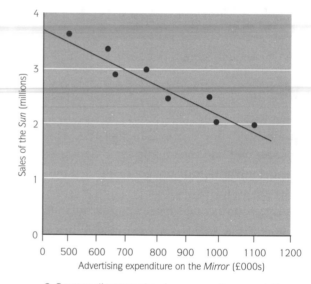

2 Scatter diagram showing a negative correlation between advertising expenditure on the Mirror and sales of the Sun

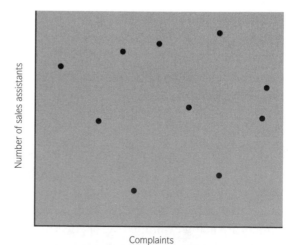

3 Scatter diagram showing no correlation between complaints and number of sales assistants

## Time series and trends

A time series is the name given to a set of figures recorded as they occur through time. The series may be plotted daily, weekly or monthly, and it is usual for the horizontal axis to be used to denote the time dimension. If there is a clear trend, these figures can be used to predict what will happen in the near future.

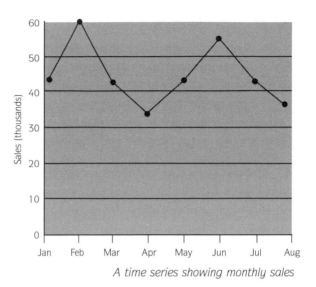

*A time series showing monthly sales*

### Case study    GT News magazine sales

GT News has a number of stores in the East Midlands. The figures in the accompanying chart show that its magazine sales vary week by week, with troughs and peaks. The company wants to know whether sales are increasing in the long term.

To identify a trend, a statistical technique known as a moving average can be calculated. GT News sales tend to peak every four weeks as the new monthly magazines appear. The moving average smoothes out the peaks so that the underlying trend can be seen.

| Week | Sales (thousands) | 4-week moving total | 4-week moving average |
|------|-------------------|---------------------|------------------------|
| 1 | 25 | - | - |
| 2 | 28 | - | - |
| 3 | 33 | - | - |
| 4 | 38 | 124 | 31 |
| 5 | 34 | 133 | 33.25 |
| 6 | 37 | | |
| 7 | 42 | | |
| 8 | 43 | | |
| 9 | 39 | | |
| 10 | 42 | | |
| 11 | 45 | | |
| 12 | 48 | | |

1 Calculate the four-week moving totals using the sales figures from the second column. Some examples have been calculated for you: 25+28+33+38=124. The total then moves by deleting the first week and adding the following or fifth week. The second total is 28+33+38+34=133.
2 Calculate the four-week moving average by dividing the four-week total by 4. For example 124 divided by 4 is 31, 133 divided by 4 is 33.25.
3 Plot the results on a graph with time on the horizontal 'y' axis and the moving average on the vertical 'x' axis.
4 Comment on the underlying trend in magazine sales.

## Use of spreadsheets for analysis

Microsoft Excel enables managers to quickly illustrate business trends diagrammatically. For example, if managers want to make a comparison between the market shares of different supermarket chains, this can be achieved graphically by using pie charts and bar charts.

In a pie chart each slice of the pie represents a component's contribution to the total amount. The 360 degrees of the circle are divided up in proportion to the figures obtained. For example, if two firms have 50% of the market each, this would be represented in a pie chart by each firm's market share being allocated half of the pie, or 180°. An example can be seen later on page 82.

Bar charts are an easily understood way of presenting information that can be used to good effect in business. Bar charts are drawn against a horizontal 'y' axis describing the variables and a vertical 'x' axis showing value. The height of each bar corresponds to the value for each variable. An example can be seen on page 82.

### Practice point

Microsoft Excel can be used to analyse the market shares of the leading supermarkets in the UK – Asda, Tesco, Sainsbury's and Morrisons.

- Click on the Microsoft Excel programme.
- A series of rows and columns will appear.
- Put the heading, starting in cell 1A, 'Market shares of supermarkets in UK'.
- Fill in the name of the supermarkets in the first column – Asda, Tesco, Sainsbury's, Morrisons and Others.
- In the second column enter the figures 16.9%, 27.1%, 16.9%, 9.4%, 29.7%.
- Now highlight the area of the table and using the mouse, go to the top of your window where you can see an icon that looks like a bar chart. Click on this to give you a list of options of different charts.
- Select pie chart and the type of pie chart that you want to illustrate. Print off the pie chart.
- Repeat the process, selecting bar chart and the type of bar chart that you want. Then print the bar chart.

Study the charts and list some market research findings.

## Appropriate uses of statistical procedures

The table below shows how the different statistical procedures might be used in business.

| Statistical procedure | Use |
|---|---|
| Mean | How much shoppers spend during each store visit. |
| | How many customers a sales assistant serves in a week. |
| | How long customers spend waiting to be served. |
| Median | Same uses as above, but with any high and low values eliminated. |
| Mode | Most popular price points for a range of products. |
| | The amount of money generally spent by consumers. |
| | Most popular times during the day for customers to arrive in store. |

| Statistical procedure | Use |
|---|---|
| Range | Difference between the prices for the basic and deluxe product. Time spent by consumers shopping in a store. |
| | Difference between the nearest and furthest delivery distances for customer orders. |
| Interquartile range | Sales by opening hour over a day. |
| | Distances generally requested by customers wishing to have orders delivered. |
| | Amount of money spent by the majority of consumers on their store cards during a year. |
| Scatter diagram | Response of sales to sales assistants' availability on shop floor. |
| | Length of checkout queues and impact on customer satisfaction. |
| | Impact of temperature on ice cream sales |
| Time series and trends | To help determine the type of new products that should be developed. |
| | To set targets for the sales team over the coming year. |
| | To suggest products that would benefit from advertising. |

# Diagrammatic analysis and presentation

Graphs and charts can help understanding by communicating information in a very succinct and effective manner. They can also maintain the interest of the audience by providing breaks from blocks of text or speech. The following section considers a number of popular diagrammatical techniques.

## *Pictograms*

A pictogram is a special type of bar chart that uses pictures of the items it is concerned with, such as bottles, cars or money, rather than bars.

### Thinking point

Smart Hats PLC produces hats, baseball caps and umbrellas. The sales team are competing for a special bonus based on the number of products sold during a month. The pictogram below shows the performance of the sales team after two weeks.

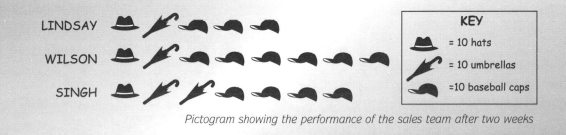

*Pictogram showing the performance of the sales team after two weeks*

1 Which member of the team looks favourite to win the special bonus?

2 Which member of the team perhaps needs more training?

## Pie charts

Pie charts show a total figure split into various categories. For example, if we wished to show how different market segments share total sales, the whole pie would represent total sales and each segment would show how much of the total was sold in each market segment.

A stacked bar chart shows the data stacked on top of each other. The advantage of this is that you can see the relevant total (for example sales) by noting the height of each bar. The sections that make up a stacked bar are normally shaded so that each individual section can be identified easily.

### Thinking point

The pie chart below shows the proportion of sales accounted for by hats, umbrellas and baseball caps for Smart Hats PLC.

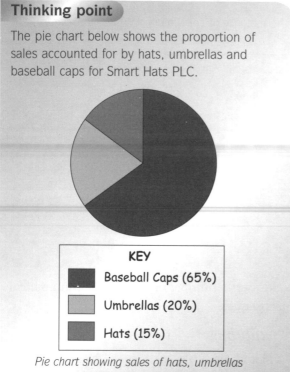

**KEY**
- Baseball Caps (65%)
- Umbrellas (20%)
- Hats (15%)

*Pie chart showing sales of hats, umbrellas and baseball caps*

1 Which product type would you select for further new product development? Explain your selection.

2 Which product type would you select for a discount promotion? Why?

### Thinking point

The bar chart below shows how many of each product each salesperson has sold.

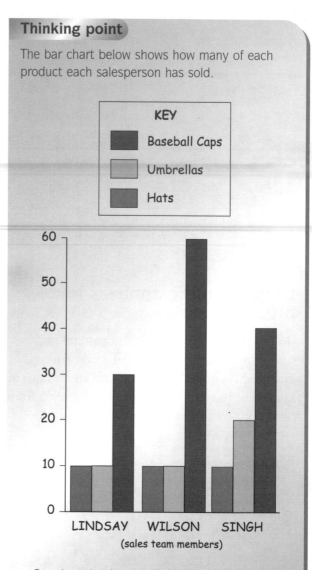

*Bar chart showing sales by sales team member and by product*

1 Which member of the sales team may require further training in baseball cap product features?

2 Which member of the team has been most successful in umbrella sales?

## Bar charts

A bar chart consists of a series of bars, positioned either horizontally or vertically, to represent the values of a variety of items.

Bar charts are used to compare data totals. A multiple bar chart shows different data side by side. For example, if you wanted to compare sales for different years, a multiple bar chart would be a good way to show the information.

## Frequency curves and histograms

The table below shows the size of hat orders, in units, taken by the Smart Hats PLC sales team, expressed in a frequency distribution table.

| Order size | Frequency |
|---|---|
| Less than 5 | 1 |
| 5 and less than 10 | 10 |
| 10 and less than 15 | 25 |
| 15 and less than 20 | 16 |
| 20 and less than 25 | 5 |
| 25 and less than 30 | 1 |

*Size of hat orders, units*

A histogram is a graphical representation of a frequency distribution table. The graph below shows the 'size of hat orders' frequency distribution table expressed as a histogram.

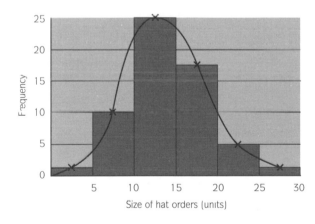

*Frequency distribution table expressed as a histogram*

A curve joining the mid-points of the tops of the rectangles of a histogram is called a frequency curve.

### Thinking point

Consider the information on hat orders above. If you showed the diagram at a sales meeting, what order size might management wish to encourage through offering a special discount?

## Line graphs

Line graphs are particularly useful in showing how values or quantities rise and fall over a period of time. On a line graph it is normal to show time along the horizontal 'y' axis and the variable on the vertical 'x' axis. Line graphs can be used to show information, such as, interest rates, unemployment rates, exchange rates, rate of growth of the economy and population changes.

Line graphs can also be used to make comparisons between two or more sets of observations. They are particularly useful for identifying patterns and trends in data such as seasonal effects (more sales in winter, for example) and turning points (such as when sales growth weakens).

### Thinking point

The line graph below shows the sales of each product over the month of a promotion.

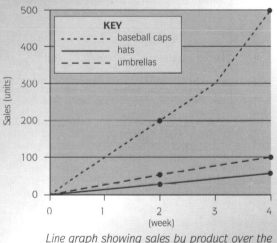

*Line graph showing sales by product over the period of a special bonus*

1 Does the graph help us understand how the approach of the sales team changed as the end of the scheme approached?

2 What change do you think took place?

## Scatter diagrams

Scatter diagrams are useful to examine relationships. Marketers are frequently interested in the degree of association between two variables, such as advertising and sales, square footage of a retail store and sales, or average queue length and customer satisfaction levels.

If you wanted to see whether there was a correlation between the amount spent on advertising and sales, you would plot the data on a graph. If there appears to be a strongly positive correlation we could say that there appears to be a strong link between advertising and sales – the more we advertise the more we sell.

## Thinking point

The scatter diagram below plots sales of umbrellas and rainfall.

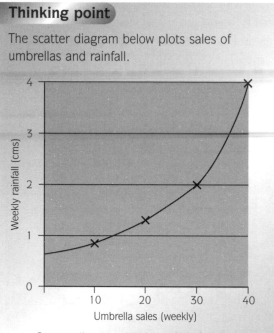

*Scatter diagram showing sales of umbrellas plotted gainst rainfall*

1  What is this correlation called?

2  What are the implications of this data for a marketing manager contemplating using further special bonus schemes to boost the sales team's performance?

## Appropriate use of techniques

The following table lists the different methods of diagrammatic analysis and presentation, and shows examples of uses for each technique.

| Technique | Appropriate use |
|---|---|
| Pie chart | Market shares of major competitors |
| | Sales from different regions of the country |
| | Orders received from different channels of distribution |
| Bar chart | Sales in a market by segment |
| | Orders received from key international markets |
| | Number of stores in major European markets |
| Frequency curve | Value of purchases by customer |
| | Time spent in store by consumers |
| | Delivery distances of customer orders |
| Histogram | Sales analysed by opening hours |
| | Number of customers moving through checkout each hour |
| | Number of purchases by price ranges |
| Line graph | Sales over three years |
| | Advertising money spent over 12 months |
| | Number of sales people employed over the year compared with sales |
| Scatter diagram | Response of sales to advertising expenditure |
| | Lengths of checkout queues and customer satisfaction levels |
| | Impact of temperature on soft drink sales |

## Practice point

Using the data gathered from the Case Study 'Students are important customers' on page 75, present some results using a selection of the techniques described above.

## Interpretation of results

The interpretation of *quantitative data* involves examining the statistics. Interpretation should draw out the implications of the data for management. While the underlying statistics are not open to subjective interpretation, therefore, the conclusions and implications for management could be.

The first step in interpreting results is to go through the evidence presented, looking at the statistics. What do the statistics indicate about the characteristics of the market?

The purpose of analysis is to uncover the relevance and significance of the data. For example, there may be trends or new factors in the competition (such as supermarkets selling financial products), market structure (such as growth in convenience store shopping) or consumer habits (such as buying over the Internet).

The analysis of *qualitative data* is, however, subjective and impressionistic. It conveys to the decision-maker insights into people's feelings about the market, the product, the advertising and their attitudes.

## Limitations of research

It is important to exercise caution when interpreting results and drawing conclusions from data, since it relates only to a sample. The more carefully the sample size and composition have been selected, the more valuable the final data, but the results can only ever be used as a guide for decision-making. There will be a certain amount of statistical error in any results and the conclusions drawn from those results. As long as marketing managers use their common sense, valuable messages can be drawn from marketing research.

### Customer databases

In the past, managers often had difficulty in gathering sufficient information to make sound decisions. Today's problems relate more to the filtering of relevant data from the explosion of information available in a wide range of formats from a wide range of sources. These sources may be internal to the organisation, coming from customer databases and electronic barcode scanning devices, or they may be from the Internet or marketing research sources.

More information does not always mean better decision-making. It is important that the levels of information presented to the decision-maker are kept to a manageable scale. Therefore managers need to be specific about the information they need.

The fact that market researchers can draw information from a number of sources does mean, however, that the reliability of the data can be confirmed by reference to other sources.

### E-business feedback

Nearly all Internet selling sites offer the consumer the chance to contact the organisation, generally by e-mail. This has resulted in organisations receiving vast amounts of information from customers as organisations have become more accessible. Customer comments, complaints or simple enquiries were traditionally considered to be a valuable source of marketing research data, but the sheer volume of data now being generated is proving difficult to cope with, process and analyse. The electronic collection of data through loyalty cards and the use of computers has enabled organisations to analyse vast amounts of consumer data, but managers are reporting that decisions are being delayed as a result of the huge amount of information available to them. In addition, a substantial amount of time is being wasted searching for and collecting information.

### Reliability of sample and accuracy

Any sample must be as representative as possible of the group being investigated. It must also be chosen in such a way as to minimise the risk of sampling error.

The sampling error of a statistic is the difference between the figure arrived at for the sample and the figure for the whole population. If we were seeking the average income of sales managers in the UK, the sampling error would be the difference between the average income of the sample chosen and the average income for all sales managers.

Some samples will produce only a small sampling error – in other words, they will produce an estimate close to the population average. Other samples will show a large sampling error, and it is therefore important to realise that even when the best sampling methods are used, there will always be the potential for error.

### Bias

Interviewer bias can be a problem if an interviewer is allowed to influence answers. This can happen when questions have to be explained to the respondent, as the interviewer will be offering an interpretation. It can be an issue when controversial topics are being investigated; it is now common practice to screen interviewers to ensure they do not hold strong views concerning the issue being researched, such as smoking, drinking or moral conduct.

Bias can also arise when interviewers are asked to approach potential respondents of a particular age group. For example, in a quota of 20- to 30-year-old women there will be a disproportionate number of 24- to 26-year-olds, because it is more difficult to judge the age of those close to either 20 or 30. There is also a tendency for interviewers to approach friendly, happy-looking, attractive people, who may hold different views and opinions from others.

Questionnaire bias can be minimised by paying particular attention to the sequence and wording of questions. The questionnaire should make it easy for the respondent to answer truthfully, and care must be taken to avoid questions or words that may lead the respondent into giving answers that do not reflect his or her true opinions or experience.

### Subjectivity

Group discussions and face-to-face interviews are the most common ways to collect qualitative data. In each case it is normally the person who was responsible for the collection of the information, the interviewer, who carries out the analysis. The analysis of qualitative data is subjective and impressionistic. The quality of the analysis and interpretation of such data depends on the individual who undertakes both the research and the analysis.

Quantitative data may be less liable to the problem of subjectivity, but the interpretation still needs to draw out the impact of the data for the organisation. So while the underlying statistics are not open to subjective interpretation, the conclusions and implications drawn from them might be.

## Presentation of findings

You will have to undertake a verbal presentation as part of your assignment. This section will provide valuable advice about presentations and general methods of presenting findings.

### Oral reports

Making an effective oral presentation is sometimes seen as more difficult than writing a report because of the direct interaction with the audience. Careful planning of an oral presentation is essential.

The basic structure for a presentation should be as follows:

**Introduction**

- Thank the audience for attending

- Introduce the people involved in the presentation

- Explain the format and structure of the presentation

- Explain the reason for the study and the objectives of the project

**Methodology**

- Give a brief description of the methodology including the data collection method, the sampling technique used, time scales and any limitations of the research

**Key findings**

- Give a brief description of the findings that are relevant to the objectives of the study, supported by graphs and tables

- Organise the material into sections, perhaps reflecting the research objectives, to make it easier for the audience to absorb the information

**Conclusions and recommendations**

- Emphasise the key points to emerge from the research and their implications for decision-making

- Highlight any recommendations

**Questions**

- Invite questions and comments from the audience

---

A wide range of software packages, such as Microsoft's PowerPoint, is now available to enable researchers to give high-quality, computer-aided presentations or to make professional-quality overheads.

There are a number of basic guidelines to follow when giving an oral report:

- check the facilities available for the presentation well beforehand

- whatever technology and software packages are being used, always ensure that the facilities and layout of the room are compatible with them

- maintain eye contact with the audience and do not simply read notes or stare at a screen

- keep the attention of the audience by ensuring there is variety in terms of the tone and pitch of your voice, visual aids and activities

- keep the message simple – use visuals aids as prompts and not as a substitute for the researcher's script

- check understanding throughout the presentation, perhaps by using questions – finding out at the end that an audience has misunderstood is too late

- provide handouts to save the audience taking notes, which allows them to pay attention and to participate fully

- stay calm and act confidently – this will give the impression of trustworthiness

- rehearse to check the timings of the presentation and practice speaking effectively

- clarify questions before answering them.

You have been asked to present a verbal marketing research report to a new client at a hotel near its head office. Produce a checklist you can use when you visit the hotel to review the facilities available.

## Written reports – formal and informal

Detailed below is a typical format for a formal written research report.

---

### Research report

**Title page**
Title, client, research organisation, date

**List of contents**
A detailed, numbered guide to report sections, followed by a list of graphs and statistical tables

**Preface**
An outline of the agreed research brief, followed by a statement of objectives and methods of research undertaken

**Summary of conclusions and recommendations**
A summary of main findings, sometimes accompanied by some creative interpretation in the form of recommendations

**Research method**
Procedures used to collect information – where, how and from whom, and techniques used in the analysis; the characteristics and size of the sample should be recorded

**Research findings**
The main body of the report, commenting on the findings in detail; emphasis should be on ease of understanding and logical presentation for the reader.

**Conclusions**
Even though the findings may speak for themselves, it is helpful to bring them together in a conclusion relating them to the objectives of the research

**Appendices**
Any detailed or technical data that is essential to a full understanding of the research report, for example a copy of the questionnaire used

---

Informal reports tend to have fewer sections and generally only include an introduction, the findings and the conclusions. They will be normally be shorter, and must be concise and precise. They might well be used to publish preliminary results for a research project or for a progress report during a lengthy programme of research activity.

### Visual aids

In both oral presentations and written reports, computer graphics, graphs and charts can help understanding by communicating information in a very succinct and effective manner. They can also maintain the interest of the audience by providing breaks from blocks of text or speech.

Too many visual aids, however, can become distracting and even boring. They should be used to clarify and reinforce a point, and should serve a real and necessary purpose.

There are numerous ways that computer graphics, graphs and charts can be produced and used, and graphical presentation can be combined with text detailing the key points.

### Conclusions and recommendations

The presentation of the conclusions and recommendations drawn by the researcher from the research results, within a written report or a verbal presentation, is the culmination of the research project. This step is particularly important, as the clarity and relevance of the conclusions and recommendations provide a lasting impression of the quality of the research long after the project is finished.

### Audience

When presenting a report the researcher should remember the following points.

- The report should be of a suitable length, and clear and relevant to the research objectives.

- The research findings should be related to the marketing decisions being considered.

- The audience will be interested in the implications of the findings for their own organisation.

- The audience will need to be convinced that the information being presented is accurate. They will want to see charts and tables, and quotations from respondents that support the findings. Researchers should think about the likely questions from the audience and answer them before they are even asked.

- Irrespective of the length of the presentation or report there needs to be a summary of the key points.

- The conclusion needs to suggest what should happen next and raise any issues that need further investigation.

Managers may return to read a report at a later date, so reports need to be easily understood months later, and the findings and recommendations need to be understood by people who have had no previous connection with the report.

## Effectiveness and quality of information

A number of issues may compromise the quality of the information being given to the audience and the effectiveness of a report or presentation.

- Some researchers present tables and graphs with very little commentary on how the figures should be interpreted. The researcher may simply display data and repeat the numbers shown. It can be very tedious for an audience to see page after page of data without any explanation of what the figures mean.

- Excessively long reports or presentations can mean that key points get lost in the detail and the results are devalued.

- Unrealistic recommendations, for example ones that are beyond the financial capabilities of the client or do not fit with its overall corporate objectives, will be of no use to the client.

- Charts for an oral presentation that are very eye-catching and colourful may fail to communicate information because clients may be distracted by the visual aspects and miss the key points.

## Outcome activity 12.4

Continue the assignment concerning CJG Electronics from Outcome Activities 12.1, 12.2 and 12.3.

### Pass

Interpret the findings from your research and present them clearly in verbal form, using written materials and diagrams to improve understanding.

Rehearse your presentation and use prompt cards to ensure you cover all your points. Interpreting the findings means explaining the meaning of the information gathered from all the marketing research you have undertaken. Your analysis might use statistical procedures such as mean, mode, median, interquartile range, scatter diagrams and time series trends. Use diagrams to help convey your important points, such as pictograms, pie charts, bar charts, frequency curves, histograms, line graphs and scatter grams.

### Merit

Analyse your own research findings, draw conclusions and make recommendations.

To obtain a merit grade you need to provide a number of high-quality, specific recommendations.

## Key terms

### Bias
the difference between the answer obtained from respondents and the truth

### CATI
Computer-Assisted Telephone Interviewing, where interviewers key answers directly into the computer. Answers automatically route respondents to the next appropriate question

### CATS
Completely Automated Telephone Surveys, where interactive voice technology is used to ask questions, with participants using touch-tone telephones to respond

### External data
secondary research information that is available outside the organisation, such as government statistics

### Internal data
secondary research information held inside the organisation, such as sales records and customer complaint reports

### Marketing mix
the combination of product, price, place (sometimes called distribution), promotion and packaging offered by an organisation to potential customers

### Marketing research
the collection and evaluation of data in order to assist organisations to better understand their consumers, competitors and market

### Non-probability sampling
using a subjective procedure to select participants, such as people who are considered typical consumers

### Primary research
research carried out to find new information required for a marketing research project, which has never previously been collected

### Probability sampling
the systematic selection of participants, for example every tenth person in the telephone directory

## Key terms

### Qualitative research
research that provides information of a qualitative nature, such as why people buy, what motivates them to buy or their impressions of, for example, products and advertisements

### Quantitative research
research that produces numbers and figures, such as the number and percentage of consumers who are aware of a brand

### Research brief
written by the organisation that has an information need, to show the objectives of the research, possible research methods, a timetable and reporting requirements

### Research proposal
written by the organisation that will conduct the research, to respond to the research brief, and include research methods to be used, costs and reporting details

### Respondent
a person who is asked and agrees to participate in a marketing research project

### Response rate
the number of people who participated in a research project compared with the total number of people approached

### Secondary research
research that makes use of work already carried out by someone else for some other marketing research project or other purpose

### Sequencing
the careful ordering of questions to reduce the impact of bias as well as putting questions into a logical order to encourage completion

### Skip questions
technique to ensure respondents only have to answer the questions relevant to them by asking them to skip certain questions on the basis of previous answers

### Subjectivity
the feature of qualitative data analysis that means the research findings and conclusions are only the opinions that the researchers formed from the research

# *End-of-unit test*

1 Describe the purpose of marketing research.

2 What clues might suggest that an interview is designed to collect selling information rather than collect marketing research data?

3 List the parts of a marketing research brief.

4 Who would write a marketing research proposal?

5 Draw a flow chart of the marketing research stages.

6 Describe what you understand by the term 'strategic research'.

7 Give three examples of internal secondary research sources.

8 Name two government publications by the Office for National Statistics (ONS) that might be useful for marketing research.

9 What are two characteristics of qualitative data analysis?

10 Define the term 'marketing research respondent'.

11 Describe three advantages of postal surveys.

12 Name two limitations of telephone surveys.

13 What is the difference between a census and a sample?

14 Describe two features of non-probability sampling.

15 Name two question types that can be used to gather the strength of feeling on a topic.

16 How would you define bias when applied to marketing research?

17 Explain the strength of the median as an average.

18 What can be calculated to establish the trend in a time series set of figures?

19 Describe some information that could be appropriately illustrated using a histogram.

20 How can the impact of bias be reduced in a marketing research project?

# Resources

## Texts

Crouch, S and Housden, M: *Marketing Research for Managers*, Butterworth Heinemann, 2000

Dransfield, R et al: *Business for Foundation Degrees and Higher Awards*, Heinemann, 2004

Dransfield, R et al: *BTEC National Business*, Heinemann, 2004

Needham, D et al: *Marketing for Higher Awards*, Heinemann, 1999

Wilson, A: *Marketing Research. An integrated approach*, FT Prentice Hall, 2003

Proctor, T: *Essentials of Marketing Research*, FT Prentice Hall, 2000

## Websites

*www.mintel.com* Mintel market research reports

*www.thomson.com* Datastream – company financial information

*www.dnb.com* Dun & Bradstreet – financial information

*www.statistics.gov.uk* Office for National Statistics (ONS)

*www.europa.eu.int/comm/eurostat/* European Union statistical office

*www.warc.com* World Advertising Research Centre

*www.carol.co.uk* Company annual reports on-line

*www.keynote.co.uk* Market research reports

*www.datamonitor.com* Datamonitor – business intelligence

An **e-business** is one that extensively – if not exclusively – uses computer systems to store and communicate digital data (data stored as 0s and 1s, known as binary code, which is understood by computers). This means that in an e-business, all or most of the important internal business processes, such as finance, human resource management, stock control, customer records, research and development and marketing, are based on computerised systems using appropriate software.

To add to this, in the past 10 years there has been a tremendous growth in the development of Web-based technologies, allowing computer systems to connect together. These technologies can create linked global computer networks and form the global community we commonly refer to as the **Internet**. All of these technologies enable the transfer and sharing of many kinds of data. Computer systems today therefore tend to be Web-based; we now live and work in the interconnected world of the Internet.

Note that the Internet and the **World Wide Web** are not the same thing. The Internet is the network of linked computers, and the World Wide Web is the web of software and applications that runs on the linked computers. The Web, in other words, exists on the Internet and moves across it.

The combination of sophisticated software and data exchange all connected via a business website to the global Internet has allowed for the development of Internet marketing, which has been defined by Dave Chaffey as:

> 'The application of the Internet and related digital technologies in conjunction with traditional communications to achieve marketing objectives.'

The Internet has considerably added to the capacity of businesses to engage in marketing and achieve marketing principles. For example, businesses can identify and track their customers and find out when they visit a website, it can monitor the rates of purchase, and can find out which pages of a site encourage purchases.

Because businesses can keep in touch with market trends, they can relate products or services more closely to customer needs and wants. The traditional principles of marketing (satisfying and anticipating customers needs) are being modified and strengthened on-line, to help businesses in the on-line world.

Using the Internet, businesses can now create better customer relationships. In this unit you will build on marketing principles and gain an insight into the importance of Internet marketing for businesses of many kinds. The hugely increased opportunities offered on-line for business organisations and consumers will be examined, as well as the challenges they bring to the on-line organisation.

Unit 14 is divided into four main sections:

- 14.1 Principles of Internet marketing
- 14.2 Benefits of Internet marketing to customers
- 14.3 Opportunities offered by Internet marketing
- 14.4 Challenges in Internet marketing.

# Principles of Internet marketing

Unit 11: Introduction to Marketing in *BTEC National Business* offers an excellent outline of the general principles of marketing. You may like to refer closely to this when you are working on the current unit.

Marketing is about an organisation's relationship with its customers. Customers make purchases in 'markets' and they may be private individuals like you and me (a business-to-consumer or **b2c** sale), or they may be other businesses (a business-to-business or **b2b** sale). There is a market for clothes and a market for cars; there are industrial markets and markets for food produce. Businesses need to know about the markets they serve so that they can serve them better. The whole process of finding out what a market wants and relating products to that market is known as 'marketing'.

Marketing is a function within business that has become increasingly important over the years. Long before the growth of the Web, it was essential for businesses – if they were to compete successfully – to think about how their products were going to meet the needs of the people who might buy them. If they failed to do this, people would stop buying them.

Before looking at the distinctive – and evolving – features of Internet marketing in the digital world, it is necessary to have some grasp of traditional marketing principles and processes in the physical world. What follows is a summary.

## Marketing in the physical world

Traditional marketing for the physical or off-line world always includes a 'marketing mix' of tactics, revolving around the so-called four Ps. These are Product, Price, Place and Promotion. The marketing function works with these to create a tactical mix designed to achieve business aims and objectives.

### Product

The marketing function considers the features of a product that is offered to a market or a part of a market (known as a segment). What is it? Who would it be aimed at? What does it do? What *should* it do? The product could be tangible (something you can touch), such as a toothbrush with a manoeuvrable head, or it could be an intangible service, such as a delivery service.

### Price

The marketing function also considers what price a product should be sold at. What sort of customers will buy at a particular price? What will be the best price to attract a particular kind of customer? What price might encourage more people to buy? What price might create the best image? What might be the effect of a change in price?

Different pricing strategies are available according to what the business is aiming to achieve:

- **penetration pricing** sets a price at a level that will gain a foothold in a market
- **destruction pricing** sets a price that will drive others out of the market
- **competitor pricing** bases the price on the prices of competitors
- **skimming (or creaming) the market** sets a high price for a unique product
- **discrimination pricing** sets different prices for different customers.

### Place

Marketing specialists have always considered how a product would find its way to consumers, to a place where they could make a purchase. This would include physical distribution and merchandising. Goods must be transported from a manufacturer into storage, through distribution centres then to wholesalers, then to the High Street retailer. Businesses working between a manufacturer and a retailer are known as **intermediaries**.

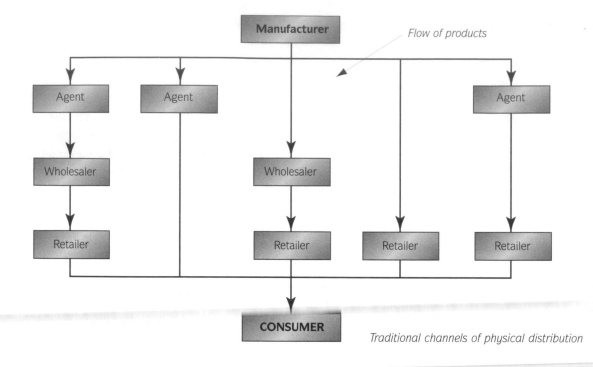

*Traditional channels of physical distribution*

## Promotion

Marketing professionals have to consider ways of bringing products to the attention of potential customers. This includes advertising in the various media, as well as other ways of promoting products in the eyes of consumers, such as special offers. These activities, in the physical world, are designed to 'push' products and services towards the eyes and ears of potential consumers.

## Marketing mix

The four Ps are a set of tactical ingredients, to be 'mixed' according to the firm's marketing strategy, but what is a marketing strategy and how is one arrived at?

### Practice point

Take as an example your favourite chocolate bar. Using the four elements of the marketing mix outlined above, describe how marketing plays a part in the success of that product.

## Identifying markets through market research

Market research is a key principle of marketing. It is about finding out who and where customers are and what their specific requirements are. Research is designed to gather information so that marketing decisions are based on useful, current and relevant data. New information, gathered by a particular business for its own purposes, is called 'primary' research, whereas information that is already available from elsewhere is called 'secondary' research.

### Practice point

1 Design and conduct a survey of students in your class to find out:
   o what percentage of the group have Internet access at home
   o what percentage have broadband Internet access at home.

2 Visit *www.ClickZ.com/stats* and search for any Internet trends about Web use and access. Make a note of your findings.

3 Prepare notes consisting of a statement explaining which of the above pieces of information is primary data and which is secondary data.

A further distinction can be made between 'qualitative' data, which is data that identifies opinions and feelings about something, and 'quantitative' data, data that is statistical or numerical in content.

Traditional market research uses a variety of methods to gather data and can be a considerable cost to a business. A company in the physical world wanting to find information about consumer preferences might consider five basic methods to collect information:

- discussions with people, in telephone surveys, focus groups and panels
- direct observation
- questionnaires and surveys
- sampling
- testing through pilots and field trials.

### Setting marketing objectives and strategy

A firm's marketing strategy, as we have seen, determines the mix of tactics to be employed, and it is designed to achieve long-term business aims. A marketing strategy can be arrived at by using careful analysis of both the external environment surrounding the business and the current state of the business itself.

These two approaches can be described as:

- an industry analysis
- a situation analysis.

These are crucial tools that can be used to ensure that a business adopts an appropriate set of marketing tactics. These tactics, in turn, will help to achieve the business aims.

### Industry analysis

Remember that marketing, by its nature, requires a business to focus outwards in order to understand the external environment it is working in and to respond accordingly. Michael Porter's 'Five Forces' model can be used to look at a whole market or industry, such as the motor industry or the cosmetics industry.

The five forces that can determine a strategy are:

- the threat of new market entrants
- the power of suppliers
- the power of buyers
- the availability of substitutes
- competitive rivalry within the industry.

These five forces are fully discussed in Unit 29: Business and Markets, on page 240. They work across an entire industry and combine to make up the business environment surrounding a particular firm. The marketing function must be completely aware of the structure of these forces and how they interact with each other.

### Practice point

You are the marketing manager of a firm manufacturing model electric train sets. Using Porter's Five Forces analysis, create a set of briefing notes for the managing director as a starting point for a strategy meeting.

### Situation analysis

An example of a situation analysis is the SWOT analysis. This results in a set of information that is closely connected to the current situation of the particular business.

In a SWOT analysis, the four categories of information about a business are:

- Strengths
- Weaknesses
- Opportunities
- Threats.

These are further divided into *internal* factors (strengths and weaknesses) and *external* factors (opportunities and threats). A business marketing team will systematically look at each factor, cataloguing the strengths the business has. For example, this might include things such as a well-established product or brands, good customer loyalty, good staff, good equipment; the weaknesses might be that equipment is dated, premises are too small or the product needs updating. Both strengths and weaknesses are within a firm's own control because they are internal.

The next two factors are external to the business. Opportunities may exist to enter new markets, to improve products or product image, or to acquire new staff; threats are those things that could damage market position. This could be an economic downturn, new competition, or new products.

By analysing both the wider industry and the company's own situation, marketing people will be better placed to ensure that marketing objectives and long-term strategic aims are soundly based.

## Practice point

Visit *www.saveanddrive.co.uk*. Do an outline SWOT analysis of this on-line business, paying particular attention to the opportunities and threats you feel are created through Internet marketing.

## Market-led and product-led approaches

In Britain, many businesses used to think that the things they made were the best of their type in the world (often they were), and that because they made the best, customers – wherever they were – would be sure to buy them. To test the wisdom of this attitude, try checking the nationality of the company that manufactured your TV, your hi-fi, or your washing machine at home, and have a look at who manufactured the cars and motor cycles in the car park. This should give you a clue about the wisdom of holding this so-called 'product-led' attitude.

The truth is that over the years, British businesses have learned that their products will fail against overseas competition if they do not provide exactly what the customer wants. Marketing is about finding out what customer needs are and setting out to meet them. This is why it should be an interesting area to look at for all of us. We are each, after all, consumers of many products.

## Thinking point

Think of a product you have bought recently. What were your main requirements from it? Can you describe how the firm that designed and made that product included the things you required?

Companies have learned that they have to look outwards – towards customers in the market – in order to be competitive. The needs of the market must lead what a business offers to it. This is the 'market-led' approach. The UK Chartered Institute of Marketing (CIM) defines marketing as:

> *'The management process responsible for identifying, anticipating and satisfying customer needs profitably.'*

## Segmentation

A business may either choose to aim a product at the mass market, with the same, undifferentiated, set of tactics for all consumers; or it may choose to **target** specific groups of consumers. This involves 'segmenting' the market (think of the segments of an orange).

In targeting market segments, the business must consider how to differentiate the product to meet the needs of different segments. It might therefore use different marketing tactics for each segment. This question of segmentation (dividing up the market) is a big issue in marketing. Traditional methods of segmentation include dividing the market according to:

- age
- sex
- geographic location
- lifestyle
- 'psychographic' profile (profiling by lifestyle characteristics, such as DINKY – Double Income No Kids Yet).

By segmenting and then targeting their marketing effort towards a segment of a market, businesses are able to create or modify products to meet this particular category of consumer's preferences and requirements.

## Thinking point

1 Consider the people within your group in college or school. How might you 'segment' them as a market?

2 You are manufacturing and selling a new soft drink product. In pairs, consider how you would target the product to the males and the females in your group. Present your findings.

### Marketing principles

Marketing principles are therefore aimed at identifying and satisfying customer needs profitably, and they apply at all times whether a business is on-line or off-line. These principles underpin the tactical tools described earlier as the four Ps; they include:

- listening to customers; finding out what they want from products

- getting as close to customers as possible

- involving customers

- serving customers well

- seeking out the best customers

- trying to nurture customers into a lifelong relationship with your firm and working to repeat this every time you do business

- constantly testing the market, measuring and improving

- adding value in everything you do for customers.

Now we will examine how the Internet can help businesses to achieve their marketing aims.

## E-marketing – marketing in the on-line world

### Marketing principles on-line

The Internet helps businesses to acquire an extensive knowledge of customers and markets. By its nature, the Web is a way of connecting everyone who is on-line. Millions of pounds, dollars, euros and many other currencies change hands through the wires linking computers all over the world.

According to Dave Chaffey, forecasts of global users of the Internet show dramatic growth over the next few years, and research complied by Nua Internet Surveys has shown a worldwide total of 605.6 million people on-line. There are as many Web pages on-line as there are stars in the sky!

Of course, eventually growth will slow down, but it will not stop completely, as more and more of the newly developing world (China, Russia, Eastern bloc countries and others in future) come on-line. The number of users will continue to grow and more importantly so will the frequency of use and the time spent on-line. Technological improvements, and increasing use of **broadband** (with much faster Internet connection and download times) will almost guarantee this. Not only will more people be on-line, but the ease with which they use the Internet will improve and fears about security issues will diminish.

In traditional marketing, specialists think of ways of 'pushing' goods and services out to consumers. For private consumers, the Internet is a 'pull medium', meaning that on the whole it is the individual consumer's choice to visit the websites he or she is interested in and to 'pull' out the desired goods or services. In this way the audience targets the business.

It is becoming commonplace to refer to a 'remix' of the traditional marketing mix, so that traditional marketing approaches can be applied in different ways in the on-line world. This marketing remix changes the traditional marketing tools and adds one or two new ingredients, described later, that are designed specifically for the on-line (sometimes called the digital) economy.

One of the specific purposes of Internet marketing is to offer something that attracts visitors from specific market segments and makes them want to stay and look around a website. This is often referred to as a site's **stickiness**. To make visitors want to 'stick' around, the site has to offer something that is of value to them. This is called an **on-line value proposition** (OVP) and it is a similar concept to the 'unique selling proposition' (USP) commonly referred to in traditional marketing.

In the case of the USP, marketers are trying to communicate something unique about a physical product or a service that will make people want to buy it more than others. Similarly, the OVP is the special set of characteristics about a website that will make people want to visit, then stay on the site and make a purchase.

To communicate an OVP successfully is one of the prime purposes of Internet marketing. The tactical means of doing this can be described within a number of elements that are referred to as the 'e-marketing remix':

1 **product**
2 **price**
3 **place**
4 **promotion**
5 **people**
6 **physical evidence**
7 **processes**

} 'personalisation'

## Practice point

Remembering that an on-line value proposition is something about a website that attracts visitors and encourages them to stay. In pairs try to identify the OVP of the following sites:

*www.diy.com*

*www.lastminute.com*

*www.elephant.co.uk*

1 Describe this OVP briefly in your own words and present your summary to the whole group.

2 How do you feel consumers might benefit from this site? Is all of your group agreed on this?

A business usually has to relate to both suppliers and its own customers:

Supplying business

↓

Buying/selling business

↓

Consumer

The buying and selling business therefore has both **buy-side** (b2b) relationships with other businesses *and* **sell-side** (b2c) relationships with the consumers it sells to. It is important that its marketing efforts enable positive messages to be directed to both contexts.

It is important to realise, therefore, that the reformulated e-marketing mix of the on-line world differs for b2b and b2c markets. We will look at each set of tactics separately.

## The on-line product

The product element of the marketing specialist's toolkit involves manipulating both the core product – the actual thing bought by the consumer (such as a camera) – and the extended product, including the additional information or services that go with it (such as details of the camera's features). Both of these can be enhanced on-line.

Obviously it is not possible to touch, smell, or taste products via the Internet, so a powerful attraction for private consumers to purchase many tangible products – using the full range of human senses – is absent on the Web. Furthermore, in Internet shopping, a consumer wishing to buy something must wait for the product to be delivered after paying for it.

Aside from convenience, why should a private consumer consider buying on-line, when there are strong instinctive reasons not to? Internet marketers have to face up to this and find ways of making the e-shopping experience worth the wait.

The Internet is ideal for adding considerable value to every product made available on-line and marketers have to think of ways this can be done. One method of doing this is to build into the product exclusive and relevant information, often personalised for the customer.

At *www.InternetDirect.co.uk*, the consumer can purchase digital cameras and supporting associated products at very competitive rates. The site offers useful technical advice and visitors can compare and contrast the specifications of many digital cameras side by side. The customer, on registration with the website, receives 100 mb of disc space in which to create his or her own on-line album to store photographs.

The InternetDirect site provides an illustration of how on-line retailers or 'e-tailers' can offer extensions to the basic core product, thereby offering increased benefit to customers. Examples of this can be seen in the screen reproduced below. The services panel on the left, for example, shows that several extra services are available from the site.

## Practice point

Visit *www.InternetDirect.co.uk* (or an alternative site).

1 Using the idea of the 'extended product', explain, using examples from the website, how this Web trader has used Internet technology to add extra value to the product.

2 Take a screen shot from the site, illustrating the value added to this Internet product.

3 Find one other example of a b2c site offering similar added value to an on-line product, and compare and contrast this with InternetDirect.

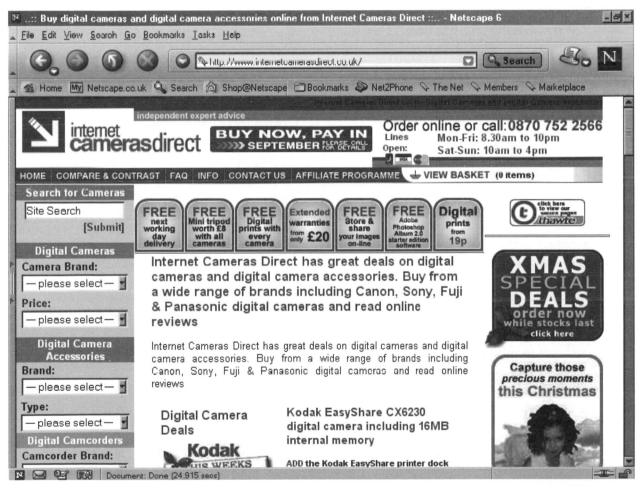

*Adding product value – www.InternetDirect.co.uk*

There are various ways of extending on-line products, by providing:

- extensive product endorsements from previous customers
- lists of customers
- warranties
- money-back offers
- additional customer back-up services
- 'cross-selling' of related or complementary products
- expert advice.

Core products can be extended too. Take the example of Mattel's *www.whatsherface.com* where the user can create an individual doll with personalised features, before deciding whether or not to buy. At *www.orange.com* it is possible to create a personalised mobile phone payment package, with agreed plans for texts or calls. Levi Strauss allows customers to personalise their jeans purchase with its 'Original Spin' programme. People can select the cut, fabric, measurements and fit. After these selections have been specified on-line, Levi Strauss will ship the product within three weeks.

In these examples the consumer is actively participating in product creation and enhancement. Internet marketing is allowing for **mass customisation** of many products.

In a 1980 book called *The Third Wave*, published long before the Internet took off, Alvin Toffler predicted that in future the things we needed to possess in order to survive (our *production* needs) and our use of them (our *consumption*) would once again be combined. In the earliest days, primitive human beings had to hunt and gather food and resources for immediate use – or they would not survive. In Toffler's view of the future, everyone would again be collaborating with each other, involved in acquiring the things they required. Toffler predicted that consumers would become **prosumers,** not just getting what was on offer from others (businesses), but participating in producing the things they required. This would involve them being knowledgeable about products (today we can get information from the Internet), being enabled to contribute to the design of products (we can participate in design via the Internet) and being enabled to interact with producers to assist in getting the products needed (we can contribute to surveys and research and can comment via the Internet).

As an illustration, look at some of the major motor manufacturers such as BMW or Citroen to see how users can actively design their own 'dream' car. The system stores this data and is able over time to monitor the most popular preferences. Has the age of 'prosumer power' arrived? One company with a policy to be at the cutting edge in using Internet technology is Kingfisher's B&Q Direct. The website is found at *www.diy.com*.

The screen shot opposite shows the services page of *www.diy.com*. Customers can access a wide range of services, from brochures giving product advice and information, to delivery details and terms. Customers can also become involved in interactively designing their own rooms, simultaneously placing orders for goods into the shopping cart as they proceed.

## Practice point

Visit *www.diy.com* (room designs) or any other website that allows you to be interactive with the content. Design a brief presentation to the whole group showing how this extends the product offering and benefits consumers.

# The on-line price

Traditional pricing models could work out desirable prices based on production costs plus a profit margin, or on set profit targets, or base prices on those of the competition in the market.

The overall effect of the Internet upon markets has been to exert a downward pressure on prices. One of the reasons for this is that production costs for many digital products have been reduced

*B&Q Direct – services to DIY customers*

to almost zero. Businesses selling on the Web have greater capacity to vary prices, and new pricing models are tending to be based upon the old question: what is the consumer prepared to pay? The means of adding value to on-line products described in the last section are therefore even more important in maintaining on-line competitiveness. The consumer's willingness to pay a profitable price could well be determined by the value a business is able to add to its on-line product offer.

In the pre-Internet economy, market research could usually tell business planners what price a market would accept and what the impact (elasticity) of an increase in price might be. Using the PED (price elasticity of demand) formula, marketers could make reasonably informed choices about price changes and their effect on demand for products and then make considered decisions.

The Internet is influential in this because, among other things, it allows a great deal of price transparency for consumers – they can compare prices easily between many potential suppliers. Prices can be stored digitally in databases and software (robot shoppers, shopping bots, or price search engines) and they can be searched for the best prices available (see *www.kelkoo.com*). Some sites, such as the BBC's Internet shopping service at *www.bbcshop.com*, provide instant price comparisons, and at *www.letsbuyit.com* customers can join together in order to lower prices.

Instead of prices being set by businesses and passively received by the market, the Internet is capable of turning this situation upside down. The site *www.priceline.co.uk*, for instance, allows consumers to set their own prices, and at several on-line auction sites (such as *www.ebay.co.uk* ) consumers are able to place bids for consumer products having been able to view the minimum (reserve) price acceptable to the seller.

In b2b markets, 'reverse auctions' are becoming more widely used on the Internet. In a reverse auction, a purchasing organisation might specify its detailed requirements and ask potential suppliers to express interest in bidding to supply. Once bidding starts, all participants can see the bids being submitted, but not whom they are from. The health-care company GlaxoSmithKline achieved significant savings of up to 25% on solvents and chemicals in this way.

**Practice point**

Prepare a short presentation about *www.ebay.co.uk*, summarising the bidding process and describing the benefits (if any) you feel are offered to users of the site.

The unit selling cost for each product is much less for an on-line product, so businesses on the Internet can make cost savings that can be passed on to consumers. Those businesses that do so the most quickly, will be the first to gain customer loyalty. This places a further downward pressure on prices. One way in which on-line traders may choose to generate revenue in this price-conscious climate is by selling many products at cost price from a website and making money by selling add-ons or services.

The effect of Internet technology on the ability of marketers to establish and maintain a pricing strategy has been dramatic. As we have seen, Internet marketers have to acknowledge that increasingly prices are being directly set by consumers and not just accepted by them. Airlines can and do offer on-line auctions for seats. Through the Internet, consumers can compare, combine, bid at auctions for most products and even establish reverse auctions, whereby potential suppliers have to compete for their custom.

Finally, prices can now be set automatically, based on the level of demand and on the stage a

product is at within its own life cycle. This phenomenon is known as **dynamic pricing** and it means that prices are not set in stone, only to be changed after major business strategy meetings; they are flexible and constantly moving in line with trading conditions.

**Practice point**

Do you think that dynamic pricing is an example of consumer power? Justify your answer.

## The on-line place

On-line distribution has caused **disintermediation** to occur in some contexts, meaning that intermediaries – businesses operating as wholesalers, distribution centres, or agents handling products between the original manufacturers of products and customers – are often no longer required. Producers can either sell directly from their own website (b2c), or to a retailer (b2b). Large cost savings can be made by selling directly to the consumer.

However, new types of middle men are appearing on the Internet. These can be neutral intermediate sites that function to bring buyers and sellers together (such as *www.bizrate.com*), or they can be **infomediaries**, sites holding information that is of benefit to both customers and suppliers. This process is known as 'reintermediation' because it introduces another new sort of intermediary.

The significance of getting products to customers is obviously huge. One of the most successful products in the world, for example, is Coca Cola. This success is not just based on an excellent product, but also on excellent distribution. Coke is available almost everywhere that people might want to drink it.

The same approach applies in the on-line world. If Amazon wants to sell books, it has to consider placing **hyperlinks** to its site in places on the Web where people might wish to buy books. Internet marketing must therefore give consideration to which, if any, other websites might be best fitted to carrying product information, or links to it.

We have already seen that, increasingly, businesses that were traditionally based on a purely physical presence ('bricks and mortar' businesses) are introducing the Internet as an additional channel for their sales (**clicks and mortar**). The example of *www.diy.com* is such a case.

Owned by the Kingfisher group, the diy.com site is the website of B&Q Direct, a subsidiary and independent organisation alongside B&Q stores. B&Q Direct management has set clear performance targets for diy.com based on a four-year plan. To achieve the level of sales required to meet the strategic plan, B&Q Direct has recognised the need to have the capacity to meet customer orders from the website. This has been achieved in the short term by contracting out the whole 'product fulfilment' function to a separate partner company, Spark Response, based at Follingsby Park, near Gateshead in Tyne and Wear. Spark Response provides warehousing and despatch services, customer service personnel and call-centre staff. Apart from the website itself and associated technical IT support, B&Q provides the whole product range and has management support permanently based at Spark Response's site, working alongside Spark Response staff.

When a customer places an Internet order, it is received by Spark Response callcentre staff and acknowledged. The warehouse is then given details of the customer's requirements and goods are prepared for packaging and despatch. Five separate carriage companies are used, depending on the weight and nature of the goods scheduled for despatch.

The parent company, the Kingfisher Group, now has within its B&Q family of companies a developing and growing 'multi-channel' approach for sales and customer service.

> **Practice point**
>
> How can the Internet change the distribution element of the marketing mix? Write a summary in your own words.

## On-line promotion

One of the first steps in Internet business promotion is to choose and purchase a **domain name** that effectively announces the business. It is often advisable, therefore, for companies to have their business name at least within the domain name. Many off-line advertisements make references to domain names.

A domain name is the means by which humans can make sense of where on the Internet a site is. Just as most of us have a home address, so that people or mail can find us among the network of roads and buildings near where we live, on the Internet every website has to have an address, so that browsers can locate it.

While computers only understand numbers, humans understand much more. So we know, for example, that .com, .co.uk, .org, .gov, .ac, and so on have meaning beyond the letters. Imagine having to search through some kind of directory containing millions of sets of 12-digit numbers! That would be no problem for computers, but for us it is far easier to have a domain name we can make sense of. Domain names mentioned so far in this chapter include diy.com, Amazon.co.uk and InternetDirect.co.uk.

A **search engine** is a software tool that makes an automatic search for key words in websites. Think of search engines as a massive index of site content. Over 80% of Web users say they use search engines for finding information. It is vital therefore, that a business seeking to promote its goods and services on the Internet is registered with the most popular search engines in order to build traffic to its website.

The next step is to 'optimise' a site for search engines. This involves ensuring that the important key words that relate to the contents of a website are present within the coding of the page. Users of search engines type in the words indicating the information they wish to find from the Web. From a promotional point of view, the marketer wants his or her site to rank highly in the search engine's results.

### Practice point

Using a specific category of product (such as car tyres), show how businesses appear to have optimised their Web presence so that search engines return their sites to Web users.

Once a website has been built and a business has a presence on the Internet, there are several ways of communicating a marketing message to consumers.

### Banner advertisements

A space across the top of a Web page, often with animated content, advertising products or services from another business, is known as a **banner**. A click on the banner by a visitor to a site leads to a referral to the advertiser's site (the 'destination site'). This is known as a **click-through**.

The choice of sites on which to place banners will be considered by marketing specialists, and there are several specialist sites offering services to help in placing, or targeting, banners. Banner ads can be exchanged between sites offering complementary products or services, or they can be specifically targeted on sites where it is felt that the audience will be appropriate. For example, in consumer markets a business selling gardening products can target an on-line gardening publication and have its banner placed on a prominent page. Retired people can be targeted through sites geared towards the elderly.

### Practice point

Search the Internet for UK-based websites that you can associate with certain hobbies, sports, or industrial sectors. Identify any banner ads placed on these sites.

Draw up a three-column table listing the URL (Web address), summarising the banner ad and commenting on whether you can identify any targeting by the business placing the banner.

The site *www.123propertynews.com* offers banner advertising slots within its on-line magazine. This is an obvious way in which anyone involved either in travel or in the property business can target a specific audience. This site offers various alternatives for banner placement, with differing prices for the most often viewed pages in the on-line magazine. Any site with a particular visitor profile can be targeted in this way.

*Banner advertisements*

Banners are of differing sizes, measured in pixels, and can be placed in rotation with others from other business organisations. Usually they are animated **.GIF** files. The banner can be arranged to appear for a while before being rotated with others – sometimes up to four or five banners may be rotated on the one space. Other types of banners are static, interstitial, or superstitial. Statics, of course, just remain in a static position on a page; interstitials usually appear between Web pages and are often seen while another page is loading; superstitials are popularly known as 'pop-ups'. Both of the latter types need to be actively closed down by the user, and marketers should be careful about using them as they can be regarded as a real nuisance!

*Page from* www.123propertynews.com

The choice for on-line marketers will be based on judging which sites attract most of the relevant target audience and where, within those sites, most visitors would view your advertisement. The content of the banner will be determined by what the business is trying to achieve. Some banners can be used to begin a **transaction**, others to inform potential customers about goods or services. Some can be used to shape attitudes or simply remind users that a company exists. Internet technology is capable of providing information about visitor numbers, numbers clicking on the banner and the place and time of the visit, so a good deal of intelligence is available for judging the effectiveness of a banner campaign.

The main drawback with a banner campaign is that it can be a relatively expensive approach. The Microsoft bCentral website (*www.bcentral.co.uk*) offers a service where business planners can examine statistics connected with Web page views. It is possible to look at the rate of click-

through to see how many people click on your banner and are referred through to your site.

The rate of click-through from banner ads has usually been calculated at less than 0.5%, and this has led some commentators to claim that banner ads are not the most cost-effective method of promotion.

Banner ads can give good results if they are used as part of a wider promotional campaign, and many off-line advertisements now include reference to Web addresses. An on-line promotional campaign will frequently make use of several channels other than the Internet to communicate a message.

A further technique is to incorporate within the banner ad something of use to a visitor to a site. A financial advisor included within a banner ad a currency converter; a life insurance company has included a quick quiz that allows users to calculate the funds they need to retire comfortably by a certain age.

## Web PR

A cheap and easy way of achieving publicity is by releasing news stories about an on-line business that are of interest to the public. This can easily be done by e-mailing press releases. The old situation in which newspaper or magazine deadlines had to be hit is now gone. A constant stream of news information is placed on the Web.

Marketers must consider the perspectives of the various consumers of Internet information. What angle on a news story might attract consumer interest? Distribution of news can be through e-mail pitches or through Web news services. A well-constructed 'About us' section on a website can spread PR content; as can an on-site newsletter. Of course, PR needs to be positive. For an example, see the award-winning *www.screwfix.com* site and go to the 'News' section on the home page.

An important facet of the Internet is its capacity to quickly turn a bad PR situation into a positive one. A firm can speedily add content to a website that can provide accurate information about a situation, stimulate interest, encourage acceptance and generate sympathy from the public.

## E-mail marketing

Every day, about 4 billion e-mail messages are sent and around 300 million text messages. The modern business can benefit enormously from e-mail. Dell Computers is reported in an Iconocast report of 2001 to have received more than $1 million per week in revenue through e-mail marketing campaigns. E-mails allow for very direct targeting and they are difficult to ignore, even if they are deleted quickly. The recipient must still see the message header.

In a b2b context the marketing effort often involves managing a quite complex set of relationships with business customers. Using customer relationship management techniques (CRM), a business can make effective use of e-mail. Customers can be acquired by using lists of e-mail addresses purchased from a list owner or list broker (an organisation that has created lists of addresses and possibly categorised them). The lists must be updated regularly.

Dave Chaffey suggests that when a firm is running an e-mail marketing campaign there are two dimensions to manage. A successful campaign, such as that of Dell mentioned above, will lead to many inbound e-mails. This calls for a successful marketing effort to handle customer enquiries effectively, and significant outbound e-mails to respond to customers.

Seth Godin pointed out that thanks to e-mail we are now bombarded with about 3,000 marketing messages a day. Godin calls traditional direct and unsolicited marketing messages 'interruption marketing'. They barge in on us and interrupt what we are doing.

The practice of sending out unsolicited e-mails is known as 'spamming' – the letters **SPAM** are said to stand for Sending Persistent Annoying e-Mail. If PR is the effort to promote an effective and positive image on the Internet, spamming tends to have the opposite effect. Maturing Internet users are simply learning to screen out and delete spam.

If Internet marketers are to tap into the potential benefits of e-mail, they need to consider ways of by-passing any accusations of spamming. To do this they might use 'opt-in' e-mailing. This means that before sending any mail they seek permission first; this is sometimes called 'permission marketing'. Users must tick a box giving the organisation permission to mail them in future.

The benefits of permission-based e-mailing are considerable, according to a survey quoted in *eMarketer* (October 2002). The survey, by Quris, found that 67% of consumers believed that the quality of opt-in e-mails positively influenced their opinions about the companies sending them, and 53% said that such e-mails had an influence on what they purchased.

Marketers must be extremely careful when considering both e-mailing and PR on the Internet. Because the Internet is a network, the effect is that news travels very quickly. Internet marketers can and do use this effect to the benefit of their businesses, but they must beware of the negative effects of bad mailing practice or bad PR. **Viral marketing** is the term used to describe the way in which marketing messages can be rapidly spread around the Internet.

### Affiliate programmes

An **affiliate** in Internet terms is an on-line business that uses a small banner or link on a site which, when clicked, will take the visitor through to a destination site. Affiliates form their own networks. Perhaps the best known is Amazon, which has over 300,000 affiliates.

> **Thinking point**
>
> How does an affiliate programme in Internet terms differ from an advertising programme? In your opinion, which is the most effective? Why?

## On-line people

If we buy on-line we buy from people, not computers. Internet marketing has to overcome the problem of gaining trust and answering an individual's personal questions about any on-line product.

The art of successful marketing of on-line products is to ensure that the service offered from the site is seen to be of value. When a user is having trouble using a site, or has a query that he or she feels should best be dealt with via a phone call, people are a crucial part of the on-line remix. See *www.easyjet.com* for a simple, three-step process for getting in touch with the company. EasyJet's policy is to try to deal with issues on-line. However, if all else fails, the company must rely on the personal skills and knowledge of a member of staff.

> **Practice point**
>
> Visit *www.easyjet.com* and view the three-step process described above. Summarise in your own words how you feel EasyJet has designed the process of getting in touch as a 'people-friendly' procedure.
>
> Find a contrasting site with a different approach. As a possible user of both sites, how do you rate the people aspect of the design? Suggest improvements if you can.

The re-emergence of e-business after the dot.com crashes of the 1990s was achieved in large part through many successful businesses combining both a physical and an on-line presence. Long-established businesses now employ an on-line channel for sales (such as Tesco and Sainsbury). From the marketing perspective, on-line customer service is the key to survival and success.

At this stage in the development of the Internet, many consumers still need the reassurance of knowing that people are available to assist or give friendly guidance if necessary, either on the telephone or by e-mail. It is becoming increasingly hard for businesses to compete on the basis of price alone.

While it is possible to compete through enhancing the on-line product with additional information or added value, excellent service from the site – offered by or designed by people with the consumer in mind – is crucial for an effective marketing effort. To be successful in Internet marketing terms requires an 'outside-in' approach – always consider the on-line offer from the point of view of the customer. To do this effectively requires good people at every stage.

### Practice point

What do you feel is meant by on-line customer service? Visit *www.diy.com* and write a list of examples of customer service from this website.

Find another site of your own choice and compare the two in customer service terms.

## On-line physical evidence

Customers often make a choice about whether to purchase goods or a service simply based upon how the business looks or feels to them. All physical things connected with the business should therefore have positive images. How can Internet marketers create appropriate physical evidence in the on-line world?

The first piece of physical evidence is the website itself. In experiencing the website, consumers need to feel they are in a professional environment. In many respects the website represents the on-line brand. Because we all have certain brand loyalties or preferences, a brand is often seen as a solidly reassuring thing; the marketing intention is to help create a quality on-line brand using the website. Reassurances to do with awards, recommendations, professional

associations or product guarantees can help, and they need to be prominent.

A site needs to be professionally designed, have clear and easy navigational aids and have a consistent look. In support of the on-line offer, the business needs to ensure that all off-line supporting activities, such as product delivery or back-up services, are communicating the right message.

### Practice point

In groups, carry out an Internet search and create a poster display showing the main features of an effective business website. Your poster can be either critical or positive about a site, but it should refer to specific aspects of site design and comment on whether you feel it represents good physical evidence for the on-line business.

## On-line processes

The ideal situation with private on-line consumers is not only to attract them to a website but to convert the visit into a sale. This is called the 'conversion rate' and it is a key measure of a business site's effectiveness. The conversion rate links closely to one of the basic principles of Internet marketing – trying to create a lifetime relationship with customers; in other words, encouraging repeat business time after time. To achieve this, as we have seen, customers' experience of the site must be positive, the presentation of goods and services on the site must be clear, the content relevant and useful, the buying process must feel straightforward and secure and, most important of all, the business must deliver on its promises.

In ensuring that all customer orders are fulfilled, Internet marketers have to consider a set of processes that lead to accurate and helpful information being available, both internally to the business and externally to customers. Processes must therefore be in place that update website information. Imagine you are buying toys for a children's party and you go to a website that informs you thirty of a certain toy are available.

Satisfied, you order them and relax. In reality however, none are in stock because the website information has not taken account of today's earlier orders. This is a calamity for the party, and disastrous for an on-line business. The following processes are vital for on-line sales success:

- responding to an enquiry
- ordering
- updating and recording stock available
- updating website information
- acknowledging an order
- tracking the progress of an order
- notifying the customer
- organising despatch (shipping).

*Customers shopping on the Web have to feel the process is easy and convenient*

The Internet marketing function needs to co-ordinate these processes, because ultimately they are all concerned with the relationship with the on-line customer. Without efficient integration with other systems internal to the business organisation the Internet presence becomes a sham and the reputation of the brand suffers. To put this simply, the website has to be accurate, and to work.

Assuming that the background processes are in place, consideration of the process that the consumer goes through in deciding on and making a purchase from the website is an important part of Internet marketing. B&Q Direct used software to analyse user interactions on its website and found that when a visitor to the site abandoned the visit, it was more often than not at the point where personal payment details were asked for. Other reports vary in their conclusions, but the drop-out rate of potential e-shoppers is a big problem. The transaction aspect of the site visit therefore has to be made very straightforward, and B&Q Direct users are reassured with the words 'Placing an order is safe, simple and secure'.

Amazon pioneered the idea of one-click shopping, so that a very easy transaction process reinforces the feeling of convenience. Customers shopping on the Web have to feel that the process

is easy, and that an error can be quickly put right by simply using the 'back' button. Ideally they should receive regular on-screen reassurance that they are doing the right things to accomplish a transaction, and the order screen should be clear and uncluttered. Internet marketing specialists have to consider all of these things from the point of view of a first-time customer.

Although private consumers are slowly but surely getting used to making purchases through the Internet, security is still a concern. Businesses hoping to make a success of on-line selling must use an SSL (Secure Sockets Layer) server to ensure credit card transactions remain secure. This server will use SSL technology, which includes encryption processes that are almost impenetrable. Many users are starting to recognise the closed padlock and key symbols at the bottom right of the screen and know that they symbolise the use of SSL.

Internet marketers will consider how to reassure customers by giving full security information. People are gaining confidence and Web designers and Internet businesses are very concerned to reassure visitors that shopping on the Web is not only convenient but secure.

## Marketing services

On-line service businesses exploit the essence of the Internet as a content-driven network. On-line businesses can use the Internet to deliver services effectively. A major difference between marketing a service and a tangible product is that whereas a tangible product order has to be fulfilled through storage and distribution to the end user, a service product does not.

On-line services nevertheless still have to be delivered with attention to quality. To successfully build an on-line service requires attention to customer expectations. Dave Chaffey lists a number of dimensions of service quality:

- Is the on-line service reliable and dependable?
- Is there a willingness to help promptly?
- Can the service convey trust and confidence?
- What does the service Web presence look like?
- Is the service provided caringly and individually?

## The marketing remix in b2b markets

The money value of on-line transactions between businesses is greater than the value of transactions with private consumers. So it's sensible for businesses in these markets to make sure their e-marketing is right.

A study by Accenture in 2001 showed that brand reputation, followed by service and price, were by far the most important variables in buyer decision-making in b2b contexts.

### How does b2b e-marketing differ from b2c?

The decision we make to purchase something in consumer markets is usually a fairly simple and straightforward one, based on social and personal criteria. An individual, or perhaps on occasions a whole family, chooses a product for private use and enjoyment. Parents choose food and drinks for family use. Sometimes the whole family might be involved in choosing a new family car. For the vast majority of household items, no great complexity is involved in the process of making the choice. The collective effect of these private purchase decisions in the b2c marketplace, however, has a dramatic effect on b2b markets.

The decision of a visitor to *www.next.co.uk* to purchase a cotton T-shirt, for example, is likely to be a simple one. However, many small-scale consumer decisions create a 'chain of derived demand', as shown opposite.

Everything from the left-hand side is pulled through the chain as a result of the demand for the end product, whether the demand comes through an on-line channel or otherwise. Businesses sell cotton to merchants, who sell it to spinners, who sell it to weavers, who sell it to clothing manufacturers, who finally sell the completed garments to Next Retail; this results in their distribution and storage somewhere, prior to delivery to the consumer. Value is being added at each stage and to add value, businesses need raw materials and equipment – things they get from other businesses.

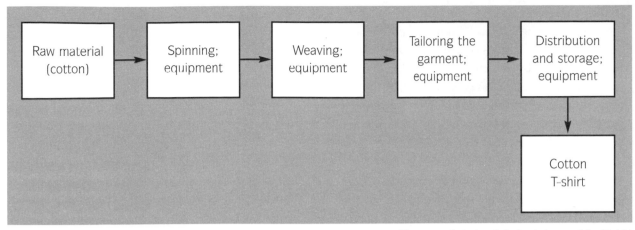

*Diagram of chain of derived demand for T-shirt*

The marketing in b2b markets is about each business meeting the needs of other businesses. The distribution company that moves clothes around on behalf of clothing e-tailers (such as Next), needs (among many other things) lorries and vans; it also needs equipment such as forklift trucks, pallets and possibly warehousing. But do managers simply have a look on the Web to see if they can find a couple of lorries? Of course not, because the decisions made to purchase industrial products such as forklift trucks, or significant quantities of raw materials, are much more complex than the decision to purchase an item of clothing. The decision to buy will probably be made by more than one individual and important criteria may be used to choose a supplier.

Whereas there are many suppliers of T-shirts, there are a limited number of forklift truck manufacturers and suppliers. Decision-makers considering the purchase of such products have to consider quality, price and delivery, just as the private consumer does. However, because of the complexity of the product and its specific purpose for a business, a degree of technical knowledge is essential.

This is the case with many b2b products. Plant and equipment, components, scientific instruments, pharmaceuticals, drugs, and raw materials of many kinds have to meet specific requirements. The marketing requirements for industrial products are therefore quite different in character from those in b2c markets. These include the following.

- Technical support must be offered from supplier to user.

- Excellent technical confidence and competence is required from suppliers.

- Confidence in quality is required.

- Product image is less important, unless it affects someone else down the supply chain. Brand, however, is important.

### *Relationship marketing in b2b markets*

Because requirements differ and are often more complex in b2b markets than for private consumers, it follows that greater emphasis is likely to be placed upon personal relationships between the firms. We have already seen that sophisticated CRM (customer relationship management) software is being used to help automate some aspects of this.

In many business contexts, technical representatives will be well known to potential buyers – they will almost certainly be on first-name terms and there must be a great deal of trust and goodwill. Often products will be marketed directly from a supplying business to a potential purchasing business. Each business will be very well known to the other, because in many cases there will be very few customers for specialist products. Considerable revenue will be generated from relatively few purchasing occasions, however; so although a firm may be involved in only a few transactions per year (or longer), the relationship between them needs to be good.

Internet technology is able to help in several ways and has the potential to transform relationships within the supply chain. Take the example of a forklift truck manufacturer.

The three companies are each enabled by Internet technology to collaborate and communicate very closely. If company C wishes to make design changes to the product, through the Web these changes can be viewed immediately; feedback and comment can come from companies A or B. Both companies can make use of Web pages that are linked to internal databases. These automatically update the Web pages of the companies with the latest data available from within the firm. Web-based e-mail platforms such as OpenMail allow employees to securely access company mailboxes from anywhere in the world. Within all three companies, design issues can be therefore be shared between specialists. The end result is that problems or complexities are avoided further along in the product development process.

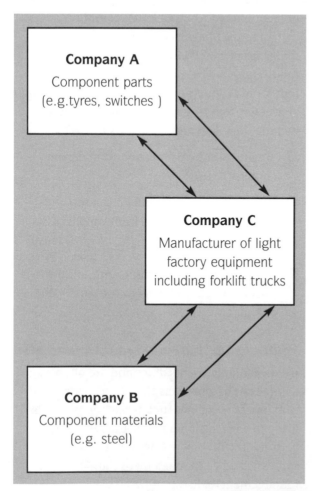

*Internet b2b relationships*

## Outcome activity 14.1

### Pass
Take two contrasting e-businesses and explain how their marketing activities illustrate the principles of Internet marketing.

You might choose a b2c site, such as diy.com, a b2b site such as RS Components, and an auction site such as eBay.

### Merit
Analyse ways in which Internet marketing activities build upon conventional off-line marketing principles and offer customers greater freedom of choice.

Give a full analysis of general marketing principles and say how the Internet is helping businesses to meet customer expectations more effectively.

### Distinction
Evaluate how the performance of contrasting businesses may be enhanced through applying the principles of Internet marketing, despite the challenges encountered.

For instance, how does a website enabling a customer to design his or her own jeans allow Levi Strauss to meet customer needs more effectively? Do you think this could be just a gimmick? Justify your comments.

# Benefits of Internet marketing to customers

Because marketing activities occur in many different market contexts, the benefits that can be achieved differ.

In b2b markets, businesses are trying to serve and meet the needs of other businesses. Transactions are often based on longer-term agreements to 'do business' with each other. The range of b2b products and services varies greatly, ranging from pencils to very sophisticated scientific or technical equipment.

The more complex the product, the greater the need to exchange detailed data and have close working relationships between expert staff. This is one of the great potential benefits of Internet marketing in b2b contexts. Data and complex information can be stored, retrieved, communicated and manipulated.

In b2c markets, private consumers tend to buy for personal reasons to do with tastes and preferences. Here too there are personal benefits to be gained from the efforts of Internet marketers.

## Practice point

Access the website at *www.BuyerZone.com*.

This is a US-based on-line marketplace enabling business buyers to access information quickly about potential suppliers.

Prepare a short presentation about the site, designed to show how Internet technology is helping the purchasing process.

Look for any similar on-line services.

What are the possible benefits of Internet marketing for all of the parties involved? Remember that marketing principles are about satisfying customer needs profitably. In b2b markets, the full benefits of the Internet tend to be felt only by those businesses that can enter into valuable collaborations with other firms that also have the right Web-based systems.

The RS Components website (*http://rswww.com*) is an example of a b2b website that is designed to help all customers take full advantage of the benefits the Internet can bring.

Research in America in 2001 by Accenture showed that larger companies tended to purchase on-line (23% of them doing so for more than a quarter of their purchases) whereas small to medium firms did less on-line purchasing (18%). At this stage in the evolution of Internet business, any firm considering moving to on-line activities needs to consider the uneven pace at which other companies are doing so. There is little point in having state-of-the-art Web-based information technology if major partner firms do not.

## Customisation

Large supermarkets and hypermarkets have tended to reduce the opportunities for a personal shopping experience. Years ago, people would tend to stay close to home and shop at different types of local outlets. Communities could be characterised by a distinctive set of shops. Increasingly, we have developed into a mass consumption society where every family tends to shop in similar ways, and is faced with similar ranges of products, throughout the country.

One benefit of the on-line shopping experience is that each of us can now enjoy a unique, personal offer from a website that is tailored to suit our individual preferences. This is mass customisation.

Customisation is important because it gets to the heart of what marketing is about – meeting customer needs. Anything that is 'customised' has been altered to suit a specific set of requirements. Some people customise cars by adding new panels, re-spraying to a fresh colour and putting stickers all over the body. This may not be to everyone's taste, but it suits the owner. In Internet marketing terms, customisation (sometimes referred to as **personalisation**) means using Internet technology to tailor websites to suit the needs (or perceived needs) of individual customers.

Take the following example from a b2c transaction involving Amazon (see *www.amazon.com*) and a private consumer.

*Amazon.co.uk – personalising the product*

The screen shot from Amazon shows that it has made use of previously gathered data to keep a log of all the purchases a specific customer has made from its website.

The example shows that this consumer has bought before from the site, and as soon as a purchase is made, Amazon's system offers other suggestions for similar books or CDs. Amazon says, 'Hello John Goymer, if you like what you've just bought, you might like these too ...' For both books and CDs, Amazon can also offer this customer – and even completely new customers – reviews of products based on other people's purchases. As with many e-tailers, Amazon uses 'shopping cart' technology. Shoppers can add many items to their cart or basket, and as they do, Amazon's system maintains the full record of the shopping visit. Each time a customer visits and re-visits the Amazon website, this customised

and up-to-date response is automatically offered, anticipating his or her needs. Each and every customer, thanks to Internet technology, can enjoy a personal shopping experience.

### Practice point

Carry out an Internet search and find three websites that offer a degree of customisation on their site.

Produce a short written description of these and include screen shots to clearly illustrate the technique. What benefits, if any, are there for both the business and the customer?

John Goymer is known to Amazon as a customer because he has 'registered' with the site. His previous buying history is known to Amazon. In many cases however, site visitors are anonymous to the website. This does not necessarily mean that they are first timers; many anonymous visitors are regular visitors to the site – they have simply chosen not to register. Marketing specialists are still able to offer the benefit of a set of customised menus for these visitors so that the site *feels* as if it is personal to them. One way this can be done is by offering facilities such as 'People who bought [item X] also often bought [item Y]' and showing a list of products to the visitor. What is important is that the user feels that the offering is personal to him or her.

Some on-line retail sites offer a gift advisory service on their site (see, for example, *www.fortnumandmason.com*). The user can be asked a set of questions: Who are you buying a gift for? What is the person interested in? What is your price range? Next to each question is a drop-down box of alternative answers. Every time the user selects an option, the screen offers an updated selection of gift suggestions. This is customisation based on user interaction, not upon asking detailed questions beforehand. It is a way of breaking down barriers and gently encouraging the user to feel a part of the site.

The thinking behind this type of on-line marketing is to try to recreate for consumers the kind of shopping experience one would expect in a high-class shopping mall. We all expect individual attention, especially if we have a problem with something.

Customer Relationship Management (CRM) software, as mentioned before, automates the whole response a business makes to its regular on-line customers or clients. Using CRM tools enables on-line businesses to be responsive and efficient. It enables them to develop an on-line relationship that is based on trust and goodwill.

It helps to think of every business as having a personality, just as people have different personalities. Two businesses trading with each other are better off if they know each other very well. The Internet offers the chance to improve on this knowledge. Studies by Accenture have shown that in b2b markets, service is what matters – in most cases more than price. The firm that offers cheapness but a poor back-up service will not compete successfully with those offering excellent customer support. This is known as 'customer orientation'. It involves constantly considering customers' needs. It is better to plan ahead carefully when developing an on-line channel, rather than rush in with an ill-conceived strategy – as the saying goes, 'e-Right is more important than e-Speed'.

## Interactive shopping

The experience of buying a product on-line can never be exactly the same as buying in a shop in town. However, some on-line businesses are attempting to use Web-based technology to create a more interactive experience for the shopper, and in doing so create a relationship that will keep him or her as a customer. It is far more productive to retain customers than only to acquire new ones.

At *www.nokey.com* an effort is made to mirror the interaction of a physical shop. At any point during the shopping or browsing process, the customer can launch a live instant messaging (IM) session to seek advice or help. The latest versions of the technology allow the on-line store to view the items a customer has added or deleted from his or her shopping cart and initiate an IM session with shoppers at any time during their visit to the site, offering help or advice at the point where it is perhaps most needed.

### Practice point

Prepare a brief set of notes outlining what is meant by the term 'interactive shopping' and explaining what, if any, benefits are gained for consumers.

## Ability to compare and select products

In both b2c and b2b markets, the Internet has offered far greater opportunities for buyers to compare the offers of businesses. For b2c markets, research quoted by Laurie Windham showed that more than a third of all Internet shoppers regarded themselves as 'comparison shoppers'. Their motivation for on-line shopping was the ability to study and compare on-line products.

In industrial markets, the evolution of e-marketplaces (sometimes called exchanges or hubs) allows firms to enter specialist on-line environments in which they can develop relationships with suppliers and choose from a broad range of offerings. Several electronic marketplaces now exist, each offering a simple, single link to a wide range of suppliers (see *www.itoi.com, www.vertical.net, www.chemdex.com*).

**Practice Point**

Visit *www.diy.com*. Prepare a presentation on the site, clearly showing how it has been designed with customer needs in mind. Consider whether consumer choices have been improved or whether they are better informed about specific products.

Make sure that you illustrate your points with reference to specific aspects of the website (such as ability to try out colour schemes).

House-hunting is one area where Internet technology is gradually transforming the process and delivering real benefits to people. Nielson/NetRatings research shows that more than 12 million Internet users accessed on-line estate agents in March 2003. Users can access comparative information about properties and agents, they can see 'virtual tours' of properties, and make use of on-line mortgage calculators.

*The Verticalnet site offers supplier selection services*

## Thinking point

Can you think of any other websites where clever use of technology enables the potential on-line purchaser to do things that might be difficult in the real world? Prepare notes to make a verbal statement about what the site provides.

The travel industry can use the Internet to offer consumers the full range of travel-related products. Virtual tours of places of interest, photo galleries and access to tourist office information can all be made available through a website.

On-line flight comparisons and reservations are now well established on the Internet, and consumers can benefit through the significantly lower transactional costs involved in on-line reservations compared to call-centre reservations. The cost of an on-line reservation is almost ten times cheaper, according to a report by Datamonitor, 1999.

## Dynamic pricing

The benefits of dynamic pricing, where the price is automatically updated to suit the particular circumstances either of the market or the buyer, are simply that everyone involved in a transaction has the chance to gain. Purchasers get the keenest price, and sellers make something from the deal because the system is set up to ensure that they do. Using dynamic pricing means that sales people are saved the need for haggling or negotiation and decisions can be made quickly. See www.lastminute.com for example of the application of dynamic pricing.

## Digital complaints and chat

On-line complaints services exist to make a business out of assisting consumers to pursue complaints about on-line products or services. Consumers benefit by being able to add their complaint to those of others gathered by the specialist firm, and thereby achieve a collective effect.

A fee is paid to the complaints service company which writes to the on-line firm concerned and

describes the concerns. Any complainant must have given the customer care staff at the company being complained about a chance to rectify the problem before it is taken up. The matter will be passed over to legal specialists by the complaints service if it is not resolved (see www.fightback.com).

The Internet offers the opportunity for people to participate in real time on-line chat groups. This is especially useful from the consumer viewpoint as they are able to contribute opinions about products and read the opinions of many others. In this respect the power of the individual consumer is enhanced both by gaining information on the perspectives of others, and by making collective representations.

## Practice point

Visit www.apple.com and navigate through 'Support' to 'Discussions' and the link about the iTunes product. Does this empower the consumer? How would you say the consumer benefits?

## Payment systems

A major benefit to on-line consumers is the ease and speed with which transactions can be completed over the Internet. A decision on the part of the private consumer to purchase tickets for an event can be quickly converted to a firm booking through a secure credit card transaction. The costs of these transactions for businesses are near zero.

In b2b transactions, the amount of funds involved is likely to be too high for credit cards to be used. In these cases invoicing is usually the preferred payment method, and this is increasingly likely to be digitised. When both parties in a transaction are well known to each other, all that is needed are passwords and log-in **authentication**. Invoicing can then be done automatically and securely.

Since 1972, Fight Back! has provided information and raised awareness to help consumers help themselves in the marketplace.  Fight Back! acts as a conduit for consumer problem solving and redress.  David Horowitz and Fight Back! assist in the legislative process through proposals for new consumer protection laws where they are needed.

**FIGHT BACK.com**

December 16, 2003

**Coming Soon**

WATCH VIDEO!

QUICKTIME
56K MODEM | BROADBAND

WINDOWS MEDIA
56K MODEM | BROADBAND

| FIGHT BACK! EVERYWHERE | BYTE BACK! | ABOUT FIGHT BACK! |
|---|---|---|
| Of Consuming Interest ▸ | Fight Back! Feed Back! Forum ▸ | David's Bio ▸ |
| Newspapers ▸ | Write Back! Complaint Form ▸ | Fight Back! History ▸ |
| On Radio ▸ | Write Back! Results ▸ | Contact Us ▸ |
| On Television ▸ | Ask David! ▸ | |
| Books & Videos ▸ | | |

**Links and More**
Consumer resources at your fingertips!

**Holiday Hints!**
Shopping, Safety and More!

**Recalls and Warnings**
for Shopping Safety!

**Fight Back! for your Consumer Rights**

Got a question?
Got a problem?

Get help now with fightback.com's
**Consumer Services!**

**Drug and Vitamin Prices Under Attack!**

Prices of medications are sky high ... and are vitamin companies fixing prices?

Read the latest about the challenges in the courts and Canada **here!**

Document: Done (5.217 secs)

*Fightback.com offers a complaints service*

## Outcome activity 14.2

### Pass

Prepare a poster display, with supporting notes, describing and illustrating the principal benefits of Internet marketing to customers of contrasting businesses.

You might select three or four key benefits of Internet marketing, such as customised Web pages, increased choice, feedback and discussion, or better customer relations in b2b markets.

# Opportunities offered by Internet marketing

The Internet offers opportunities for businesses to re-launch themselves on-line. A well-established off-line business can create an entirely new on-line personality and tap new markets on a global scale if it chooses to adopt such a strategy.

To be able to serve a market properly, and more importantly to target a particular segment of a market, an on-line business needs to know as much about that market as possible. It must be an intelligent business, in terms of being well informed about trends or changes. Information is the lifeblood of the Internet, and marketing information is readily available. Who is using a site? Where are they? What are they like? This is marketing intelligence, and it is vital.

# Acquiring marketing intelligence

The Internet makes it possible to gather business information from all over the world, to monitor competitor activities, to find out the opinions and feelings of potential customers (see *www.ciao.co.uk* for an example of a consumer product-rating site) and to study changes in the on-line market a business is working in.

Trends and fluctuations that may affect a firm's on-line activity can be analysed quickly. It is possible, by using the services of a specialist Web analytics firm such as *www.accrue.com*, to gain an insight into the impact and performance of your website and any advertising campaigns it contains.

Traffic to a website can be analysed, and the most popular areas of a site can be found. Marketing specialists can establish which content has been most interesting to visitors and make sure the best content is developed.

A vast resource of secondary data is easily available on-line – data that has already been researched by others. New, primary data can also be discovered. This primary data can be researched from the firm's own website, as illustrated in the Black and Decker case study below.

Visitor use or navigation patterns can be established by tracking the pages visited, the most common entry page, and the page people most often leave a site from. Obviously visitor numbers can be checked, as well as the numbers of visitors who are converted to customers. A whole new industry supplying Webanalysis tools and services has developed. Businesses of all sizes now find that quite sophisticated marketing research tools are within their grasp.

In the CIM definition of marketing given earlier (page 98), identifying, anticipating and (as we shall see) satisfying customer needs can all be assisted by effective use of Internet marketing intelligence.

## Case study    Black and Decker

Black and Decker (USA), the leading global manufacturer and supplier of power tools and accessories, set up a consumer website at *www.blackanddecker.com* designed to support customers throughout the buying and home-improvement process. The company wanted to build better relationships with consumers by getting them to become registered members of the site.

Its challenges were to:

o maximise registrations of users as members
o effectively monitor the success of the effort to build better relationships, to find whether people were registering as members of the site.

The company appointed WebTrends (*www.webtrends.com*) to provide detailed analysis of the traffic on the Black and Decker website.

One question was where was the most effective place on the site to locate a registration button. The solution was found by varying the position of the button and measuring the registrations gained from each. By doing this through the WebTrends Reporting Centre, Black and Decker discovered the best location and increased registrations by 40%.

1 In what ways do you think Black and Decker has engaged in more effective marketing through its website?
2 What issues are involved in encouraging site users to register?

## Affiliate marketing

We saw earlier that the process of carrying advertising links from one website to the website of another business is known as affiliate marketing. This is an agreed arrangement between two on-line businesses.

Internet technology allows businesses to track how many visitors pass through a particular link on another site to their own site. The affiliate business – the one carrying the link – will be paid either a flat fee or commission from sales generated by the referral. Commissions vary; some businesses pay a higher rate if more than, say, fifty sales per month are generated.

Being an affiliate can be quite lucrative for some on-line businesses, depending on the value of the products concerned. If a product is worth £400 and an affiliate receives 2.5% per sale, this can add significant sums to revenue. From the point of view of Internet marketing policy and strategy, the decision to add an affiliate programme to a company's on-line presence could be a very significant addition to distribution channels.

## Analysis of competitor activity

The Internet offers the opportunity to carry out careful and accurate analysis of what competitors are doing on-line. Each company that goes on-line immediately becomes more open and transparent. By its nature, the Internet is open and everyone can view its content. Marketing activities have to include keeping a close eye on the tactics, ideas and offerings of competitor firms.

The websites themselves can be monitored and are a primary source of information. The marketer will look for new ideas, for offers and tactical manoeuvres, particularly from firms competing for the same segment of the market. The idea is not to copy a website, but to gain an insight into competitor strategy. There are organisations offering this kind of intelligence as a service on the Web. At *http://finance.yahoo.com* it is possible to gather information about many companies around the world. Dunn and Bradstreet has a database on more than 64 million companies across the globe and on 3.4 million in the UK alone (see *www.accountancyage.com*).

## Identifying customers

On-line businesses in both b2c and b2b markets can discover much information about customers. Only a few years ago, the typical Internet user was a young white male, probably from an academic background. Today there is a much more diverse pattern of Internet usage. Because of this there are many more diverse markets segments for on-line marketers to target.

As the Internet is a global phenomenon, there is no single ethnic group that does not have some access to the Internet. Virtually every country on every continent has Internet connection and it is essential for businesses to remember that what is offered via the Web has to be tailored to meet the needs of local populations. 'Think globally, act locally' has become a common requirement for Internet marketers. Remember, a fundamental principle of any marketing strategy is to identify and get to know customers, whether we are dealing with them globally, nationally or regionally.

The production of statistics about Internet use and trends ('webographics') has therefore become an industry in itself, and several options are available for gaining such data.

The website of the International Telecommunications Union (ITU) – *www.itu.int* – makes available data about Internet access across countries and continents. The site *www.nua.com/surveys* offers statistical data based on European Internet trends. The British Market Research Bureau (*www.bmrb.co.uk*) provides data on consumer buying behaviour.

We can categorise data about the on-line population in a number of ways:

- by demographics – age, gender
- by geographic location – continent, nationality, region
- by 'psychographic' profile – characterising Internet users according to major tendencies identified via research (see below)
- by access device – personal computer, mobile, TV
- by lifestyle characteristics – interests, home ownership, car ownership
- by social class – based on work status, occupation, income.

## Psychographics

The 'psychographics' of on-line shoppers were categorised by Harris Interactive (*www.harrisinteractive.com*) into six main groupings, and these illustrate what is meant by the term psychographics. Harris suggested six main types of on-line shopper, as shown below.

- **E-bivalent newbies** (5%) – new to the Internet and less interested in buying on-line. Mainly older and less often on-line.
- **Time-sensitive materialists** (17%) – interested in maximum convenience, not bothered about product reviews or comparisons.
- **Clicks and mortar** (23%) – tend to shop on-line but buy off-line. Probably female home builders who have privacy and security concerns.
- **Hooked, on-line and single** (16%) – more likely to be young, single males with a high income; have been on the Internet longest and play games, download software, bank and invest on-line.
- **Hunter gatherers** (20%) – married, aged 30–49 with two children; often go to sites to compare prices and read analyses and product reviews.
- **Brand loyalists** (19%) – people who go directly to a shopping site they know, are satisfied with on-line shopping and spend most on-line.

### Practice point

In groups, design a questionnaire about attitudes to on-line shopping. Try to discover whether you can categorise a significant group of people you know, according to the types identified by Harris.

## Getting to know business customers

Business users of the Internet can be profiled in much the same way as private individuals.

- Do they have Internet access?
- Who within the firm has Internet access?
- What is their main market? Which industrial sector? Which products?
- Do they purchase on-line?
- What is the size of the firm?
- Is it private or public sector?
- Which country or region is it based in?

It is very important to profile potential business customers. It has already been stressed that it is essential to consider the state of 'Internet readiness' of firms that may be crucial business partners, either as suppliers or purchasers of your products. So called 'vertical **portals**' are gateway websites to communities of firms working in specific industries; they are important means of targeting firms (see *www.vertical.net*).

## On-line and off-line marketing

Marketing people may not only exploit the opportunities offered by the Internet but can add to their total communication effort by integrating off-line promotional work. This could include the following:

- promoting the domain name (via livery, posters or other advertising)

*Off-line promotional work helps highlight on-line services*

- brand building by stressing the on-line value proposition (see page 99)
- promotional offers.

Increasingly, on-line businesses are building a brand identity and people are referring quite naturally to dot.com brands, often adding to a physical business as with diy.com. Through word of mouth, websites are able to gain a powerful reputation and this, known as **viral marketing**, is increasingly a major concern.

Similarly, Webpublic relations can be a low-cost but very effective form of promoting a site. Also, direct mailing of website offers can be used, together with Web address promotion via business cards, magazine inserts, catalogues or brochures.

## Marketing through search engines

Over 80% of Web users are reported to use search engines, so it makes sense for an on-line

business to register with one. There are now over 3 billion Web pages on the Internet, yet most of them are not registered with one of the search engines. This makes them largely inaccessible to all but a relatively few users. Marketers must – at a cost – submit the URL of the website to the appropriate search engine after making sure that the main Web page includes important 'meta data' (data about the information on the site) at its <HEAD>. If the site is accepted, key words from the meta data on the site are added to the search engine's database and an index is created. When people search this engine, the index is searched.

## Other on-line marketing opportunities

### Promotional microsites

Sometimes a small business may not have either the resources or the time to invest in the design of a website. The cost of planning, design and ongoing maintenance can be expensive. An alternative way to achieve some form of on-line presence is to create a promotional 'microsite'. Such a small-scale site can be placed within other on-line services and be used for either general or specific promotional efforts. Microsites can include all the usual features of a website, including graphics.

### Hot links

So-called 'hot' links or hyperlinks are simply active links that connect a user to a site of particular interest. A web surfer who might be looking for information about gardening products might look at an index of hot links relating to gardening. It is obviously important to a business in that market that its site is included in such a list of links.

### Syndication

When a Web-based retailer has an on-line presence, it is crucial that the contents of the website are regularly updated. This can be a costly process, whatever the context.

Imagine an on-line business dealing with electrical products; these can change constantly. Some Web-based services provide for 'syndicated' content. This means that information is put together by a central source and can be purchased and used by many businesses. The idea is similar to the long-established practice of syndicating articles from newspapers or magazines.

### Collaborative design and engineering

Web-based collaboration (working together) is now a reality for some firms, especially in the construction industry. By using software effectively, firms can share information on design questions and work co-operatively on-line. The north-east firm Leighton Group (*www.leighton.com*) has been at the forefront of such collaborative technology and has marketed '4Projects' as a tool to help in this (see *www.4Projects.com*). By being able and willing to participate in such collaborative work, firms can engage in fruitful on-line relationships.

## Equality of Internet presence

In the physical world, a small business is often perceived as inferior to the big, well-established firm. This perception can make the difference between success and failure. Some buyers or consumers might feel that the SME (small to medium enterprise) is likely to be unreliable or of poorer quality. The lack of status can also be a problem.

In the on-line world, these differences are minimised. On-line, the SME competes on equal terms as long as its website works well. The Internet therefore offers small businesses an opportunity for increased competitive power.

## Challenges in Internet marketing

While the Internet is offering marketing benefits and opportunities, it also throws up many challenges. These challenges have to be faced and overcome if a business is to successfully compete in the on-line world. Traditional thinking about business activity looks at a chain of value-adding processes; businesses acquire materials, store materials, work with materials to produce something, package the product, warehouse (or store) the product, market the product, sell it, and move it. Modern businesses

### Outcome activity 14.3

**Pass**

Explain how Internet marketing may create new business opportunities for contrasting businesses.

One way of achieving this outcome might be to create your own case study showing how two businesses have responded to the opportunities offered by Internet marketing.

You might select two firms, one offering a service to other businesses and another selling a product both on-line and off-line (such as B&Q and RS Components). Outline – among other things – how the Internet can allow access to new markets; how market knowledge can be improved; how new distribution channels can be used; and how new suppliers might be sourced.

**Merit**

Analyse ways in which Internet marketing has created new business opportunities and also presented new challenges for contrasting businesses.

You could so this as a SWOT analysis in which you detail the strengths and opportunities that a particular business could have. This might be strong product, excellent staff, good skills, growing market, good client relations and strong reputation. Weaknesses and threats could include lack of completely effective distribution and product fulfilment capability, and vulnerability to competitors from overseas.

have grown to encompass several of these spheres of activity within one organisation.

According to Dave Chaffey, one way of looking at e-business as a whole is to see at it as two overlapping sets of business processes: on the one hand buying and on the other selling.

These sets of activities are at the heart of what business is about. The Internet offers a new channel through which the processes involved in adding value take place, but just as it represents a new channel of opportunities, so it has the potential to cause conflict and challenges. The Chaffey perspective is useful for putting these challenges into perspective.

## The challenge of channel conflict

The Internet offers the chance to use a direct channel of supply to clients or customers. As we have seen, this disintermediation process is the tendency to cut out the middle man. This creates obvious efficiencies and savings, but also brings the danger of destabilising many older, traditional channels that are still valuable sources of revenue to the business. Several scenarios might serve to show how this can occur.

**Example 1:** a manufacturer (such as Dell) sells PCs directly to customers. Several long-established and valued retail outlets for the product object to this and refuse to sell its products any more.

**Example 2:** a distributor is employed to deal with physical placement of products and is made redundant for some products, but not others.

Established businesses considering adding an on-line distribution channel (either to their 'buy side' or 'sell side') therefore have to consider the impact such a move may have on existing methods of distributing products. Where a new on-line channel causes problems with an established set of business relationships, this is **channel conflict**.

Dave Chaffey argues that today's firm has to identify what its 'core competency' is. What does it do best? Once the core business is identified, it can build key channel partnerships to collaborate with other firms that do other things better. Some examples will again help.

**Example:** a manufacturer works with a retailer to offer better on-line customer support. Both share customer data; both work to create the brand identity.

**Example:** B&Q Direct (at *www.diy.com*) works in partnership with Spark Response. The latter provides customer service, call centre, warehousing and product fulfilment (see page 105).

**Example:** Ford in the US works in collaboration with its dealer network on an 'Internet Approved' programme, giving training and expertise to promote Internet-based customer relationships. In this way, Ford has developed direct customer relationships over the Internet without conflict with its highly valued dealership network.

> ### Thinking point
>
> What do you understand by the term 'channel conflict'? Do you feel this should deter a business from a possible on-line venture?

## Meeting customer expectations

The Internet is significantly raising customer expectations and this is a real challenge to all on-line business. The uninterrupted availability and convenience of the Internet has been reinforced with increased personalisation and price transparency. Even more importantly, customers are starting to expect higher levels of reliability and responsiveness, and are increasingly expecting not only convenience but speed – in terms of both deliveries once an order is placed and while using the website. Taken together, these are heavy demands on an on-line business.

Through the Internet, merchandise is becoming available in 'mass customised' form, allowing customers to enter personal measurements for trousers (for example) before ordering; or allowing a computer manufacturer to encourage customers to configure their machines on-line as they order. Customers will increasingly demand or expect this one-to-one on-line attention.

The process of engaging the customer is fundamental to good on-line marketing. Yet it generates a fierce level of expectation that what is asked for is what is delivered, and that all supporting information is available and correct. A beautifully constructed website, with tremendously informative content, competitive prices, and smooth and easy transaction arrangements all counts for nothing if a customer's product expectations or customer service requirements are not fulfilled.

A Forrester Technographics survey of 9,000 users who have made on-line purchases found that 80% of them had visited a manufacturer's site first before visiting the retailer selling the item. These people then re-visited throughout the buying cycle and knew exactly what they wanted. Buyers on the Internet are increasingly showing this willingness to by-pass the retailer for product information. The Internet buyer can be very well informed indeed.

### Thinking point

It is harder to meet customer expectations on-line than it is off-line. Do you agree with this statement?

The challenge for on-line marketers is to anticipate and understand what customer expectations will be, whatever the market context. One of the best-known failures of the dot.com boom was the US on-line delivery service called Kozmo. This was a retailer promising delivery of *any* on-line order. The idea was born in busy New York City, where many people living in apartments might decide they suddenly wanted a DVD or a pizza at any time. Kozmo promised to

deliver free of charge. The business was neither realistic nor cost effective, however. Marketing should lead to customer expectations being met *profitably* – the moral is, do not make outrageous promises.

A business strategy for managing customer expectations has been suggested by Chaffey.

- Find out what customers expect by doing some research. Include a feedback form on the site if necessary. Always work to rectify any shortcomings.

- Make realistic promises and communicate them clearly. Do not make impossible promises.

- Deliver commitments with the help of staff as well as physical fulfilment.

### Practice Point

Visit *www.bizrate.com* and look at customer comments. Make a note of some of the complaints made by customers.

Draft a statement for the management of a business that is proposing going on-line, specifying what you see as the most important things to consider in meeting customer expectations.

## Information overload

Because marketing requires a business to focus beyond and outside of itself, in order to discover information about the market it hopes to serve, its customers and its competitors, the business will naturally gather large amounts of data. Employees and systems can be overloaded with information. There is therefore a need at the outset to consider the types of data that are crucial to the business, and the processes and information systems that will be required to handle such data.

In b2b markets especially, customer profiles can usefully be built up. These will characterise each customer in terms of products bought, specialist input from customer buying staff, location and size. This sort of information allows the customer to be placed in a market segment, and from this an appropriate marketing relationship should be formed. It is vital to capture the relevant information and to act appropriately upon it.

Information is not knowledge – data has to be interpreted and made sense of before it becomes knowledge. Managers and individual staff within the organisation should have good access to relevant data and assistance with its interpretation and the ability to act upon it. This of course generates more information and so the cycle goes on. Eventually, people can be faced with overload, and this is known as 'information fatigue'.

Many organisations incorporate on their site a frequently asked questions (FAQ) panel. Most serious on-line businesses include an e-mail contact and telephone number within a 'Contact us' link. This facility is likely to generate a considerable degree of feedback. The on-line business must be prepared to allocate resources to deal with this effectively, otherwise it risks damaging its reputation. If necessary, large portions of a marketing strategy may need to be revised in response to feedback. The business must process feedback and be prepared to act upon it if required.

## Keeping pace with technological change

As the global world of e-business gathers pace, every business is having to face up to the challenges of what to do, when to do it and how. Technological change has always been with us; our economies have evolved from agriculture to manufacturing to services. Now we are in a digital economy in which change is accelerating at a faster pace than ever before. Businesses are having to innovate (find new ways of doing things) in virtually all markets. They are having to respond to new ways of working by partner firms as well as competitors. The digital economy is a knowledge-based economy, based on providing better products, more quickly and more efficiently than others. In this economy, speed wins, and for management this is pressure.

## Ensuring maximum exposure through search engines and ISPs

Internet service providers (ISPs) are firms that offer an Internet connection service to both private householders and businesses. Their primary function is to provide a link to the World Wide Web, and many ISPs also host websites on their own servers.

The crucial point for business management is to ensure that the ISP is offering a satisfactory level of service for a reasonable price. ISPs have to be able to deal with fluctuating and perhaps growing traffic. Speed of access is crucial; we have already seen that customers on line demand speed.

One way of improving speed is to have a dedicated server, that is one that is serving content only from your business. Additionally, bandwidth is an important factor in governing the speed of content delivery, and the bandwidth between the ISP and the Internet needs to be considered. The bigger the bandwidth, the quicker data can pass through (like water through a pipe). Bandwidth is measured in kilobits (1,000 bits) per second, which is written as Kbps. A typical modem operates at 56.6 Kbps and will often be used by a small business. ISDN (Integrated Services Digital Network) is usually twice as fast.

A further issue with ISPs is the amount of time that a website is made available to customers. Ideally a business needs to ensure that the site is available all the time. Not all sites are, and of course time unavailable means lost revenue.

Search engines are extremely important for the promotion of a website, as we saw earlier. Over 80% of Web users are known to use them and if a business has not registered with the search engines it is unlikely to be found unless it has an extremely well-known brand name. The registration process and the website design process are fundamental to the site profile; the former for making the search engines aware of the site, and the latter for elevating the site in the search engine listings.

# Security and payment systems

The Internet has become a global phenomenon because it is an open network, but it is also an insecure network. Despite this, millions of Internet-based business transactions are taking place every minute. Confidential, sensitive and potentially damaging company data is increasingly being made available to Internet-based access.

Viruses and hackers are a constant danger. Malicious individuals (or firms) can attack a company's data, to make fraudulent claims or simply to thieve. Vital information can be open to attack.

Almost 50% of all credit card fraud is known to be Internet related. For the e-tailer there is known to be a significant risk of fraudulent purchases. Repudiation of orders is a common problem – this is where people order goods then deny that they did. The security of private individuals is just as open to attack, and it is a real fear for on-line consumers. It is a task of the e-business to re-assure consumers about security.

The challenge for business leaders is to plan for security. This means devising an e-business strategy that right at the outset takes security issues seriously. There are several ways of doing this.

## Authorisation

Authorisation involves determining who has access to certain applications and information. A consistent policy needs to be established and this must be centrally controlled and monitored.

## Encryption

Changing data into a hidden format is called encryption. The true text or numbers become almost impossible to retrieve by anyone who does not have access to the 'key'.

Businesses in the digital world *must* embrace encryption. Confidential documents such as contracts, personal data, pricing details, and product research data can all be vulnerable to theft or attack. Encryption of e-mails is the equivalent of putting a document into an envelope to keep it private.

Both SSL (Secure Sockets Layer) and SET (Secure Electronic Transactions) are standards that ensure the encryption of Internet traffic. SET encompasses a whole payments system, while SSL encrypts only traffic between a Web browser and server.

## Authentication

**Authentication** procedures can be put in place to require customers to identify themselves through a log-in and password procedure.

> ### Thinking point
> How important do you think security concerns are for a potential e-business?

# Linguistic and cultural issues

## Language barriers

As use of the Internet continues to grow, more and more people on-line are expected to be non-English speakers. According to Jupiter Research, almost 60% of the Internet population are likely to live outside the US by 2005. English-speaking audiences are unlikely to dominate the Internet for too long. Obviously it is important for an expanding business to consider translations of its site. Remember, marketers must 'think globally, act locally'. But how?

It is important to remember that literal linguistic translations (from one language to another) are only the first step in providing a truly local service; a website needs to take account of local cultural expectations. Translations can cause problems – things can and do go badly wrong when local knowledge is lacking.

- The Pepsi slogan 'Come alive with the Pepsi Generation' was translated for Taiwan as 'Pepsi will bring your ancestors back from the dead'.

- The Kentucky Fried Chicken slogan 'Finger-lickin' good' was translated into Chinese as 'Eat your fingers off'.

- US car-maker General Motors realised why it wasn't selling any Chevy Novas in South America when it found out that *no va* means 'it doesn't go' in Spanish. The company renamed the Nova for Spanish-speaking markets as the Caribe.

### Cultural attitudes to payments

A report by NetSmartAmerica ('America.com: What makes America click', 2000) showed that 70% of on-line shoppers in the US paid by credit card. In Japan, the most common payment method (in May 2000) was cash on delivery. This is said to reflect the Japanese preference for cash-based payment. A spin-off from this was that in Japan many more websites were obliged to be based on membership, reflecting the fact that customers preferred to pay by direct bank deposit.

Web designers of the future will increasingly need to consider cultural differences at great length. Differences in perception are significant. Oriental scripts (Japanese, Korean, Chinese) are read vertically, Arabic is read from right to left, and European languages including English are read from left to right. These differences are very significant. Does a Chinese user view a left-justified Web page as appealing?

Some societies can be said to be very family or group oriented (such as China), while others are much more individualistic (such as the US, UK, and Western Europe). This difference can be reflected in marketing communications. If the message is wrong, real long-term on-line damage can be caused. In marketing, as we know by now, it is vital to know your market.

## Additional legal complexity

One of the challenges posed by the global nature of the Internet is the legal complexity of trading internationally, especially when things go wrong. If you buy a product from an on-line retailer based in the US, and it sends you the product but you are not satisfied with it, whose legal system applies? The UK or the US system? What rate, if any, of taxation applies to the purchase?

Imagine setting up a website from which you are hoping to sell across Europe, possibly worldwide; how do you satisfy the legal requirements that might exist in the different European states? What laws exist covering on-line promotions? What are the regulations about offensive material?

In 2002 the European Union enforced an Electronic Commerce Directive designed to set a framework for electronic commerce in the EU. There is a useful summary on the Department of Trade and Industry website, and other information for small businesses (*www.dti.gov.uk*). There is little doubt that legal regulations are an important issue for any business intending to sell on-line.

### Outcome activity 14.4

**Pass**

Identify and describe key challenges presented by Internet marketing activity to contrasting businesses.

One way of doing this might be to take a local business that you know does not have an Internet presence. You could take each of the above sections and produce a summary of what the business might have to consider.

Alternatively, you could consider *www.saveanddrive.co.uk* and, going through each of the sections in the unit, consider each issue from the viewpoint of the management of this innovative on-line business. The Terms and Conditions section of the website is informative about the legal complexities involved.

## Key terms

**Affiliate**
in Internet terms, a business that provides a link on its website to another site in return for a payment from any resulting sales

**Authentication**
methods by which parties to a transaction can prove who they are

**Banner advertisement**
typically a rectangular graphic, often animated, at the top of a Web page, designed to promote a brand or a business service

**Broadband**
a fast method of transferring data across the Internet

**Buy-side**
transactions in which a business makes purchases

**B2B**
business to business – transactions between organisations

**B2C**
business to consumer – transactions between businesses and individual consumers

**Channel conflict**
where an Internet method of direct selling threatens existing business partnerships

**Clicks and mortar**
a business combining an on-line and an off-line presence

**Click-through**
where a website visitor clicks on a banner that takes them through to another Web page

**Disintermediation**
removing intermediaries and cutting out the middle man

**Domain name**
a Web address

**Dynamic pricing**
updating prices in real time according to market conditions

**E-business**
where all exchanges between business processes and with external business stakeholders and partners are digitally (electronically) based

**GIF**
Graphics Interchange Format, used for images

**Hyperlink**
the means by which a visitor can move from one page to another by clicking on a link, usually underlined on the page

**Infomediary**
a business that captures consumer information, profiles it and sells it on to third parties

**Intermediary**
in Internet terms, an on-line site bringing together buyers and sellers

**Internet**
the physical network of computer networks across the globe

**Mass customisation**
the capacity offered by Internet technology to create individually tailored on-line products or marketing messages

**On-line value proposition (OVP)**
something of value offered by a specific on-line service that makes it distinct from other offerings

**Personalisation**
where Web page content is made personal to the individual user

**Portal**
a gateway website to other Web services

## Key terms

**Prosumer**
a pro-active consumer – the tendency is for on-line customers to be closely involved in specifying their requirements

**Search engine**
specialised websites used to search out key words from indexes of registered Web pages

**Sell-side**
transactions between a supplier and a consumer

**Site stickiness**
the factor that determines how long visitors stay on a website

**SPAM**
e-mail messages that are not wanted

**Targeting**
aiming a marketing message at a specific segment of a market

**Transaction**
an exchange between two parties, such as exchanging a product for cash

**Viral marketing**
rapid transfer of marketing messages to potential customers via e-mail

**World Wide Web**
the worldwide body of software designed to operate across the Internet that enables access to and communication of data

# End-of-unit test

1 In your own words, define the term 'marketing'.

2 What is meant by 'primary' and 'secondary' research?

3 What is a SWOT analysis, and how does it differ from an industry analysis?

4 How does a 'market-led' approach differ from a 'product-led' approach?

5 The Internet is a 'pull medium'. What does this mean?

6 What is meant by an on-line value proposition? Describe two examples from websites you are familiar with.

7 What is the on-line marketing remix? What do you think are the main differences with the traditional marketing mix?

8 Describe what is meant by 'personalisation' and 'mass customisation'.

9 How is it possible to 'extend' an on line product?

10 What is meant by the term 'prosumer'?

11 Do you feel that the Internet offers the potential for more of us to become 'prosumers' rather than 'consumers'? Justify your response.

12 How does the Internet cause 'disintermediation'? Is this always a good thing?

13 What is an 'infomediary'?

14 Describe how a search engine can assist in promoting a business.

15 What is 'viral marketing'? Is it important to an on-line business? Justify your response.

16 Why is the on-line 'process' important?

17 What is meant by buy-side and sell-side relationships?

18 How does the Internet assist in market research? Specify two websites that can assist in researching a market.

19 What is meant by 'dynamic pricing'?

20 Describe two challenges and two opportunities offered to businesses by Internet marketing.

# Resources

## Texts

Amor, D: *The e-Business Revolution*, Prentice Hall, 2001

Chaffey D: *e-business and e-commerce Management*, Prentice Hall, 2001

Chaffey, Mayer, Johnston and Ellis-Chadwick: *Internet Marketing, Strategy, Implementation and Practice*, Prentice Hall, 2003

Godin, S: *Permission Marketing, Strangers into Friends into Customers*, Simon Schuster, 1999

Haig, M: *The e-Marketing Handbook*, Kogan Page, 2001

Mathewson, J: *e-Business, A Jargon Free Practical Guide*, Butterworth Heinemann, 2001

Windham, L: *The Soul of the New Consumer*, Allworth Press, 2001

## Magazines

*Marketing Weekly*

*Business Review*

## Newspapers

*Guardian On-line Supplement* (Thursdays)

## Websites

*www.ClickZ.com/stats* Useful for Internet trends and statistics

*www.saveanddrive.co.uk* A good example of small business entrepreneurs successfully using the Web

*www.diy.com* The B&Q on-line service, using a variety of interactive features

*www.lastminute.com* Dynamic pricing in practice

*www.elephant.co.uk* Purely on-line insurance service

*www.InternetDirect.co.uk* Direct selling website

*www.whatsherface.com* A good example of consumer interaction via the Web

*www.orange.com* Mobile phone service provider

*www.kelkoo.com* An example of a shopping intermediary helping consumers

*www.bbcshop.com* BBC on-line shop with affiliates

*www.ciao.co.uk* On-line price comparison service

*www.fightback.com* Consumer response service

*www.chemdex.com* Portal site to other on-line services

*www.vertical.net* Excellent on-line service for e-business development

*www.letsbuyit.com* Well-known shopping intermediary

*www.ebay.com* On-line auction site connecting private consumers

*www.bizrate.com* On-line consumer feedback service

*www.bccntral.co.uk* Microsoft's small business service

*www.easyjet.com* The low cost airline's dynamic pricing facility

*www.next.co.uk* On-line retail service

*www.buyerzone.com* On-line service for b2b buying

*www.amazon.com* Successful on-line bookseller

*www.nokey.com* Security device website

*www.accrue.com* Web analytics service helping e-businesses develop

*www.blackanddecker.com* The power tools website

*www.webtrends.com* Web analytics service

*www.affiliate.com* Useful site about affiliate programmes

*http://finance.yahoo.com* On-line portal with an 'ask' service

*www.nua.com/surveys* Useful for Web trends and surveys

*www.bmrb.co.uk* Market research site

*www.harrisinteractive.com* Market data site on many industrial sectors

*www.leighton.com* Cutting-edge north east-based e-business

You have already studied the concept of management in several of the BTEC National Business core units, including the organising and monitoring of resources such as goods and services. This unit describes the human resources within business and the factors that affect their operation.

The first area covered in this unit is the skills that are needed by employees in order to be able to run businesses effectively. This section also looks at skills shortages and the effect that these can have on any business.

Company culture is explored in the human resource management section, together with the effect on employees if the organisation is either forward thinking or more traditional, and what is meant by motivating or demotivating employees at work.

The section on human resource planning considers how businesses plan for their future workforce, both inside and outside the company. It also considers what happens when working methods change and employees need to consider doing new types of jobs at work.

The unit ends with a discussion of the management of human performance, by looking at how that performance can be measured. These measurements can be used to compare the business to others through the use of benchmarking, or to reward individual employees for good performance.

Unit 18 is therefore divided into four main sections:

- 18.1 Issues of human resource skill
- 18.2 Human resource management and motivational practice
- 18.3 Human resource planning
- 18.4 Management of human performance.

# Issues of human resource skill

All businesses, whether they are large or small, have human input. This input might be physical, such as making something by hand; technical, using computer software to design a new product; or financial, such as providing money to invest in businesses. When investigating human resource skills there are three areas to be considered: the human resources themselves, how those human resources fit in with the other resources accessible to the business, and the skills of those human resources.

## Human resources

Human resources is the term used for employees within a business. Human resources are also referred to as labour. **Labour** strictly speaking means the physical and mental effort given by employees within the workplace, but can also be used as a measuring tool, such as how many people are employed by an organisation or how those people are used.

Human resources are just one type of resource available to organisations, and because of this they are in competition with other resources. Investment in human resources brings an **opportunity cost** to the business in that it cannot spend the money elsewhere.

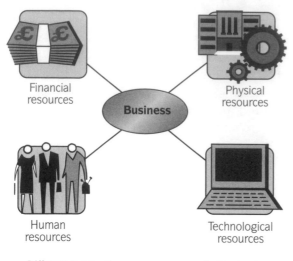

*Different types of resources are needed in business*

## Competition between resources

The level of competition between human resources and other resources will depend on the nature of the business, its size and its methods of production.

Human resources, like finance or buildings, need to be used efficiently. They need to be paid and planned for, especially if the skills required are hard to find.

As human resources are just one part of the set of resources available to any organisation, humans should be considered in an objective way and treated like any other resource. This is easier said than done, however, because unlike other resources, humans have feelings and need to be dealt with sensitively in order to achieve the best outcomes and maximise efficiency for the business.

## Human resource skill set

The type of work an organisation does will affect the level of human resources needed and the level of skill required. Some organisations invest heavily in machinery and have fewer employees. These types of businesses are known as **capital-intensive**, because a lot of financial resources, known as capital, are invested in machinery or technology to support production. Examples of capital-intensive businesses include food manufacturing and car-making.

Other organisations need human involvement rather more than machinery. Such organisations are known as **labour-intensive**, which simply means they need a lot of people to achieve their production. Examples of labour-intensive businesses include hairdressing and house-building.

The term *production* can be used in two ways. It can describe products being made or the provision of a service such as hairdressing. Both can be labour-intensive.

---

### Case study    Whitbread PLC

Whitbread PLC is one of the leading hospitality companies in the UK and employs around 40,000 people. Whitbread manages some of the leading hotels, restaurants and health and fitness clubs including Premier Travel Inn, Brewers Fayre, Beefeater, Costa, TGI Friday's and David Lloyd Leisure.

Across the chain, 10 million customers are served each month, and in the year to March 2004 Whitbread made a pre-tax profit of £240.8 million.

Whitbread's businesses are all very labour-intensive, as they provide services. David Lloyd Leisure needs employees to run every aspect of the fitness club, from working in the restaurants, to coaching tennis, giving advice on fitness or maintaining the facilities. Premier Travel Inn is a hotel chain and again it needs many staff to look after guests and keep their rooms in working order. The other part of Whitbread's chain is the restaurant business, again relying on staff to produce and serve food in more than 1,000 outlets across the UK.

Whitbread shows that using labour-intensive working methods can be very successful and very profitable.

1  Why do Whitbread's chain of companies need to be so labour-intensive?
2  What possible problems might Whitbread have when operating in this way?
3  What are the implications for the training budget of being so labour-intensive?
4  How might low levels of unemployment affect Whitbread?

## Types of skills needed

Both capital- and labour-intensive businesses need employees to maintain production, but the type of employees required and their levels of skill are likely to be quite different. Capital-intensive businesses, with heavy investment in technology and machinery, are likely to need fewer employees. Robots or other machinery may perform most of the production, and humans are needed only to identify problems and improve processes. Employees need to have good training and experience in order to make sure that production is as efficient as possible.

Business organisations that are more labour-intensive might need more lower-skilled workers, such as waiting staff or kitchen porters in a restaurant. The level of skill required will depend on the complexity of the job, and this will in turn determine the level of education expected and how easy it is to replace a person.

## Levels of skills needed

Different jobs have different levels of skills. A complicated job that requires a high level of education and training is said to be a highly skilled job. A job that can be performed with a minimum amount of training is more likely to be low-skilled. Taking into account the range and complexity of skills that are needed is an important task for management.

A porter's job in a hotel might require a low level of skill, but within that a range of tasks may need to be performed; carrying luggage, giving directions, opening doors and taking messages for customers may be included. An employee in a highly skilled job might centre on only one task, but need to be an expert in that field. An example is a computer programmer for a specific piece of software.

A senior occupational therapist, on the other hand, might need to be highly skilled and also able to demonstrate a range of complex skills including leadership, supervision, planning, development, management of patient case loads and appraisals.

### Replacing employees

Within any sector of business, it is important to consider how easy it would be to replace a member of staff with a particular set of skills. The more difficult to acquire a person's skills are, the more of a problem it is to replace him or her, so there will be competition between organisations in that sector to employ the best people. The demand for such people means that is likely that their pay will increase, because of the rules of supply and demand – employees can ask for higher salaries if they are in short supply. Unless organisations can recruit enough skilled workers, they will have vacancies in their workforce and may not be able to cover the required workload.

Competition between organisations to attract specialist workers may lead to the offer of extra incentives such as paid travel, accommodation or private healthcare plans. Companies may also use headhunting agencies to recruit the right people; these agencies will approach potential employees and negotiate with them directly. One such headhunting agency is Jefferson Maguire (*www.jeffersonmaguire.co.uk,*) which headhunts on behalf of Siemens, Sara Lee Bakery and SunValley Foods, among others.

### Transferring skills

Some specialist jobs such as doctor, teacher or quantity surveyor have skills that can easily be transferred from one organisation to another. This means that it is relatively easy for employees to leave and get a job elsewhere. Organisations have to look after employees who have highly transferable skills, to try to make sure they don't leave. Some organisations have a high dependence on specific workers and if they cannot get them within the UK, they may need to take steps to source such workers from other parts of the world.

### Case study    Network Rail

In August 2004, Network Rail faced the problem of not having enough staff to carry out important work on signal boxes in the Stockport area.

Essential operations had to be completed quickly in order for £8 billion of works to be completed on time, but the company was unable to recruit enough rail engineers. The whole project was in danger of being delayed.

As no rail engineers were available in the UK because of a skills shortage, Network Rail's solution was to fly in 12 mechanical engineers from India to work alongside the UK team.

This is an example of the fact that skills cannot always be transferred from one industry to another. An aircraft engineer may not be able to transfer his or her skills in order to work as a rail engineer, and this can make organisations very dependent on specialists. Problems can be caused if companies cannot recruit and retain the right staff.

1  What are the disadvantages of having to bring in specialist staff from another country to carry out essential work?
2  What might the benefits be?
3  How could this situation have been prevented in the first place?

### Specific and specialist skills

Employees can also experience problems if their skills are so specific that they cannot be transferred to another organisation, or if they are employed by the only organisation of its type in an area. For example, in April 2005 it was announced that the car-maker Rover was to close with the loss of around 6,000 jobs. As Rover was the only company manufacturing cars in the Longbridge area of Birmingham, workers were unable to transfer their skills to another business in the same industry. Instead, workers were encouraged either to relocate – as far away as Australia – to take their skills to other car manufacturers, or to consider retraining in other types of manufacturing that were experiencing skills shortages in the area.

There can be shortages of highly skilled and specialist workers in a number of different occupational areas. While there are usually a limited number of unemployed people seeking jobs, they often don't have the right skills to supply the shortages. The UK generally suffers from a skills shortage and is reliant on a low-skilled workforce. It is not just advanced skills that are in short supply; research from the CBI showed that 47% of employers were unhappy with young people's basic skills.

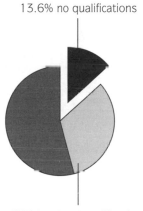

13.6% no qualifications

33% low-level qualifications

*Levels of education in the UK in 2005*

Other figures announced by the government's Department for Education and Skills in February 2005 suggest that around 33% of the UK workforce possess low-level qualifications and of those just under 13.6% have no qualifications at all. This makes it difficult for employers to recruit suitably qualified staff and be able to grow their businesses and the economy as a whole.

## Outcome activity 18.1

### Pass

Using an organisation you are familiar with or a case study from this unit, describe the skill profile of staff employed in the business.

Make sure you include information on whether the business is capital- or labour-intensive. What type of skills are needed in that organisation? Are there any skills shortages?

# Human resource management and motivational practice

The skills of the employees involved in a business are crucial to its success, but there are also other factors that influence the way things happen in a business. **Corporate culture** determines how people behave within a business, and the level of motivating as opposed to demotivating factors within a business. This can determine how hard people work, and how successful they are.

## Corporate culture

Corporate culture is often described as 'the way we do things around here'. It is like a set of rules that everyone in the organisation learns to abide by, and which influences the behaviour of employees. It could be as simple as using first names for the company directors or remembering to bring cakes into the office on your birthday. The culture of an organisation can influence how forward-thinking or traditional it is in the way it operates.

### The effect of tradition on culture

As you have already seen, corporate culture can also be affected by tradition. Businesses that have operated over a number of years may have policies and procedures that make it clear that you should not speak to a senior manager directly without speaking to your own manager first. Some industries might have traditionally attracted more of one gender than another; for example in IT there are many more young men than women in full-time employment and the culture may be geared to young male attitudes.

## Case study  Fire fighters' culture

Some aspects of corporate culture can work across whole industries, as well as within individual organisations. One example is the culture of fire fighters. Their culture is based on tradition and values that have been passed down over generations.

When dealing with dangerous incidents, fire fighters have to have complete confidence in their colleagues, as they must trust each other with their lives. Their culture is therefore based on strong leadership and respect, and as each fire fighter joins the service he or she becomes part of that culture. Some of the influences on the culture come from the need to wear a uniform and to follow orders as part of drills and safety checks each day.

There are approximately 38,000 full-time fire fighters and 15,000 part-time fire fighters in the UK, most of whom are members of the Fire Brigades Union (FBU). Between 2002 and 2003, members of the FBU agreed by ballot to take industrial action. They went on strike for varying lengths of time. They were protesting that:

- their pay was inadequate
- changes were being made to their jobs, such as different shift patterns and arrangements for overtime
- fire fighters were due to lose their jobs.

During the strikes the police and armed forces undertook fire-fighting duties, but some fire

fighters helped out at very serious fires while they were officially on strike. This was partly to do with the culture of the organisation. Fire fighters feel a strong duty to protect each other and the general public. Therefore, although they were willing to take industrial action, they were prepared to assist in difficult situations.

1  What do you think is meant by a culture of 'strong leadership and respect'?
2  Why do you think it is so important to have a strong culture in an organisation such as the fire service?
3  How could changing working conditions affect the culture of an organisation?

Some of the culture within a business is also affected by the history of industrial relations within that organisation, such as whether the business recognises a union or whether there has ever been industrial action such as a strike. Some businesses have traditions and these will influence whether people feel valued and whether they receive benefits such as sick pay.

Two businesses that work in the same sector may have differing cultures, because a culture is always changing and is influenced by the people who are working there now as well as those who have worked there in the past. As people join the company they bring their own values and experiences with them, and therefore start to influence the culture.

## Practice point

| Office Angels | Data Connection Limited |
|---|---|
| Founded in 1986, Office Angels had 585 staff in 2005 and annual sales of £124 million. The company is a recruitment consultant that organises work for people on a permanent and short-term basis. | Data Connection Limited was founded in 1981 and is a computer software company. In 2005 it was also voted one of the Best 100 Companies to work for. Annual sales are £30 million. |
| Typical salaries at Office Angels are around £35,000, 76% of staff are under 35, and 80% are female. | Data Connection Limited employs 264 staff. Staff are 79% male, and of those 61% are under 35. Staff are allowed to work flexible hours in consultation with their managers. Managers look after just three to five staff, and therefore people feel looked after. Employees are rewarded with profit-sharing and performance-related pay. Everyone gets 25 days' holiday per year and people work well in teams. The company also donates 2% of its annual profits to local and national charities. |
| It was voted one of the Best 100 Companies to work for in 2005. The culture at Office Angels is said to include clear career planning, good rewards for hard work and a fun working environment. | |
| Employees are said to have a strong sense of family at work and to be able to laugh a lot. Teamworking is seen as essential and teams spend social time together as well as being able to work for unlimited bonuses. | |

1 Based on the information provided above, describe the company culture that you believe exists in Office Angels and at Data Connection Ltd.

2 How are they similar? How are they different?

3 Thinking about organisational cultures that you have experienced through education or in your part-time job, produce a checklist of the most important features of a good organisational culture. Exchange these with other students in your class – what similarities and differences do you notice?

### Other influences on culture

Some organisations' cultures reflect their very reason for being in existence, for example Oxfam. The aim of this charity is to overcome poverty and suffering and see all lives being equally valued. With this in mind, it has a 'gender-sensitive' culture. This means Oxfam promotes equality between men and women. In some organisations the culture supports the development of men more than women, so women do not often achieve the top jobs.

The culture of an organisation will also influence the way that work is carried out and how policies and procedures are drawn up to support or punish employees. Organisations will have different ways to deal with absenteeism in the workplace or time off sick, for example.

The Royal Mail started a scheme to reward employees who had good attendance records and had not taken time off sick by putting their names into a prize draw to win cars or holiday vouchers. As a result, sickness levels between August 2004 and January 2005 were reduced because employees aimed to earn more opportunities to enter the competitions. This saved the company money and improved customer satisfaction as the business was able to complete more work. Such incentive schemes are designed to reward certain behaviour at work and to change the culture.

*The Royal Mail rewards employees with good attendance records*

Tesco used a different method of trying to reduce the amount of absenteeism among its employees when it introduced a new policy to deal with sickness in the workplace in 2004. This scheme cancelled sickness payments for all employees during the first three days of sickness to try to reduce the number of people taking time off sick. The culture at Tesco, unlike the Royal Mail, sought to punish people for being absent rather than reward those who had good attendance. The culture of the company will influence the method chosen to deal with problems and will also influence how well that method works.

### The effect of culture on communities

Corporate culture includes attitudes towards both local and national communities. Some businesses have such a long history and tradition within a particular area, they become a central part of the local community and promote investment in it. One example is Cadbury in Bourneville, Birmingham. The area was created in the early nineteenth century to site a factory and housing for Cadbury employees. Another example is Guinness in Dublin, Ireland; the Guinness family introduced pensions, hospital treatment and social facilities for employees from the 1850s. The Guinness family invested money in the local community and paid workers well, and this resulted in great loyalty from employees and a strong local community. Even today Guinness supports education, enterprise and learning in Ireland.

Another example of such an approach to looking after communities was that of the Rowntree family, who were based in York in the 1800s and owned the Rowntree Chocolate Company. Starting as a small enterprise of only 30 employees, the factory went from strength to strength. This was partly due to the paternalistic attitude of Joseph Rowntree, the

---

### Real lives — Perween Warsi

Perween Warsi is the matriarchal leader of S&A Foods, one of the most successful ready meal manufacturing companies in the UK. It supplies food to many UK supermarkets and also to continental Europe, and in doing so has a turnover of £100 million. It employs around 1,500 staff across four factories.

Perweeen built up the business from scratch by developing recipes in her own kitchen and selling the finished products to a local takeaway. She was then discovered by Asda at a blind tasting, and the business has now developed on a huge scale.

One of the strengths of the business is the 'family culture' that Perween has developed, based on her own understanding of what it is like to be both a businesswoman and a mother. She views her employees as needing to be looked after rather than as just resources of the business. This creates a culture that recognises the importance of its employees and displays care for them.

For more information about S&A Foods, see www.sa-foods.co.uk.

1  What is meant by a 'family culture'?
2  To what extent has culture been responsible for the success of S&A Foods?

founder, who provided a number of extra benefits for employees and their families including a free library in the factory, education for anyone under the age of 17, a welfare officer, doctor and dentist. He also made a large contribution to a pension fund for retiring employees. Rowntree was keen to reduce poverty in the area and invested in land and housing in order to help his workers. He set up Quaker schools and special trusts to help people in the area. In York today there are still schools named after him, and parks in the city today still have the Rowntree name.

### Outsourcing and worsening conditions

Other employers have been perceived to be treating their employees and local community less fairly, such as General Motors in Flint, Michigan, in the US in 1998, when employees felt that General Motors was cutting jobs at its local factories and **outsourcing** the work to lower-paid workers to cut costs. More recently, Learning Support Assistants in the Brighton and Hove area of the UK took strike action in late 2004 because their employer, the council, was threatening to cut the number of weeks they were paid.

### Thinking point

In small groups, produce a mind map of all the cases of industrial action that you have ever heard of in your local area or nationally, such as work-to-rule or strike action. For how long did the action take place, and what was the final outcome of the dispute? You may find it useful to access material from the Internet and newspapers to help you with this task.

### Perceived attitudes of employee groups

The attitude of employee groups towards employers can vary significantly between organisations. If an employee group, such as a committee, focus group or union, has the perception that employees are treated well it is likely that its attitude towards the employer will be positive. However, if an employee group has the perception that employees are likely to be treated unfavourably it is more likely to risk taking industrial action such as working to rule or strike action, which may damage the business directly or its customers. For example, car

manufacturing in the 1970s had such a poor 'them and us' relationship between employees and management that deep mistrust built up. This meant that employees perceived they were treated less favourably than they should have been.

The Royal Mail has had industrial problems in the past – at one stage thousands of worker-days were lost each year. As the culture at Royal Mail has changed, so too have industrial relations. Until recently it was estimated that the Royal Mail was losing up to 50,000 worker-days due to industrial action, but new management practices have come into place and the business has become increasingly profitable.

### Case study    Gate Gourmet

During August 2005, an industrial dispute involving former employees of Gate Gourmet brought British Airways (BA) flights to a standstill and left travellers stranded in many parts of the world. Gate Gourmet is the supplier of in-flight meals for all BA flights and is the second-largest airline catering service in the world.

The original dispute arose because of the sacking of 670 staff, which led to strike action by workers and a picket outside the company's factory. Strikers were accused of intimidating workers who went through the pickets. Ground staff employed by British Airways went on strike in sympathy and made the situation even more chaotic. A deal was finally reached between Gate Gourmet and the Transport and General Workers Union, which represented employees, offering employees voluntary redundancy compensation or their jobs back. BA agreed to sign a two-year contract with Gate Gourmet subject to it sorting out its labour problems.

1 What effect did the Gate Gourmet strike have on other businesses?
2 What is a picket?
3 How was the strike perceived by other employees working in related businesses?
4 Why was it important for BA to have a contract with Gate Gourmet that was subject to it sorting out its labour problems?

The culture of an organisation will influence how much power a **trade union** has within an organisation and whether or not industrial action can take place. The attitudes of employees towards the employer will very much depend, therefore, on a business' history, its way of doing things and the actions of the organisation in the local and national community.

## Motivation in practice

Motivation means stimulating someone to do something. To be successful, organisations need to motivate their employees to perform well. Some people are motivated by money, and so money is the stimulus to make them work harder; others are motivated by the job itself, teamworking or the desire to do well.

### Thinking point

In small groups, discuss what motivates you to work hard on your BTEC National course. Some ideas are:

o the possibility of a good future career
o being with friends
o getting a good qualification
o the thought of running your own business
o the chance of going to university
o the opportunity to learn more about business.

Which idea is the most popular in your group? Can you think of any other factors that motivate you?

### The positive effects of motivation

Everyone needs some motivation each day to function in society. The extent to which an employee can feel motivated in the workplace will be influenced by the culture and techniques that employers use to improve motivation within their workforce. Improving motivation will mean that employees are happier in their jobs and this should increase **productivity**.

Motivated and productive employees are more likely to make higher quality products, answer more telephone calls or give better customer satisfaction. This should lead to a better company image and, in profit-making companies, increased sales, which should bring bigger profits. In non-profit-making organisations, better value for money can be obtained.

### Case study  St Ann's Hospice

St Ann's Hospice is based in Greater Manchester and aims to improve the quality of life for people with life-threatening illnesses, and their families and carers. It employs 298 people. Most of the employees earn less than £25,000 per year and have no company travel or bonuses, but receive free tea, coffee, toast and vouchers as extra benefits. Two thirds of employees are happy with their pay and benefits.

Pay is clearly not the main motivator for these staff. Their motivation to work is about making a positive difference for vulnerable people. The staff respect each other and use teamwork to help each other. The local community is also involved with the hospice and helps with fundraising. It also supports other hospices in countries such as South Africa and Romania.

The atmosphere at the hospice is said to be warm and friendly even though the patients are suffering from serious illnesses, and staff feel proud to work there. Education and skills are important at the hospice and there is regular training, including job shadowing. Staff have 27 days' annual holiday and are able to spend time away from the job undergoing training.

1 What are the biggest motivators for staff at St Ann's Hospice?
2 Why is it important that pay is not the main motivator for staff?
3 What difference do you think a warm and friendly atmosphere makes to staff motivation?
4 Name three other types of job where pay is not the main motivator.

## Ways to make employees feel happier in their jobs

There are a number of ways that employers can seek to increase the motivation of their employees.

One of the most basic ways is to make them feel secure. This is known as giving employees **job security**. If employees feel that their job is safe they are more likely to work harder and to try to progress within the business.

If jobs are safe, the motivation of employees is likely to be improved by making their jobs more interesting or challenging, such as increasing their responsibility or giving tasks that require more effort. Making a job more interesting to employees is known as **job enrichment**. An example of job enrichment might be for a junior assistant in a hairdressing salon, who is usually responsible for sweeping the floors, making tea and answering the telephone, to be given responsibility for keeping the reception area looking attractive and for taking bookings. These are additional, higher level tasks that will challenge and motivate the employee.

**Job enlargement** is another method of motivating employees. Unlike enrichment, where tasks are made more difficult and challenging, job enlargement gives the employee more tasks of a similar nature. This means the employee is less likely to be bored as he or she has a range of tasks to do. For example, a customer service assistant may answer the telephone, word process letters,

deal with e-mails and do some basic data entry. These tasks are all at a similar level but too much repetitive work is avoided and therefore interest is increased.

## Home and work life balance

Employees may feel more valued if they are given special working arrangements to help them balance their home and working lives. This issue is known as the **home and work life balance**. Some employees might prefer **flexible working practices**, including flexi-time, which means working a certain number of hours per week but choosing the hours within guidelines set by the employer, for example between 6 am and 8 pm. Other employers allow employees to work additional hours and claim extra days' holiday rather than overtime pay. This may motivate employees to work as hard as they can.

Achieving a balance between home and work may be difficult for some employees, and **job sharing** might help them to do so. Job sharing involves two or more employees sharing the workload of one job, and making the equivalent of one full-time person. Usually, one person will work either afternoons or mornings, or two or three days per week, and the other person will work at the other times. This can be ideal for people who like a job with full-time responsibility, but for only part of the time.

*Balancing home and work life is difficult for some*

## Consultation and empowerment

Consulting workers about how they feel and giving them responsibility for contributing to decision-making makes them feel more valued.

Giving such responsibility is known as **empowerment**, and should also increase motivation. Sometimes empowerment can be formalised by making teams entirely responsible for their own working methods and decision-making. This is known as team autonomy. The benefits of greater autonomy should include higher quality products, reduced costs and greater satisfaction, because employees feel more interested in and responsible for what they do.

### Alternative methods of working

**Teleworking** is another alternative and potentially motivating method of working for some employees. Teleworkers are people who work from home and don't need to travel to an office or factory every day. This type of working may suit people with disabilities who find travel difficult, those who live in areas of the country that are isolated, and those who have responsibilities that make it easier to work from home. Examples of teleworking jobs include accountants, web designers and book editors. This type of work can be motivating for employees as they can fit it in around their other commitments, but it can also be very isolating as they may not have much contact with other people, and then in fact they can become demotivated!

### On-the-job training

Even if employees are working in a standard, full-time nine-to-five job, there are plenty of ways to make them feel more motivated at work. On-the-job training – being trained while you are working – can help employees feel that an interest is being taken in their skills and their future, and therefore make them try harder. The company benefits because the employee is being trained while still being productive.

### Investors in People

Motivation isn't just about motivating each single employee. Some companies aim to motivate the whole workforce at the same time, by pursuing a status award associated with good practice. One of the best-known awards is that of Investors in People (IIP), which requires employers to provide evidence of four key elements: commitment to employees; planning for their development; taking action to develop them; and evaluating success. In 2002, IIP conducted research with employers which showed that IIP status brought an increase in employee commitment and productivity. Other bodies also provide accreditation to employers investing in developing their employees; a number are sector-specific, such as the Institute of Chartered Accountants, the Institute of Business Advisers and People First.

For some people, flexible working hours or recognition of status within the organisation is not motivating enough, and these employees need different motivators. Companies may decide to offer enhanced packages that improve on the legal requirements for **maternity** or **paternity leave** or **pay** (when employees become parents) to make them want to return to the workplace. Other employers offer what are known as fringe benefits. These are benefits that are paid to the employees in kind rather than money, such as private healthcare, gym membership, sports facilities, social events or discounts in shops.

> **Practice point**
>
> Write a list of all the fringe benefits you have ever heard of. Now carry out a small survey in your class to find out how many students are receiving fringe benefits in their part-time jobs.
>
> 1 Which fringe benefits are most common?
>
> 2 Which fringe benefits are least common?
>
> 3 Which factors do you think influence the benefits that organisations choose to offer?

### Linking motivation with promotion

Employers often try to link motivation with promotion opportunities for employees. You may have already learned in Unit 15 of your qualification about the concept of the **glass ceiling**. This is an invisible barrier that in many businesses seems to prevent women from reaching the top jobs. They are held down to more junior levels in the organisation for a number of reasons, such as taking time out of a career to care for a family, or being channelled to jobs that are more associated with women such as human resources or administration. Giving opportunities for men and women to be treated equally helps employees to feel valued and therefore motivated. Oxfam is one organisation that is trying to dismantle barriers in the workplace by encouraging both men and women to advance themselves for promotion on an equal basis.

## Pay scales

**Pay scales** are another way of motivating employees. Where pay scales are in place, an employee is assigned to a certain level or grade when he or she starts at a company and is able to progress up the scale according to his or her level of effort and responsibility. Knowing it is possible to rise up that scale can motivate employees to work harder.

In many organisations there are two pay scales, one for the workers and one for the managers. Some organisations have rejected this, however, and opted for one pay scale for all employees. This helps to make management and employees seem closer and therefore potentially better able to communicate and co-operate. Where there are the same pay scales and working conditions for all employees, whether they are managers or workers on the shop floor, this is known as a single-status pay scale.

### Practice point

The pay scale below shows you how a single-status pay scale works. Local government employees join at a point on the pay scale and then are given opportunities to progress up the scale based on reviews of their progress. All workers, whether they are managers or junior employees, start somewhere on this pay scale and then have the chance to move up.

| SCP 1 | Apr 04 | Apr 05 |
|---|---|---|
| 4 | £10,560 | £10,872 |
| 5 | £10,809 | £11,127 |
| 6 | £10,962 | £11,286 |
| 7 | £11,316 | £11,649 |
| 8 | £11,673 | £12,018 |
| 9 | £12,027 | £12,381 |
| 10 | £12,279 | £12,642 |
| 11 | £13,071 | £13,458 |
| 12 | £13,344 | £13,737 |
| 13 | £13,701 | £14,106 |
| 14 | £13,953 | £14,364 |
| 15 | £14,244 | £14,664 |
| 16 | £14,586 | £15,015 |
| 17 | £14,931 | £15,372 |
| 18 | £15,225 | £15,675 |
| 19 | £15,795 | £16,260 |

| SCP 1 | Apr 04 | Apr 05 |
|---|---|---|
| 20 | £16,371 | £16,854 |
| 21 | £16,968 | £17,469 |
| 22 | £17,409 | £17,922 |
| 23 | £17,922 | £18,450 |
| 24 | £18,507 | £19,053 |
| 25 | £19,092 | £19,656 |
| 26 | £19,713 | £20,295 |
| 27 | £20,370 | £20,970 |
| 28 | £21,033 | £21,654 |
| 29 | £21,867 | £22,512 |
| 30 | £22,599 | £23,265 |
| 31 | £23,313 | £24,000 |
| 32 | £24,000 | £24,708 |
| 33 | £24,708 | £25,437 |
| 34 | £25,407 | £26,157 |
| 35 | £25,938 | £26,703 |

| SCP 1 | Apr 04 | Apr 05 |
|---|---|---|
| 36 | £26,625 | £27,411 |
| 37 | £27,372 | £28,179 |
| 38 | £28,173 | £29,004 |
| 39 | £29,100 | £29,958 |
| 40 | £29,865 | £30,747 |
| 41 | £30,654 | £31,557 |
| 42 | £31,434 | £32,361 |
| 43 | £32,217 | £33,168 |
| 44 | £33,009 | £33,984 |
| 45 | £33,750 | £34,746 |
| 46 | £34,566 | £35,586 |
| 47 | £35,358 | £36,402 |
| 48 | £36,147 | £37,212 |
| 49 | £36,921 | £38,010 |

*Source*: NJC Local Government Pay Scales 2004/5 (*http://www.unison.org.uk/pay/payscales.asp*)
For more information about these and other pay scales, *see www.unison.org.uk*.

1 What are the advantages of using pay scales like this one?

2 What are the disadvantages of using them?

3 How effective do you think single-status pay scales might be in motivating workers?

Pay, as we have already seen, is a powerful tool for motivating employees and is a way of rewarding them for good performance. A formal system of rewarding good work with extra pay is known as performance-related pay (PRP). This can take many different forms.

Some organisations, such as banks, monitor and reward performance by using individual appraisals to judge how well employees are doing. If they do well, they receive a bonus payment or an increase in their pay. Other companies, such as Tesco, award free shares to virtually all of their employees if the company does well. Many teachers in further education receive performance-related pay based on how well pupils succeed in their GCSEs or BTEC Nationals.

The main point to remember about performance-related pay is that the method used to calculate the pay must be easily measurable and avoid any type of **inequality**. It must be accessible for all employees regardless of race, gender or religion.

If a formalised system of PRP is not available in a company, there is still the possibility of financial rewards for employees who work hard. This can be achieved by offering incentive payments, such as a one-off payment related to company profits, or overtime pay for working late.

Some organisations give a cash bonus at different times of the year, or awards to particularly hard-working employees. Whichever method a company chooses to implement, the linking of performance with pay should build a loyal, stable, skilled and committed workforce. People will want to stay with the employer to receive these extra payments, and they will feel more motivated and therefore become more productive at work.

## Real lives          Carole Nash Insurance Consultants

Carole Nash returned to work aged 39 after bringing up her family by taking a job at her local insurance company. She demonstrated competence at work and although she was not keen on motorbikes was put in charge of motorbike policies. For the next four years she helped staff who worked for her by introducing schemes such as flexible working to help motivate them and support their work and home life balances. In 1989, however, the office closed and the insurance company decided to discontinue the insurance policy for classic motorbikes as it was making a loss.

Carole was made redundant, but knowing that there was no other classic motorbike insurer around, she took on the scheme from her former employer and set up her own phone line and professional insurance to start trading.

At first, policy holders were concerned about the change from one system to another, but soon word spread that Carole was able to offer a friendly service and other motorbike owners started to join the scheme. Carole took £30,000 in premiums in her first year. She started to promote the business at motorbike events and the business really started to expand, until five years later she was taking £1 million in premiums each year. At this point she decided she needed professional help to run the business, so she sold 49% of her business and took on a managing director.

The business has since continued to go from strength to strength and in 2004 achieved sales of £70 million. With sales this large you could be fooled into thinking that Carole was only motivated to set up the business to make money. However, she would suggest that she did it because she enjoyed it and that the money is a bonus!

For more information about Carole see *www.carolenash.com*.

1 What motivated Carole Nash to start her business?
2 Discuss the extent to which personal interest rather than skills and competencies was the key to her success.

This will in turn enhance the reputation of the organisation, as products and services will improve and people outside the organisation will want to join it.

An example of a business with a stable and loyal workforce is Barcardi-Martini in Southampton. It has always been voted in the top ten in the Time's 'Best Companies to Work For' surveys since 2001. It offers incentives and makes employees feel they are part of a team. In March 2005, 40% of employees had worked for the company for five years or more. Bacardi-Martini beats its competition by having excellent productivity levels as a result of the quality of its staff, and this allows it to reduce costs.

## Reasons for employee demotivation

Motivation is about stimulating employees to work as hard as they possibly can. Demotivation has the opposite effect. It is important to recognise that sometimes employees feel they are unable to apply themselves to the job and have bad feelings about their work.

Some of the most basic needs that have to be satisfied before employees can work are having adequate food and drink, feeling safe and secure, and feeling they are part of a group. These ideas about basic needs are based on the work of a famous theorist called Abraham Maslow. If an employee has poor working conditions, he or she is not likely to feel safe and therefore may become demotivated. Employees in this situation will not be able to focus on working hard at their jobs because they are worried. Some examples of industries that may have poor working conditions include cleaning, mining or clothes manufacturing. These jobs may require the use of chemicals, be carried out in unpleasant conditions or involve very repetitive, boring tasks that must be performed over and over again, causing both physical and psychological stresses for employees.

*Some types of employment may include repetitive or boring tasks*

Not all companies involved in these industries will have problems. But if working conditions are not good, employees will become demotivated. A company may also be prosecuted by the Health and Safety Executive (HSE) if health and safety standards are not maintained. Poor working conditions investigated by the HSE include employees being exposed to dangerous substances such as asbestos, or poor seating in offices causing employees back pain.

The more job satisfaction an employee has, the more motivated he or she is likely to be. If job satisfaction is low, employees are likely to feel demotivated. How much people feel satisfied with their jobs will depend partly on their personality and approach to life, but in some industries low job satisfaction is widespread among workers.

## Case study  Stress calling?

Call centres have been described as 'twenty-first century sweatshops', and as very stressful places to work. In these centres large teams of people work all day answering telephone calls. You might have come across them if you have telephoned your bank, an insurance company, or placed an order with a catalogue company over the telephone. There are estimated to be between 250,000 and 400,000 people working in call centres, answering people's need to access these services day or night.

While there are differences in the way that individual call centres work, some key problems have been identified with them. Some call centres are extremely strict about how long employees can spend on toilet breaks, and sometimes time them. Others monitor telephone calls for how long staff talk with a customer before they move on to the next one.

Call centres often have an electronic screen in the centre of the room showing how many calls are coming in at that time and how quickly they are answered, such as within four rings. There is little interaction between employees because their time is spent dealing with customers on the phone, so it can be isolating.

Call centres want to be as productive as possible so it is a very pressurised environment. The businesses operating the centres will have a target number of customers they want to deal with each day. Some centres have team systems, so each member of the team must work as hard as possible to make sure they don't let down their fellow team members and risk losing a bonus at the end of the month.

Possible health problems associated with call centres include eye problems from looking at screens, hearing and voice problems as well as other common problems associated with working for long stretches of time at an office desk, such as back problems.

1 What are some of the possible issues about working in a call centre?
2 Why do some organisations monitor their staff so much?
3 In small groups, produce a presentation giving ideas for how call centres could make staff feel more motivated at work. Suggest ways to reduce demotivation and describe some possible new ways of working.

Some workers may have jobs that they really enjoy but feel demotivated by the poor pay. For example, a care assistant may really like looking after the elderly or young children, but be disappointed with the pay.

### The impact on corporate culture of demotivation

Where demotivation is a problem, the business culture as a whole will become more negative. If a number of employees are demotivated, they are less likely to work hard and feel satisfied, and their attitudes can spread throughout the organisation. If an organisation has a negative business culture, workers can feel alienated from management and feel they are not cared for. They will work to the minimum level expected, but this is likely to increase costs, and in a profit-making business reduce profits.

If workers feel resentful towards management they will be less likely to welcome new ideas at work. This makes change more difficult to implement in the business, potentially making the business less efficient.

### Culture and inequality

In negative business cultures, there may be perceived inequalities between the employees who produce the product or service and the managers and shareholders who control the business. Sometimes, top executives receive very high pay increases based on good company performance or record profits, and high dividends may be given to shareholders, while the ordinary employees receive a minimal wage increase. This can make employees feel unfairly treated and demotivated, which is likely to then affect customer satisfaction and eventually the reputation of the company and its profitability.

## Working conditions

As already mentioned, poor working conditions can make employees feel demotivated, and there may be hazards in the workplace such as asbestos, unsafe structures, equipment without safety guards, or lack of protective clothing when dealing with chemicals. These are physical hazards, but employees can also be demotivated by psychological hazards in the workplace such as harassment.

## Harassment and victimisation

Harassment can take many different forms, but it could include gossip being spread about an employee, unwelcome sexual advances being made, or blocking an employee's progress within the organisation. Victimisation could include the employee being singled out for different treatment, such as being continually criticised for his or her work or being refused requests for time off. Harassment and victimisation can demotivate employees because they damage the psychological well-being of those employees.

If harassment or victimisation take place in the workplace the employee might ultimately be unfairly dismissed. A claim of **unfair dismissal** is investigated at an industrial tribunal. More information about laws relating to the workplace can be found in Unit 15 of BTEC National Business.

As you have already learned, employees can also be demotivated because of lack of advancement at work as a result of a 'glass ceiling' preventing progression on the basis of age or gender.

## The effects of casual and fixed-term working

So far we have concentrated on employees who have permanent jobs, but an increasing number of workers have less job security and consequent demotivation because they are employed on a casual basis. Casual workers are usually employed on **fixed-term contracts**, such as for six months or one year. As they are not permanent employees they are often not entitled to company benefits such as sick pay, holiday pay

or pension contributions. Casual workers are less likely to feel loyal to the business and much more likely to leave to get a more secure job.

Trade unions can play an important role in a business. Unions will negotiate with management on behalf of a number of workers about pay or working conditions. Some organisations may not want to recognise a union and this may demotivate employees as they may feel they have no one to speak on their behalf. ACAS (the Advisory, Conciliation and Arbitration Service) can help employees to try to get union recognition in their workplace by law, but this can be complicated and take a long time.

### Practice point

Copy the following table about trade unions. Complete it to show the advantages to both the employee and employer or having a recognised union. What are the possible disadvantages?

You may find it useful to consult websites such as ACAS (*www.acas.org.uk*), Business Link (*www.businesslink.gov.uk*) and the Department of Trade and Industry (*www.dti.gov.uk*).

|  | Trade unions |
| --- | --- |
| Advantages to the employer | |
| Advantages to the employee | |
| Disadvantages to the employer | |
| Disadvantages to the employee | |

As you have already seen in the case of General Motors, some organisations use outsourcing to save costs. This may be done on a temporary or permanent basis and therefore make employees worry about their job security, again leading to demotivation. Outsourcing has become more common in the IT and banking industries in recent years, with a lot of work now taking place in countries such as India. Employees in these industries have, in some cases, become demotivated and been more likely to take part in industrial action.

## Consequences of employee demotivation

What are the consequences for employers of having a demotivated workforce? First, it is likely that the business will experience high **staff turnover**. This is the measurement of employees leaving, calculated as a percentage of the average number of employees over the same period of time.

Staff turnover =

$$\frac{\text{Number of staff leaving in a time period}}{\text{Average number of staff employed in that time period}} \times 100$$

If staff turnover is high, this means that a lot of staff are leaving and taking valuable human experience with them. It also means the business needs to recruit new staff to replace them, and this will increase recruitment and training costs.

Another possible consequence of demotivation is that employees may take more time off such as days sick. This will increase absenteeism levels in the workplace.

Staff sickness levels =

$$\frac{\text{Number of staff off sick in a time period}}{\text{Average number of staff employed in that time period}} \times 100$$

This same calculation can be adapted to calculate the percentages of staff who are absent for other reasons.

If employees are away, either less work will be done or costs will have to rise, as more people need to be called in to cover them. If cover is not provided this may lead to further demotivation for the remaining employees, who will have more work to do.

## Workplace vandalism and theft

Demotivated employees can resort to workplace vandalism and theft as a way to get some kind of revenge on their employer. This can take many forms, from stealing stationery and pens to deliberately damaging equipment or materials.

The way that employers deal with employees who are found to have been vandalising or stealing

will depend very much on the employer and the nature of the incident. Employees who are caught will face disciplinary action and in some cases dismissal.

### Thinking point

Theft from work doesn't just mean stealing money kept on the premises; there are a number of different types of theft, all very damaging to a business. Some examples are:

- stealing pens or paper from work to use at home
- pretending you are ill and cannot come to work when you are well
- coming back from lunch late
- spending time booking holidays on the Internet during working hours
- leaving work early
- eating food that was intended for customers
- making personal telephone calls
- putting in exaggerated claims for expenses
- taking frequent breaks to chat to colleagues and friends
- using the photocopier for personal matters
- taking money from the till
- taking free samples that were intended for customers.

1 In small groups, look at the list of different types of theft listed above and rank them in order of seriousness.

2 Why do some types of theft seem more serious than others?

3 Should all types of theft at work be treated in the same way?

4 What are the consequences for business and for its customers of such thefts?

## The purpose of exit interviews

One way of finding out in detail how demotivated or motivated employees are in the workplace is to conduct what are known as **exit interviews** with staff who are leaving. These interviews can provide valuable information to the business as they can find out people's opinions on their pay and working conditions, and the reasons why they are leaving. If poor working conditions or poor pay are reasons for high staff turnover, the business may be able to change these conditions in order to prevent the loss of more employees.

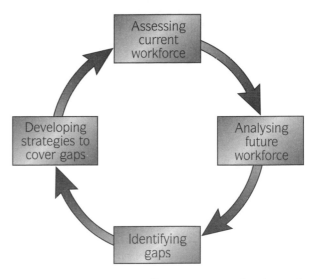

*Human resource planning cycle*

## Outcome activity 18.2

### Pass
Using an organisation you are familiar with or a case study from this unit, describe evidence of motivational practice in that business.

Which techniques does the organisation use? Job enlargement, enrichment, empowerment, teamworking?

### Merit
Analyse the impact of motivational practice in the business, taking account of skill levels.

Thinking about these practices, what influence do skills levels have on motivation? How do they affect the way in which the organisation motivates its employees? How can the necessary skills restrict what a business can do? Are there any aspects of the jobs that are demotivating?

### Distinction
Evaluate the extent to which motivational practice is a clear priority for human resource managers in your selected business.

Give a judgement about how important motivational practice is to the organisation – do managers see it as very important, or less important? What evidence do you have of this? What other considerations do human resource managers have to take into account?

# *Human resource planning*

Human resource planning looks at the current skills and motivation in the workforce and compares them with what will be needed in the future. To make this analysis the business has to take into account both internal (inside the business) and external (outside the business) considerations.

## Internal planning considerations

Assessing the skills of the current workforce is an essential part of planning as it enables the business to build up a profile of the training, experience and qualifications that employees already have. This is very important, whether the business is capital- or labour-intensive.

### *Workforce skills profiling*

A workforce skills profile provides business managers with information about whether skills are adequate for the business' needs, and whether extra training and skills development need to take place. Planning is about deciding when and where such training should take place based on predicted future demand for a product or service.

Some organisations that experience rapid changes in demand or technology may plan for 12 months ahead, while others will look at the longer term such as the next 10 or 20 years. The chosen length of time is called the *planning horizon*.

Estimates of future demand for the products and services and future business growth allow the business to plan the size of workforce needed. Technological changes will bring the need to take on additional workers in some businesses, while others will need to reduce the number of workers that they employ. Increasing the number of workers is called *expansion* of the workforce. Reducing the number of workers is called *contraction*.

Technological change may also require workers to be transferred from one area of production to another. This is likely to involve retraining in different skills.

### Equal opportunity monitoring

When managers are looking at the current workforce they not only take into account its overall skills but also the balance of age, race and gender within the organisation at each level. This allows them to carry out equal opportunity monitoring, which means making sure that there is an appropriate mix of employees working within the business, and that there is no discrimination in employment or promotion against people of particular races, religions or genders.

### Analysing the workforce

Building up a workforce profile can also give clear information to the management team about potential problems in the structure of the workforce. If an area is identified as being a weakness within the organisation, for example if the majority of the workforce belongs to older age groups and many are due to retire in the next five years, plans must be put in place to recruit new employees to take the place of those staff if the jobs will still exist. There may also be concerns about heavy reliance on casual labour or on large amounts of overtime being worked. Relying too much on either of these ways of working may lead to the workforce losing motivation or becoming over-worked. Overtime is also an expensive way of paying for production, and increases costs to the business.

Staff turnover can also be examined in the workplace profile, to calculate the number of staff leaving compared to the average number of staff employed. The higher the staff turnover, the more people are leaving, which could reveal demotivation among employees and increases costs.

As we have already seen, exit interview results can also be used for planning purposes as they can indicate potential problems in certain areas of the business. If there is a shortage of a particular type of skill and employees are leaving for higher wages elsewhere, this should be evident in the feedback from exit interviews.

### Empowering the workforce to multi-task

Workforce planning for the future, especially if technological changes are likely to be happening, may conclude that employees need to be moved within the organisation to a different role. Deploying human resources successfully – allocating employees in the most efficient way – can ensure that the workforce is developed to meet the business' future needs.

**Multi-tasking** can also help the business plan successfully for the future; it involves training employees to do a number of tasks, so that they can be more flexible in coping with the changing needs of the business. An example of multi-tasking is a restaurant manager who:

- oversees the kitchen
- supervises the waiting staff
- checks there is enough change in the till
- monitors the availability of ingredients and drinks
- deals with customer complaints
- organises staff rotas.

Training employees to do as many different tasks as possible means that the business will become more flexible.

## Assessing the capacity for training

Once a skills gap has been identified, management can plan the type of training needed. It can often take place inside the business, and be provided by employees or managers while working (on-the-job training), thus saving both time and money. Organisations may also have a training room and offer lectures or self study, which is known as off-the-job training.

On-the-job training can include work shadowing, which means that the employee to be trained works with and watches another employee to learn about the job. This type of training is often used when a new employee starts a job, such as serving food to customers while learning the skills of waiting staff. On-the-job training can be a very cost-effective way of training a workforce as employees are still productive while being trained.

### Thinking point

Look at the list of different types of training below and work out which are on-the-job and which are off-the-job training.

- Following a training manual while working at your desk.
- Spending the day performing role plays with colleagues as part of a training day.
- Watching a video in the training room.
- Attending an evening class at college.
- Going to a lecture at the local university.
- Watching the accountant to see how to improve your auditing skills.
- Accessing an on-line course in your lunch break.

Identifying the gap between the skills the business will need in the future and those it has now allows management to plan for the costs of training and development. This investment planning is critical to the success of the business, as unless sufficient money and time are allocated for training it will not take place.

# External planning considerations

The business also needs to take into account what is happening to the labour force outside the organisation and estimate the influence it will have in the future.

## Estimating future industry trends

As a business plans its workforce for the future, other businesses in that industry will be doing the same, and if the industry is expanding there may not be enough potential employees to supply all the recruitment needs of the future. A lack of potential future employees means there will be a labour shortage and companies are likely to need to pay higher wages in order to attract the right people to work for them. If one organisation pays less than others in the same industry it is not likely to be able to attract the best recruits, or even sufficient numbers of recruits if demand is high.

## Budget implications of pay comparability

A company needs to ensure that the pay and conditions it offers are comparable to those offered by others in the same industry. But there is a need to strike a careful balance as an increase in costs for the company may lead to lower profits in the future. Paying the appropriate rate to attract suitable employees must be balanced against managing funds carefully in order to make a profit.

## Technology and the changing nature of work

When considering external influences on human resource planning, it is also necessary to consider what is happening to the nature of work on a local and national scale. Over the past 50 years there has been a shift towards greater use of technology and the Internet in the workplace. This has changed the way employees work and the type of work they do.

In the past, telephone operators connected all telephone calls, but technology now does this automatically. Data entry clerks used to be employed in great numbers to input order information into computers, but now many customers order for themselves on-line. Managing orders on-line is about managing the overall process and identifying problems, rather than inputting data. Such changes in working methods are happening on a national scale and people with IT skills are in demand for a huge variety of jobs.

Some parts of the UK have seen dramatic local changes as a result of a shift in the nature of work. The north east of England has seen a change in the nature of employment from mostly primary and manufacturing industry to new industries such as microelectronics and biotechnology, and service industries including retail, education and tourism. This presents a huge training challenge for the area as a high number of people may have skills in manufacturing but fewer are skilled in retail or tourism, where jobs are available. This training gap needs to be dealt with by both local businesses and agencies such as colleges to give local people the skills they need.

## Practice point

1 Using the National Statistics website *www.statistics.gov.uk*, look at what is happening to employment in your neighbourhood by researching your own postcode. This will give you information about employment levels and the types of jobs in your area.

2 Look at the national statistics on the number of hours worked on average, and the types of employment for the nation as a whole.

3 Make a note summarising your findings on both your local area and the national employment situation.

### Analysing labour information by sector and region

As you have seen, the government publishes national and local statistics on employment. If a business wants to investigate conditions in its local area to find the skills levels available and the likely availability of potential workers, it can find this information on an area and sector basis. To use this information to their best advantage, businesses need to consider their future needs and those of their competitors in order to make sure they attract the right people to work for them, especially if they are working in a skills-shortage area.

This may mean they need to offer extra benefits or better working conditions in order to recruit the right people. In some areas it may not be possible to find people with the right skills, and then the business may need to recruit further afield or even abroad in order to get suitably qualified staff.

Areas with shortages in 2005 included doctors, nurses, teachers and IT staff. Doctors and nurses were being recruited from developing countries such as India and the Philippines, and teachers from countries such as Australia and Canada, to fill these gaps.

### Adapting and developing other resources

As human resources must be planned in order to meet expected demands in the future, so too must the other resources needed to meet those needs. Employing more people will require more equipment for them to use, more finances to pay their wages and more investment in buildings for them to work in.

The reverse is true of a reduction in employees; if fewer employees are needed the business may be able to reduce the number of managers or amount of equipment needed, as staff are replaced by machines or different methods of working come into force.

Either way, it is important to recognise that human resource needs are constantly adapting and developing, and that the resources to support those staff need to adapt too.

## Outcome activity 18.3

**Pass**

Using an organisation you are familiar with or a case study from this unit, describe internal and external issues which may affect workforce planning.

To do this you will need to consider the following:

| Internal | External |
|---|---|
| Workforce skills profile | Skills shortages |
| Results from exit interviews | Structural employment change in the area or industry |
| Staff turnover | Training |
| Resources available | Technological change |
| Organisational objectives | Future plans, e.g. expansion |

**Merit**

Explain how a business may undertake effective workforce planning.

Using the issues outlined above, explain how such issues can be used to make workforce planning more effective.

# *Management of human performance*

Managing human resources needs to include measuring performance and rewarding it in some way. It also involves dealing with stress in the workplace.

## Measuring and rewarding performance

While motivation is the key to encouraging employees to work as hard as possible, a business can only find out how hard employees are working if it measures their performance to see how productive each employee is.

Businesses have different ways of measuring employee performance. For example, they might calculate how many customers an employee has served on a till per day, how many products he or she has made in a factory or how many reports have been written in a week. Measurements like these gives management a tool for comparing employees.

Some industries find it more difficult to measure productivity than others. If employees are sewing slippers in a factory, it is relatively easy to compare the number made; for example, Sunita made twenty pairs today and James made nine – Sunita has been more productive than James. But in some industries, such as services industries, it is difficult to draw accurate comparisons. This is because some measurements are quantitative (linked to numbers and statistics) whereas others are qualitative (based on opinions and judgements). In service industries, more qualitative measurements may be made. Each method has its place within different organisations but they must be used carefully and appropriately so both the employee and employer feel their needs are being met.

In the National Health Service, for example, it may be possible to compare bed occupancy rates of hospitals throughout the UK, but some may be in areas of higher ill health. This may mean one area appears more productive than the other, and may not be a good method of comparing the efficiency of the service. Health care is difficult to measure as it is not just about numbers and processing 'products' – it is about offering people care and attention.

### Target setting and the appraisal system

Worker performance measurements will be different, as you have already learned, depending on the type of industry. In banking and other office-based environments measurement is often linked with the employer's appraisal system. Under this system the employer and employee measure performance against objectives or targets that were set in a previous review. These reviews can take place at different intervals such as three, six or even twelve months. Examples of targets that may be set for an employee might include learning a new software package or taking part in training and putting a new skill into practice.

Some employers may give an employee six or eight relatively simple targets, whereas others may concentrate on only one or two more difficult targets that require a high level of performance.

It is important that targets are relevant to the employee as well as the employer, so that everyone is aware of what needs to be achieved and the way in which the targets will help to meet the business' and employee's needs.

### The purpose of appraisal systems

Appraisal systems in any organisation should be designed to motivate and encourage employees to give their best performance. The targets that are set by employer and employee should strike a balance between what is needed for the business and what the employee needs. An employee may feel he or she would like to attend a particular course in the coming appraisal period, but if it does not meet a business need the manager may need to persuade him or her to undertake different training.

### Practice point

Consider the following businesses. What type of measurement could be used for productivity, and which method of performance management could be used? The first example has been completed for you.

| Organisation | Method of measuring productivity | Method of management and review |
| --- | --- | --- |
| Restaurant | Number of dishes produced Number of customers served Spend per customer Amount of waste produced Mystery shopper results | Daily target setting with weekly review by restaurant manager Mystery shopper results analysed monthly Action plans drawn up weekly to deal with shortfalls Annual appraisal of individual staff performance |
| Police force | | |
| Bank | | |
| Charity | | |
| Estate agent | | |

| Advantages of appraisal systems | Disadvantages of appraisal systems |
|---|---|
| Allow an employer and employee to discuss and work together on improving performance, leading to better use of resources or more profits | Need tight control so that all appraisers set the same level of target and standards are fair |
| Provide a formal system for monitoring and measuring performance | Targets need to be achievable but if they are too easy costs may go up |
| Rewards can be given for good performance, such as pay rises, prizes or time off | If targets are too difficult to meet, employees may feel demotivated |
| Allow business objectives to be filtered down an organisation and 'owned' by all employees, therefore more likely to be achieved | Will only be useful if both the employer and employee believe in the system and regard it as valuable |
| Allow the employee and employer to learn more about each other and therefore improve their working relationship | Need time and effort to be done successfully – a bad appraisal interview is far worse than none at all |
| Allow the business to plan training and development so that future needs can be met, for example planning for people to take over when someone is about to retire. | Budgetary constraints may mean a limited amount of money is available for training and therefore needs identified within the appraisal system cannot be met |

The inclusion of unpopular targets requires careful management if the appraiser is to persuade the employee that such targets are in his or her best interest. Targets such as cutting costs often need to be cascaded down from senior managers to more junior managers so that overall business objectives are met.

The advantages and disadvantages of appraisal systems are summarised above.

### Self-assessment as part of appraisal

Good appraisal systems often include a method of self-assessment. This allows employees to review their own progress and to consider what they need to do at every point in the review cycle. If employees 'own' their targets and carefully consider what they need to do to improve their own performance, they are more likely to work harder and thus help the organisation in the long run.

Employees can assess their own performance and plan how they are going to improve by setting themselves targets. Three, six or even twelve months later, the employee can review those targets and judge their own success. The key to successful self-assessment is to make sure that targets are linked to the best interests of the employee as well as the business.

An example of such targets is to link attendance with bonuses. This means if the employee has very good attendance at work he or she will receive a bonus, and at the same will be more productive and therefore earn more money for the company. Both the employee and company will benefit.

## Practice point

Complete the mini self-assessment below by considering your performance so far on your BTEC National course. Be honest with yourself – have you given your best performance, or have there been times when you could have made improvements or given extra effort?

Read each of the following statements and tick which most applies to you.

| Statement | Very like me | A bit like me | Not like me | Very unlike me |
|---|---|---|---|---|
| I have been excellent at planning and have always handed my assignments in on time. | | | | |
| I have coped with various difficulties during the course but have overcome them. | | | | |
| I have spent time giving detailed analysis within my work. | | | | |
| I have developed my listening skills during the course in order to more fully understand what I am being asked to do. | | | | |
| I am gradually developing more skills in order to succeed at the higher levels on the BTEC National course. | | | | |
| I am determined to earn a Merit or Distinction on this course. | | | | |

This mini self-assessment should have given you some idea of why reviewing yourself can be important. Discuss your results with your teacher so that you can set targets for your course that will help you to achieve to the highest level possible. Produce a self-assessment document that could be used by future students on your course in order to improve their own productivity and performance.

### Benchmarking

One way for a business to gain a basis for the comparison of performance is through the use of industry-wide benchmarks. Benchmarking seeks to provide data in an industry so that competitors within that industry can judge how they are doing against the best possible standards. The best organisation in an industry becomes the standard to which all other competitors should aspire.

Benchmarking can be used to compare many industries, from the performance of pupils in schools using school performance league tables, to the number of products made and their sales value for the manufacturers of parts for fridges and freezers.

Benchmarking allows businesses to measure their performance against competitors in the same industry but also to monitor and reward performance within the organisation. One way of doing this, as you have already seen, is by using performance-related pay. Linking pay to performance is relatively simple for manufacturing or sales staff – the more products made or sold, the higher the performance level. But in some industries applying performance-related pay is more complicated. One such area is education. Many teachers and lecturers are given

Sweet Chocs is a fairly new company producing handmade chocolates and trading on-line. In order to compare its performance against other on-line chocolate sellers, it looks at the following benchmark data.

|  | Sweet Chocs | Handmade Delight | Chocolate Dreams | Caramel Corner |
|---|---|---|---|---|
| Price per 250g box | £3.50 | £4.00 | £2.99 | £5.00 |
| Delivery time from order to receipt, in days | 10 | 12 | 8 | 18 |
| Cost of order processing per order | £1.50 | £2.00 | £1.00 | £1.50 |
| Customer complaints as a percentage of orders | 10% | 6% | 10% | 15% |

1 Which company's performance would you suggest Sweet Chocs should choose as a benchmark, and why?

2 Which factors could Sweet Chocs' managers consider in order to improve their performance?

performance-related pay on the basis of retaining students in classes and those students passing their courses. If teachers' performance is above the average expected at a national level, they are likely to be rewarded with a performance-related element in their pay. However, some students may not stay on or succeed in a course because of difficult personal problems that have nothing to do with the teacher, although this will still affect the results of the teacher's class.

### Linking pay to performance

When linking pay to performance it is important that the indicators used to measure performance are applied in a sensitive and careful way. Drawing comparisons from unsuitable indicators is worse than not measuring at all, as it will give a false impression of how the organisation is performing.

Some measurements are easy to apply, such as monitoring attendance, employees' punctuality and whether they have met specific production targets. Other ways of measuring performance can be more difficult to judge, such as rewarding positive attitudes and increased effort, for example in providing better customer service. Rewards for goodwill of this kind may be appropriate across the whole company if results and customer satisfaction are improving; alternatively, individual employees may be rewarded based on indicators such as customer recommendations, or if they have offered useful suggestions that have helped to improve the company's operations.

## Stress management

So far within this unit the emphasis has been on making the best use of human resources within the organisation. This has meant analysing and planning for the skills needed by the business now and in the future, and persuading employees to work harder by motivating, monitoring and rewarding their performance. However, humans, unlike machines, do feel stress in the workplace.

*A plant-filled environment can lower stress levels*

### The impact of environment on stress levels

While employers want employees to work as hard as they possibly can, they also need to understand and put in place methods of helping their employees to deal with pressure. There are many different ways this can be done. For example, something as simple as increasing the number of plants in offices has been found in the Netherlands to increase productivity and reduce stress. Job Centres in the UK were recently given a softer décor to make the environment more relaxing for both staff and customers.

Making the environment at work as healthy and relaxing as possible should help employees to feel happier at work, but they also need to feel safe in order to feel less stressed. Stress may be reduced for bank workers if they are behind security screens, or for bus drivers if two-way radios are available. In many large cities taxi drivers not only have two-way radios but also have CCTV in their cabs to make them feel safer when they are transporting passengers. These measures all help to make employees feel safer and therefore less stressed.

### The need for training to reduce stress levels

Some jobs by their very nature are more stressful than others, particularly if they involve dealing with upset or dissatisfied customers. Employees need specific training in how to deal with these confrontational situations so that they don't experience too much stress.

Employees need the opportunity to talk to others about how they are feeling, and organisations often use confidential counsellors, or set up employee assistance programmes or discussion services. Agencies such as the Employee Advisory Resource can provide these services for employers, or they can employ their own staff within the company.

### Sharing the workload

One of the ways of making sure that employees don't feel under too much pressure at work is to ensure that everyone has a fair share of the workload. Employees should not given too much while others have little to do. This sounds very easy in theory but requires careful management to make sure that it is done properly. Flexible working hours and the use of part-time staff may also help to even out the workload, as extra employees can be brought in to deal with a higher workload at certain times in the week or month on a permanent basis.

## Technological change

You have already learned that technological change has led to a change in the skills needed in some jobs, with others ceasing to exist altogether. Managing this process of change needs to be done carefully to ensure employees can cope with new methods of working.

Some employees might be resistant to technology and find such a change difficult. They will need support during the time of change to avoid excessive stress. In some areas of the country there may be a huge structural change, where large numbers of people need to change the type of job they do and work, for example, in service-based jobs rather than manufacturing. Dealing with such a change in working environment can be extremely stressful.

Whether it is caused by a structural or technological change to the working environment, stress can be reduced by making sure that the environment is as ergonomically sound as possible. This means that the workplace should be designed so that it is comfortable and safe for employees.

In an office environment this may mean making sure that ergonomically designed chairs with adjustable backs are used, so that employees can have proper back support. Managers in a factory need to examine how products are lifted and moved about to ensure employee comfort and safety. The more ergonomically sound a workplace is, the higher productivity is likely to be.

## E-mail as a stressor

Stress management involves looking at many different aspects of the working environment, including changes made to that environment as a result of new technology. One of the top stressors in the workplace now, it is suggested, is e-mail. E-mail is a stressor because it involves people having to read and deal with an increasing number of messages on a daily basis. It is predicted that the number of these messages is likely to multiply by at least a factor of four in the next few years.

Teaching employees how to manage e-mails is one way to help them to manage their stress levels and therefore be more productive in the workplace. Some employers have even introduced the idea of having 'e-mail-free Fridays' when e-mails are ignored for the day, to be dealt with on Mondays.

## Outcome activity 18.4

### Pass

Using an organisation you are familiar with or a case study from this unit, identify and describe effective ways of managing human performance in that organisation.

- How is worker performance measured?
- Does the organisation use benchmarking?
- What procedures does the organisation have for assessment and self-assessment?
- Which rewards are offered for good performance?
- What happens if workers give a poor performance?

### Merit

Analyse ways in which human performance may be enhanced in a selected business.

How can the organisation use the methods you have described to make employees work even harder?

What are the benefits and costs to an employer of extra training?

How can productivity be increased without increasing stress in the workplace?

### Distinction

Evaluate the effectiveness of human performance management in the achievement of business objectives.

Give a judgement about how well human performance is monitored in the organisation you have chosen, based on evidence you have provided at Pass and Merit level in relation to business objectives, for example. How does monitoring of productivity help the business to achieve its objectives? What impact does the management of stress levels have?

## Key terms

### Capital-intensive
making more investment in use of technology and machinery than humans during production

### Corporate culture
the way people usually behave within a particular business; the formal or informal set of rules that influence employees' behaviour

### Empowerment
giving responsibility and decision-making powers to employees

### Exit interviews
interviews that take place when employees leave a business, to find out why individuals are leaving and whether improvements can be made

### Fixed-term contract
a contract that is set for a specific amount of time

### Flexible working practices
the ability to make work fit in with an employee's needs, e.g. flexi-time when employees can choose starting and finishing times as long as they work the agreed number of hours in a week (or over a longer period)

### Glass ceiling
a concealed limit to the amount of advancement an individual can achieve because of racial, age or sex discrimination

## Key terms

### Home and work life balance
making sure that work and home lives have equal status so that employees can, for example, control the number of hours they work and work doesn't have a negative effect on their families

### Inequality
unfair treatment; treating an employee differently because of age, race or gender

### Job enlargement
giving employees additional tasks at the same level

### Job enrichment
redesigning employees' jobs to give them more challenging tasks to do and/or increased responsibility

### Job security
the feeling that your job is safe

### Job share
an arrangement where two or more employees share the hours of one full-time job

### Labour
the physical and mental effort given by employees

### Labour-intensive
needing a lot of labour as part of business production, as opposed to technology or machinery

### Maternity leave and pay
the time off and money paid to a female employee when she has a baby

### Multi-tasking
doing more than one task at the same time

### Opportunity cost
the cost to the business of investing money in one area of a business rather than elsewhere

### Outsourcing
the arrangement whereby a business pays another to do work for it that has previously been performed by employees

### Paternity leave and pay
the time off work and pay given to a male employee when his partner has had a baby

### Pay scales
the list of different salary levels that an employee can receive in a workplace

### Productivity
the output of either individual workers or whole groups of workers

### Staff turnover
the measurement of how many staff are leaving an organisation, expressed as a percentage of the average size of the workforce

### Teleworking
working from home using computer and/or telephone technology for communication

### Trade union
a group of workers who join together to negotiate pay and working conditions, for example the National Union of Teachers

### Unfair dismissal
when an employee is dismissed from an organisation because of race, gender, religion or other unfair reason

# End-of-unit test

1 What does 'capital-intensive' mean?

2 Give two examples of labour-intensive businesses.

3 Name three types of specialist jobs that have transferable skills.

4 What is meant by a skills shortage?

5 Describe what is meant by 'corporate culture'.

6 What does 'industrial action' mean?

7 Name two trade unions.

8 Describe what is meant by 'empowerment'.

9 What is one advantage of job sharing?

10 Why might pay scales motivate employees?

11 Describe one disadvantage of performance-related pay.

12 Name two causes of employee demotivation.

13 What does ACAS do?

14 Which ratio is used to measure sickness levels?

15 What is meant by human resource planning?

16 Why is a workforce profile useful?

17 What might a high staff turnover show?

18 How can exit interviews help an organisation?

19 What is the difference between on-the-job and off-the-job training?

20 How can benchmarking help an organisation become more successful?

# Resources

## Texts

Bartol and Martin: *Management*, Irwin/McGraw-Hill, 1997

Bradburn, R: *Understanding Business Ethics*, Continuum, 1997

Dransfield, R et al: *BTEC National Business*, Heinemann, 2004

Gillespie, A: *Business in Action*, Hodder and Stoughton, 2002

Lockton, Deborah: *Employment Law*, Palgrave MacMillan, 2003

Martin, M and Jackson, T: *Personnel Practice (People and Organisations)*, Chartered Institute of Personnel and Development, 2002

## Journals

*Personnel Today*

*Personnel Review*

*Personnel Management*

## Websites

*www.acas.org.uk* The Advisory, Conciliation and Arbitration Service

*www.bbc.co.uk* BBC website

*www.bestcompanies.co.uk* Best Companies website giving awards to companies displaying excellence

*www.cbi.org.uk* Confederation of Business and Industry

*www.cipd.co.uk* Chartered Institute of Personnel and Development

*www.dti.gov.uk* Department of Trade and Industry

*www.ear.co.uk* Employee Advisory Resource

*www.elliotmarsh.com* Elliot Marsh recruitment consultants

*http://education.guardian.co.uk* Education pages as part of the Guardian newspaper on-line

*www.equality-online.org.uk* 'Equal' website offering information on equal opportunities

*www.guinness.com* Guinness website with company information and history

*www.hse.gov.uk* Health and Safety Executive

*www.iba.org.uk* Institute of Business Advisers

*www.icaew.co.uk* Institute of Chartered Accountants in England and Wales

*www.investorsinpeople.co.uk* Investors in People website

*www.lg-employers.gov.uk* Employers' organisation for local government

*www.managementqualifications.co.uk* Management qualifications website

*www.onrec.com* OnRec recruitment website

*www.people1st.co.uk* Website aimed at improving standards in hospitality, leisure, travel and tourism

*www.personneltoday.com* Personnel Today human resource information provider (US)

*www.personneltoday.co.uk* Personnel Today human resource information provider (UK)

*www.plants-in-buildings.com* Website dedicated to improving the number of plants in offices

*www.statistics.gov.uk* National Statistics published by the government

*www.voluntarysectorskills.org.uk* Voluntary skills promotion website

*www.workingintheuk.gov.uk* Home Office website providing details about what it is like to work in the UK

# Unit 26 Business Ethics

Does it bother you (*should* it bother you?) if an innocent young child in another part of the world worked for 10 hours a day in a sweltering factory in order to make the trendy trainers or fashionable top you are wearing? (The minimum hourly rate in Fujian province, China, is 16 pence.)

Does it bother you that the banana you might have had with your breakfast this morning cost *you* 30 pence in the store, yet the worker who toiled on the plantation that grew it received less than a penny of that?

Are you worried if you hear that multinational armament firms are making billions of pounds from selling guns to squabbling nations all around the world?

Can the planet Earth – on which we all depend – sustain future economic development?

These are all serious *ethical* questions. They are about businesses doing right or wrong. The word **ethics** comes from the Greek word *ethikos* meaning 'character'. In this unit it could be said you are looking into aspects of the 'character' of business the world over.

The unit will introduce you to many ethical questions to do with business, raising many of the dilemmas businesses face in the modern world. The unit is intended to make you think and help you to understand, to investigate and explore a little further some of these fundamental business and human issues.

Unit 26 is divided into four main areas:

- 26.1 Business activities, aims and objectives
- 26.2 Ethical consequences of business activity for employees
- 26.3 Ethical consequences of business activity for consumers
- 26.4 Ethical consequences of business activity for other stakeholders.

---

## *Business activities, aims and objectives*

### Key drivers of organisational behaviour

In a free market economy like ours, the primary purpose of business activity is to produce the things we as a society – increasingly, a global society – need or want. The major incentive for people to set up in business is to generate wealth, and this is always going to be one of their basic **objectives**.

The owners of businesses must continue to benefit, otherwise the business will be judged to have failed. If the owners don't benefit, business activity ceases and the things that were produced by it – either products or services – stop being produced and are no longer offered. This is part of the 'free' aspect of the market; business decision-makers can enter markets as they choose, and leave them when they choose.

Very often in business studies, therefore, the basic objective of business activity – above all else – is assumed to be the creation of wealth for the owners (the **shareholders** in the case of many private business). This traditional view tells us that for all businesses, at least in the **private sector**, short-term goals and wider strategic **aims** must all eventually serve to maximise profit. By maximising profits, shareholders become richer.

Unit 1 in *BTEC National Business* (page 21) sets out very clearly the ways in which a typical private sector business can set about trying to maximise profit. Maximum profit for a firm is achieved when the difference between the revenue that is received from sales is at its greatest in relation to the costs associated with producing something. If business managers set out to follow a strict and unbending policy of profit maximisation, they will always try to increase sales and lower costs.

*Thousands of public limited companies are listed on the London Stock Exchange.*

### Thinking point

In April 2005, Tesco reported profits in excess of £2 billion. In small groups, look in a national newspaper and investigate the current share price of Tesco. If you were a group of shareholders in the company, would you want to encourage management always to go for maximum profit? Write a short statement justifying your answer to this.

is whether they should *always* seek to achieve the maximum profit. As we shall see later, to pursue maximum profit at all times might mean causing other problems. It is quite reasonable for a business manager to follow an alternative policy to maximising profit in the short term, in order to achieve better profitability in the long term.

### Shareholder push for sales maximisation

Large business corporations are operated on a day-to-day basis by professional managers. These people are usually not the owners of the business. They are paid by the shareholders and must answer to them for their performance. This means there is intense pressure on them to achieve results.

When a PLC (public limited company) publishes its annual report to shareholders, the shareholders are keen to see how the business has performed in terms of profitability, because the value of the shares they hold is dramatically affected by this. The problem faced by managers and executives who are taking business decisions

### Thinking point

An executive is under pressure to get maximum profit figures because she knows that shareholders are hoping for good results. She decides to postpone important investment in safety equipment in premises around the country. From the point of view of shareholders, has she made the right decision? Be prepared to justify your response.

In pursuing business aims and objectives, decision-makers will often be aware that there is a trade-off between one objective and another.

Maximising profits might not be good for business in the long run because eventually something would happen that would be damaging to the firm.

The executive who decides to cut corners on safety measures might regret it if accidents occur that cause public relations damage to the business. Paying low wages or not investing in clean processes could lead to scandal. The wise manager settles for reduced profits in the short term, while channelling resources into other priorities. This means that reporting to shareholders and engaging with them in a positive and open way becomes very important. Shareholders must be kept informed and made to understand why dividends might be reduced. Strong management will ensure that such decisions are understood.

### Stakeholder push for attainment of service targets

Shareholders are one type of **stakeholder**, and they have a direct *financial* interest in a business; they have invested their cash in the hope of a good return on their investment.

Stakeholders are those people, or groups, who are affected by the actions of a business. People who live close to a business are stakeholders in it; they will soon complain if traffic increases dramatically, or the business creates an environmental problem. Other stakeholders are employees, suppliers, customers, shareholders, and the government; all of these groups have a stake for different reasons.

**Thinking point**

A local DIY business decides to create an on-line sales channel. It has purchased a large warehousing unit on an industrial estate, located near a large housing estate and not far from a motorway. It is acknowledged that sales volume will dramatically increase if the firm fulfils its delivery promise. In such a case, who are the stakeholders in the business? Why are they stakeholders?

Stakeholders might exert different kinds of pressure on a business, depending on the type of organisation. The following are examples.

| Type of business organisation | Stakeholders |
|---|---|
| Manufacturing company | Employees, suppliers, neighbours |
| Retail store | Employees, customers, suppliers |
| Hospital | Patients, staff, the community, government |
| School | Parents, pupils, teachers, governors |
| Local council | Citizens, councillors, officers |

Each business has to look around itself in order to balance the concerns and interests of different stakeholder groups. Sometimes it might not be possible to please them all.

**Thinking point**

Do shareholders and other stakeholders have different concerns? Illustrate your answer with examples.

Several kinds of public sector organisations have in recent years been held to account by one very important stakeholder, the government. They are expected to achieve levels of service that provide citizens with good value for the taxes they pay. Schools have to achieve targets for passes at Key Stages in the curriculum and for examination performance. School league tables are published, and an inspection body (Ofsted) publishes school data.

Hospitals similarly are called to account for waiting times, bed occupancy rates, and patient outcomes. Health trusts have to monitor hospital performance, and all staff from senior consultants down to porters and cleaners feel the effects of these service targets.

By setting targets, the government acts on behalf of all citizens. The intention is to drive up standards of public service in those areas where we all benefit. However, for some stakeholders the effects are bad. Teachers feel the pressure to get good results (ask them!), doctors and nurses feel under pressure to deal efficiently and quickly with patients, and managers feel the same pressures.

## Practice point

Visit *www.Royalmail.com* and access the 'Customer service' link. Write a summary of what is meant by 'service targets'. How important do you feel these are for stakeholders of the Royal Mail?

## Sources of organisational culture

All business organisations possess an **organisational culture**, and this has a lot to do with the way they view business ethics. A good way to think about this is to regard each business organisation as if it had a personality, just as each one of us has. Some people are quiet and reserved, some are loud and brash, some mild, and others fairly aggressive. Often in humans these traits or characteristics are hidden for most of the time.

When you get inside business organisations, you will find that they too tend to have strong characteristics that can affect many things they do.

Some organisations are very formally run and rely heavily on enforcing rules and procedures. These are called 'bureaucratic', and they tend to be slow in the way they make decisions. Staff know their place in the hierarchy, there may be a formal dress code, the bosses might have authoritarian styles, and employees do as they are told without discussion or question.

Many organisations today are much less formal and will encourage staff to be more relaxed. Procedures might be less rigid, and managers will encourage initiative, consultation and flexibility.

The communication styles in such a culture can be informal, and instead of people being fixed in their job roles they will be multi-skilled, with teamwork being the preferred style.

There is another way in which organisational culture can show itself. This has to do with the 'external personality' of the business. How do people outside the business perceive it? One of the best ways of understanding this is to examine a classic case of a business deliberately adopting a very specific corporate personality – the Body Shop.

*Reproduced with permission of The Body Shop International plc*

The Body Shop presents a very clear and identifiable corporate culture. This is based on several core **values**:

- 'We consider testing products or ingredients on animals to be morally and scientifically indefensible.'

- 'We support small producer communities around the world who supply us with accessories and natural ingredients.'

- 'We know you're unique, and we'll always treat you like an individual; we like you just the way you are.'

- 'We believe that it is the responsibility of every individual to actively support those who have human rights denied to them.'

- 'We believe that a business has the responsibility to protect the environment in which it operates, locally and globally.'

The Body Shop corporate culture comes from the philosophy of the founder of the business, Anita Roddick:

*Businesses have the power to do good. That's why the Body Shop's Mission Statement opens with the overriding commitment, 'To dedicate our business to the pursuit of social and environmental change'. We use our stores and our products to help communicate human rights and environmental issues.*

(Source: www.AnitaRoddick.com)

### Industry norms

In the industrial economies of advanced nations such as the UK, each sector of industry can be identified as a group. On the website of the Department of Trade and Industry, at *www.dti.gov.uk*, almost 50 different sectors of business are listed; these include agriculture, jewellery, pharmaceuticals, chemicals, tableware, food and drink, oil and gas, retailing and clothing.

Each of these sectors has some form of representative body that serves to bring together the many participants, and forms a collective voice for that particular type of firm. For example, there is a British Giftware and Jewellers Federation. This organisation into industrial sectors helps the government to relate to an entire group of companies and assists specific industrial sectors to impose particular values on their members. These values help to create industry-wide 'norms' of behaviour and practice.

An example of an industrial sector that attempts to establish clear norms is the chemical industry. This industry, perhaps more than most, must strive to maintain a positive public image. In 1984 in Bhopal, India, almost 4,000 people died after a leak of deadly gas from a Union Carbide chemical plant.

### Other sources of organisational culture

*Historical practices* are another source of organisational culture. In many businesses, things have been done in a certain way for generations. If something has worked over many years, why should it be changed? A business might always have practised a centralised style of management where decisions were passed down a hierarchy. Thus a practice involving, say, the use of a particular method of production will be unlikely to change without a massive process of re-formulating policy. This is a huge task.

**Lobbying** by **pressure group**s happens when a representative body works to exert pressure on a company, an industry or the government. (The word 'lobbying' comes from the fact that people used to go to the lobby of the House of Commons in order to question or harangue Members of Parliament.)

The effect that pressure groups can have is significant. For example, the Trades Union Congress (TUC) is a fairly powerful group representing large portions of the union movement.

*A chemical catastrophe in Bhopal, India killed thousands*

If the TUC adopts a position on an issue, this can reverberate around companies and affect the way they work.

Other pressure groups can be single-issue groups. These include such organisations as Greenpeace, Friends of the Earth, the Royal Society for the Prevention of Cruelty to Animals, and the Campaign for Real Ale.

## Values

In mathematics, a value is a number, a quantity. In economics, a value is a measure of what something is worth. But personal values are not written down anywhere because they are a state of mind. They are ideas that a person holds to be important, and they consciously or unconsciously determine how that person behaves.

In a business context, too, the values held by certain key individuals are often translated into specific corporate behaviour. We saw the example of Anita Roddick earlier.

### Thinking point

Draft a statement in which you try to identify your own personal set of values. If you were to start your own business, how would these affect the way you worked?

## Power and authority

Questions of **power** and **authority** are very important both at an organisational level and at the widest global level. To illustrate these two concepts, let's look at a global issue.

The US is the most *powerful* state on earth. It can send military forces almost anywhere in the world (as it did of course in Iraq) and try to enforce its will. The power of the US comes from its economic and military might. Power can be seen as an ability to cause people (or nations) to do something they might not otherwise have done.

By this definition, the bully in the school playground might be said to have power. The biggest, rudest and strongest person can often make others do things they don't really want to.

Some people have powers given to them. They might have the power to clamp vehicles parked in particular places; the power to issue parking tickets; the power to move you on; the power to prevent you entering a club. This form of power is acquired by virtue of a job role. Power, then, causes things to happen.

In business organisations some people have a lot of power. This is not always because they have great *personal* strength. Very often, power is given to them by virtue of their position in the organisation. A problem can arise when someone uses this power irresponsibly – this can lead to an abuse of power.

The owner of a business employing staff has enormous power simply because of the nature of the employer–employee relationship. A manager has power over subordinate staff.

### Case study    Management power

A new member of staff, Ahmed, has joined the business. He has a relevant university degree and is highly academic; his manager, Mrs Huntley, has few academic qualifications but her position has been well earned through both aptitude and experience. However, she has taken a personal dislike to Ahmed and has quietly determined to make life difficult for him.

Today Mrs Huntley has refused Ahmed leave to attend his sister's wedding, and has insisted that he attend a meeting at 5 pm on Friday. She has also suggested to one of the company directors that Ahmed be moved to a remote depot, a move that appears logical but will be seriously harmful to Ahmed's chances of gaining good experience in the firm. In the meantime, Ahmed is being given increasingly tedious tasks to perform.

1 Is Mrs Huntley exercising power?
2 What can Ahmed do about this?

*Authority* often includes power, but it is not the same. Consider the case of Ahmed and his line manager Mrs Huntley above. Mrs Huntley obviously has power because she can refuse Ahmed permission to take a holiday. She also has authority over him because of her job role. But imagine that a technical question arises to do with work. Ahmed knows that Mrs Huntley is not recently qualified and prefers to take the advice of another colleague. Now who has authority?

This often happens in workplaces. Authority can come from experience and personal qualities as well as a person's official job title. It can be acquired from diverse sources. Your local council acquires 'authority' because central government gives it powers to do certain things.

# Ethical evaluation

Questions to do with ethics are very hard to resolve. In your personal life, you will often be faced with decisions that produce a dilemma – where it seems impossible to do the right thing. For example, you are invited to a friend's party on a certain date but it's also your grandparents' anniversary celebration. Obviously the friend's party would be more fun for you, but you don't want to hurt your grandparents. You might try to compromise and go to both.

Ethical questions in business can bring more serious dilemmas. In the private sector there is a need to make profits, but at what cost? Do you compromise on worker safety? Do you buy from the cheapest source, irrespective of its workers' conditions? Do you operate processes that damage the environment? Do you transfer large chunks of operations abroad, making people in this country redundant, to take advantage of cheaper labour? To what extent does the profit motive dominate your business policy?

## *Conflicting values*

Values can conflict with each other. In our society there are many different groups holding different values. Some people value individual freedom above all else, and will argue passionately that people should enjoy liberty. Others value law and order, and insist that the police should be able to arrest people on suspicion, to listen in to phone calls and to intercept e-mails.

In a business context, conflicting values can result in internal tensions when it comes to deciding on strategy. Some of the examples already mentioned could be the result of value conflict; other potential conflicts are social responsibility versus maximum profits; creating local employment opportunities versus maximum cost efficiency; and technological progress versus traditional, time-honoured methods.

## Thinking point

Work together with a fellow student. Research a local or national business example where there are, or might be, conflicting values. These could be within a business, or involve a business and an external pressure group (such as a trade union). Make a set of notes and create a visual display capturing the essence of the conflict.

## Practice point

In pairs, consider the following situation.

A company is involved in a chemical process that is known to create emissions harmful to the ozone layer. After pressure group activity, the company considers the installation of new equipment and the adoption of a new process. However, this would involve 40 workers losing their jobs and at least two local suppliers also suffering.

Why is this an ethical dilemma, and how would you justify your decision?

## Loyalties and responsibilities

It is clear that when business leaders have to make a choice between one course of action and another, they are often faced with deep ethical problems. Often they must fall back upon non-ethical criteria in order to arrive at a decision. One of these is loyalty. Loyalty might relate to one's nation, region, family, workforce, trade, speciality, industry, company or religion.

Every business forges partnerships with other firms, and every employee creates relationships both within and beyond his or her own office or workshop. Decisions might frequently be made on the basis of these, and they might help resolve an ethical question at least in the short term.

A firm might feel that it is responsible for the economic well-being of a region; some companies are responsible for employing very large portions of a regional labour force. It might feel a responsibility for its workforce; it might feel that it has contractual responsibilities.

### Thinking point

Recently the Rover Group plant at Longbridge in Birmingham ceased trading and went into receivership. This was a massive blow to the regional economy.

Research in newspapers or on the Internet the story of this business failure.

1 What do you think Rover management's responsibilities should be?

2 Why might local communities feel they are owed loyalty?

## Winners and losers: stakeholder groups

Business owners want good financial performance from their investments, so business managers know their first responsibility is to deliver good financial results. However, while it has always been acknowledged that a firm exists in a diverse social, economic and political environment, today it is also accepted that businesses should be managed with the interests of *all* stakeholders (including shareholders) in mind.

As we saw earlier, businesses today have to balance the sometimes conflicting aims of a number of stakeholders.

### Shareholders

Shares in UK businesses might be held by private individuals or by institutions holding blocks of company shares as investments for pension funds or mortgage endowments. If a business is performing very well, it is likely that the share value – and therefore the value of the business – will rise. The big question is, which decisions will help the business to prosper? What about those that sacrifice short-term profit for long-term security?

### Practice point

You are employed by a large pub/restaurant chain and you are considering implementing a 'No smoking' policy throughout all public bars and restaurants in the chain.

1 How might you convince shareholders that such a policy might be for the best in the long term?

2 Consider the various stakeholders in the situation. Who might be the 'winners' and who the 'losers'?

### Employees

Ordinary citizens benefit from business activity because it creates employment and wealth. One of the basic tensions in our type of economy is that labour is a major cost of business. In centuries past, in the UK, business owners would be ruthless about employing even children to work in mines and factories; workers could be exploited and made to work long hours, and sacked when they were no longer needed.

Nowadays it is expected that employers will provide satisfactory working conditions and that workers – who after all are the ones directly adding value to provide products or services – will be safe and fairly rewarded. It is illegal to employ children, and there is a minimum wage. In modern business, the needs of employees must be taken into account by managers.

## Customers

If you have a favourite takeaway, it becomes an important issue to you if the business is suddenly sold. The regular customers of any business can be assumed to be satisfied with the service they receive. They are stakeholders in the business because they hope to continue to be satisfied.

In many industrial markets, this relationship can be very important. The existence of one business can be affected by the success or performance of another; if one significant firm fails, or takes dramatic decisions about strategy, a whole network of other firms, especially suppliers, are affected. In each market there can be a chain of businesses relating to each other as customers. The decisions of one can have a major impact on the others.

### Practice point

Research the 2005 collapse of Rover at Longbridge. Write a clear set of notes describing the ways in which various stakeholder groups were affected. Pay particular attention to the suppliers and distributors.

## Local and national communities

Business activity occurs within a community, and it is important that the local population is considered in major business decisions. Many firms adopt a specific company mission to do 'good work' in the community – Procter and Gamble is an example. This is in part why public relations is such a key feature of business.

Many businesses are of national importance and their activities become of crucial significance to communities. Tesco, for example, is a powerful presence in any community; it can have an influence in many ways. Issues such as traffic, new buildings, employment, and the impact on established businesses are all important considerations.

Sometimes a business or a government agency takes a strategic decision that has an effect on the natural environment. A common example might be where a business park is developed. Some derelict land might be put to effective use, jobs might be created and building firms get work. These are good things for the people who benefit. However, in the background there may be other consequences: open space is lost, wildlife loses a habitat and some plant species are destroyed. The natural environment – plants, trees, wildlife — can suffer as soon as human beings intervene.

The whole world is a global community. We all have a stake in the well-being of our planet. When natural disasters occur, such as the 2004 Indian Ocean tsunami, or hurricanes Katrina and Rita in 2005 on the US Gulf Coast, business concerns are placed in perspective. The world seems – temporarily at least – to come together. We can quickly realise how much we all have in common.

## Bankers, stock markets and financial commentators

Public companies are listed on the stock exchange and attract investment from wealthy individuals and professional investors, such as insurance companies or pension funds. These groups and individuals constantly monitor the performance of companies and entire markets. They sell shares in companies that are expected to do less well (because their value might fall) and buy shares in companies that are expected to do better (because their value is expected to rise).

Financial commentators can have a big influence on what people or investment professionals do. The expert opinion of the banks, markets and commentators can sway the stock markets one way or another.

## Outcome activity 26.1

### Pass

Identify and describe possible ethical dilemmas resulting from the pursuit of business aims by a selected organisation.

Select and research a specific business case. There are many issues you could identify: businesses relocating call-centre work abroad; retailers selling clothes manufactured by cheap labour abroad; a firm's activities harming the natural environment. While it is not a specified part of the assessment, it is a good idea to make your work local and topical.

### Merit

Using examples, analyse reasons why the pursuit of business aims by a selected organisation may result in ethical dilemmas.

In your sample case you need to consider the many ways in which a businesses strategy might impact on people or communities at home and overseas. Think globally and be clear about the impact of a policy of profit maximisation.

### Distinction

Using examples, evaluate the consequences for stakeholders of business activity.

You might take each category of stakeholder in your chosen business and offer your own views about the degree of impact upon their interests. Some may be winners and others losers. How?

# *Ethical consequences of business activity for employees*

## Implications of cost reduction

In the twenty-first century the world is dominated by **capitalism**. After a century of disagreement (almost leading to war between the eastern and western blocs of countries) about the fairness of *private* capitalist enterprise, the world seems now to be broadly accepting that this is the most effective way to produce what we need.

Capitalism, however, has many in-built tensions and inequalities. A capitalist world economy consists of private companies (owned by private shareholders) that are under pressure to compete and make profits. Professional managers are judged by their firm's profits.

The biggest and richest private businesses are controlled from only a few wealthy countries and they tend to be constantly looking for ways of cutting costs. They are doing this, increasingly, on a global scale.

Because securing a labour force is a serious cost for any firm, business leaders the world over naturally look for ways of reducing labour costs, and some of these ways can be unethical. National governments, and economic and political blocs such as the **European Union** and the **United Nations**, have all therefore enacted laws and codes to attempt to control employers of human labour.

The United Nations Declaration of Human Rights was first produced in 1948, soon after the Second World War. All over the world at that time there was an intense desire to create a better world, based on fairness and justice. Part of the declaration covered the question of paid employment.

> **Article 23 of UN Declaration of Human Rights**
>
> (1) Everyone has the right to work, to free choice of employment, to just and favourable conditions of work and to protection against unemployment.
>
> (2) Everyone, without any discrimination, has the right to equal pay for equal work.
>
> (3) Everyone who works has the right to just and favourable remuneration (pay) ensuring for himself and his family an existence worthy of human dignity, and supplemented (added to), if necessary, by other means of social protection.
>
> (4) Everyone has the right to form and join trade unions for the protection of his interests.

There are several serious ethical questions about employment and protection of workers. The following issues should be considered on a global scale. All relate to possibly unethical cost-cutting practices in business organisations.

### Child labour

UNICEF, the UN child welfare agency, has said that globally 352 million children between five and seventeen are engaged in some kind of employment, with 97% of all working children employed in developing countries, many in forced labour and extremely bad conditions.

Children continue to be forced into work because they are a cheap source of labour and in some cases a child's work can make the difference between survival or starvation for his or her family.

Poverty is therefore the root cause of child exploitation. In the 43 countries with an average family income of US$500 or less per person, child labour runs at 30–60%; where average income is between US$500 and US$1,000, the figure falls to between 10% and 30% of all children.

## Case study — 'Make Poverty History' wristbands

Pop stars, footballers and politicians, including Prime Minister Tony Blair, have been seen wearing wristbands promoting the 'Make Poverty History' campaign. Made in fabric or silicon, they cost £1, of which 70 pence went to the charities involved, and hundreds of thousands were sold. Reports in May 2005 showed, however, that the Chinese factories making the silicon versions fell woefully short of ethical standards. A report on the Tat Shing Rubber Manufacturing Company in Shenzhen accused it of using 'forced labour' by taking financial deposits from new employees.

The audit also showed 'weaknesses' including poor health and safety provision, long hours, a seven-day week, workers cheated out of pay, inadequate insurance, no rights to annual leave and no right of freedom of association.

The report on the Fuzhou Xing Chun Trade Company found that some workers were paid as little as 9 pence an hour; overtime was worked beyond the legal limit, there was no paid annual leave and no guarantee of a day off each week.

1 What was the purpose of the wristbands?
2 What if anything could be done to minimise the PR damage caused by the Chinese workers scandal?

*Child labour is a global issue*

## Low pay

For a worker making clothes for Nike, Adidas and Gap in a hot, dirty factory in Thailand, the pay for an eight-hour day can be as low as £2.80. Eleven-hour days are considered normal. In China, garment workers earn between 13 and 22 pence per hour. Is low pay a problem?

We have already seen that Article 23 of the UN Declaration of Human Rights refers to the right of all workers to a rate of pay that ensures a level of 'human dignity'. However, 57 years after the declaration there is still a huge problem of low pay within the UK as well as across the world. **Multinationals** work in several countries and

### Thinking point

Multinational corporations setting up in low-wage economies pay wages on average twice that of local businesses. US multinationals have the reputation of paying most.

What do you think about multinationals setting up in poorer countries? Are the multinationals a good thing for a local population?

can relocate just about anywhere. Many are relocating at least part of their work to cheap labour areas to save costs.

In the UK, there are national minimum wage rates. 'Low pay' is defined in relation to these rates. However, low pay in the UK remains a problem, with several groups of workers falling into this category. The latest available figures showed 5.4 million (23.2% of all employees) earn low pay.

Women in the UK tend to suffer low pay more than men; working mothers even more so. Of the 5.4 million low-paid workers, 3.2 million were women. Low pay is a recognised problem addressed by government action in the UK. People who fall into poverty because of low pay can seek state help in the form of income support and tax benefits.

## Duty of care over health and safety

The International Labour Organisation, an agency of the United Nations consisting of employers, governments and unions, asserts that globally there is one death every 15 seconds – 6,000 a day – at work, and almost 270 million accidents at work are recorded each year.

Employers the world over have immense responsibility for worker health and safety. Do they take this as seriously as they should in relation to profits?

Health and safety law in the UK places joint responsibility onto both employers and employees. Employees (staff) must be informed by management about their health and safety responsibilities. This includes basic things such as the location of fire exits, provision of first aid, and procedures and safe practices in carrying out all duties. Induction and ongoing training will be the basis of this.

An employer carries a major responsibility to ensure the safety and health of employees and this can be a costly task. Employers are expected to give full and proper training to staff and to maintain equipment. Failure to do so can lead to horrific accidents.

There are many risk factors in all industries and managers are expected to carry out risk assessment on a regular basis so that they are aware of and can address any dangers. Employers are also required to arrange any training necessary for health and safety reasons, and to ensure adequate maintenance of plant and equipment. A particular concern is work involving hazardous materials.

### Hazardous materials

Some workers have to work with radioactive materials. Radioactivity is an invisible, silent, odourless but deadly form of contamination that can cause several forms of cancer and deformity in all living things. Protective clothing is essential when handling radioactive material, and great care must be taken in waste disposal. In all workplaces where radioactivity is present, even in small doses, contamination must be monitored. In cases where foodstuffs are possibly subjected to contamination, there are several sets of EU regulations to be complied with.

Asbestos was thought to be an excellent fireproof construction material in the 1950s and 1960s, and used extensively for insulation. It is estimated that there is up to 6 million tonnes of asbestos in schools, hospitals, offices, factories and ships.

It is now known that asbestos has been a hidden killer for years. Around 5,000 people die each year from asbestos-related cancers.

Today, many construction workers remain exposed to asbestos in their work and it is the duty of their employer to make sure that workers

*People wearing protective clothing for work.*

are issued with appropriate warnings and protective clothing.

### Protective clothing

On your way to college or school today you may well have seen workers employed on highway maintenance work, school crossing patrols or street cleaners. These people will probably have been wearing fluorescent jackets or coats so that they can be seen easily by drivers.

This is a simple example of the personal protective equipment that employers are expected to provide for their staff. Failure to do so may save money in the short term but will be a very costly mistake if an incident occurs that could have been avoided. Footwear, helmets, waistcoats, jackets, masks, goggles and earmuffs are examples of other equipment that employers must make available under the Personal Protective Equipment at Work Regulations (1992).

### EU working time directive

EU directives tell member states that they must implement law in a particular area. The 1993 Directive 93/104/EC is the **working time**

**directive** and it lays down provisions for a maximum 48-hour working week (including overtime), rest periods and breaks, and a minimum of four weeks' paid leave per year for employees.

The working time directive was introduced because the link between long working hours and health and safety problems was clear. Long hours lead to tiredness and tiredness leads to accidents.

The UK government, however, negotiated an 'opt-out' from the working time directive by introducing the following conditions:

● the worker can agree to work more than 48 hours (but must not be disadvantaged for deciding not to do so)

● the employer must keep records of all workers who carry out such work

● records must be made available to the authorities on request.

Employers must still provide adequate facilities for rest breaks, as specified in the directive.

In 2005, the EU voted to stop this opt-out from the working time directive. The UK is the only member state where working time has increased over the past decade.

**Thinking point**

The UK government is trying to ensure that UK employers have some flexibility within the EU working time directive. Investigate the UK position on this. Describe it and write about your own views. (For a useful starting point on this, see *www.guardian.co.uk/business*.)

## Abuse of workplace power

People in paid employment receive pay and benefits in return for their labour. These must be clearly laid out in contracts of employment (described below). Work is rarely done purely for fun; it is essential to earn a living for one's family.

People need their jobs, and they spend a good deal of their life at work. Employers are therefore in a position of power in relation to workers. This power needs to be exercised with responsibility.

In the UK, the government has established certain key laws in this area, generally known as 'employment law'. Several important aspects of employment law were outlined in Unit 5: Business Enterprise (page 211) in *BTEC National Business*.

The contract of employment outlines an employee's basic entitlements. The law states that a new employee must receive a written statement (the contract) informing him or her of the main terms of employment within two months of starting work. The contract must show the hours of work, method of payment, sick pay arrangements, pension rights, grievance procedure, job title and holiday pay. Sadly, some employers abuse this requirement, either by not issuing employment contracts to staff, or by simply ignoring their terms. Trade unions exist to help support staff in protecting their rights.

Despite the existence of laws on employee rights, it is still possible for some employers to abuse their position of power over an employee. Employees are entitled to be free from **harassment** at work; they should also be free from **discrimination**, unfair treatment and any kind of bullying. For example, workers should not be forced to work excessive unpaid overtime.

Harassment can take many forms and can leave staff feeling anxious and fearful in their workplace. The most typical and common form of harassment is where a woman suffers unwanted sexual advances from male bosses. Discrimination is a different matter but can flow on from harassment.

A person suffers discrimination if he or she is treated less favourably on grounds that have nothing to do with the job. The following case study illustrates this perfectly.

## Case study    Discrimination

The Equal Opportunities Commission investigated the case of Mrs W, a human resources manager working for a firm called Gefco (UK) Ltd. One day she learned that part of her job was being taken from her and given to a French national, Mr R, despite the fact that he had neither the experience nor the training to compare with Mrs W.

Mrs W claimed that she was being discriminated against on grounds of both her sex and her nationality. The holding company of Gefco (UK) Ltd was appointing more French people to the company for its own reasons.

Mrs W resigned as a result, and an employment tribunal agreed that she had been discriminated against because of her nationality. Had Mr R not been French he would not have been given the job role.

The tribunal did not, however, agree that Mrs W had been discriminated against on the grounds of her sex. The selection of Mr R had been purely because of his French nationality, not his gender.

Mrs W won her case of unfair dismissal.

1 Why do you think that the tribunal judged that Mrs W had been discriminated against on the grounds of her nationality but not her gender?
2 Research a case in which the Equal Opportunities Commission has found gender discrimination to be taking place.

Another form of discrimination can occur through the application of discriminatory benefits. An employer might base a payment structure upon age, for example paying anyone under 21 less, regardless of the job, or alternatively paying anyone over 50 less. People in the middle age bracket automatically receive more. This might happen because of labour market conditions. In some cases, an employer might choose to withdraw medical or life insurance for employees after a certain age. Once again, EU directives require governments to take action on such discrimination.

Discrimination by employers on grounds of ethnic background, religion, disability or sex are all illegal. In some countries – Kenya has been identified as a problem area – compulsory pregnancy testing of female employees by employers has been seen. Consumer pressure organisations are trying to highlight where this practice is going on.

### Duty of care

Employers have a 'duty of care' towards employees, and the law expects them to protect vulnerable people. This includes those who might encounter hazards of any sort in their work, as well as those who might suffer from a disability or a medical condition such as HIV/AIDS. Employers have to constantly monitor the work environment with risk assessment in mind. For many managers, these are costly and time-consuming distractions.

### Thinking point

George, the owner of a successful fish and chip shop, employs eight people doing a range of jobs from selling at the counter to cutting fish and cleaning.

George is visited by an officer from the local authority, who informs him about the latest health and safety regulations covering storage of foodstuffs, cleanliness and staff safety.

'These regulations are ridiculous!', George says. 'Are you serious? Am I supposed to do all this and still make a profit?'

In response to George's comment, outline an ethical case for government regulations supporting staff interests.

### Corporate manslaughter

An individual can be held to have committed manslaughter if he or she causes the death of another person through gross negligence. **Corporate manslaughter** is a crime that can be committed by a company (a corporation) responsible for a work-related death.

## Case study    Corporate manslaughter

A company was employed by a port authority to load and unload cargo from ships. The unloading process involved the use of cranes that lowered mechanical 'grabs' into the holds of vessels to pick up material.

The managing director of the company had agreed with his supervisors that these grabs could be modified to use metal chains which would help speed up the process. These chains, however, had to be manipulated by a worker standing under the grab in the hold of the ship, who located them on cargoes.

A temporary worker beginning his first morning's work in the hold was given only brief instructions about what to do and about safety procedures. Tragically, when he was standing under the grab and attempting to place the metal chains, the grab suddenly closed on him and he was killed instantly.

Efforts to save time and increase the efficiency of the loading and unloading process had unwittingly caused the death of an employee.

1 Do you think the managing director was guilty of gross negligence?
2 Could the managing director blame the crane operator, by saying it was not management's fault if an operator made a mistake?

### Membership of trade unions

Employees have more power when they act as a group. Some employers make it hard for staff to join a trade union, however, believing that unions are disruptive and restrictive.

In the UK the law gives workers the right to be union members – if a majority of workers want union rights and vote for this in a ballot, employers have to recognise the union. The United Nations Declaration of Human Rights, mentioned earlier, also reinforces workers' rights to collective union representation (see *www.tuc.org.uk*).

## Practice point

From a newspaper or Internet search, find an example in which a trade union has attempted to intervene in a dispute where employer abuse of workplace power has been alleged.

Make a written summary, then verbally describe this case to another member of your group, explaining how the abuse of power might have occurred.

## Response of employees

There are a number of steps that can be taken by employees of businesses where the owners or management engage in unethical practices:

- **Non-co-operation** – members of staff may simply refuse to go along with something that they regard as ethically questionable. This can range from relatively small-scale issues such as refusing to participate in a discriminatory selection process, to serious matters such as an attempt to cover up a major environmental incident.

- **'Whistleblowing'** – the Public Interest Disclosures Act, 1998, made it an offence to discipline anyone who made a disclosure about something that was in the 'public interest'. This is called 'whistleblowing', because it involves alerting everyone to something that is wrong.

- **Pressure group participation** – workers are always free to campaign alongside one of the many organised groups that exert pressure on governments and industries, such as Friends of the Earth or Greenpeace.

- **Litigation** – employees can take action in the courts, which is known as litigation.

- **Involving investigative journalists** – the press or TV journalists will often take an interest in something that is wrong, and are guaranteed to raise publicity if there is a genuine story to be told.

- **Sabotage** – this means destroying or damaging something. Responses that amount to sabotage could be said to be unethical in themselves, and place a worker in a poor legal position.

## Incentives to adopt ethically questionable practices

There is a danger that employees who are a party to ethically questionable activities at work might be put under pressure to keep quiet and to go along with what is happening. Workers want to keep their jobs, and most staff wish to succeed and gain favour from managers. There are intense pressures on staff, sometimes creating dilemmas between loyalty to an employer and loyalty to some possibly vaguer notion of the 'public interest'.

Bribes could be offered to them in the form of promotion, extra cash, or better conditions. All of this involves dishonesty and possible non-disclosure of information.

### Defamation

**Defamation** is a legal term for what happens when a person's reputation is damaged in the eyes of other people. In a case where defamatory statements are written down, libel is committed; where they are verbal comments, this is called slander.

A ruthless employer might defame an individual because he or she has refused to go along with something that is questionable. The difficulty is in proving to a court that an individual had a good reputation in the first place, and that the defamatory statements are untrue.

# *Ethical consequences of business activity for consumers*

## Supply of products and services

As consumers we are the ones who use the services or products that result from business activity. Is it acceptable that some of the products we are invited to consume, or services we are encouraged to use, can *kill* us? Do we need protection? Over the years businesses all over the world have occasionally supplied goods and services that were a direct danger to users and consumers, or indulged in practices that were harmful to consumers. It is possible to divide these areas into various categories, as discussed below.

## Cigarettes and alcohol

Cigarettes and alcohol are the two obvious but very serious cases where companies make huge profits but consumers suffer directly as a result. According to Cancer Research UK, every day 450 children in the UK start to smoke; by the age of 11, one third of children have experimented with smoking. Since the 1980s, girls have been more likely to smoke than boys.

Advertising tobacco is known to encourage children to smoke and in the UK direct cigarette advertising is banned. However, across the world the tobacco companies are known to target youngsters, especially in developing countries. Messages linking smoking with independence, rebellion, self-expression, freedom and confidence are all deliberately directed at children.

### Thinking point

Surveys show that approximately 60% of smokers start by the age of 13 and 90% start before the age of 20. This is the paradox of the cigarette industry – it is both socially and legally unacceptable to advertise to teenagers and children, yet it is to this age group that cigarette manufacturers have to advertise in order to survive.

1 What do you feel are the consequences of cigarette advertising for consumers?

2 Is there a conflict between banning smoking and personal freedom?

The brewing industry is huge, and several companies make massive profits from the sale of alcohol in many forms. On a global scale there is growing harmonisation of markets and media. These shape young people's views and perceptions. Youngsters now see drinking as socially acceptable and they increasingly have more disposable income, so there are greater opportunities for youngsters to experiment with alcohol.

### Practice point

In pairs, create a table showing the different kinds of businesses that are involved in selling and distributing alcohol. Show as many different sectors as you can.

Is there a cost of youth drinking to society? What causes this cost?

So called 'binge drinking' among teenagers and young adults often leads to violence and anti-social behaviour. Meanwhile brewers, pub chains and nightclubs make businesses more successful by opening for longer and promoting 'happy hours' that encourage binge consumption of alcohol.

### Practice point

Organise your class into two groups. Prepare a discussion or debate on the proposition: 'Alcohol is bad for young people and those around them; businesses are wrong to sell it to them.'

One group should prepare a case for this statement, and the other against.

Drinking and smoking could be said to be a question of personal choice. Perhaps people should be free to kill themselves if they want to! Sometimes, however, businesses do things that cause death and injury to completely innocent consumers.

## Deception and suppression of information

It is in the interests of some businesses, indeed some entire industries, to try to keep consumers in ignorance of the true nature of their products. It is one thing to agree to include a large panel on the side of a cigarette packet announcing that 'Smoking kills', and another to ensure that people know exactly *how* it kills. Do young people know, for instance, that tobacco is one of the most addictive of drugs, and what this means? The question of choice does not arise once a person becomes addicted to tobacco. This is why 69% of smokers say they would like to quit, but can't.

Another modern form of deception is the claim made by many food manufacturers that their products promote health. They claim that if you eat this or drink that, you will be fit and healthy.

**Practice point**

In groups, identify at least three products that are marketed as promoting good health, or which claim to contain ingredients that are 'good for you'.

What are your views about this? Are these claims well founded?

### 'Gas-guzzling' cars and aircraft

One question that often exercises the minds of motor manufacturers and motoring writers is the issue of how much fuel vehicles use. Not only are 'gas guzzlers' expensive to the individual pocket, they are harmful to the planet.

The ever-increasing numbers of aircraft in the skies is another huge source of pollution. How much do we have a right to travel by air anywhere in the world?

### Dangerous products and services

We rely on service providers to ensure that the services offered are managed with safety, as well as efficiency, in mind. With transport services there is an obvious requirement that people and goods are moved safely, so that they arrive at their destinations intact. People also expect to be transported in reasonable comfort. Sadly, over the years there have been tragic instances where business organisations have failed to balance efficiency with safety.

Another classic example of cutting corners on product safety in order to save time and money was the 1960s American case involving the Ford Motor Company. It designed and produced the Ford Pinto in 18 months. This vehicle was designed to be cheap and lightweight; suitable for mass production.

**Case study    Paddington and Clapham rail disasters**

On Tuesday 5 October 1999, the 6.03 am Intercity express smashed into the 8.06 am Thames commuter service at Paddington, causing a raging inferno in which 40 people died and dozens more were seriously injured.

Investigations into the accident pointed clearly to the fact that Railtrack, the private company responsible for selling track paths to train companies, was fully aware that there were many places where signals were in need of maintenance and improvements. Because the company was driven primarily by the profit motive, it was unwilling or unable to devote time and money to improvements that would have ensured the safety of passengers.

It is known that there are several ways in which private companies involved in the railways have felt forced to cut costs, including cutting down on driver training and putting inexperienced drivers in charge of trains.

In 1988, long before the Paddington crash, 35 people were killed in a rail accident at Clapham. The investigation into this incident found that major investment was required to install an automatic train protection system (ATP) that would prevent such collisions occurring. This would, however, cost an estimated £380 million and as the millennium year approached the private companies involved in the railway industry had still not committed themselves to investing in safety.

1 Investigate the meaning of the term 'privatisation' in relation to the UK railways.
2 Find out and describe the overall structure of the railway industry.
3 State your views as to whether this structure might have reduced rail safety.

## Case study | The *Herald of Free Enterprise*

*Commercial pressures can cause tragic mistakes, as in the case of the Herald of Free Enterprise in 1987*

The *Herald of Free Enterprise* was a roll-on roll-off ferry operated by P&O European Ferries. On 6 March 1987, it sailed some way out of the Belgian port of Zeebrugge with its bow doors left open, allowing sea water to flood the lower deck. The ferry capsized with the loss of 190 lives.

The captain and his crew were under tremendous pressure to meet tight turnaround times, and had hurried the vehicle-loading process, with tragic consequences.

P&O was charged with corporate manslaughter (see page 182) and although the case collapsed, a new set of safety regulations was put in place enforcing better ferry-loading procedures.

1 What kinds of commercial pressures would cause the type of accident that occurred at Zeebrugge?
2 Are there any other industries where you feel commercial pressures for profit and efficiency might cause problems with public safety?

When the car was tested it soon became clear that it was likely to become a firetrap in the event of a rear-end collision at more than 40 mph. The petrol tank often exploded and the rear doors tended to jam closed. There was no doubt that the vehicle was highly dangerous.

Questions of safety were not high on the list of Ford's priorities, however. Market considerations such as cheapness, lightness, economy, and ease of manufacture were what mattered.

### The social acceptability of products and services

The concept of the free market means that private enterprise can respond to the demands of consumers by offering to the market the goods and services that are wanted. The problem with this is that some of these goods and services are clearly not in the general interests of consumers. The government is then forced to step in and introduce regulation.

Social acceptability revolves around the question of what is *generally* acceptable. There are many examples of products and services that are acceptable to some, but cause offence to others. These include pornography, gambling and prostitution.

## Product liability

Sometimes it may be in the interests of businesses to cut corners in manufacture or save on costs associated with safety or cleanliness. However, in the UK there are clear regulations associated with bringing products to market.

If a business manufactures or sells a product that causes harm to the consumer, the Consumer Protection Act 1987 and EU regulations place strict **product liability** on it. Local authority Trading Standards officers have day-to-day powers to enforce safety laws. Fines of up to £5,000 or a prison term of up to six months can be imposed.

The laws on product safety cover a whole range of goods – everything from food products to toys must be safe. Attempts on the part of a manufacturer to suppress information about products or even to actively deceive the public can be dangerous, but sadly there is real tension in some cases between commercial survival and the public's well-being.

### Practice point

Investigate the role of your local Trading Standards office and create an informative leaflet explaining its work.

## Financial advice

The debt of the typical UK family today is so high that about a quarter of families have debts they cannot afford to repay. Businesses that prey on indebted people by offering expensive loans that only serve to get them into deeper financial trouble are increasingly subjected to scrutiny.

Financial advice given several years ago caused many people to invest in mortgage endowment schemes that have failed to bring the expected returns. For these reasons, financial services have increasingly become regulated.

## Pharmaceuticals

Anti-retrovirals are powerful anti-AIDS drugs that are a major help in combating the HIV/AIDS virus. They can extend the life of HIV-positive patients by many years. The drugs companies have been under intense pressure for some time to provide these drugs at heavily discounted prices, or even free, to poor African and Eastern European nations that have been badly affected by HIV.

But this diversion of drugs towards those areas of the world where they are most badly needed has been hampered by some companies that have re-imported them back into Europe and tried to re-sell them at massive profit. The market for these drugs has become highly valuable.

### Case study

Warwick-based pharmaceutical company Dowelhurst supplied the NHS with anti-retroviral drugs meant for Africa. GlaxoSmithKline said it had earmarked the batch of drugs for countries such as Senegal, the Democratic Republic of Congo and Chad, but some came back into the UK via Switzerland.

The company took legal action, claiming Dowelhurst must have known the drugs were meant for charities in Africa because of the cheap price it had paid. Dowelhurst would not comment, but during the court case it conceded that the Swiss trader from whom it bought the drugs, Claude Horn, was not licensed to sell them in the EU. The firm said it did not realise that at the time. It also strenuously denied it ever suspected the drugs were meant for Africa, saying it had paid normal market prices for them.

1 What is the case for earmarking ant-retrovirals for countries such as Senegal, the Congo or Chad?
2 Do the companies doing so have anything to gain? How would you argue that this is a good thing for the industry?

# Promotional communication and sales activity

## Targeting children in advertising

Both the tobacco and alcohol industries are accused of investing millions in targeting specific groups, including children. The Independent Television Commission (ITC) in the UK restricts adverts that take advantage of children. There are rules on transmission time for advertisements for alcohol, medicines and slimming products so that children should not be influenced.

Since restrictions curtail direct advertising of cigarettes in Britain, the tobacco companies seem to target developing nations. Both alcohol and tobacco are promoted in such a way that children are encouraged to regard these products as desirable. Research by the ITC has shown clearly that children are heavily influenced by adverts that are shown in conjunction with their favourite programmes.

### Thinking point

1 In Greece, adverts for children's toys are banned between 7 am and 10 pm and there is a total ban on all war toys. Should this be the case in the UK?

2 Work in a small team and research the promotion of alcohol. Write a joint statement saying what you think the message of advertisements is. Create an alternative advert of your own which is designed to deliver a different message about the effects of alcohol.

It's not just the obvious cases of cigarettes and alcohol that cause concern. The promotion of certain kinds of foodstuff to children is now causing widespread condemnation. The reasons are related to children's general health, fitness and dental hygiene.

The TV chef Jamie Oliver recently played a big part in raising awareness of the need for healthier food in children's diets. Yet, on prime-time television and elsewhere, companies continue to promote junk food for commercial gain.

Many breakfast cereals are marketed to children by using popular cartoon characters and to parents by emphasising health benefits. However, many of the most popular breakfast cereals are coated in sugar – damaging for teeth and harmful to long-term health. A Which? report in March 2004 ('Cereal Offenders') found that 85% of the breakfast cereals surveyed contained 'a lot' of sugar and 40% contained 'a lot' of salt. The Food Standards Agency called for the industry to reduce these levels.

## Direct marketing

How many times have you seen people open envelopes containing glossy leaflets only to throw them straight in the bin? Have you ever been irritated when you are on-line by constant pop-ups on your screen? Is your e-mail in-box clogged by junk mail or 'spam'? These are all examples of direct marketing and the sending of unsolicited information.

Many firms make use of call centres that directly target potential customers by making random calls inviting consumers to take up offers such as insurance, or changing their bank account or utility provider. The firm does not promote to everyone at once; it targets us as individuals.

## Taste and decency

In an increasingly global world, advertisers sometimes cross the boundaries of good taste and offend people. Different countries and even different regions within the same country have cultural variations, and what is considered acceptable in one place might not be so in another. This makes global advertising a potentially tricky business.

The Internet has offered a huge business opportunity for many people and organisations. The 'dot.com' crash of the 1990s burst the bubble of many purely Internet-based business ideas, but what has emerged is a healthy on-line world consisting of numerous well-established 'clicks-and-mortar' businesses capable of working both on-line and off-line. Questions of taste and decency arise quite strongly in the on-line world; Internet pornography is a huge source of business activity.

### Gambling

Lotteries, scratchcards, slot machines, casinos, greyhound and horse racing, bingo, football pools ... the list could go on; there are many, many ways in which people can gamble today. With modern technology, people can take part in each of these activities from the comfort of their own homes, through the Internet or interactive television, or just by picking up the telephone. Approximately 76% of men and 68% of women gambled in the past year. Amazingly, 75% of teenagers gamble.

In 1998 Sue Fisher conducted a survey of 12–15-year-olds and published the following figures:

- 75% played slot machines
- 47% played National Lottery scratchcards
- 40% played the National Lottery draw
- 7% had been illegally sold tickets
- 5% showed signs of gambling addiction.

(See *www.gamcare.org.uk*.)

Gambling can become a 'hidden' addiction that shows no physical symptoms. Individuals and families can suffer, yet the industry makes huge profits and gambling is promoted as socially acceptable and fun.

### Thinking point

Should the National Lottery be freely advertised so that people as young as 16 are encouraged to take up gambling?

### Aggressive selling

The traditional view of a business offering something for sale is that the offer is made available and the consumer is the one who chooses to make a move. As consumers, we like to feel we control the purchasing situation – we don't go into a furniture shop unless we are considering buying furniture.

However, in competitive markets aggressive selling by some businesses has become a problem.

Aggressive selling occurs where businesses approach potential consumers and push their products. This is occurring more frequently than ever; as mentioned before, many companies now employ staff to make telephone calls inviting people to sign up for a product. Very rarely in such situations does the consumer get the chance to make a reasoned decision based on the full information.

### Thinking point

'It is the essence of a free economy that consumers make a choice based on comparisons between the offers of different businesses. This is competition. Aggressive selling is diminishing this freedom and should be outlawed.'

Do you agree with this statement? Why?

## Ethical awareness as a USP

In today's business world many ethical questions are held to be so important that they are paraded in mission statements and even in some cases used as a USP – a unique selling proposition that will make people want to buy from the business. This new, ethically aware consumer market has become a niche area that can be targeted by progressive businesses.

Two examples of businesses that have specialised in ethical awareness are the Body Shop and the Co-operative Bank.

### Practice point

Research the Body Shop and the Co-operative Bank. In what ways do these two businesses use ethical awareness as a selling point? Describe with examples how they do this. Do you feel this is successful?

Another area in which consumers can choose to buy 'ethically' is by buying 'fair trade' products. A range of such products is available.

**Practice point**

Access the Fairtrade Foundation website at *www.fairtrade.org.uk*. Make a list of FAIRTRADE Mark products. In pairs, select two products each and make a verbal presentation about them and the work of the Fairtrade Foundation.

Guarantees a **better deal** for Third World Producers

FAIRTRADE ®

## Societal marketing

Marketing, as you know, is about a business satisfying consumer (or market) needs and wants. Traditionally, businesses have aimed for profit maximisation; they have sought to increase sales, broaden market share and extend their reach within markets. Some definitions of marketing highlight these priorities and speak of the marketing process as being primarily aimed at sales and profit. But Philip Kotler, one of the world's most respected marketing academics, has said that modern marketing involves satisfying not only a company's *commercial* needs, but the wider needs of society too.

**Practice point**

In what ways do you think a business can operate successfully, but at the same time take account of the wider needs of society?

Can you think of an example local to you?

**Outcome activity 26.3**

**Pass**

Identify and describe the ethical consequences of business activity for the consumers of a selected organisation's products or services.

You might find an enjoyable way to do this by researching local press stories. Are there any local issues where people have been affected by the work of a particular business or industry?

If you feel it is better to choose a more global issue, you could create an imaginary news story yourself and include visual displays to show how each issue has consequences for various people.

# Ethical consequences of business activity for other stakeholders

We saw earlier that many people and groups can be stakeholders in businesses, not just those directly involved in the company. The actions of a particular business or industry can have 'ripple effects' – like a pebble thrown in a pond – that can touch many individuals, groups and communities across the globe.

## Local communities

Business activity across the world is having a dramatic effect on many local communities. Some of these are tribal peoples whose entire way of life is threatened by business corporations seeking more profit. Many others are agricultural or rural communities.

The South American Amazon Basin is a vast area, the majority of which is in Brazil. The area used to contain more than 2 million square miles of rainforest. Over the past 30 years the Brazilian government has allowed **deforestation** in order to permit industrialisation and the creation of a network of roads. This has had a serious impact on the scattered communities living there as well as the forest itself.

The same process has occurred in Africa, where commercial logging, mining, drilling and clearing for living space have all led to large areas of deforestation. Other communities have suffered in Australia.

In the Philippines, mining companies are not only granted mineral mining rights, they are also granted a logging concession allowing them to chop down trees to supply timber for pit props and sluices.

The problems associated with deforestation and mining are dramatic for local populations. Tribal groups suffer loss of land, total disruption to their way of life, loss of cultures, damage to their health and pollution of the local water supplies.

*The communities in the Amazon rainforest have experienced the impact of industrial development*

Some global corporations go some way towards involving the local populations in their corporate activities. Levi-Strauss has a training and education programme involving over 12,000 employees worldwide. The Levi-Strauss Foundation engages in local charitable causes and offers matched funding to help local people.

**Practice point**

Investigate the Levi-Strauss Foundation. What kind of support activities does it offer to assist local communities? Prepare a verbal report on this to give to another member of your group.

**Case study    Shell and the Ogoni people of Nigeria**

In June 2001, the Shell oil pipeline that passes through the Baraale community of the Ogoni people ruptured and started spilling crude oil into nearby forests, farmlands and houses. As reported by the Environmental Rights Action group in Nigeria, Aseme Mbani, chief of the community, was at his farm when the pipeline ruptured. 'I saw crude oil rushing into my cassava farm. Then I went to the pipeline and I saw where it was leaking.' The oil flowed into people's houses and they had to be abandoned.

The chief of the community said he took steps to ensure that Shell repaired the ruptured pipeline. 'I reported the matter to the Shell contractors in charge of the pipeline and also to the police. After that we wrote Shell a "Save Our Soul" letter. When there was no response I went to Shell. They told me they have seen the letter I wrote. They said we should suffer the spillage because we caused it. They said we have been cutting pipelines and we should reap what we sow.' Chief Mbani said the oil continued to leak and he kept repeating his visits to Shell to urge them to act fast before the situation worsened, but Shell failed to respond.

1  In what ways, if any, do you think the local people in the Ogoni community of Nigeria benefit from Shell's oil activities on their land?
2  Do you think that multinationals like Shell have a responsibility to people like the Ogoni? Why?

# The national community

Some business activities have an effect on entire national economies. One such practice is business **tax avoidance**. This is the lawful practice of arranging a company's affairs so that it pays the least possible tax, notably re-locating business activities 'offshore' in order to take advantage of reduced rates or exemptions from corporate (business) taxation. Over half of Europe's top 500 companies have some form of subsidiary located offshore. Multinational corporations can plan on a global scale to manipulate local tax regulations to their best advantage.

The opportunities offered by the Internet are considerable in this respect. There are no borders in the on-line world. It is thought that in 2001 Britain might have lost up to £10 billion in tax revenue.

If large portions of the business community succeed in avoiding tax, then the ability of the government to deliver vital public services such as health and education is diminished. This is a major concern to governments everywhere.

Illegal **tax evasion** by the business community has the same effect. The difference is that tax evasion and money-laundering schemes break the law, so authorities can pursue and take action against the businesses concerned.

Businesses may also try to influence what governments do. Multinational corporations straddle the globe and it is no exaggeration to say that national governments, even powerful ones such as the US, can be relatively powerless to interfere in their activities.

Multinationals looking to expand or relocate are a very good catch for some national governments hoping to develop their economies and create jobs. Such firms often bring subsidiaries (secondary businesses that are part of the bigger corporation).

One way of inducing a multinational to locate in a certain area is by offering 'tax holidays'. This means that the firm is given a zero rate of tax for a number of years. Other incentives can also be offered, such as subsidised training, low tariffs and cheap loans.

## Thinking point

A large US multinational is looking to locate a major operation in a foreign country. Investigate the meaning of the terms:

- tax holiday
- zero tariffs
- zero training costs.

Why do you think a government such as, say, Thailand might offer these?

'Soft loans' are another form of help offered to businesses. The banks will often not support a firm if it cannot offer security for its loan repayments. A government or a local authority, however, can offer a so-called soft loan on favourable terms to a promising business if other sources of funding have failed. The ethical question involved is whether this a good use of public money.

Some multinational businesses are given government assistance in the form of export credit guarantees in order to help them do business in foreign countries. This means that governments insure them against the risk of not being paid. Unfortunately some of these contracts are for arms to areas of the world where trouble exists. Others can be for controversial dams, mines or power stations. An additional problem is that local companies can be frozen out of contracts while these large corporations, from comparatively wealthy nations, gain profitable business. In some cases, local peoples are displaced.

### Business lobbying

In democratic societies such as Britain and the US, the government is in theory representative of everyone. All groups in society – workers, businesses of all kinds, pressure groups and voluntary societies – are entitled to have their views heard by government.

To influence government decision-makers, the business community will try to lobby politicians, so that public policies are likely to help their activities. Problems of balance arise, however, because government resources may be spent on public welfare issues such as unemployment or disability benefits, schools and hospitals in a way that is not to the advantage of certain businesses; also, a policy that helps a certain industry may not help another. For example, a public policy that favours nuclear power has a detrimental impact on the coal industry.

### Practice point

Research the work of the Confederation of British Industry (*www.cbi.org.uk*). What is this body for? Write a short summary of the work of the CBI. Give examples of how this pressure group tries to influence government policy to favour business (see the 'Policy work' link on the website).

Can you find any local examples of the business community coming together to pressurise the local council?

'Media barons' are business people who own significant portions of the national or international mass media. The most influential of them all, Rupert Murdoch, owns News Corporation, an international business worth billions, with a global reach. The ethical question is whether media barons have too much power and influence, because they can influence what is reported in the media.

### Thinking point

To what extent do you think that a media baron such as Rupert Murdoch might have too much influence? Justify your response.

## The global community and the natural environment

We can see that business and industrial activities can do direct harm to local communities and that sometimes entire countries can be harmed. However, perhaps the most serious problems of all are those to do with how our economic activities damage the planet Earth.

War, terrorism, exploitation and division were all plagues of the twentieth century. Perhaps as great a threat as all of these, however, is the threat posed to the planet we all depend on. There are now major fears about whether the Earth can sustain continued economic development. While economic development may improve the standard of life in rich countries, it can not only harm local communities but exhaust the resources of the planet.

The following sections highlight some of the major concerns.

### Global warming

While there is not universal agreement on this, the evidence is strong that our planet cannot survive ever-increasing levels of industrial development, particularly development that uses carbon dioxide-producing technology (such as the car engine, the aircraft engine, and oil burning).

- Since the start of the twentieth century, Earth's average surface temperature has increased by $1.1°$ F $(0.6°$ C).

- The twentieth century saw temperature increases greater than the previous 400–600 years.

- Seven of the warmest years in the twentieth century were in the 1990s.

This is what we know as 'global warming', and the effects are:

- mountain glaciers all over the world are melting

- the Arctic ice pack has lost about 40% of its thickness in the past 40 years

- global sea levels have risen three times faster over the past 100 years than over the previous 3,000 years

- plants and animals are changing their range and behaviours in response to climate change.

*Global warming is part of significant climate change that has taken place over the past 50 years*

It is now widely felt that most of the global warming that has taken place over the past 50 years has been caused by human activity. The emissions of carbon dioxide into the Earth's atmosphere, from petrol engines, oil burning and coal burning among other industrial activities, have a caused a 'greenhouse effect' that effectively warms the Earth's surface. A barrier is formed by these gases that prevents the sun's rays from bouncing back from the Earth.

All of this is causing potentially significant climate change. The Kyoto Protocol (part of a United Nations framework) was initially agreed in 2001 and the decision was made to reduce 'greenhouse gas' emissions by 5%. However, in March 2001, the US President George W. Bush, under intense pressure from US corporate lobbying – especially from the fossil fuel industry – announced that the US would not accept the protocol.

**Practice point**

Research the pressure group Greenpeace (*www.greenpeace.org.uk*). What does this group do? Create a poster display that effectively communicates some of the present worries about climate change and global warming. To what extent do you think industry has a responsibility to address these?

## Ozone depletion

The Earth is surrounded by a layer of ozone that acts as a shield protecting every living thing on the planet from the harmful effects of radiation from the sun. Skin cancers are one such harmful effect. For years scientists have known that certain products, particularly those used in refrigeration units, gave out gases (called CFCs) that damage the protective layer of ozone, leading to **ozone depletion**.

By 1986 it was realised that the ozone layer had become so seriously damaged that something had to be done. Some big firms such as Coca Cola, McDonald's and Unilever promised to phase out use of any climate-harming chemicals. The worry today is that even those chemicals that have replaced CFCs have been found to damage the ozone layer.

**Practice point**

Divide your group into three sections. Select one of the three corporations mentioned above:

- McDonald's
- Coca Cola
- Unilever.

Research what these businesses say about environmental damage to the Earth and summarise their present policies. Present your findings to the other group members.

As already mentioned, in certain parts of the world – most notably South America – huge tracts of rainforest are being cleared to make way for new forms of economic development. Deforestation is a major cause of concern because of its alleged effects on the planet's ability to maintain the protective ozone layer (see *www.rainforestconcern.org*).

## Other environmental issues

As well as these concerns, controversy also rages about such issues as genetically modified crops, and their effect on the natural environment as well as on the people who consume them; about the increase in air pollution, affecting people's health; and about dwindling fresh water supplies and the spread of tropical diseases such as malaria in the less developed nations.

Quite apart from business and industrial activities that might accelerate damage to the planet and to people's health, there are harmful business activities of other kinds that are directed towards more specific stakeholders.

## Competitors

Within particular markets, businesses are always aware of who their main competitors are. Unilever, mentioned above, is a big competitor and rival to another major multinational business, Procter and Gamble. Many of their products are in direct competition with each other.

Competition is the way the free market works. In theory, we as consumers benefit from it as businesses try to undercut the prices of their rivals and to offer greater benefits or a better service.

Problems can arise when some businesses attempt to damage a competitor by undermining the reputation of a product or a service, or to steal business secrets through **commercial espionage** (spying).

*Commercial espionage has now entered the digital age*

Aside from spying, there are several other ways in which a competing business may try to undermine the trading position of its rivals. It could attempt to:

- deceive by withholding key facts
- coerce and harass by abusing a superior trading position
- impose unfair terms of contract
- exploit other people's work
- imitate or copy a product
- distribute unfair criticisms of a business, or spread malicious rumours about it.

Some companies can go further and directly attack a rival firm by engaging in activities that affect an entire market. This can be done by dumping goods or by buying at inflated prices. Businesses can also be subjected to software attacks, in which computer 'hackers' try to gain access to systems in order to introduce harmful viruses, steal information or corrupt computer records.

## Stock markets and other business finance

The stock markets depend on full and accurate information from companies so that investors can be aware of how well a firm has been doing, what it has achieved and what it intends to do in the future. In this way, people who might wish to buy stocks in companies can base their decisions on a firm foundation.

### Case study    Gillette

In 1997, Gillette was in the process of designing and developing a new shaving system. It had sub-contracted some aspects of production to another firm, Wright Industries. An employee of Wright Industries was removed from his position as a process control engineer at Gillette's request, and then made some crucial technical drawings available to a major foreign competitor, Bic.

1 Is commercial espionage a bad thing for consumers?
2 What can businesses do to protect their commercial secrets?

The Gillette case illustrates one kind of commercial espionage, and it is well known that in this digital age, spying and surveillance can be widespread.

Because the stock markets value businesses on the basis of the published figures, there can be a real temptation for some managers or executives to indulge in what is known as **creative accounting** – manipulating figures in such a way that a company's finances look healthy so that stock values stay high.

It is a primary function of professional accountants that their audits and accounts are produced with integrity, objectivity and independence. Issues such as the way a company accounts for the depreciation of its assets, and the valuation of stock and work in progress (see Unit 10: Final Accounts) are all important to providing a fair picture of its financial position.

On a smaller scale, there are many ways in which a business may account for its finances in such a way that either responsibilities or taxes are avoided.

### Thinking point

George is a successful sole trader running a very busy and therefore profitable fish and chip shop in the north of England. He and his wife and two children decide on a short summer break at a high class hotel in Torquay on the south Devon coast.

George is lawfully entitled to claim tax relief on his business expenses. So, advised by his accountant, George finds out that a fish and chip shop in Torquay uses some high-tech frying equipment that might just be what he needs. Suddenly, the family trip to Torquay becomes a 'business journey', and George saves a good deal on the cost.

Is this good sensible business planning, or unethical accounting?

One of the effects of a company having highly valued stock might be to deter another business from launching a so-called 'predatory takeover bid'. A predator in the wild is an animal that hunts smaller creatures; in the business world, larger or more wealthy companies may attempt to buy smaller ones in unwelcome takeovers. If the stock value is high, however, the target business will simply cost too much.

There are many ways in which accounting practices can be used to alter the stock market's perception of a firm. In 2004, the Anglo-Dutch oil company Shell caused a scandal when it over-estimated its reserves of oil by a massive amount.

How a firm is valued is obviously of vital importance to potential investors and people who already hold stocks in the firm. The issue of 'insider trading' arises when senior managers, for example, trade in a company's stocks when they are in possession of information that outsiders do not have. They may sell when they are aware of factors that might cause the value to fall, or buy when they know that stocks are bound to rise. This is illegal. Other ways in which senior managers may benefit unethically from a company include situations where they buy out the company or create share repurchase schemes for personal gain.

## Regulatory bodies

Several regulatory bodies exist in order to protect the interests of stakeholder groups and prevent many of the unethical practices described in this unit. These include:

- the Financial Services Authority (*www.fsa.gov.uk*)
- the Food Standards Agency (*www.food.gov.uk*)
- the Advertising Standards Authority (*www.asa.org.uk*).

### Practice point

Investigate each of the above regulatory bodies and write a concise report saying what it tries to do.

## Influences

In an increasingly global economy, the forces of private profit are immense and they cross national boundaries and entire continents. National governments have needed to join forces and collaborate, partly to strengthen their economic position and thereby assist private corporations, and partly to create good systems of regulation that can enforce standards across wider areas.

One of the long-established features of democratic countries is the tolerance of protest and pressure groups. These groups can try to change government policies and raise public awareness of certain issues. Friends of The Earth and Greenpeace are two of the most well-known environmental pressure groups.

Single-issue groups exist to prompt action about a single cause. Action on Smoking and Health (ASH) works to combat tobacco smoking, and a counter group called FOREST (Freedom Organisation for the Right to Enjoy Smoking Tobacco) tries to argue the opposite case.

In the UK, the trade union movement exists to represent workers' interests and help to defend the rights of employees against the potentially damaging acts of employers. Most groups of workers have the opportunity to join a union dedicated to their industry or sector, and the over-

arching body, the Trades Union Congress (TUC), tries to speak for all unions.

It is part of the essence of a democratic society such as the UK that pressure groups can try to change government decisions and raise public awareness of unethical business practices.

### Practice point

Take the following categories of pressure groups and find examples of issues where they have tried to influence business leaders or government bodies:

- trade unions
- environmental groups
- single-issue groups (such as ASH).

Other influences upon business activity come from investigative journalists, including film makers as well as press and TV reporters, who are interested in exposing wrongdoing; and from lawyers who are concerned with protecting human rights and combating exploitation. All of these are part of society's defence against unethical business activity.

### Outcome activity 26.4

**Pass**

Identify and describe the ethical consequences of a selected organisation's business activity for other stakeholders concerned.

You might take a corporation such as McDonald's and examine various ethical questions. An example is the question of CFC emissions and the harm done to the Earth's ozone layer, or the question of childhood obesity. You might look at where McDonald's locates its outlets. You might even know of someone who works at a McDonald's in order to give a wider view of the effect on stakeholders.

**Merit**

Using examples, analyse ways in which relevant stakeholders may influence business behaviour.

You might search for examples of trade union activities or look at pressure groups such as Greenpeace. Say how they might have influenced business behaviour. Have the oil companies done anything differently under pressure from environmental groups?

**Distinction**

Using examples, make supported recommendations for ways in which the ethical behaviour of business organisations may be influenced.

Take some general issues such as smoking or alcohol sales to children, and suggest ways in which the business community could be persuaded to change its attitudes. One example might be to examine recent changes in the attitudes of bar owners towards 'happy hour' sales, which seem to encourage binge drinking. How have they been persuaded to change tactic?

# Key terms

**Aims**
long-term business goals

**Authority**
power given to bodies by Parliament through the law; or to individuals either by virtue of job position, expertise, qualifications or ability

**Capitalism**
the economic system based on private enterprise

**Commercial espionage**
one firm spying on another

**Corporate manslaughter**
the offence of a corporation causing death

**Creative accounting**
organising and presenting company accounts in a way that might benefit the company concerned, but relies on unethical or dishonest accounting practices

**Defamation**
damaging a person's good reputation by use of untrue comment

**Deforestation**
clearance of large areas of rainforest to allow other forms of development

**Discrimination**
treating an individual or group differently based on race, nationality, sex, age or religion

**Ethics**
questions to do with right and wrong

**European Union**
the political and economic union of 25 nation states that is subject to governance from Brussels and Strasbourg

**Harassment**
unwanted behaviour towards a person based on his or her race, nationality, sex, religion or some other factor

**Litigation**
legal action – referring a matter to a court of law

**Lobbying**
asking questions of and making demands from politicians

**Multinational**
a company with operational activities in several nations, often world-wide

**Objectives**
short to medium-term, measurable business targets (such as to achieve 2.5% growth next year)

**Organisational culture**
the collective attitudes within a business, led by management, that determine the way the organisation works

**Ozone depletion**
the thinning of the Earth's protective ozone layer

**Power**
the capacity to cause someone, or a group, to take actions they would not otherwise have done

**Pressure group**
an organised body existing to put pressure on government or business to follow certain courses of action

**Private sector**
that part of an economy that is privately owned and controlled, usually profit-seeking businesses

**Product liability**
the liability of a manufacturer for any faulty product that could cause harm

**Shareholders**
people who have a financial share in the value of a business and are therefore often entitled to a share of the profits

## Key terms

**Stakeholders**
groups or individuals with any kind of vested interest in what an organisation does

**Sustainability**
the general question of whether the Earth's natural resources can continue to keep up with economic development

**Tax avoidance**
lawfully taking steps to avoid taxation by, for example, moving a firm's location

**Tax evasion**
illegally taking measures to avoid taxation, such as deception and false accounting

**United Nations**
New York-based body representing the collective views of world nations

**Values**
things a person or organisation holds to be important

**Whistleblowing**
alerting relevant authorities or the media to malpractice within an organisation

**Working time directive**
an EU instruction to introduce a maximum 48-hour working week and rules for rest breaks

# End-of-unit test

1 Write a brief paragraph describing in your own words what you understand by the term 'business ethics'.

2 What is the difference between a shareholder and a stakeholder?

3 Take a business of your own choice, list at least four stakeholders and explain why they are stakeholders.

4 Do shareholders always demand 'maximum profit'? Would this be wise?

5 What is 'organisational culture'? Why might this be important in understanding the approach a business takes to ethical questions?

6 What is meant by the term 'values'?

7 How have the values of Body Shop founder Anita Roddick shaped the business?

8 In what ways do 'capitalist' values of profit-seeking and cost efficiencies generate ethical dilemmas?

9 In your own words, describe what the UN Declaration of Human Rights says.

10 What is meant by an employer having a 'duty of care' for staff?

11 What is the 'working time directive'?

12 What does a contract of employment do, and why is it important to an employee?

13 Outline three ways in which an aggrieved member of staff might respond to unethical activities by an employer.

14 Describe three ways in which consumers might be harmed by unethical activities of businesses.

15 Choose one business organisation that uses ethical awareness as a unique selling proposition. Describe how this is done and give your own views as to the effect.

16 What is tax evasion?

17 What is a predatory takeover?

18 What is global warming? What are alleged to be its causes and effects?

19 What is deforestation?

20 What is meant by 'sustainability'?

# Resources

## Texts

Bradburn, R: *Understanding Business Ethics*, Continuum, 2001

Hogg, C: *Internet and e-Mail Use and Abuse*, CIPD, 2000

Kotler, P: *Principles of Marketing*, Prentice Hall, 2005

Pilger, J: *Distant Voices*, Vintage, 1994

Pilger, J: *The New Rulers of the World*, Verso Books, 2002

## Websites

*www.jusbiz.org* Useful site highlighting ethical business issues

*www.ibe.org.uk* The Institute of Business Ethics

*www.AnitaRoddick.com* The Body Shop founder's personal website

*www.dti.gov.uk* The Department of Trade and Industry

*www.hse.gov.uk* The Health and Safety Executive

*www.tuc.org.uk* The Trades Union Congress

*www.fairtrade.org.uk* The Fairtrade Foundation

*www.cbi.org.uk* The Confederation of British Industry

*www.greenpeace.org.uk* Environmental pressure group website

*www.rainforestconcern.org* Single-issue pressure group website

*www.whitbread.co.uk* Whitbread, the brewing firm

*www.levistrauss.com/responsibility* Levi-Strauss social responsibility site

*www.corpwatch.org* Website keeping a watch on corporate activities globally

*www.gamcare.org.uk* Website on the perils of gambling

## Magazines

*Business Review* (published by Philip Allan)

*The Ethical Consumer* (published by SAGE Publications Ltd)

In your studies so far you have looked at the way organisations work within a business framework. All the concepts you have learned so far must, however, be set against the background of the rules of business law, which will affect the day-to-day running of any organisation. This unit describes the rules of business law and how they affect the operation of business.

The first legal concepts to be described are the requirement for valid contracts, and the way a business contract is formed. This includes what to do if something goes wrong with the contract and the remedies that might be available in law.

The rights of consumers under contract law are examined by exploring the statutory consumer protection laws that are currently in force in relation to contracts. These relate to the sale of consumer goods and the supply of other goods and services.

The section on employment legislation considers contractual issues between organisations and their employees. The different types of contracts of employment are discussed, together with the various rights employees have, such as those connected with:

- working time rules
- holiday and sick pay
- maternity and parental leave
- issues such as discrimination, unfair dismissal and redundancy.

This unit ends by considering the impact data protection legislation has on organisations, particularly the way businesses deal with various types of data and communication methods.

Throughout the unit, real scenarios from case law are described, and references for those cases can be found in the bibliography entitled 'Case references' on page 238.

Unit 27 is therefore divided into four main sections:

- 27.1 Requirements for a valid contract
- 27.2 Statutory consumer protection
- 27.3 Employment legislation
- 27.4 Data protection legislation.

# Requirements for a valid contract

Whether a business is a huge multinational concern like Microsoft, or a small local trader selling clothes from a market stall, its day-to-day existence will rely on the legal rules relating to contract. Buying goods from suppliers, selling products to consumers, and employing staff all rely on the principles of contract law.

The first thing to consider, therefore, is what is meant by the term **contract**.

## Definition of a contract

A contract is an agreement or set of promises enforceable by law, made between two or more persons, to do or refrain from doing something. In the business world it is more than a mere promise. There must be an intention to create a legally binding agreement between the parties and they must intend to give something of value as **consideration** to add value to the set of promises.

The starting point for an enforceable contract is the **offer** and **acceptance**.

Contracts can occur in many ways and in different forms in the business world. Examples could include contracts for the buying and selling of business premises, machinery or equipment, the buying and selling of products for the business, and contracts for the hiring of staff. Contracts can be for anything from the purchase of some photocopier paper to the purchase of a fleet of Boeing 747 aircraft, running into many millions of pounds. Whatever the size or value of the contract, the essential elements remain the same.

The first thing that must happen is that a person offers to be bound by a contract.

### Offers

An offer is a definite promise from one of the parties to the agreement, made with the intention that it shall become binding upon the person making it as soon as it is accepted by the person receiving.

An offer must be communicated to the other party, usually in writing (although verbal offers are still valid).

There is, however, an exception to this rule about communication. In certain situations known as 'reward cases', an offer to make a contract can be made to many people at once, or even (in theory) the whole world. The term has come from the idea that if you were to lose your dog and put cards in shop windows offering a reward for its safe return, you would be making a universal offer to any person who might accept the challenge and begin to look for the dog.

The offer must be certain and not vague, or it will be invalid. A person entering into contract negotiations must know for certain what it is that he or she is agreeing to.

### Invitations to treat

In business law there is a situation known as an 'invitation to treat'. In this sense, 'treat' means 'trade' or 'do business'. This is nothing more than an indication that a person is prepared to *receive* offers from another person. The person who makes an invitation to treat can accept or reject the offers subsequently received.

An invitation to treat can exist in many forms. The display of goods with a price ticket attached in a shop window or supermarket is not an offer for sale but an invitation to treat. The customer is invited to make an offer to buy, and this can be accepted or rejected by the seller at any time until it is accepted.

When products are displayed in advertisements, catalogues, brochures and on the Internet this will be deemed to be an invitation to treat, even if the word 'Offer' is used by sellers to promote their goods.

The company prospectus issued when a company is selling its shares is an invitation to treat, as potential investors can offer to buy the shares at a price that the directors can accept (through allocation) or reject.

At an auction, items for sale are invitations to treat. The bid is the offer, which is accepted when the auctioneer's hammer falls.

Invitations to treat can sometimes cause confusion and embarrassment when mistakes have been made about product information (usually price). This has resulted in businesses having to tell disappointed customers that their products, strangely, are 'not for sale', as although an invitation to treat has been given it cannot then be followed up.

### Case study    Amazon

In March 2003 the Amazon UK website temporarily closed after an advertisement showed a Hewlett Packard pocket personal computer, which should retail at around £200, at the amazing price of £7.32.

The website was jammed with excited customers wanting to get their hands on such bargains. Amazon refused to deliver the wrongly priced items and thousands of disappointed customers were left without their products.

From a legal point of view, the company was not obliged to sell the products at the price stated as the advertisement was considered an invitation to treat, and the company was free to reject customers' offers to buy at any time.

1  Do you think this is a fair rule?
2  Can you think of reasons why this might be the most effective approach?

### Distinguishing invitations to treat and declarations of intention

It is important to recognise at an early stage in any negotiation whether you are intending to form a contract (by making a definite offer) or whether you are merely making enquiries about the possibility of making a contract in the future (for example, an invitation to treat).

One way to do this is look at the intentions of the parties, and from their actions decide whether a definite offer had been made or whether the parties were still merely negotiating. This can be very difficult to establish and it is normally the person relying on the offer who must prove that a contractual intention was to be formed.

### Acceptance of the offer

**Acceptance** of the offer is a vital part of the formation of the contract. The normal way of accepting an offer is either in writing or by word of mouth.

The principle of acceptance is that the offer must be accepted on the same terms as it was made. One factor that will stop the offer is the existence of a **counter-offer**.

### Case study    Hyde v Wrench (1840)

On 6 June, Mr Wrench offered to sell some property to Mr Hyde for £1,000. Two days later, Mr Hyde made a new offer to buy the property at the lower price of £950. This counter-offer was rejected by Mr Wrench. Mr Hyde then said he would accept the original offer and buy the property at the price of £1,000, but Mr Wrench refused to sell.

1  Do you think Mr Wrench's original offer to sell was still valid, or had it ceased to exist?
2  Mr Hyde sued Mr Wrench for the right to buy the property at £1,000. What do you think the outcome was?

## Methods of communication

Whatever method is used to accept the offer, at some point and in some way there must be a communication to the person making the offer that it has been accepted. This must be a positive act: silence is not communication.

In the modern world, businesses use technology to imply acceptance of offers through instant communications. An offer that is accepted by telex, telephone, facsimile, electronic mail or the Internet will be deemed to have been made the moment the acceptance is made. As long as it has been communicated and received by the person making the offer, a contract will have been formed.

In Entores v Miles Far East Corporation (1955), Entores (based in London) made an offer to the Miles Far East Corporation agent in Holland via a telex message. The agents accepted by telex.

A dispute arose and Entores wanted to serve a writ for breach of contract. It could do this only if the contract was deemed to have been made in England.

The court held that the contract was enforceable in London because through the use of telex it was as though an agreement had been made in the presence of the parties, similar to a telephone conversation. The acceptance was deemed to have been made in London when the agent's telex was read.

### Practice point

Amy was browsing on the Internet when she saw a new coat she wished to purchase. Having completed her selection and filled in the necessary payment details, she presses the 'submit' button and awaited delivery. When no coat arrived a disappointed Amy sued the company, which argued that no contract existed as the offer to buy the coat had not been received or accepted by them.

1 What could have gone wrong in this case?

2 Was Amy's communication sufficient to form a valid contract?

It is quite usual in business contracts for the person making the offer to stipulate at the negotiating stage of the contract exactly how acceptance is to be communicated by the other party. This is called **acceptance by specified means**. Unless a method of communication has been specifically mentioned, acceptance may be in another form that does not prejudice the party making the offer.

One of the most common ways an offer can be accepted is through the post. It is normal in business for the person making an offer to include the information that they expect acceptance by letter through the ordinary course of post. The **postal rule** has been developed by lawyers to cover this area of business law. The rule is very clear. Where the use of the post is expected by both parties, acceptance of an offer is complete

### Case study    Yates Building Co v R J Pulleyn & Sons (York) (1975)

In this case, the offer called for acceptance by 'registered or recorded delivery letter'. Acceptance was sent by ordinary letter post and arrived without delay. The person making the offer was not disadvantaged in any way by the other side using this method of acceptance.

1 Do you think this acceptance was valid?

2 Would it make a difference if the use of the ordinary post had caused delay or prejudiced the person who was expecting to receive it by 'registered or recorded delivery'?

and effective as soon as the letter (if correctly addressed and stamped) is posted, even in circumstances where the letter might be delayed or lost altogether. There is an exception to the postal rule in cases where the person making the offer expressly states that acceptances have to be returned by a certain date to be valid.

### Standard form contracts

Many difficulties can arise in law when companies deal with one another. Often they use their own **standard form contracts**. These forms often contain terms that amount to custom-made offers and acceptances that fit individual business needs. So it is quite possible for one company to make an offer on its own standard form contract and the other company to accept it on its own standard form contract.

However, this can lead to contractual disputes known as 'battle of the forms' cases, and the courts may have to decide which standard form contract applies to the transaction.

### Consideration

Under contract law the agreement between the parties will not in itself create a legally binding contract. Another element necessary for a valid contract is some degree of **consideration** between the parties.

Consideration is defined as something given, promised or done in exchange by each party to the agreement. Consideration can take two forms:

- **Executed consideration** is an act in exchange for a promise, such as in a reward case. The promise of the person making the offer to pay the reward is consideration for the act of completing the task that earns the reward.

- **Executory consideration** is a promise yet to be fulfilled; the parties exchange promises to perform acts in the future. Most contracts begin in this way. An example is the promise of a seller to deliver goods to a buyer in consideration for the buyer's promise to buy at the agreed price. Consideration from the buyer is the promise to pay the price on completion.

---

**Practice point**

In groups, list different examples of executed consideration and executory consideration.

---

There are various other rules of consideration that have to be considered. For a contract to exist, consideration can never be 'past consideration', something already completed by a party. This can never be deemed to be consideration for a promise later made by the other party.

In the case Re McArdle (1951), Mr McArdle died leaving his wife a life interest in their house, after which it was to be given to their children.

While the widow was still alive one of the children and his wife moved in and made improvements voluntarily to the house valued at £488. The other children agreed to reimburse them for the work done.

Later a dispute arose and they refused to pay. It was held that the promise to pay was not legally binding as it was made after the work had been done, so the consideration was in the past and invalid.

---

**Thinking point**

Conor is away on holiday and Don, without being asked, paints Conor's house for him. On Conor's return he agrees to pay Don for the work.

1  Has Don provided any consideration?

2  If Conor changes his mind and refuses to pay, can Don enforce a contract?

---

The rule that 'consideration must always move from the promisee' emphasises the idea that there must be consideration in some form from both parties to a contract. If X (the **promisor**) makes a promise to Y (the **promisee**), Y must show consideration for that promise. Consideration cannot be one-sided.

**Case study**  **Chappell and Co v Nestle and Co (1959)**

As part of a promotional campaign, Nestle offered to supply a record to consumers who sent in a postal order for one shilling and sixpence plus three wrappers from sixpenny bars of Nestle chocolate.

A dispute arose between Nestle and the owners of the copyright of the music, in which the copyright owners claimed Nestle was selling the record for money, which would require a separate agreement. Nestle claimed it was not selling the record for money, so under the Copyright Act 1956 all it was required to do was give the owners notice and 6.25% of the retail selling price as payment. Nestle argued that the wrappers had no value and could not be consideration in the agreement.

The House of Lords disagreed, and held that the wrappers were consideration in the transaction as the offer by Nestle was to supply the record in return for cash *plus* the wrappers.

1 Where did the real value of the wrappers lie for Nestle?
2 Can you think of any other similar types of promotion? What types of consideration are provided?

Consideration must also not be illegal. A contract will not be valid if the consideration involved is illegal or considered immoral.

Consideration must also be sufficient. This means that in all valid contracts, consideration must have some value, but there is no requirement that the consideration must be adequate in the particular case. The value of consideration is agreed by the parties and the courts will not help people who agree consideration and then complain of making a bad bargain.

## Capacity to enter into a contract

Having looked at offer, acceptance and consideration it is important now to consider whether a person has legal capacity to enter into an agreement. This is vital if a contract is to exist between the parties. **Capacity** means the legal power to enter into a contract.

There are certain classes of person who have only limited capacity to enter into legal agreements: minors, incapacitated persons and certain organisations.

*The courts will not help people who simply make a bad bargain*

## Minors

Legal rules have been developed to protect **minors** (people aged under 18) from contractual liability and to allow them to enter into agreements in limited circumstances.

Generally there are two types of contract that will bind a minor when dealing with adults: contracts for the supply of necessary goods and services, and beneficial contracts of service. The position is clarified under the Sale of Goods Act 1979. Under this Act, necessities are defined as:

> goods suitable to the condition in life of the minor and to his actual requirements at the time of sale and delivery.

Here the definition will be looked at by the courts in the context of the social and financial background of the minor involved. Luxury goods are generally excluded, as are items or services that the minor already has. Duplicate items and services are not seen to be necessities of life.

### Practice point

If a minor made contracts to purchase the following, which do you think would be legally binding?

- a set of tailor-made suits
- a motor car
- a copy of this text book (as a business studies student)
- a mobile phone
- a new coat
- a train ticket to attend a hospital appointment
- a holiday in Australia
- emergency private dental treatment.

A minor is bound by contracts of employment, apprenticeship and education as long as the whole contract is for the benefit of the minor. This will include contracts such as football apprenticeships and music scholarships.

Minors who set themselves up in business will not be bound by trading contracts even if they are deemed to be for the minors' benefit, unless the contract was created out of fraud, in which case it will be binding upon the minor. So minors who set up a business will not be liable to repay the price of goods if they fail to deliver them!

## Incapacitated persons

Mental patients (medically diagnosed) cannot enter into a valid contract, as they are deemed not to have sufficient mental capacity to understand what they are doing.

However, under the Mental Health Act 1983, the court may enter into valid contracts on a patient's behalf and continue contracts entered into before the illness affected the person and before the person was sectioned under the above Act.

If a person is suffering from temporary insanity, or a drink- or drug-related problem, any contract made by that person during that time will be **voidable** by the person, providing he or she can prove that at the time of negotiation he or she had no understanding of what was going on and the other party to the agreement knew this or should have known it.

## Organisations

It is necessary to consider the legal position when entering into an agreement with various types of organisations.

- **Registered companies** are created by registration under the Companies Act 1985 (as amended). The company has a legal identity of its own and can sue and be sued on contracts made in its name.

  Under this Act, the company's power or capacity to contract was limited and confined to the powers in its Memorandum of Association in the objects clause.

  The Companies Act 1989 has amended the 1985 Act, allowing a company to change its objects clause by Special Resolution so that it can carry on 'any trade or business whatsoever'.

  A company has no legal power to enter into binding contracts before it is properly formed.

Any person 'acting on behalf of the company' before the date of incorporation (the date when it legally came into existence) will be personally liable on the contract.

---

**Case study**    **Kelner v Baxter (1866)**

In this case the promoters of a proposed hotel, an unincorporated company, agreed to buy a stock of wine on its behalf.

After the company was incorporated they tried to enforce the contract in the name of the company, but a dispute arose. The court had to decide whether a contract existed at all, and if so, between whom.

1  Who do you think was liable for the contracts before the company was incorporated?
2  Why would a person who claims to be acting on behalf of a company be held liable, if the company is not in fact legally incorporated?

---

● **Unincorporated associations** are groups of people joined to further a common interest such as a sporting, social or political group.

  In general terms these groups are not considered legal entities, and capacity to contract belongs to members jointly and not to the group or association in its own right.

● **Partnerships** are made between two or more people. Many partnerships are in fact associations formed for business purposes, and are governed by the Partnership Act 1890. Under this Act each partner has capacity to contract on behalf of all the partners, and therefore each is liable jointly on any contract entered into on behalf of the partnership. Here it is not the partnership that has legal capacity, but the individual partners themselves.

● **Local authorities** have power from either Royal Charter or the Local Government Act 1972. Local authorities are separate legal entities and have capacity to contract in their own right. Local authorities are subject to the *ultra vires* rule, which means they can be found to have acted beyond their powers.

## Intention to create legal relations

Even if all other elements of a contract are present in law, there will be no binding contract between the parties unless there is an **intention to create legal relations**.

If there is doubt about this, then certain presumptions are brought into play allowing the law to decide what the parties intended.

These presumptions can be divided into 'business agreements' and 'social agreements'.

### Business agreements

There is an automatic legal presumption that parties in business transactions always intend to create legal relations and to create legally enforceable contracts. This presumption exists unless there is an express statement to the contrary in the agreement.

There are other situations when commercial agreements are not binding. Under the Trade Union and Labour Relations (Consolidation) Act 1992 agreements (joint agreements) made between employers and trade unions are not intended to be legally binding unless they expressly state so.

Also, vague promises and guarantees in advertisements are not generally held to be intended to create legal relations as they are invitations to treat. And in an agreement where one of the parties is a public body bound by statute to provide goods or services (such as the BBC), there is no intention to enter into contracts with customers.

### Social or domestic agreements

Agreements of a domestic, social or friendly nature raise a very strong presumption that no legal relations were intended between the parties.

## Case study    Domestic agreements

Compare the following cases.

In Balfour v Balfour (1919), when Mr Balfour went abroad to work, leaving his wife in England, he agreed to pay her £30 per month. The marriage later broke down and the wife sued for non-payment. The Court of Appeal held that there was no enforceable contract because in this type of situation it must be assumed no legal relations were intended to be created. There was nothing in the conduct of the parties to suggest a binding agreement.

In Merritt v Merritt (1970), the husband left the matrimonial home to live with another woman. He agreed in writing to pay his wife £40 per month to allow her to keep up mortgage payments on the matrimonial home. He also agreed to have the property transferred to her when the mortgage was paid off. The mortgage was paid, but he refused to transfer the property. It was held that there was an intention to create legal relations and the transfer had to be made.

The crucial difference between these cases is the intention of the parties to create legal relations. In Merritt v Merritt they made an agreement after the husband had left the marriage and this was therefore seen as an intention to make a contract. In Balfour v Balfour a social agreement was made between husband and wife at the breakfast table, and this was therefore not regarded as enforceable.

## Distinguishing contracts from agreements

The law of contract is concerned with enforceable agreements between parties. Most people would assume that the difference between contracts and other agreements is that the contract is written in a formal document. In reality, any agreement between parties can be a contract as long as the elements that form a valid contract are in place.

Certain types of agreements, however, do have to be more formal in order to create valid contracts. For example, agreements for the sale of land must be in writing to formalise the particulars within the agreement. Another example is in employment, where a new employee must be given a written statement of the terms of the agreement made with the employer. Failure to formalise these types of agreement will mean that no contract has been formed.

### Thinking point

Consider your own part-time job, or a friend's job. What kind of terms are written into the contract?

### Business implications of failure to establish contracts

Failing to establish proper contractual agreements can have serious consequences for a business. Poorly drawn-up agreements may make it impossible for businesses to trade effectively, and disputes may arise between them that may have to be dealt with in the courts. Such disputes can lead to:

- loss of business efficiency
- loss of trade
- damage to reputations
- loss of confidence in an organisation
- opportunity costs, as time and money are spent in court instead of on the business.

## Referral to civil 'first instance' courts

In the event of a contractual dispute, it may be necessary to apply to the civil courts for a claim to be heard.

The civil court system was transformed under the Woolf reforms, a series of changes to the civil courts made under Lord Woolf when he was Master of the Rolls in the late 1990s. This resulted in the Civil Procedure Act 1997 and Civil Procedure Rules 1998. The three main civil courts that can hear cases initially (at **first instance**) are the Small Claims Court, the County Court and the High Court.

If you are in dispute with an individual or company, you must apply to the court and your case will be passed to a judge who will be assigned as case manager for your case. It will be allocated to the correct court depending on the seriousness of the case. This is known as the **track system**.

The small claims track deals with small claims court cases; the fast track deals with County Court cases; and the multi-track system deals with complex High Court cases.

### Small claims court

The small claims court is a special part of the County Court which deals with minor claims, including contractual and business disputes where the claim does not exceed £5,000. This includes claims such as failure to supply goods, failure to pay for goods and other business disputes. The cases accepted are not expected to raise any difficult questions of law.

If the case is a simple one and both parties agree, the district judge may make a decision on the documents alone, without a hearing. Otherwise, the judge gives directions (for example, about producing certain documents in advance, and about the number of witnesses allowed) and sets a date for a hearing.

It is usual for parties to be encouraged not to have legal representation by a solicitor or barrister, as no help for payment of legal fees is allowed. The courts try to reduce both parties' cost burden.

If the case goes to full hearing, the proceedings are very informal and are often uncontested – meaning that the other party does not disagree.

Help with a claim is available on *www.hmcourts-service.gov.uk*.

### County Court

The County Court deals with fast-track cases worth between £5,000 and £15,000. The County Court also has jurisdiction (power) to hear cases concerning the recovery of land, bankruptcies, company windings up, consumer credit and copyright matters.

A case at the County Court is more formal and will be heard by a circuit judge. It is normal for the parties to have legal representation.

As with the small claims court, however, help and advice are available from the court itself and a person can now even make a claim against another person on-line, at *www.moneyclaim.gov.uk*.

### High Court

The High Court is the most senior of the first-instance civil courts. Based in London and other large cities, it is split into three divisions dealing with different branches of civil law.

- The **Queen's Bench division** will hear contract cases – multi-track cases involving large sums of money or complex points of law. It sits as a commercial court dealing with business matters such as insurance, banking and the meaning of commercial documents. Its divisional court will also hear civil appeals from the County Court.

- The **Chancery division** deals with matters of **equity** (or fairness) including trusts, mortgages, partnerships, companies, bankruptcies and taxation.

- The **Family division** deals primarily with family law matters such as divorce and adoption, so it has little part to play in the law relating to businesses.

## Alternatives to the civil courts

There are many reasons why a person may not want to use the courts to resolve a dispute.

The costs associated with **civil litigation** are still high, with many people simply not being able to afford the high bills lawyers charge for such work. People don't want to take risks if they think they may not win the case.

There are also considerable delays in cases coming to court, although this is improving. It has not been uncommon for cases to take up to three years to come to the County Court and up to five years to come to the High Court.

*Legal delays are becoming more common as cases become increasingly complex*

Legislation is becoming increasingly complex, and this increases the delay and pushes up the cost of a case.

Because of these problems, more and more civil cases are being negotiated and settled out of court. There has been a movement towards an alternative method of resolving disputes. Currently various schemes are available, all playing an important part in solving commercial disputes.

## Arbitration

Arbitration is a system whereby both sides voluntarily agree to have an independent third party make a decision about their case. The process is governed by the Arbitration Act 1996. The details of all cases are put into writing to keep everything clear. The process itself can be very formal or informal, depending on the parties involved. The courts can enforce awards made by the arbitrator. There are three main types of arbitration, which are detailed in the table below.

## Mediation

Mediation involves a third party trying to find some common ground between the disputing parties. The mediator acts as message carrier, but the process will only work if there is some midway point that the two parties actively attempt to find. See *www.mediation.org.uk*.

It is quite normal for a mediator to be appointed by an organisation that is trying to change its working practices or re-structure itself. If a third party is involved, organisations hope the change-management process can be better explained and dealt with to avoid costly industrial disputes.

## Negotiation

One of the jobs of the judge before a case starts is to try to get both sides in the dispute together to negotiate a settlement of the case without the need for a full trial.

It may be possible for businesses that are in dispute to negotiate a settlement of the matter to avoid court action or prevent industrial action. After the strike at British Airways in summer 2005, the parties involved (British Airways and the business providing in-flight meals, Gate Gourmet) were involved in negotiations to try to resolve the contract dispute, which had cost the airline around £40 million.

## Conciliation

Conciliation involves a neutral third party attempting to solve a dispute. The conciliator

| Industrial | Consumer | Commercial |
|---|---|---|
| One of the best-known services is ACAS (Arbitration and Conciliation Advisory Service), which is government funded. It often helps resolve disputes between unions and employers and is well respected. See *www.acas.org.uk*. | Many industries have introduced arbitration schemes to help relationships between consumers and businesses, e.g. ABTA (Association of British Travel Agents). See *www.abta.com*. | The complexity of business contracts makes disputes likely. To limit the damage and expense caused by such disagreements a safety valve is often built in. The two parties will seek arbitration if they cannot quickly solve a problem that arises between them. |

raises relevant issues and actively suggests appropriate solutions. A number of official bodies offer this support, including the Centre for Dispute Resolution. The service is quick and cheap, although the two parties in dispute are not bound by the process and can break off at any point they choose.

The Glass & Glazing Federation currently has a conciliation scheme in place which covers disputes between the public and its members in areas such as installation of double glazing or the building of conservatories.

# Remedies for breach of contract

If a valid contract is not fulfilled, the person who has not completed his or her side of the bargain will be liable for **breach of contract**.

In law, every breach of contract gives the injured party the right to recover damages. Other remedies are available, such as specific performance and injunctions (see below). These are equitable remedies granted at the discretion of the court.

## *Damages*

Two types of damages are available to a person who has suffered from a breach of contract.

It is quite common for parties to agree in advance the amount of damages that would be paid in the event of a breach of contract. These are known as liquidated damages.

Unliquidated damages, on the other hand, are those awarded for breach of contract where there is no prior agreement between the parties as to the amount of damages to be awarded.

The aim of unliquidated damages is to restore the person to the position he or she would have been in had the contract been carried out correctly. They are designed to compensate only for losses suffered, so if no loss has been suffered, the damages awarded will only be nominal (small) to recognise the fact of the breach of contract.

Breaches of contract can cause a chain of events. In law, there has to come a point after which the damage becomes too remote from the original contract to be recoverable.

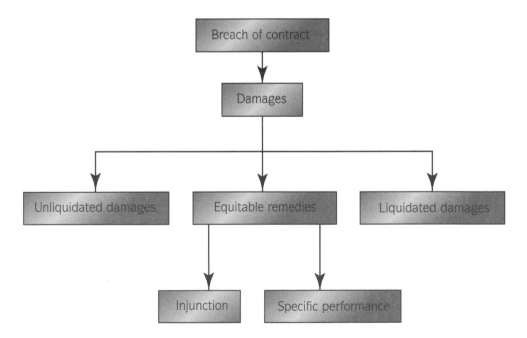

*Remedies for breach of contract*

## Mitigation of loss

Once a breach of contract has occurred, the innocent party is under a duty to mitigate (reduce) his or her loss. This means that victims of a breach of contract cannot simply stand back and allow their losses to mount up. For example, a seller whose goods have been rejected must attempt to get the best price for them elsewhere.

## Equitable remedies

There are some situations where monetary damages are neither adequate nor appropriate. **Equity** developed other forms of relief to ensure that justice is done, for example injunctions and the doctrine of specific performance.

- An **injunction** is an order of the court requiring the party at fault not to break the contract. Its main use is to enforce negative promises in certain contracts such as employment contracts, restraining employees from working in a similar capacity for rival employers.

- **Specific performance** is an equitable remedy that requires the party in breach of contract to carry out his or her contractual promises. An example would be where a person is compelled to fulfil a contract for a personal performance, such as a DJ employed by a nightclub. No amount of damages would make up for the loss of a DJ particularly chosen for a specific occasion.

  Specific performance would be refused in cases where an award of damages would be more appropriate. For example, if a company employed a painter to paint its building, it would not be able to force the painter to complete the work if he or she stopped half-way through, as an award of damages would be more appropriate to enable the company to employ another painter to finish the job.

## Limitation of actions

The right to claim for breach of contract does not last forever. The Limitation Act 1980 imposes time limits on bringing actions. Simple contract disputes must be brought within six years of the breach, and for contracts made under deed (such as the sale of land) the time limit is within 12 years of the breach. This time limit can be extended where fraud is involved, or where the person making the claim is suffering from a disability or lacks capacity.

### Outcome activity 27.1

**Pass**

Using a business scenario of your choice, describe the requirements of a contract it might use, and explain the remedies that might be available to both parties in the event of a breach of contract.

Include the elements for the requirement of a valid contract and the types of remedies that are available under contract law and equity.

# Statutory consumer protection

Contract law is an important tool to protect businesses but also consumers when they purchase products. Without really knowing it, consumers enter into countless contracts every day for the purchase of items ranging from bars of chocolate to cars and computers. Even though these contracts are diverse, one thing that is certain in all of them is that consumers in the United Kingdom are well protected by law when things go wrong with the products purchased.

If, for example, a newly purchased MP3 player fails to work properly, the purchaser can expect to have the product replaced or the money refunded. The reason is that there is a powerful set of legal guidelines to ensure that businesses do not, as far as possible, get away with selling inferior (or even dangerous) products to consumers.

In this section we will examine the legal rules that regulate contracts for the sale of goods and the supply of goods and services.

The primary source for these rules is the agreement between the parties, but Parliament has become increasingly involved in this area of law to provide a statutory framework for such transactions.

# Sale of goods

The law relating to contracts for the sale of goods is the Sale of Goods Act 1979, as amended. It provides the framework for the relationship between the buyer and the seller and covers such matters as the rights and duties of the parties and their remedy in the event of a breach. The key sections that protect the consumer within the Act are sections 12 to 15, which deal with the seller having the legal right to sell the product, the fact that products sold by description must match the description, the requirement that the goods sold are fit for the purpose intended and of satisfactory quality, and that if a purchaser buys products after seeing a sample, the bulk delivery must match the sample.

The Act applies to all contracts for the sale of goods, from buying a sandwich to multi-million-pound deals.

## Definitions

Section 2 (1) of the Sale of Goods Act defines a contract of sale of goods as:

> a contract by which the seller transfers or agrees to transfer the property in goods to the buyer for a money consideration called price.

This definition is very important, because only those contracts that fall within it will be covered by the Act.

Goods are defined as all items of property such as food, clothes and furniture. Land and money are excluded from the definition.

## Implied terms

Parties are generally free to agree between themselves the details of their contract. But the Act automatically includes a series of conditions in every contract for the sale of goods. These are known as 'implied terms' and are dealt with in sections 12 to 15 of the Sale of Goods Act 1979, as discussed below.

## Title

There is an implied condition in Section 12 (1) on the part of the seller that he or she has the right to sell the goods.

For example, a car dealer implies confirmation that the cars she sells actually belong to her and that she can legally pass ownership (title) to another person. If the seller cannot pass good title (the right of ownership) to the buyer, he or she will be liable for breach of contract.

## Description

Where there is a contract for the sale of goods by description, there is an implied term that the goods will correspond with that description. The description of the goods may cover such matters as size, quantity, weight, ingredients, origin or even how they are packed.

The slightest departure from this description will entitle the buyer to reject the goods for breach of condition of the contract.

## Fitness and satisfactory quality

No general duty is placed on sellers who sell in private to ensure that the goods sold are of correct quality and suitability. This preserves the principle of *caveat emptor* or 'let the buyer beware' – if you buy a camera from a friend and it does not work, little remedy will be available to you.

---

**Case study** | **Moore & Co v Landauer & Co (1921)**

The claimants agreed to supply 3,000 tins of Australian canned fruit, packed in cases containing 30 tins each. When the goods were delivered it was discovered that about half the consignment was packed in cases of 24 tins.

The courts agreed that the recipient could reject the whole consignment.

1 Do you think it is fair that a contract should be ended because of small deviations from what is expected?
2 What do you think is the reason for this rule?

However, if your friend was selling the camera in the course of his or her business, Section 14 of the Sale of Good Act implies two conditions:

**(1)** the goods are of satisfactory quality

**(2)** they are fit for a particular purpose.

Under the Sale and Supply of Goods Act 1994, where a seller sells goods in the course of a business there is an implied condition that the goods supplied are of satisfactory quality, except to the extent of defects which are brought to the buyer's attention before the contract is made, or which ought to have been noticed by the buyer if he or she has examined the goods. The quality of goods includes their state and condition.

Fitness for purpose means suitability for the purposes for which goods of the kind in question are commonly supplied, in terms of their appearance and finish; that they are safe, free from minor defects and durable (long lasting).

The law does not impose absolute standards of quality with which all goods must comply, but goods must be satisfactory to a reasonable person, taking into consideration the price paid. This means that goods do not have to be absolutely perfect, but satisfactory in the usual way.

Where the seller sells goods in the course of a business, there is an implied condition that they will be reasonably fit for the purpose that the buyer has expressly or impliedly made known to the seller. It is vital that a seller is told if a particular product is to be used for a particular purpose, as this will offer the buyer a degree of protection under the legislation.

*Goods have to be of satisfactory quality and fit for purpose*

### Case study    Fitness for purpose

In Grant v Australian Knitting Mills (1936), the buyer bought a pair of woollen underpants from a shop. The pants contained a chemical that should have been removed before sale, and the buyer suffered a skin reaction (dermatitis).

It was held that the items were not fit for purpose as the buyer had impliedly made known to the seller that they were to be worn next to the skin.

In Griffiths v Peter Conway (1939), the buyer bought a tweed coat from the defendants. Unknown to them, she suffered from exceptionally sensitive skin. She also contracted dermatitis.

In this case it was held that the defendants were not liable as the buyer had not made her condition known to the sellers, and the coat was a normal coat fit for ordinary wear.

**1** Do you think this level of protection is necessary for sellers of products?

**2** How does the existence of such protection help reputable businesses?

### Case study    Rogers v Parish (Scarborough) Ltd (1987)

The buyer bought an expensive new car for £16,000. Within six months of delivery the engine became defective and the bodywork began to deteriorate. The purchaser wished to reject the vehicle.

It was held that the buyer was entitled to reject it. The vehicle was not of merchantable quality as the buyer did not receive the appropriate degree of comfort and reliability from the new car.

**1** Do you think that this level of protection is necessary for purchasers?

**2** How does the existence of such protection help to promote reputable businesses?

## Sale by sample

The Sale of Goods Act provides that in a contract of sale by sample there is an implied condition:

- that the bulk will correspond with the sample in quality

- that the buyer will have a reasonable opportunity of comparing the bulk with the sample

- that the goods will be free from any defect making their quality unsatisfactory which would not be apparent on reasonable examination of the sample.

## Remedies for breach of consumer contracts

Inevitably things go wrong in some contracts, and the parties can find that they have broken the terms of the contract. This is known as breach of contract and can take many forms.

Common examples of breach of contract are failure to pay for goods, delivering damaged goods, or delivering incomplete work by the agreed date. Whatever type of breach has occurred, various remedies are available for the person who has suffered the loss. These fall into two categories.

A seller who suffers a breach of contract by the buyer can sue for the contract price, sue for damages for non-acceptance of the goods by the buyer, stop the goods being delivered in transit, and re-sell them.

Buyers' remedies for breach of contract by the seller include rejection of the goods, damages for non-delivery or breach of contract, and an order for specific performance (see page 214).

## Exclusion of liability using exemption clauses

An **exemption clause** is a term in a contract that attempts to exempt or limit the liability of a party who is in breach of that agreement.

Parliament regulates exemption clauses under the Unfair Contract Terms Act 1977. This is a vitally important piece of legislation but is not applied universally to all contracts. It was intended to be used primarily for contracts of sale by commercial organisations and businesses, and not by individuals. The Act does not apply to contracts for land, insurance, company promotions, shares and debentures, and patents (copyrights).

Exemption clauses are regulated under the Act in two ways:

- they can be rendered void and ineffective

- they can be made subject to a test of reasonableness.

The reasonableness of an exemption clause will be a matter for a court to decide in the light of all the circumstances of the case, such as the relative strength of the parties concerned.

## Exclusion of liability in standard term and consumer contracts

When they do business with consumers on their standard term (pre-written) contracts, organisations will almost certainly try to limit their liability when things go wrong. To be effective, the clauses in a standard term contract must be deemed to be reasonable.

---

**Case study**    **R W Green Ltd v Cade Brothers Farm (1978)**

A farmer bought seed potatoes from a supplier. An exclusion clause in the supplier's standard form contract stated that any complaint had to be brought within three days of delivery of the product.

When the potatoes grew they were not of the correct quality, and the farmer complained, but the supplier tried to rely on the exemption clause in the contract.

1 Do you think this clause would be a reasonable one?
2 Why is it important to regulate exemption clauses?

Under Section 5 of the Unfair Contract Terms Act, a manufacturer or distributor cannot restrict his liability in negligence for losses arising from defective goods by means of a term in a guarantee. For example, a manufacturer of a washing machine would not be able to rely on a term in the guarantee stating that it was not liable in negligence (for, say, a flooded kitchen) if the product turned out to be faulty.

Under Section 8 of the Unfair Contract Terms Act, any clause that excludes or restricts liability for misrepresentation will be ineffective unless it satisfies the reasonableness test. Misrepresentation occurs when a person makes false representations that persuade a person to enter into a contract. For example, a telephone salesperson for an energy provider who makes claims about its services being the cheapest would have to ensure that the claims satisfied the reasonableness test to avoid being declared ineffective in the event of a dispute.

The law relating to exclusion clauses has been expanded by the creation of the Unfair Terms in Consumer Contracts Regulations 1999, which apply only to consumer contracts and mean that the court can strike out any term in a contract that the court deems to be unfair. The test of unfairness is to look at whether the parties have acted in 'good faith', a judgement that will be made on the basis of the strength of the parties, whether any inducements were offered to make the consumer agree to the contract, and whether the seller had dealt fairly with the consumer.

Unlike the Unfair Contract Terms Act, which renders void the whole contract, the regulations allow the court to strike out the unfair term while leaving the rest of the contract intact.

# Supply of goods and services

The Sale of Goods legislation applies only to contracts where goods are sold for a money consideration. It does not cover methods of obtaining goods by means other than money purchase, nor does it cover the provision of services such as hire-purchase services.

Legislation has been passed to protect commercial transactions that are not covered under the Sale of Goods Act, including contracts for work and material (building work, car repairs, installation work such as central heating and double glazing, hairdressing and gardening); contracts where no money changes hands (exchange or barter deals); contracts for 'free gifts' (where a buyer is given a free product if he or she buys another); and contracts for hire of goods (including the hire of cars, machinery and clothing).

The Supply of Goods and Services Act 1982 was passed to place on a statutory footing the terms that had previously been implied by common law in contracts for services.

### Implied terms

Section 2 of the Supply of Goods and Services Act contains an implied condition that the transferor (the person who is providing the goods or services) has the right to transfer the property or goods and they are free from undisclosed third-party rights.

Section 3 provides that where the transfer is for goods by description, there is an implied condition that the goods will correspond to that description. For example, if your computer broke down and it was sent to a computer shop to be repaired, when the invoice described the work and the parts fitted it would be implied in the contract that the work and parts described had been provided.

Section 4 provides that where goods are transferred in the ordinary course of business there is an implied condition that the goods are of suitable quality and fit for the purpose.

Section 5 provides that where there is a transfer of goods by reference to a sample, there is an implied condition that the bulk will correspond with the sample.

### Contracts for the hire of goods

Contracts for the hire of goods apply to contracts where one person agrees to bail (lend) goods to another by way of hire, such as the hire of cars or machinery. Again the Supply of Goods and Services Act deals with this.

Section 7 states that there is an implied condition that the bailor (the person providing the hire) has the right to transfer the goods. For example, if a person arranges to hire a car from Hertz for a holiday via the Internet, it is implied that the car will be owned by Hertz and that Hertz will allow the hire to take place.

Section 8 provides that where there is a contract for the hire of goods by description, there is an implied condition that the goods will match that description.

Section 9 provides that where goods are hired in the course a business, there is an implied condition that the goods are of a satisfactory quality and reasonably fit for the purpose.

Section 10 covers implied conditions in relation to contracts for the hire of goods by sample – the bulk must match the sample.

Remedies for breach of contract will be broadly the same as for contracts for the sale of goods.

### Exclusion of liability

The Supply of Goods and Services Act 1982 provides that liability can be excluded or limited subject to the terms of the Unfair Contract Terms Act 1977 and the Unfair Terms in Consumer Contracts Regulations 1999.

## Consumer protection

### Defective goods

There are circumstances where a person responsible for putting defective goods into circulation will be made liable for his or her actions.

Under Part 1 of the Consumer Protection Act 1987, a claimant who is injured by an unsafe product can sue the manufacturer of the product without the need to prove the tort of negligence.

Under the Act, liability is strict, which means that unless one of the defences listed in the Act can be proved, consumers injured by a product will always gain damages from the producer of that product.

The Act gives the right to sue to any person who is injured by a product, 'the safety of which was not such as persons generally are entitled to expect'.

Under the Act, liability is on the producer of the product, and producer is defined as:

- the manufacturer of the product
- the extractor of raw materials
- industrial processors of agricultural produce
- 'own branders' who add their own label to products that they do not produce
- anyone who imports the product into the EU.

Section 3 of the Consumer Protection Act 1987 provides that:

- products can be regarded as defective if their safety is not such as people are generally entitled to expect
- products include not only finished products but component parts of other products and raw materials.

For example, a new car is a product, but so are all its component parts such as radios, batteries, rubber for the tyres, and so on.

The court will consider all the circumstances of the case in deciding whether the standards of care that the Act expects have been broken. Factors will include:

- the way the product was marketed
- any instructions and warnings with the product
- what is expected to be done with the product
- the time at which the product was supplied, so that if new versions of a product are produced, older versions are not necessarily considered unsafe.

Section 5 of the Consumer Protection Act allows a claimant to claim damages for death or personal injury caused by an unsafe product.

**Practice point**

Using a set of guidelines such as those at *www.bbc.co.uk/watchdog*, *www.consumerdirect.gov.uk* and *www.tradingstandards.gov.uk*, produce a poster giving advice to fellow consumers about their rights under consumer protection legislation.

## Supplying defective products

In business dealings, when things go wrong it is normal for the parties involved to sort out their problems in the civil courts.

But the criminal law has imposed very strict rules protecting consumers from rogue traders and manufacturers who breach safety standards and supply dangerous products. There are many pieces of legislation that protect consumers, such as the Trade Descriptions Act 1968, which makes it a criminal offence to mislead a consumer by a false description.

At the heart of the drive towards consumer safety is the Consumer Protection Act 1987, which creates an offence of supplying consumer goods that fail to comply with general safety requirements. These requirements have been given further backing by Parliament through the General Product Safety Regulations 1994. This is a wide-ranging set of rules ensuring manufacturers and suppliers of goods comply with safety regulations, including the content, design and packaging of goods, the requirements of safety testing, and the inclusion of warnings, instructions and other information about the goods.

Businesses that fail to comply with these rules can be prevented by Trading Standards officers from supplying goods that are in breach of the law. Officers can seize the prohibited goods and in extreme cases seek a criminal prosecution, where a guilty person may be fined up to £5,000 and/or given six months' imprisonment.

*The Consumer Protection Act is at the heart of the drive towards consumer safety*

## Case study — Oxford Products Ltd

Oxford Products Ltd was fined £2,500 and ordered to pay £13,700 in costs when it was prosecuted in 2003 for selling a luggage carrier to Jennifer Brereton for her high-powered Suzuki motorcycle without sufficient fitting instructions.

The tailpack was not fitted correctly and it came loose, causing the bike to crash. Twenty-year-old Jennifer was killed.

1 In small groups, discuss whether you think the punishment for this type of offence is suitable.
2 To what extent could such instances be avoided in the future?

# Unsolicited goods and services

There are controls in place to protect consumers who receive goods and products that they have not ordered. These are known as unsolicited goods, and are examples of a technique known as **inertia selling** where manufacturers and suppliers send goods to us and then expect us to pay for them.

The Unsolicited Goods and Services Act 1971, now updated by the Consumer Protection (Distance Selling) Regulations 2000, make it a criminal offence for suppliers to send unsolicited goods and services to unsuspecting consumers and demand payment for them.

The recipient of these goods or services is under no obligation to return the items and may treat them as an unconditional gift; there will be no duty to pay for them. A supplier who demands payment will be committing a criminal offence.

## Outcome activity 27.2

### Pass
Using a case that you are familiar with, a case study from this unit, or the following case study, describe the impact of relevant statutory consumer protection on both consumers and businesses.

Babycare UK are sellers of baby products and are struggling financially. They were given the opportunity to purchase some very cheap car seats for babies from a supplier in the Far East. The products do not conform to UK or EU safety standards, but would allow Babycare to make some much-needed profit.

Babycare UK took delivery of 5,000 of these seats and sold them. Unfortunately, over the next few weeks some babies were injured as a result of sitting in the seats when involved in car accidents.

### Merit
Explain and apply contract and statutory consumer provisions in your selected case study, illustrating appropriate legal authority, and making reference to relevant courts and remedies.

Analyse the law relating to contract controls and consumer protection that is relevant to your case. Show how the case was or should be dealt with by the business and the court, including descriptions of available remedies.

### Distinction
Evaluate the application of contract and consumer protection requirements in your selected case study, giving a reasoned conclusion.

Give judgements as to why we need contractual controls and consumer protection in the selected case study, and how effective they are both for the organisation selected and its customers.

# Employment legislation

The law relating to the relationship between an employer and an employee has changed dramatically over the past few years, and there now is now a complex framework provided by UK law and influenced by European law. Employees have more rights than ever before and consequently employers have more duties imposed on them. In the next section we examine some of the main provisions of this relationship.

## Employee or independent contractor?

In employment law there are two main types of workers: employees, who are part of the organisation and have a contract of service; and self-employed workers, who are independent contractors working for the organisation under a contract for service. Both technically work for the organisation but they have distinctly different rights under their contracts.

## Terms of an employment contract

The main rights and duties of both employers and employees will be found in the contract of employment. These rights are specified in the terms of the contract, which can be either express terms or implied terms.

Express terms are the main part of the individual contract, and will have been discussed at an interview and confirmed in writing. They will include pay, hours and holiday entitlement.

Implied terms are provisions in the contract that are not included as written terms but are understood to be included automatically. These include terms such as the right to equal pay and the right not to suffer discrimination.

Some terms may be included in a contract through custom or tradition. For example, the business might close every Wednesday afternoon but be open every Saturday morning, and working according to those times may form part of a contract of employment.

The key differences are shown in the following table.

| | Employee | Independent contractor |
|---|---|---|
| Contractual status | Contract *of* service | Contract *for* service |
| Insurance and welfare benefits | Entitled to unemployment benefit, statutory sick pay, industrial injury benefit and state pension, provided the employee has contributed to these state schemes via National Insurance contributions | Very little welfare benefit and no statutory sick pay |
| Taxation | Income tax and National Insurance payments deducted at source by employer | May be liable for own tax and National Insurance payments; criminally liable for failure to pay |
| Vicarious liability | Employers can be liable for the civil wrongs of their employees | No such protection |
| Safety | High standards of care imposed on employers towards their staff | Much lower standard of care required |
| Employment protection rights | Right not to be unfairly dismissed, right to redundancy pay, maternity and sick pay, right to belong to a trade union and time off for union duties; freedom from discrimination | No such rights other than freedom from discrimination |

Below is an example of a standard type of employment contract. This is the basic contract, but a particular contract is likely to include many more terms.

## Statement of particulars of employment (Standard form)

Name of Employee     [                            ]

   ('You')

Name of Employer:    [                           ]

('the Employer')

### Duration of employment
Your employment commenced on [      ] and no employment with a previous employer counts as part of a period of continuous employment.

### Probationary period
The first [  ] month period of your employment shall be regarded as a probationary period, during which time your progress will be closely monitored and the [disciplinary procedure], sick pay and pension provisions (if applicable) will not apply to you.

During the probationary period:

a)  you may, for any reason, give the Employer not less than [  ] weeks' notice in writing to terminate your employment;

b   the Employer may, if your performance is considered unsatisfactory, give you not less than [  ] notice terminating your employment

### Job title
You shall be employed as [                ].

### Duties
You are required to undertake the duties as set out in your Job Description attached.

You may from time to time be required to undertake such other duties as the Employer may reasonably require.

You will report to [           ].

During your employment by the Employer you must not engage in any business activity or act as an employee of any other organisation or person without the Employer's written permission.

### Place of employment
Your place of employment shall be at [              ] or such other place(s) as the Employer may require.

You may be required to travel within the UK and overseas on the Employer's business.

During the period you will be working in [country outside the UK] your salary will be paid in [currency] and you will be entitled to [additional benefits available during this period] and, upon your return to the UK, [terms and conditions relating to the employee's return to the UK].

### Remuneration

Your salary amounts to £ [      ] per annum. Your entitlement to salary accrues on a daily basis, payable monthly in arrears on the last day of the month.

You hereby agree that the Employer is authorised to deduct any sums due to it from you from your salary or any other sums due to you in respect of your employment or its termination.

### Hours of work and overtime

Your normal working hours are as follows:

Monday to Friday: [  ] to [  ] with [  ] hour(s) off for lunch.

You are required to work such hours as are necessary to complete satisfactorily your duties. Accordingly the Employer may require you to work overtime as and when necessary. There are no overtime payments/You will be paid [   ] per hour/given time off in lieu for each hour of overtime worked provided advance authorisation is obtained from [     ].

### Timekeeping

You are required to attend the office as specified above. If unable to do so you are required to notify [          ] immediately.

### Pensions

The Employer operates a contributory pension scheme commencing after one year's employment. Details can be obtained from [       ].

### Holidays and holiday pay

The Holiday Year runs from 1 January to 31 December.

From the commencement of your employment your paid holiday entitlement will be at the rate of [   ] days per calendar year plus Bank and other usual statutory holidays. Your holiday accrues on a daily basis.

Should you leave the Employer before earning the holiday entitlement you have taken, you agree that a deduction will be made from your final salary payment equivalent to the amount of time so taken.

Holidays not taken by 31 December may not be carried forward to the following Holiday Year without the Employer's written permission. Payment will not be made for holidays not taken.

Holidays may only be taken at times convenient to the Employer as previously arranged by reasonable notice.

If you leave the Employer with some holiday entitlement not taken in the current Holiday Year, you will be paid on your last day of employment in addition to any other sums due to you, a sum representing pay for the number of days not taken.

Your paid holiday entitlement will be lost if:

a)   you are dismissed with or without notice for serious misconduct or breach of contract

b)   you terminate your employment without giving proper notice.

### Absence due to sickness or injury

A self-certification system operates for absence from work due to sickness and injury not exceeding [  ] days.

If you cannot attend work because of sickness or injury you must, unless there is some good reason to the contrary, advise your manager of the reason for non-attendance by 9.30 am on the first working day of absence. Failure to do so may result in sickness pay not being paid.

Immediately on your return to work you must obtain, complete and return to your manager before the end of the day of your return to work, a self-certification form (or provide a Doctor's Certificate for periods exceeding [   ] days).

Sickness or injury absence exceeding [   ] days must be covered by a Doctor's Certificate.

All sickness or injury absence will be entered on your employment record.

The Employer operates the Statutory Sick Pay scheme and you are required to co-operate in the maintenance of necessary records for the purposes of calculating your entitlement to Statutory Sick Pay. 'Qualifying days' are those days on which you are normally required to work.

During sickness you will receive sick pay from the Employer at your normal rate of pay for a total of [   ] weeks' sickness followed by a further [   ] weeks' sickness at half the normal pay in any period of 52 weeks commencing on the first day of sickness absence. Payment thereafter will be at the Employer's discretion. There will be deducted from sickness pay an amount equal to SSP or State Sickness Benefit whether or not claimed or received.

The Employer reserves the right to require you to undergo a medical examination at its request after [   ] weeks' absence due to sickness in any period of [   ] weeks commencing with the first day of sickness absence. The Employer will pay the cost of any such examination and you agree that all information and documents in connection with it and any report produced shall be fully disclosed to the Employer.

## Disciplinary and dismissal procedure

For rules and procedures relating to disciplinary matters and dismissals, please see the attached disciplinary and dismissal procedure. The procedure does not form part of your contract.

## Notice of termination of employment

Without prejudice to the provisions regarding the Probationary Period set out above, this contract may be terminated at any time by the following periods of notice given in writing:

Employer's notice to you:

Continuous service from 1 month to 2 years – 1 week

2 years or more service – 1 week for each year of continuous employment up to a maximum of 12 weeks.

Your notice to the Employer:

[   ] weeks.

I, the Employee, acknowledge that this Agreement constitutes a statement of the particulars of my employment and I confirm that this Agreement constitutes my contract of employment with the Employer.

SIGNED:   ................................................................ (on behalf of the Employer)

DATE:   ................................................................

SIGNED:   ................................................................ (Employee)

DATE:   ................................................................

# Employment Act 2002

Employees enjoy a range of rights thanks to the extensive changes made to employment legislation in recent years. One of the most important pieces of legislation is the Employment Act 2002, which has changed many employee rights such as maternity leave, paternity leave and disciplinary matters. The effect of this has been to extend employee protection to an unprecedented level. The main rights employees possess are detailed below.

### Maternity leave

The Employment Act 2002 has extended the rights to maternity leave. Before the baby is born, a pregnant employee is entitled to reasonable time off for ante-natal classes, and as soon as the baby is born the mother is entitled to 26 weeks' maternity leave, which will be paid leave as long as she has been in continuous employment for 26 weeks by the fifteenth week before the child is born. Mothers who do not qualify for this may still receive a maternity allowance at a lower level. The employee must also give the employer notification of when her maternity leave is expected to begin.

### Parental leave

Employment legislation also aims to help parents who have to balance family responsibilities and work. The Employment Rights Act 1996 and the Parental Leave Directive 1996 provide the right for parents who have responsibility for caring for children born after 15 December 1999 to take up to 13 weeks' leave for each child up to the age of five. If the child is disabled, this leave can be up to 18 weeks and can be taken up to the child's eighteenth birthday, and if the child is adopted, leave can be taken up to the fifth anniversary of the child's adoption.

Parental leave must normally be taken in blocks or multiples of one week at a time for up to four weeks in a year, unless the child is disabled, when the leave can be in blocks of single days or up to four weeks.

Parental leave will be unpaid (unless the contract allows for such payment) and it is normal for the employer to insist on up to 21 days' notice of the leave. The employer must guarantee that the employee will suffer no disadvantage for taking leave in terms of promotion or loss of status.

# Working time rights

Employment legislation has introduced a series of rules that protect workers' rights during their time at work. The main rights are detailed below.

### Holidays and pay

The Working Time Regulations 1998 state that all full-time employees must be given four weeks' paid holiday per year. Part-time employees are entitled to holiday in proportion to the time they work; this is known as *pro rata*.

The leave year begins in 1 October for employees who began work before 1 October 1989, and for employees starting after that time it begins on the anniversary of the beginning of their employment or the date agreed in their contract of employment.

Normally employees can take holiday only in the year in which it is due and it cannot be carried over to the next year nor must a payment in lieu of holiday not taken be made.

Employers will expect employees to give adequate notification of the intention to take holiday, and it may be the case that certain employers will prohibit staff taking holiday during certain times of the year, as the business dictates. For example, many retailers will not allow their staff to take holiday in December as it is usually a peak trading period.

### Break periods and rest periods

All employees are entitled to breaks and rest from work. Those who work more than six hours a day

*Employees are entitled to adequate rest periods*

are entitled to a rest break, which must be at least 20 minutes' uninterrupted break away from their work. Ideally this should be taken during the six-hour period and not at the start or end of the shift, to allow workers a real break from work.

Adult employees are also entitled to a complete rest period of not less than 11 continuous hours in any 24-hour period. Longer periods of rest should be given to night workers and younger employees.

## Maximum working week

There are rules to protect workers from having to work too many hours each week. The Working Time Regulations state that an employee should not work more than 48 hours on average in each week.

This is not straightforward, however. An employee has the right to opt out of this arrangement and can work as many hours as he or she wishes. Also, the calculation is complicated by the fact that the 48-hour guide is an average, normally calculated over 17 weeks, so it is possible for an employee to work over the 48 hours on occasions, provided that the overall average does not exceed that figure.

## Minimum wage

Employees' rates of pay will be an express term in the initial contract of employment. By law, the rate cannot fall below what is known as the national minimum wage. Currently this is as follows:

- adult workers £5.05 per hour (rising to £5.35 per hour in October 2006)
- workers aged 18–21 £4.25 per hour (rising to £4.45 per hour in October 2006)
- workers aged 16–17 £3.00 per hour (under review).

## Sunday working

Traditionally, Sunday was considered a day of rest. But since the Sunday Trading Act 1994, small shops and betting shops have been allowed to trade on a Sunday, with larger stores such as Tesco and Asda being allowed to trade for a maximum of six hours.

This has given employers potential difficulties to overcome. The Act gives all employees the right to choose not to work on Sundays. The situation is made more complicated by the fact that there are three types of employee to consider.

- Employees who were employed by their current employer before 26 August 1994 may simply refuse to work on a Sunday.
- Workers first employed after 26 August 1994, but whose contract does not require them to work on Sundays, may refuse any request from an employer to work on a Sunday.
- Those employed after the above date in businesses where Sunday trading is normal will be given a written statement within eight weeks of beginning their employment. This will set out the law relating to Sunday trading and inform them that they can opt out of working on Sundays by giving written notice to the employer.

Employers should not discriminate against an employee who refuses to work Sundays, and any dismissal for such refusal will be classed as unfair.

Andy has sought legal advice about his working conditions. He is 20 and works as a shop assistant at a local shop. He is being paid £3 per hour and has been working for at least 50 hours each week. His working day is very long and the owner of the shop has said that he can have a 15-minute break for each eight hours he works. Now the shop is to open on a Sunday, Andy has been threatened with the sack unless he works Sundays as well.

1  What advice can you give Andy?

2  What should be his first step in protecting his employment rights?

# Protection from discrimination

All employees in this country should be protected from being discriminated against. This can take many forms but we will focus on three.

## *Sex discrimination*

Under the Sex Discrimination Act 1975, employers must not discriminate on grounds of sex, marital status or because someone intends to undergo, is undergoing or has undergone gender reassignment or sex change. Discrimination can be direct, where an individual is treated less well than another person on grounds of sex; or indirect, where a whole class of person is disadvantaged because of gender. An example of indirect discrimination would be an employer insisting (without reasonable cause) that all employees need to be above a certain height. This would tend to discriminate against women, because the average woman is shorter than the average man.

Sex discrimination covers all aspects of employment – from recruitment to pay, training and the termination of a contract.

Discrimination includes applying conditions which, though applied equally to all, have a bad effect on one sex or on married people and which cannot be shown to be justifiable.

There are limited exceptions. The Act permits employers, under certain conditions, to train employees of one sex in order to fit them for particular work in which their sex has recently been under-represented. Also, certain jobs may require a particular sex, for example a female community worker may be employed to look after women in refuges.

A female British Airways pilot who claimed sex discrimination in a dispute over working hours in 2005 won her case.

Jessica Starmer, a pilot aged 26, was denied a request to work part-time so that she could look after her one-year-old daughter. Male pilots had been allowed such time off but Jessica was denied such rights, and despite claims from BA that they had not been discriminatory, they were found liable.

1  Where was the sex discrimination in this case?

2  What defences could British Airways have brought?

## *Racial discrimination*

Under the Race Relations Act 1976, it is unlawful for a person to discriminate on racial grounds against another. The Act defines racial grounds as including race, colour, nationality or ethnic or national origin.

To bring a case under the Race Relations Act, the victim must show he or she has been discriminated against in one of the following ways.

● **Direct racial discrimination** occurs when a person is able to prove he or she has been treated less favourably on racial grounds than others in similar circumstances. Racist abuse and harassment are forms of direct discrimination and are unlawful under the Act.

● **Indirect racial discrimination** may fall into one of two categories. The first is on grounds of colour or nationality, under the original definition in the Race Relations Act. It happens when there is a non-discriminatory requirement which applies to everyone, but the proportion of the victim's racial group who can comply is considerably smaller than the proportion of those in other groups who can comply. The requirement must be unjustified, irrespective of race, and it must be to the victim's disadvantage that he or she cannot comply with it.

The second category is on grounds of race, ethnic or national origin. This was introduced by the Race Relations Act (Amendment) Regulations 2003. This is broadly the same as under the Act but takes into account a broader approach, as it also outlaws discrimination on the basis of ethnic origin.

*People who use wheelchairs need suitable access and facilities at work*

## Practice point

Harpreet Singh has worked for a couple of years for the financial services firm owned by John. John had noticed that some of his employees were scruffy and had got into the habit of wearing baseball caps in the office. He decided to ban the wearing of all headgear and hats in the office.

Harpreet is a Sikh, and he wears a turban. In the spirit of fairness to the other workers, John said that he must not wear his turban to work. This angered Harpreet and he explained to John that there is a religious significance to his turban. He refused to obey the rule.

When a promotion opportunity was advertised, Harpreet was the obvious candidate for the job but as he still insisted on wearing his turban, John ignored his application and gave the job to someone far more junior.

Harpreet believes he is being racially discriminated against.

1 Do you agree with Harpreet?

2 How might John have handled the situation more successfully?

### Disability discrimination

Employers must be aware that they have duties placed on them when they employ disabled workers. The Disability Discrimination Act 1995 prevents the discrimination that many disabled people used to face in many areas of their lives, including employment.

Since December 1996 it has been unlawful for businesses and organisations to treat disabled people less favourably than other people for a reason related to their disability. Since October 1999 they have had to make reasonable adjustments for disabled people, such as providing extra help or making changes to the way they provide their services. Since October 2004 they have had to make reasonable adjustments to the physical features of their premises to overcome physical barriers to access. For example, a business employing people who use wheelchairs must allow ramp access to its building and lifts to enable them to have the same access to the building and work environment.

## Equal pay

One of the oldest employment rights is the right to equal pay between men and women.

Legislation has existed since 1970 with the Equal Pay Act. This was extended by the European Union's Equal Pay Directive (1975), which states that employers must give men and women equal treatment in the terms and conditions of their employment contract if they are employed on work that is the same or broadly similar, or work found to be of equal value.

## Statutory sick pay

The majority of employers pay their workers full pay if they are sick for a certain period of time. The terms will be included as part of the contract of employment. When this entitlement runs out, or if it is not part of the contract, by law employers have to provide Statutory Sick Pay (SSP) – an earnings replacement for employees who are off work through sickness.

At present the rate of SSP payable by an employer is £68.20 per week and is available for 28 weeks in each period of illness.

## Unfair dismissal

Inevitably cases arise where employers have to discipline employees. The ultimate disciplinary sanction is to dismiss an employee.

- **Summary dismissal** is where a person has been found guilty of gross misconduct, for example violence towards a customer or staff member, or a serious theft. A person dismissed in this way will be given no notice and will have to leave immediately after the disciplinary hearing.

- **Dismissal with notice** will be for reasons such as persistent lateness, poor performance or failing to follow instructions. Here the person dismissed will be given a paid notice period and will leave after that has finished.

The Employment Act 2002 lays down guidelines that should be followed. Failure to follow the statutory guidelines could lead to the former employee claiming unfair dismissal.

There is now a standard statutory procedure for dismissal. The first thing that must happen is that the person must be told in writing of the alleged misconduct, and invited to attend a meeting. Then there must be a hearing where the person can argue his or her case. The decision will then be reached and the employee will have a right of appeal. After any appeal hearing the employee should be told of the final decision.

In the case of gross misconduct, the procedure is different in that the employee is given written information to stating the alleged misconduct that led to dismissal and informing him or her of the appeal procedure. An appeal should be held if requested.

These procedures are implied terms in a contract and neither side can opt out of them. Failure to follow these procedures will mean that the dismissal is automatically deemed unfair.

Other reasons for dismissal that are always judged unfair include dismissing an employee because he or she has taken maternity or parental leave, is pregnant, is proposing to join a trade union, is seeking to claim employment rights such as equal pay, has disclosed wrongdoing in the workplace (**whistleblowing**, see page 233), has been unfairly selected for redundancy or is involved in a grievance claim against the company.

The wronged person may be able to take out a claim for unfair dismissal at an employment tribunal, where it may be ordered that the person is reinstated to his or her job, re-engaged in the business but in a different job, or given financial compensation by way of damages.

## Redundancy

Redundancy occurs when staff are no longer required. Legally, redundancy is classed as a dismissal of staff.

There are three situations in which redundancy can occur:

- the employer closes down the business completely, as at the MG Rover car plant in Longbridge, Birmingham in spring 2005

*Many redundancies can occur when a business closes*

- the employer closes down the employee's place of work, such as when British American Tobacco (BAT) announced hundreds of redundancies at its Southampton factory in 2005 to move its operation to the Far East

- there is a reduced need for employees to do work of a particular type, for example where computerised, automated systems have replaced workers, such as in the increasing use of on-line banking.

In the event of redundancy, employees have certain rights under the Employment Rights Act 1996. Where the redundancy is through the closure of the business, the employer has little more to do other than ensure that redundancy payments are made correctly. Where an employer closes part of the business, but the business as a whole continues, the employer must try to find suitable employment for the employee in the company. This has to be reasonable for both sides. Clearly BAT workers in the example cited above would not be expected to re-locate to the Far East and they would be made redundant.

The most problematic redundancies are in areas where rationalisation of the workforce takes place. The biggest problem for an employer is to select who is to be made redundant. The best

practice is to involve the relevant trade union from the start to help manage the process. This would include explaining the situation to staff and perhaps asking for voluntary redundancies first – this may be attractive to some workers. The union could also advise in the drawing up of an objective list of employees to be made redundant. The employer must not draw up this list in a discriminatory way as that would constitute unfair dismissal.

Redundancy payments are calculated on the basis of years' service with the employer, up to a maximum of 20 years. The amount payable is:

- one and a half weeks' pay for each year employed between the ages of 41 and 65

- one week's pay for each year employed between the ages of 22 and 40

- half a week's pay for each year employed between the ages of 18 and 21.

More details of employer and employee rights can be found at *www.businesslink.gov.uk* and *www.dti.gov.uk*.

---

**Outcome activity 27.3**

**Pass**

As a personnel manager, you have been asked to prepare a report describing the implications of employment legislation for the rights of your employees.

Explain the relevant provisions of contract law and statutory provisions regarding the employment rights of workers.

---

# Data protection legislation

As businesses have become increasingly sophisticated and responsive to technological advances, more and more information is being stored and used to gain competitive advantage and to manage businesses more effectively.

The widespread use and storage of this information or data has led to the development of many new laws to protect against its misuse. The amount of data held about individuals is often felt to be excessive and intrusive into people's lives. Effective management of information in a business needs to follow the legal rules carefully.

## Data Protection Act 1998

The Data Protection Act 1998 aims to protect individuals' rights to privacy with respect to the processing of personal data. Personal data means any facts or opinions relating to a living individual.

A business may keep data about its employees, including addresses, dates of birth, bank details and personnel issues such as pay, pension and disciplinary record. To manage the information properly and ensure confidentiality, businesses that hold data must appoint a person known as a **data controller**, who manages the accuracy and validity of information held. This person must be registered with the Information Commissioner, who is appointed by the government to be responsible for data protection. Businesses should be aware that it is a criminal offence to hold data without the permission of the Information Commissioner.

Information can only be stored if an individual has consented, or if it is necessary for the performance of the individual's job or to protect the individual in some way (such as holding medical information).

The Data Protection Act seeks to strike a balance between the interests of an organisation that holds data and the individual who is the subject of the data. The individual has certain rights under the Act. The main ones are:

- the right to access the information held about himself or herself
- the right to refuse permission for information to be held
- the right to prevent information being used for marketing purposes or passed to third parties

- the right to compensation for mistakes made
- the right to ask the data controller to rectify errors.

For further information see *www.informationcommissioner.gov.uk*.

### Practice point

What must a data controller ensure happens to information held about a person?

### Case study    Criminal records

A woman applied for a job as a foster carer and for a place on a nursing course. A Criminal Records Bureau check was carried out. The 'disclosure' showed that between 1995 and 1999 she had associated with people who were allegedly responsible for local drug dealing.

Upon enquiry, the police ascertained that the allegations did not relate to the applicant but to associates of her ex-husband who was still living in the marital home during the course of their separation. The police deleted this information from their records.

1  What rights would the woman in this case have?
2  What are some of the possible consequences of inaccurate information being held about a person?

## Telecommunication interceptions

An even more controversial area involving privacy is where employers monitor communications made by an employee. The law regulating this practice is laid down in the Telecommunications (Lawful Business Practice) (Interception of Communications) Regulations 2000.

The regulations establish what is lawful business practice in terms of telephone and e-mail monitoring without consent. An employer has to show is that there is a 'business motive' for the interception of any communication and has to make reasonable efforts to warn those using the system that communications on it may be monitored.

Consent from an employee is not strictly relevant. The important thing is that a responsible employer must warn staff and other potential senders and recipients of telephone calls and e-mails that their messages may be monitored. It is advisable therefore to include such a warning on the footer of all outgoing e-mails and to give a recorded message at the beginning of each telephone call.

This is potentially a very sensitive issue and one that has to be dealt with professionally. More guidelines are available at *www.dti.gov.uk*.

> **Practice point**
>
> In your own business, why might you need to intercept communications? What would you tell your staff about the issue?

## Whistleblowing

Another difficult area to manage in the workplace is where an employee publicly discloses poor working practices – known as **whistleblowing**. A whistleblower who, for example, brings dangerous working practices to the attention of senior management or the authorities risks being victimised by fellow workers and managers.

To protect those who have witnessed poor practice and need to disclose it, the Public Interest Disclosure Act was passed in 1998. The Act protects workers from being subjected to any reprisals by their employer. These may take a number of forms, such as denial of promotion, facilities or training opportunities. Employees may make a claim for unfair dismissal if they are dismissed for making a disclosure.

Only certain kinds of disclosures qualify for protection. Qualifying disclosures are those where the worker reasonably believes that one or more of the following is happening now, took place in the past, or is likely to happen in the future:

- a criminal offence
- the breach of a legal obligation
- a miscarriage of justice
- a danger to the health or safety of any individual
- damage to the environment
- deliberate covering up of information tending to show any of the above.

Anyone disclosing such information outside the organisation must also prove the existence of at least one of the following conditions to gain protected status:

- they reasonably believed that they would be victimised if they raised the matter internally
- they reasonably believed that the disclosure related to a criminal offence and was a 'qualifying disclosure'
- there was no prescribed regulator and they reasonably believed the evidence was likely to be concealed or destroyed
- the concern had already been raised with the employer or a prescribed regulator
- the concern is of an 'exceptionally serious' nature
- they had suffered an identifiable detriment.

Protecting workers who disclose any of the above matters will have to be managed carefully. As this a particularly difficult area to deal with,

**Case study**    **Carroll v Greater Manchester County Fire Service (2001)**

Carroll was a retained, on-call fire fighter. After being assured that his identity would remain confidential, he reported internally that his station had put in a false alarm call to generate fee income. Carroll and his colleagues were arrested, and then disciplined. Contrary to the assurances he had been given, the fire service revealed Carroll's identity to his colleagues as the source of the information. Carroll was shunned by his workmates and his colleagues were encouraged to complain about him. Carroll resigned, for other reasons, and was awarded £1,000 in damages for the breach of confidence and injury to his feelings.

1 Explain what is meant by 'whistleblowing'.
2 When should an employee be protected from adverse consequences for disclosing information?

employers' organisations and trade unions have set up support groups to help workers deal with a whistleblowing situation. An example is 'Safecall', a government-sponsored help line dealing with this type of case. See *www.safecall.co.uk*.

# Computer misuse

The Computer Misuse Act 1990 deals with attacks against computer systems or data in the workplace, or in other organisations such as schools and colleges. It provides protection against misuse of systems and data, or attacks on their confidentiality, integrity, or availability. The Act provides for three offences, as described below.

## Unauthorised access to computer material

It is an offence to cause a computer to perform any function with intent to gain unauthorised access to any program or data held in a computer. Under the Act, it is necessary to prove that the access to the computer was unauthorised and the person knew that this was the case.

This offence is commonly referred to as 'hacking'. It includes entering a computer system without permission having guessed or discovered another individual's password, or having obtained it through the use of other software tools.

If a person is found guilty of such an offence and takes information unlawfully from the computer, he or she may go to prison for up to six months.

## Unauthorised access with intent to commit further offences

This offence is committed where a person has gained unlawful access to a computer, but with the intention of committing a further criminal offence such as the distribution of obscene material. This is viewed as a more serious offence and is punishable on conviction by a term of imprisonment of up to five years.

## Unauthorised modification of computer material

Any act that causes the unauthorised modification of the contents of any computer is an offence. There must have been the intent to cause the modification and knowledge that the modification has not been authorised. This offence covers the introduction of harmful worms and viruses to a system, and denial of service attacks. On conviction it is punishable by a term of imprisonment of up to five years.

**Case study    Computer viruses**

In January 2003 Simon Vallor, a 22-year-old web designer from North Wales, was jailed for two years at Southwark Crown Court having been convicted under the Act of writing and distributing three computer viruses. His actions were proven to have infected 27,000 PCs in 42 countries.

1 What type of damage can be caused by computer viruses?
2 How can businesses attempt to protect themselves from such viruses?
For more information see *www.homeoffice.gov. uk/crime/internetcrime/index.html*.

Compliance with the Computer Misuse Act, along with the other types of legislation dealing with the storage and management of data, will be dealt with in the workplace through training and induction. It is an important area, and as with all aspects of data protection must be dealt with effectively to avoid problems for both employees and the business itself.

---

### Outcome activity 27.4

**Pass**

Select a workplace and describe the impact of data protection legislation and regulations upon it.

You might choose your own workplace, or perhaps your college or a business you have studied for another unit. Explain how data protection legislation impacts on it. You might examine a scenario such as being asked to investigate a case where a male employee is reported to be sending malicious and pornographic e-mail on the company intranet to a female employee who is too upset and afraid to complain.

**Merit**

Explain and apply employment and data protection legislation to the selected case study, providing relevant legal authority.

Using information from this and other units, analyse how a selected business is affected by both employment and data protection legislation. Use relevant legal authority to support your arguments.

**Distinction**

Evaluate the application and impact of employment and data protection legislation on your selected workplace.

Evaluate the way your chosen businesses is affected by employment and data protection legislation, with clear references to the impact these factors have on the business.

---

### Key terms

**Acceptance**
a positive act by a person accepting an offer to create a contract

**Acceptance by specified means**
an acceptance of an offer in a particular way, as demanded in the offer

**Breach of contract**
where a person fails to fulfil his or her side of the contract

**Capacity**
the ability of a person to enter into legal relationships

**Civil litigation**
the collective name for court action when civil law matters need to be resolved

**Consideration**
the value given to the promises on a contract

**Contract**
an agreement that the law will enforce

**Counter-offer**
a new offer that will cancel out an earlier offer

**Data controllers**
the persons responsible in a business for looking after data

## Key terms

**Equity**
fairness in the law

**Exemption clause**
a term in a contract that attempts to limit the liability of a party who is in breach of the agreement

**First instance courts**
courts that hear cases for the first time

**Inertia selling**
sending out goods to people who have not asked for them (unsolicited goods) in the hope of gaining payment for them

**Intention to create legal relations**
the necessary intention to form an enforceable contract

**Minors**
persons aged under 18 – they normally cannot form contracts

**Offer**
a statement of the terms on which a person or business is willing to be contractually bound

**Postal rules**
the rules of acceptance whereby an offer is deemed to be accepted as soon as the acceptance is placed in the post box

**Promisee**
a person who receives a promise

**Promisor**
a person who makes an offer

**Standard form contracts**
pre-written contracts used by individual companies

**Track system**
the three types of track or court that civil cases are allocated to: the small claims track, the fast track and the multi-track

**Voidable term**
a valid term of a contract but one that can be declared void at the request of the parties

**Whistleblowers**
workers who disclose unsafe practices to their employers or the authorities

# End-of-unit test

1 What is the definition of a contract?

2 What is the difference between an offer and an invitation to treat?

3 What is consideration?

4 What is the small claims track?

5 Explain the difference between liquidated and unliquidated damages.

6 What implied terms are in a contract for sale of goods?

7 What remedies are available for breach of a consumer contract?

8 What is the purpose of an exclusion clause?

9 What punishment might a seller of a defective product receive?

10 How can an individual treat goods he or she has received but not ordered?

11 What are the main differences between employees and independent contractors?

12 Explain maternity leave rights.

13 What is the minimum wage for a 20-year-old worker?

14 Do all employees have to work on Sundays if asked?

15 Explain some of the grounds for claiming unfair dismissal.

16 What is the purpose of the Data Protection Act 1998?

17 What does a data controller do?

18 When is it lawful to monitor telephone and e-mail communications?

19 What is whistleblowing?

20 What is computer misuse?

# Resources

## Texts

Abbott, K: *Business Law*, DP Publications, 1994

Beale, Beatson et al (eds): *Chitty on Contracts*, Sweet & Maxwell, 1994

Keenan, D and Riches, S: *Business Law*, Longman, 2002

Lockton, D: *Employment Law*, Palgrave, 2003

Sparrow, A: *The E-Commerce Handbook*, Fitzwarren Handbooks, 2001

## Statutes and legislation

Arbitration Act 1996

Civil Procedure Act 1997

Computer Misuse Act 1990

Consumer Protection Act 1987

Consumer Protection (Distance Selling) Regulations 2000

Companies Act 1985

Data Protection Act 1998

Disability Discrimination Act 1996

Employment Act 2002

Equal Pay Act 1970

General Product Safety Regulations 1994

Local Government Act 1972

Mental Health Act 1983

Parental Leave Directive 1996

Partnership Act 1890

Public Interest Disclosure Act 1998

Race Relations Act 1976

Race Relations (Amendment) Regulations 2003

Sale of Goods Act 1979

Sale and Supply of Goods Act 1994

Sex Discrimination Act 1975

Sunday Trading Act 1994

Supply of Goods and Services Act 1982

Telecommunications (Lawful Business Practice) (Interception of Communications) Regulations 2000

Trade Descriptions Act 1968

Unfair Contract Terms Act 1977

Unfair Terms in Consumer Contracts Regulations 1999

Unsolicited Goods and Services Act 1971

Working Time Regulations 1998

## Case references

Balfour v Balfour [1919] 2 KB 571

Chappell & Co Ltd v Nestle Co Ltd [1960] 2 All ER 701

Grant v Australian Knitting Mills Ltd [1936] AC 85

Green (R W) Ltd v Cade Bros [1978] 1 Lloyd's Rep 602

Griffiths v Peter Conway Ltd [1939] 1 All ER 685

Entores v Miles Far East Corp [1955] 2 All ER 493

Hyde v Wrench [1840] 3 Beav 334

Kelner v Baxter [1866] LR 2 CP 174

McArdle re [1951] 1 All ER 905

Merritt v Merritt [1970] 2 All ER 760

Moore & Co and Landauer & Co re [1921] 2 KB 519

Rogers v Parish (Scarborough) Ltd [1987] 2 All ER 232

Yates Building Co Ltd v R J Pulleyn & Sons (York) Ltd [1975] 119 Sol Jo 370

## Websites

*www.abta.com* Association of British Travel Agents

*www.acas.org.uk* Arbitration and Conciliation Advisory Service

*www.bbc.co.uk/watchdog* Watchdog consumer advice television programme

*www.businesslink.gov.uk* Business Link government advice for businesses

*www.consumerdirect.gov.uk* Consumer advice from the government

*www.dti.gov.uk* Department of Trade and Industry, major government department dealing with companies

*www.hmcourts-service.gov.uk* Courts services

*www.homeoffice.gov.uk/crime/internetcrime/index.html* Home Office advice for dealing with internet crime

*www.informationcommissioner.gov.uk* Information Commissioner, government department responsible for data protection

*www.nationalmediationhelpline.com* Dispute settlement organisation

*www.moneyclaim.gov.uk* Advice agency to help with civil claims

*www.safecall.co.uk* Organisation to support whistleblowers

Businesses rely on their markets, but what exactly is the market for a firm's products? We might say these days that the market for a product or service is everyone in the world; but that is not a very useful definition, as we are unlikely to sell to everybody. We could qualify the definition by saying that it is everyone in the world who would like to buy our product; this is getting closer, but that definition contains a large number of people who might want it but can't afford it. Perhaps a market is those who want it and can afford it as well.

But even that definition might be considered to be a little too broad. Most firms tend to identify a particular group of people to target with their product (their target market), but even that may overstate the position because no company attracts all of its target market, so a true market is probably only a relatively small number of its target market.

However we define it, successful interaction with its market is vital to the success of any business, and it is that relationship that we will examine in this unit.

Unit 29 is divided into four main areas:

- 29.1 Business and customers
- 29.2 Competitive business environments
- 29.3 Impact of stakeholders on business decision-making
- 29.4 The impact of e-business.

## Businesses and customers

The relationship between businesses and their customers is a very complex one, but some understanding of this relationship is vital to success in business. One of the main problems is that customers are basically unpredictable. Economists like to believe that customer buying decisions are made as a result of rational behaviour and as such are predictable to a certain extent. A lot of economic theory is based on the principle that faced with alternative buying choices, the customer will weigh up the options in terms of quality and value and will buy the best deal. But the truth seems to be that many buying decisions are made on impulse and seem completely irrational.

However, we have to work with our customers and all their unpredictabilities, so let us examine the relationship in some detail.

## Factors determining producer supply

The two most important factors to consider in the relationship between businesses and their customers are the level of demand from consumers and the amounts that firms are prepared to supply. It is these factors that comprise the true market for the product. Here we consider each in turn, beginning with the factors that influence levels of supply (sometimes known as the **determinants of supply**).

### Consumer or customer demand

The basic factor to consider when a company is preparing to supply a product is the level of potential demand for that product. Clearly a firm will not supply something that is unlikely to sell. Therefore it will use market research to identify, analyse, understand and react to customer needs (you can learn more about this topic and the value of using both primary and secondary research methods in Unit 12: Marketing Research, page 45).

Research is also about anticipating customer demand, which can be important since customers' needs change very rapidly. Steve Jobs, the co-founder of Apple Computer Inc, makers of Apple computers and the iPod, said 'You can't just ask customers what they want and then try to give that to them. By the time you get it built, they'll want something new'. Forecasting customer behaviour is also important and will inform supply decisions.

## Product design, research and development and technological change

Once a product is being sold it is possible to get further market information from customers that will also inform the supply of that product. Customer feedback will include ideas for improved product design, any research and development needed on the product, and technological changes required to keep up with customer needs.

### Practice point

In groups, consider one of the following products. Each group should decide on the key factors that will determine whether you would decide to supply that product. Put your ideas on flip-chart paper so that you can share them with the class.

- Group 1: Laptop computers
- Group 2: Flowering plants in pots
- Group 3: A new soft drink
- Group 4: A set of children's building bricks (like Lego)
- Group 5: A range of clothing

## Cost and availability of input materials

If the costs of production for a particular product fall, this encourages businesses to produce more of that product and it may also encourage new firms to enter the market, thus increasing overall production. The same may also happen if new sources of raw materials are found.

The converse is also true of course – if costs rise, businesses will either produce less of the product or may withdraw from producing it altogether.

## Production technology

As methods of production and technology improve, companies are able to make more and increase the level of supply. Consider the mining or extraction industries – 100 years ago the level of technology employed was limited to a shovel and a bucket, whereas today grinding machinery means that one worker can produce far more than before.

## Subsidies or government support

Subsidies are payments made by governments to producers to help them with the costs of production. Businesses often choose to make those items that attract subsidies or to set up in areas that attract government grants, and so such payments do influence the level of supply of particular products in certain areas.

## Economies of scale

The more a firm produces of a particular item, the cheaper it becomes to produce each individual item as a result of cost savings such as bulk buying of raw materials. There is a strong drive, therefore, for firms to increase the scale of production, and the more economies of scale are available, the more supply will increase. There is more information on economies of scale later in this unit.

## Impact of supply arrangements

Other factors that businesses take into account when deciding what products or services to supply are:

- **timing** – how frequently and how quickly customers will need supplying; clearly in some industries this could be burdensome and more difficult to maintain

- **packaging** – whether the product requires special packaging, which may involve special and more expensive production processes

- **where it will be sold** – transportation of the finished product will be more of a problem to some destinations than others.

## Market information on consumer demand

The availability of market research information will vary from industry to industry, and some sources are clearly more reliable than others. You can learn more about this topic in Unit 12: Marketing Research on page 45–93.

# Factors determining consumer demand

Of course many buying decisions are based on the price of the product, but we often consider that price is the main influence over whether a person buys a product or service, and that is not necessarily the case. Items of clothing, for example, are often bought because of style, fashion or branding; price is often a secondary consideration, and many people buy more expensive rather than cheaper items of clothing.

The factors that determine customer demand are often referred to as the **determinants of demand**. A few of the most influential ones are described below.

### Changes in consumer tastes and preferences

People's tastes change on a regular basis. For example, today people are much more likely to

buy products that are produced in an environmentally friendly way, whereas in the 1960s and 1970s people were less aware of such issues so this did not affect their buying behaviour.

### Income levels

When income levels in the country rise, people have more money to spend and consequently they buy more. Conversely, if the economy is doing poorly and wages are static or going down, general spending in the economy is reduced.

Consumer confidence is an important influence over demand levels. When people are confident about their future they are happy to spend; when they are uncertain, spending levels drop. We measure the impact of consumer incomes on demand using **income elasticity of demand**, which we will examine in detail later in this unit (see page 256).

### Quality of products/services

Companies can create higher demand by improving the quality of their product or service, but they can equally reduce demand if they allow quality to decline.

---

### Case study    Burberry

Burberry is a producer of designer clothes, many of which are made from a very distinctive beige check. During 2004 these clothes became very popular with a group of young people known as 'chavs'. According to the ChavWorld website (*www.chavworld.co.uk*), a chav is a young person, often without a high level of education, who follows a particular fashion; chavs usually wear designer labels including the chav favourite Burberry, and if they're girls, very short skirts, large hoop earrings and stilettos.

Initially this change in fashion undoubtedly gave a boost to Burberry sales, but many people began to form a very negative opinion of chavs. Consequently, a number of people who would ordinarily have bought Burberry clothes began to desert the company for fear of being associated with chavs. At the end of 2004 Burberry was reporting that sales were not growing nearly as quickly as anticipated – indeed sales in the UK became their weakest market at the time. It is clear, therefore, that fashion can be a negative influence as easily as a positive one.

1 What companies/products can you think of that might be particularly susceptible to changes in tastes or fashions?
2 What can companies do to protect their sales levels in such a situation?

## Availability of products/services in relation to competition

The more outlets that are available for potential customers to buy your product, the more sales you are likely to make. If your product is available in more outlets than your competitors', then you are likely to take a greater share of the total market demand for the product. Therefore ensuring that your product is available in a wide range of stores, over the Internet and in many places where people congregate (such as railway stations or at concert venues) will boost demand for the product.

## Promotional activity

Demand can be increased by well-focused promotions such as advertising, direct mailing, packaging redesign, good availability of information on the product and effective branding.

## Diversification

An effective way of increasing demand for a company's products is to produce a wider range; in this way the company is likely to be addressing the needs of a wider range of customers, which gives more opportunities for sales. This is called **diversification**.

## Incidence of producer-controlled markets

Some companies find themselves in the position where they are the dominant supplier in a market. In this situation they are able to manipulate levels of demand to some extent. You will study this in more detail later in this unit.

## Price of substitutes

The classic example of substitute products is butter and margarine. Since each is potentially a substitute for the other, if the price of one rises, some consumers may switch to buying the alternative. A rise in the price of margarine, for example, might cause more people to buy butter, so demand for one product is influenced by the price of another.

## Price of complements

**Complements** or complementary products are those that we have to buy together, such as DVDs and DVD players – one is no use without the other. As the price of DVD players has dropped, that has had the effect of increasing demand for DVDs. Therefore the demand for one is influenced by the price and demand for the other.

We measure the impact of the prices of complementary and substitute products on demand using **cross elasticity of demand**, which we will examine in detail later in this unit (see page 257).

## Population changes

Population changes can affect demand in two ways:

● the size of the population affects demand – the larger the population, the more people are likely to want to buy

● the structure of the population also has an effect. We have an ageing population in the UK, meaning that there are more older people in society today. This has increased demand for those products that older people use, especially some types of medicines or nursing care.

## The state of the economy

During the recession in the early 1990s, many consumers were worried about their jobs and demand for many products went down. In recent years there have been better economic times and consumer confidence has been high, so demand has improved.

## Availability of credit

A business can increase demand for its products by making loans easily available to its potential customers. This might be done in the form of interest-free credit or in-store credit cards. These will encourage more people to buy and boost demand.

---

**Thinking point**

In groups, identify five products or services – three that have grown in popularity recently and two that have become less popular. Identify the determinants of demand that have influenced each of those products in recent times. Put your ideas on flip-chart paper so that you can share them with the class.

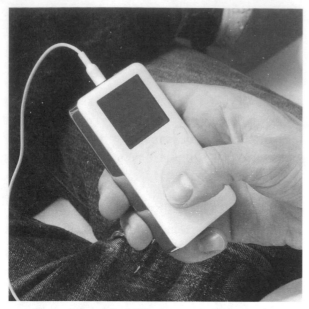

*Likely demand for MP3 players at different prices can be shown in a demand curve*

## Market interaction

### *Operation of the 'price mechanism' and 'market clearing'*

Prices in a market are determined by the influence of demand and supply upon one another. Let us consider the market for hard-drive-based MP3 players, such as the Apple iPod.

If a company were to survey the general public to find out how many hard-drive-based MP3 players were likely to be sold at different prices, the results could be put into a table that would be known as the demand schedule for the product. The company could then put this information into a graph and draw up a **demand curve** that would look like this:

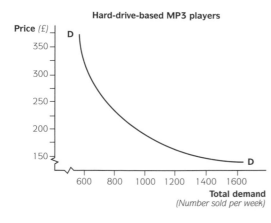

This is the demand curve for hard-drive-based MP3 players. Almost all demand curves look similar to this – they slope downwards from left to right, although the gradients of the curves vary considerably. Whenever you draw up a demand curve you should always remember the following rules:

- the graph is always given a title using the name of the product
- prices always go on the vertical axis
- total demand always goes on the horizontal axis
- state the units you are using on your axes (for example, £)
- label the curve 'D' – it is customary to label both ends of the curve.

As prices rise, we expect fewer people to buy a product, and conversely as the price falls we expect more people to buy the product. A demand curve illustrates this relationship and enables us to quantify how much demand rises or falls when the price changes. A demand curve illustrates the relationship between the price of the product and the demand for it.

We can do a similar exercise with supply for the product. If we researched the potential supply for the product, the resulting curve might look like this:

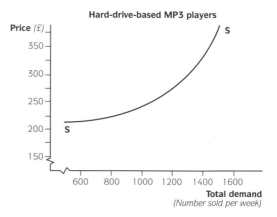

In general terms, as the price of product rises, producers will be inclined to produce more of that item as there is more profit to be made. There is therefore a direct relationship between price and supply – the higher the price, the more the supply. That is why the **supply curve** slopes upwards as in the diagram above.

If we allow demand and supply to interact without interference, they will determine prices for products and they will also determine how much producers should make of the items. If we take our demand and supply curves for hard-drive-based MP3 players and put them together on one graph, we get a new graph like this:

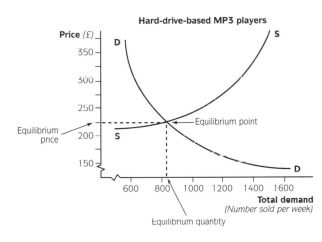

The point at which the two curves cross is particularly significant, as it is this point that establishes the price and quantity supplied of the product. This point is known as the **equilibrium point**. We can read horizontally left from this point to identify the **equilibrium price**, and vertically down from this point to establish the **equilibrium quantity**. This is also known as the **market clearing** position. What our graph shows us is that if free market forces (demand and supply) are allowed to dictate conditions in the market for the MP3 player, 825 items per week will be produced and they will be sold at a price of £225 each.

### Changes in markets over time

This market situation is a dynamic one, however, which means that it is always changing. As the determinants of demand and supply change, so demand and supply curves will move. For example, if incomes rose in the UK we would expect more people to buy the product. This increase in demand will shift the demand curve to

the right, and our new diagram would look like this:

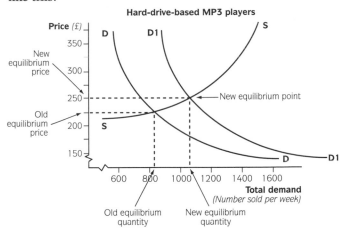

You can see that the increasing demand for the product has pushed up the price, in this case from £225 to £250.

The same thing could happen to the supply of the product, if one of the determinants of supply changes – for example if the costs of production should change, this would shift the supply curve. If the costs of production fall, this will encourage more supply, so the supply curve shifts to the right:

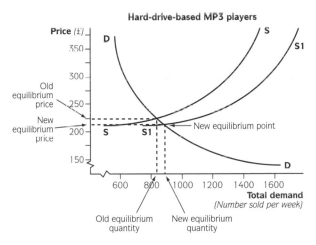

This time the increased supply of the product has caused a reduction in price.

The effect of changes is summarised below.

● A change in the determinants of demand that will *increase demand* will shift the demand curve to the *right*.

● A change in the determinants of demand that will *decrease demand* will shift the demand curve to the *left*.

● A change in the determinants of supply that will *increase supply* will shift the supply curve to the *right*.

● A change in the determinants of supply that will *decrease supply* will shift the supply curve to the *left*.

Note that the new curves are labelled either D1 for a new demand curve or S1 for a new supply curve.

Re-read the sections entitled 'Factors determining producer supply' and 'Factors determining consumer demand' (pages 240–243) to remind yourself of the different determinants that can shift demand and supply curves. All of the factors listed in these sections will shift either demand or supply curves.

## Case study    Demand and supply

The changes in the demand and supply for DVD players in recent years has been dramatic. In 2000, sales were considerably less than 1 million units, but by 2004 this had risen to nearly 7 million units per year. At the same time a number of new companies have begun producing DVD players. The most notable increase has been in own-brand products, particularly from supermarkets. At the same time the average price for a DVD player has fallen from £311 to just £90.

Source: *www.mintel.com*: 'DVD and VCR Players – UK – May 2005'

1 Draw a demand and supply diagram to represent the market for DVD players in 2000. Make sure you label it fully (refer back to the diagram on page 244 for guidance).
2 Add more demand and supply curves to illustrate the changes described above.

## Case study    Phil's Electricals

Phil's Electricals has been offered the chance to produce a new portable digital radio/MP3 player. The company has researched the potential demand for its new model, to be known as the MZ69, and the market demand schedule for the machine is made up of the expected demand from six key towns as follows:

| Price (£) | Quantity demanded in sales per week | | | | | | Market demand (D) | D1 | D2 |
|---|---|---|---|---|---|---|---|---|---|
| | Town 1 | Town 2 | Town 3 | Town 4 | Town 5 | Town 6 | | | |
| 110 | 114 | 58 | 286 | 103 | 137 | 102 | | | |
| 120 | 92 | 46 | 230 | 80 | 109 | 73 | | | |
| 130 | 82 | 39 | 195 | 69 | 92 | 63 | | | |
| 140 | 63 | 31 | 169 | 58 | 83 | 56 | | | |
| 150 | 51 | 26 | 152 | 49 | 74 | 48 | | | |
| 160 | 47 | 22 | 138 | 45 | 64 | 44 | | | |
| 170 | 43 | 20 | 123 | 40 | 54 | 40 | | | |
| 180 | 41 | 18 | 114 | 39 | 49 | 39 | | | |

1 Calculate the market demand schedule for the MZ69 (by adding across each of the rows) and from the data plot the demand curve (D) on graph paper. Vertical axis = price, horizontal axis = quantity demanded.

**Case study    Phil's Electricals** (*continued*)

This table shows the supply situation at the company:

| Price (£) | Quantity supplied per week |
|---|---|
| 110 | 0 |
| 120 | 58 |
| 130 | 288 |
| 140 | 460 |
| 150 | 575 |
| 160 | 660 |
| 170 | 719 |
| 180 | 748 |

**2** Now plot the supply curve (S) on top of the demand curve that you drew previously.

Use the demand and supply curves that you have already constructed for the MZ69 to answer the following questions.

**3** What was the equilibrium price and the equilibrium quantity for the MZ69?
**4** What would happen in the market if Phil's Electricals set the price at £170?
**5** What would happen in the market if the firm set the price at £125?

Let us examine what will happen following a change in the real disposable incomes of the company's customers.

**Situation 1**

Assume that the income levels for the UK went up by 20%, which leads to a 20% rise in the level of demand at all prices. Using the table above, calculate the new demand schedule (D1) for the MZ69 and plot the curve on the original graph drawn.

What is the new price and equilibrium quantity?

**Situation 2**

Assume that the income levels for the UK went down by 15%, which leads to a 15% fall in the level of demand at all prices. Turn back to the original table and using the original market demand figures, calculate the new demand schedule (D2) for the MZ69 and plot the curve on the original graph drawn.

What is the new price and equilibrium quantity?

**Extra task**

Draw demand and supply diagrams to illustrate the following situations. Create a separate diagram for each task and remember to label each diagram fully. Explain why the changes you have drawn have taken place. All of the tasks relate to the demand and supply situation for the MZ69.

**1** The government passes strict new laws preventing the downloading of music onto MP3s.
**2** The cost of components for the new players increases considerably.
**3** In an attempt to boost the export trade, the UK government offers financial help to the companies producing the players.
**4** The marketing team at Phil's Electricals creates a very successful advertising campaign for the MZ69.

## Impact of unsold stocks

Sometimes companies price their products wrongly, that is above or below the equilibrium or market clearing position. In such a case we get an imbalance of demand and supply. The good news is that the market will rectify such problems for us. For example, let us examine what would happen if the manufacturers of hard-disk-based MP3 players pitched their prices too high, at £300. This would be the result:

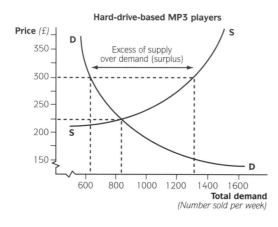

In this situation we get an excess of supply over demand – in other words, at that price the companies are keen to supply the product (as there is a lot of profit to be made so they are supplying over 1,300 per week) but customers consider it to be too expensive so demand is low (only just over 600 per week).

This is known as a disequilibrium situation, meaning that demand and supply are not in balance. In this case the companies are making about 700 items per week that are not being sold. In this situation manufacturers will be forced to reduce prices to clear unsold stocks. The price will continue to fall until the equilibrium position is established (at £225).

## Impact of rapid stock sell-out

Sometimes, however, companies pitch the price too low, in which case the opposite happens. What would happen if the companies producing hard-drive-based MP3 players set their price at £215?

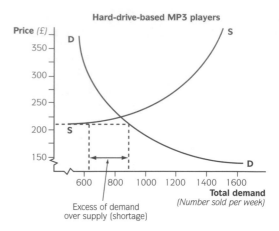

This is another disequilibrium situation. In this case, customers will be keen to buy the product as they consider it to be cheap; nearly 900 per week are keen to buy. However, companies are less willing to supply, since less profit can be made on a low price, so only just over 600 per week are being produced. This time we have a shortage situation, of just under 300 items per week. In such a situation the price will start to rise as companies will see the possibility of exploiting high demand. The price will continue to rise until equilibrium is established at £225.

## Importance of information in market clearing

Timely and accurate information about changes in the market conditions is clearly vital for a firm to avoid the problems of disequilibrium. Changes in customer expectations or the firm's ability to produce need to be known quickly if the firm is to respond and avoid excesses of demand or supply. On-line markets are able to respond significantly more quickly to such changes. You will learn about an example of this, known as 'dynamic pricing', later in this unit on page 254.

The market mechanism is therefore a very useful tool for solving disequilibrium situations. The forces of supply and demand will force prices up to eradicate shortages or down to get rid of surplus production. Either way an equilibrium will be established where a fair price is set and the right number of products are produced.

# Consumer representation

How do you feel about the level of service you receive from companies? Is it always first class, or does it sometimes leave something to be desired? Businesses ought to be responsive to customer needs, but that is not always the case. It is easy for customers to feel powerless in the face of an uncaring and unsympathetic company, but there are a number of organisations who work to support consumers when we feel this way.

## Practice point

Check local and national newspapers and TV programmes for the next week looking for cases where customers feel they have been given poor service by companies.

Discuss the cases that you have discovered with a partner. In pairs, complete the following tasks:

1 Choose the case that you feel is most interesting.

2 Prepare a role-play to be performed in front of the class. One of you will play the customer and the other will play a representative of the company. The role-play will outline the facts of the case that you have chosen, highlighting exactly why the customer felt so aggrieved.

3 Host a discussion with the rest of the class about:
   - whether the customer truly had a grievance
   - what the company should have done to solve the problem
   - what the customer could do if the company fails to resolve the problem satisfactorily.

## Office of Fair Trading (OFT)

The OFT is a government department that has been set up to look after the interests of consumers. The OFT website (*www.oft.gov.uk*) states its purpose to be as follows:

*'The OFT's goal is to make markets work well for consumers. Markets work well when there is vigorous competition between fair-dealing businesses. When markets work well, good businesses flourish.'*

The OFT's activities in pursuit of this goal involve:
- enforcement – of competition and consumer protection rules
- market studies – into how markets are working
- communication – to explain and improve awareness and understanding.

The OFT invites customers to contact it if they feel that they have been given a poor deal by a company or group of companies, and it also invites firms to contact it for advice on how to deal more effectively with customers. If it finds that firms have acted against UK competition law, it also has rigorous powers to investigate and prosecute offending companies.

Consumers often find it difficult to find out about their rights when buying goods and services, and they do not know what to do to solve problems when things go wrong. The OFT aims to give consumers clear and consistent information on these issues and to improve their knowledge of consumer issues. It provides a wide range of publications giving information about consumer rights and advice, along with guides to particular subjects such as shopping, credit and debt, and home improvements.

An excellent guide to the operations of the OFT is available for download on its website at *www.oft.gov.uk/About/default.htm*.

## Local authority trading standards departments

While the OFT deals with issues relating to lack of competitive behaviour in markets, trading standards departments are there to protect consumers from sharp practices, fakes, frauds and scams by companies, as well as offering general advice on consumer rights. These local government departments offer a wide range of advice concerning issues such as buying on credit, warranties, how to complain effectively, your rights when buying second-hand vehicles, and how to sue a company that has provided unsatisfactory service.

Many local councils have their own trading standards departments, but the central source for information is the Trading Standards Institute, and its main website is at *www.tradingstandards.gov.uk/index.cfm.*

### Environmental health departments

Environmental health departments are also run by local councils and they are responsible for protecting public health and safety and improving environmental conditions in their areas. They monitor levels of food safety, occupational health and safety, consumer protection, home safety, environmental protection and licensing of a wide range of services such as street trading, the sale of alcohol, and tattooing parlours.

In the area of consumer protection they will monitor the safety of consumer goods such as electrical goods, toys and furniture, in order to protect the public against risk of injury from unsafe goods.

### Which? – The Consumers' Association

The Consumers' Association is a charity that now trades under the name of Which?. It publishes a monthly magazine (also called *Which?*) and a range of books that, according to its website, aim to 'help people make the right choice when buying products and services, tell consumers their rights, expose company wrongdoing ... and also campaign to stop businesses ripping off or endangering customers.'

Which? also offer a legal service to subscribers who need advice on consumer matters, and also does extensive research testing products and services, and finding out what people think of them. Which? runs an extensive website that can be found at *www.which.co.uk/index.jsp.* Visit this site to see some of the latest campaigns that it is running.

### National Consumer Council

The NCC was set up in 1975 by the UK government to ensure that consumer interests and opinions are considered when major decisions are taken. The council carries out research into potential consumer issues and, when it identifies changes that are needed, develops solutions and works with businesses and public bodies as providers of goods and services to ensure that policy solutions work.

Unlike Which?, it is not involved in testing products, nor does it give direct advice to the public or enforce legislation as the OFT does. Instead, it represents consumers through seminars and lobbying the UK government and public bodies. It delivers carefully researched reports to decision-makers at national or international level.

You can learn more about its activities at *www.ncc.org.uk/index.htm.*

### Utility regulators

Many of the companies that supply essential services such as water, gas and electricity to UK citizens were formerly owned and controlled by the government. This has now changed, and many of them are now privately owned, but often those companies have naturally very strong positions in their particular markets. Many of them face only limited levels of competition and consequently there is a danger that they may not give customers a good deal.

As a result the government has created a number of regulators whose job it is to monitor the activities of these companies and to step in if they act against the best interests of their customers. Here are a number of the main regulators.

| Name | Industry regulated | Website |
|------|-------------------|---------|
| OFGEM | The Office of Gas and Electricity Markets | *www.ofgem.gov.uk* |
| OFWAT | Regulator for the water and sewerage industry | *www.ofwat.gov.uk* |
| OFCOM | Regulator for the communications industries including TV, radio, telecommunications and wireless | *www.ofcom.org.uk* |
| ORR | Office of Rail Regulation | *www.rail-reg.gov.uk* |
| POSTCOMM | The Postal Services Commission | *www.postcomm.gov.uk* |

The following case study illustrates well the difficulty that regulators have in balancing the needs of consumers and the industry that they are regulating.

## Case study    Postcomm

In June 2005, the *Sunday Telegraph* reported that the Royal Mail was seeking to increase the price of first class stamps from 30p to 48p by 2010 in order to invest in technology that would enable it to compete effectively against new competitors. The UK mail market will be opened to full competition in 2006, breaking the Royal Mail's current monopoly on the delivery of letters.

The regulator, Postcomm, was keen to limit the increase to 34p in order to protect the interests of Royal Mail customers. The chairman of Royal Mail, Alan Leighton, threatened to complain to the Competition Commission if Postcomm did not back down. He said: 'We are trying to reconstruct this business so it is a modern mail service that is profitable, and if it is profitable it can afford to invest back into itself. We need to put another £2 billion into the business to move it on.'

1  To what extent do you agree that regulators should have the power to dictate prices to businesses such as the Royal Mail?
2  What are the likely effects on individuals and businesses should the Royal Mail go ahead with the planned price increases?
3  Whose interests do you believe are paramount in this case, the customers who wish to see limited price increases or the Royal Mail wanting to increase prices to develop and improve its service to customers?
4  It is likely that the Royal Mail will face stiff competition from foreign mail carriers when the market opens up in 2006. Does this change your opinion in any way?

### Citizens Advice Bureaux

Citizens Advice is a registered charity running a network of 3,200 Citizens Advice Bureaux across the country. These offer advice to people about a very wide range of subjects including debt problems, benefits, housing issues, legal problems, discrimination, jobs, immigration and also consumer issues. Advisors help clients to talk through their problems and discuss the options available to them. More information is available on the website *www.citizensadvice.org.uk*.

### Response opportunities via the media

The media are also interested in promoting consumer rights – companies that have ripped off unwitting customers make good TV and newspaper stories! One of the popular BBC TV programmes that is involved with such issues is *Watchdog*, and you can see stories featured in the programme at *www.bbc.co.uk/watchdog*. People with complaints can contact *Watchdog* and, if they are lucky, their problems may be pursued by the programme. Threatening a firm with press coverage is often enough to encourage it to sort out your grievances.

### Thinking point

Review the research and role-play activity that you took part in earlier in this section (page 249). For each of the cases you discussed, outline which of the organisations described above would be able to help.

# Competitive business environments

Being competitive is vital to the survival of modern business, and this is not something that is unique to modern life. The eighteenth-century writer Oliver Goldsmith said 'the best way to meet the enemy is head on in the field and not wait till they plunder our very homes'. If we sit back and ignore the competition, we will be overrun. Being competitive makes sure that a business survives to fight another day. In this section we will examine how the degree of competition in a firm's market shapes the behaviour of the companies in that market.

## The nature of markets

If we go back in history, the market that a firm operated in was made up of a group of business people who came together to sell their products to each other, which is how famous markets such as the Portobello Road Market and Petticoat Lane grew up. Today, however, the market that a firm may operate in could be very much bigger and more widespread than these.

A market is simply the coming together of buyers and sellers, and while this

might happen on a very localised basis, such as with a small newsagent shop or a local greengrocer, many firms operate on a national or even international scale. With the advent of e-commerce over the Internet, even many small firms find it feasible to offer products and services for sale to a very wide audience.

Consequently a business might now find that its main competitors are local firms, but it is equally likely that they may stretch across the local region, the whole country or throughout the globe. This, of course, makes it increasingly difficult to be precise about who are the main competitors to a company.

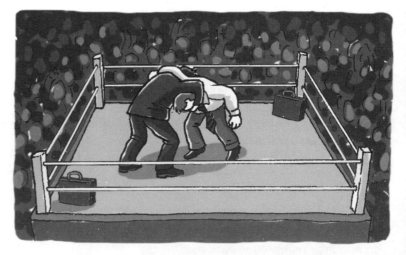

*Competitive business people strive to overcome the opposition*

**Thinking point**

In pairs, select a business that operates close to where you live. Discuss and list the key competitors for that business. To do this well you should firstly list all of the products or services offered by the business, and then identify the range of competitors for each product or service.

See which pair in the class is able to find the most competitors for their business.

In past times, Mr Brown the butcher simply had to look around the town to spot his competitors. There might be another butcher providing direct competition, but perhaps the local grocer might also be selling some meat products, and the local baker might be selling meat pies similar to those available in Mr Brown's shop. Although it might take a walk around the town, it was not hard to identify who Mr Brown's key competitors were.

Today it is not so simple. With the increasing trend for shops to sell wider and wider varieties of goods, it is possible for a large number of firms to sell competing products. With good communications, delivery and postal services, it is entirely possible for a firm's competition to lie well away from its immediate vicinity, in other regions of the country or elsewhere in the UK. With the Internet, the key competitors could be spread right across the world.

Today some markets are conducted purely via communications technology and use very little human contact; others rely on technology substantially for information exchange. Commodity markets and stock markets, for example, are run principally via computer networks and the Internet.

## Competitive behaviour

### The degree of competition within a market

The more firms there are in a market, the more competitive that market becomes. Some businesses find themselves with very few competitors, while others are in markets containing many firms.

We can illustrate the variety of different types of market by considering the following continuum:

Perfectly competitive market          Oligopoly  Duopoly  Monopoly

The two extremes of market are the **monopoly**, where there is only one supplier of a particular good or service, and the **perfectly competitive market**, where there are a large number of suppliers of any one good or service. A **duopoly** is a market with only two producers and an **oligopoly** is one where there are just a small number, say between three and six. While the perfect market is seen as an ideal situation, the monopoly may exhibit many of the worst excesses of anti-competitive behaviour. We shall examine these later.

Competition is healthy, especially from the point of view of consumers, as it tends to deliver lower prices, higher quality products, good service and innovative ideas for new or improved products. The perfectly competitive market should contain the following features.

- It should have a large number of buyers and sellers of the good or service, so that no one person can affect the market price through his or her own actions.

- There should be freedom of entry and exit to the market for both buyers and sellers, so that any new company may trade freely within the market and any firm is free to withdraw when it wishes.

- Products should be homogenous, that is all goods sold should be identical in quality, so we would never buy a product and then wish we had bought it elsewhere because the quality was inferior.

- There should be perfect knowledge of the market on the part of both the buyers and sellers, so that no buyer would ever pay more than necessary and all sellers would know exactly what their competitors were doing.

- It should be possible to buy or sell any amount of the commodity at the market price.

- Buyers should be perfectly mobile. This ensures that buyers can travel to a bargain rather than having to remain close to home and pay higher prices.

- The factors of production should also be perfectly mobile, so that they can therefore be moved to the production of those products or services that are in heavy demand relatively easily.

Of course, the perfectly competitive market will never exist, as it is impossible to achieve perfection. It is a theoretical concept identifying all that is best about markets. It gives us a set of standards by which we may judge real markets.

Comparing a real market with this ideal will highlight shortcomings in the market so that we can identify which aspects of the market ought to be improved. For example, sometimes businesses in a market attempt to maintain their market position by making it hard for new entrants to establish themselves in the market, so that 'freedom of entry' is restricted. This is clearly anti-competitive and as a result may mean that the customer does not get such a good deal. We will examine such activities later in this unit.

### Competitive business strategies

In competitive markets, firms are compelled to adopt a number of strategies to ensure that they continue to sell to their customers. A wide range of tactics are used, some of which are described below. Possible pricing strategies are described first.

- **Skimming pricing** is a tactic used by firms launching new products when they are confident that the product is likely to sell very well when launched. It involves setting a very high initial price to maximise profits in the short term. This technique is often used with new technology items and in the computer games industry. The PlayStation 2, for example, was launched at the premium price of £299 in the UK because Sony knew demand would be great and the market could stand a high price. Three years later you could buy the same model for little more than

£100. This is also typical of skimming strategies – the price is dropped later in order to attract further customers who are not prepared to pay the high price to be one of the first to own the product.

- **Penetration pricing** is the opposite of skimming. In this case a low price is set initially in order to break into a market. This is used when a business is entering a competitive market or is launching a new product where there is doubt as to whether it is likely to be successful. The product is launched cheaply to build up market share. Once a good market share is established, the price will be increased to one that is more realistic from the point of view of profit. Caution should be exercised when increasing the price, as if the demand is too price elastic (customers buy it only because it is cheap), many customers may be lost once the price is increased.

- **Competitor pricing** is used in many retail markets where price competition is so fierce that companies have to keep a close eye on what the opposition is doing. A strategy of competitor pricing involves monitoring closely the prices charged by competitors and reacting immediately when they change by matching them. This is used a lot in the petrol retail market, where demand is very price elastic. In this market it is known that customers will drive to another petrol station rather than have to pay higher prices.

- **Price wars** take place when firms continually and deliberately undercut each other in order to keep market advantage. As a result, average prices in the market move downwards, which can be very harmful to company revenues but is healthy for consumers. Price wars regularly break out in the supermarket industry.

Price leadership and predatory or destruction pricing are dealt with later in the section entitled 'non-competitive behaviour' (page 259).

Non-price strategies are strategies designed to keep the firm ahead of the competition without manipulating prices. There are many of these.

- **Product differentiation** is a marketing activity that encourages customers to believe that the company's product is different from and better than that of a competitor. Sometimes the differences can be genuine where additional features are incorporated, but often this can involve only changing customer perceptions of a product: 'Our soap powder washes whiter than our competitors'.

- **Unique selling points** (USPs) are unique features of your product or service that make it stand out from the competition. Featuring a USP in advertising can encourage sales at the expense of competitors.

- **Branding** exploits the fact that modern consumers love strong brands. A good brand image can sell a product more effectively than many other methods. Branding gives consumers the confidence to buy, and a brand image that is stronger than your competitors' can be worth a large number of sales. It is no wonder that businesses spend large amounts of money not just featuring products in advertising but stressing the brand name and its association with quality.

- **Packaging** can also help a product to sell. Many a flagging product has been revitalised by putting it in a different box or wrapper.

- **Advertising** can be informative but most of all it should make the product or brand familiar to potential customers.

## Thinking point

Consider five different products or services with which you are familiar.

1 Identify the different methods being used by the businesses concerned to keep them ahead of the competition.

2 Identify the pricing strategy being used for each.

3 Identify and explain the non-price strategies being used for each.

4 Put your results on flip-chart paper so that you can share them with the rest of the group.

### Price elasticity of demand

Pricing is clearly a significant method for capturing customers and being competitive, but it can be a slightly unpredictable strategy. When we lower our price we expect to achieve more sales, but whether we do or not depends on the reactions of our customers to the price drop. We may see a substantial rise in sales in which case our revenue will undoubtedly rise, but sometimes customer reactions can be much more modest and as a result we only gain a small number of customers. In this situation we can expect our revenue to fall as we are charging less for the product. The degree of reaction to a price change is known as the **price elasticity of demand** for the product.

If we change the price of our product and this results in a big change in demand for it, we describe the product as price elastic over that particular range of prices. In this situation, a rise in price tends to reduce revenue from the product (because we lose a lot of customers) and a fall in price tends to increase the firm's revenue (because we gain a lot of customers). A price elastic product or service gains a big response from customers to a change in price, which is very good if you are planning to discount the product, but seriously bad if you have to increase prices.

If we change the price of our product and this results in a small change in demand for it, we describe the product as price inelastic over that particular range of prices. In this situation, a rise in price tends to increase revenue from the product (because we do not lose many customers) and a fall in price tends to decrease the firm's revenue (because we do not gain many customers). A price inelastic product or service gains a small response from customers to a change in price, which is good if you have to increase prices, but not good if you are considering holding a cut-price sale.

Clearly it is important for a firm to have a good understanding of the level of price elasticity for a product before price changes are considered.

There are a number of factors that can influence the elasticity:

- **the size of the price rise or fall** – a proportionately small change may result in a very different degree of elasticity from that produced by a proportionately large change

- **how competitive the market is** – products with many close substitutes tend to be more price elastic than those with few competitors, simply because if one company raises prices there are plenty of other firms to buy from

- **whether the product is an essential item** – necessities such as basic food items tend to have much more inelastic demand, as people have to buy them regardless of the price

- **how addictive the product is** – smokers tend to continue buying cigarettes regardless of regular price increases, so demand for them is relatively inelastic.

**Thinking point**

Consider the following products and services and classify them as either price elastic or price inelastic over the price ranges mentioned. Explain your answers so that you can discuss them with the class.

1 Beer. Assume a 10% increase in price.

2 First class stamps. Compare an increase of 1p to an increase of 20p.

3 Bread. Assume a price increase of 15p per loaf.

4 Rail travel. Assume a 10% increase in price.

5 Margarine. Assume a 50% reduction in price.

6 Apple iPod. Assume a 50% reduction in price.

7 Ticket to a Chelsea football match. Assume an increase of £15 per ticket. (In 2004–2005 most adult tickets sold for between £45 and £48 per game.)

8 Designer label clothes. Assume a 30% reduction in price.

### Income elasticity of demand

Another key factor influencing demand is the incomes of customers. Some products and services are more responsive to changes in income than others – **income elasticity of demand** measures this responsiveness.

As people get richer they choose to buy more of some products. These are described as having income elastic demand. They are often luxury products.

With some products, however, people tend to buy the same amount regardless of how much richer they become. These products are described as having income inelastic demand and they are usually necessities.

There are some products, however, that people buy less of as they become richer, and these products are said to have negative income elastic demand. These are inferior products that people buy only because they are cheap, and as people get richer they buy fewer of them and buy higher quality substitutes instead.

**Thinking point**

Consider the following products and services and classify them as having income elastic demand, income inelastic demand or negative income elastic demand. Bear in mind that you will be looking at them from your own point of view, which may differ from that of other people. You might like to discuss alternative answers with your colleagues in class. The important thing is to be able to explain your reasoning.

- Restaurant meals
- Public transport
- Margarine
- Bread
- Foreign holidays

## Cross elasticity of demand

The demand for some products directly influences the demand for others. For example, as demand for DVD players has increased in recent years (as a result of falling prices), this has had the knock-on effect of increasing the demand for DVD discs. The disc manufacturers have seen demand increase, not as a result of anything they have done but because of something out of their control. **Cross elasticity of demand** measures the change in demand for one product following a change in price for another.

Some products, such as DVDs and DVD discs, find that their demand changes in similar ways – in other words, as one becomes more popular so does the other. These are known as complementary products (meaning that we tend to buy them together) and are described as having negative cross elasticity of demand.

Other products are substitutes for each other, and as the price for one increases, customers tend to buy the substitute instead because it is cheaper. Products that have very close substitutes tend to have demand that is very responsive to changes in price, and we describe them as having positive cross elasticity of demand. Different brands of soap powder tend to be good substitutes for each other, for example, and the manufacturers may find that they have positive cross elasticity – if one becomes cheaper people switch from buying the more expensive alternative.

### Case study   Cross elasticity

A good example of cross elasticity in recent years has been in the DVD player and video player markets. The average price of a DVD player has dropped from £311 in 2000 to just £90 in 2005, and consequently there has been a massive increase in sales of DVDs of over 700%. Over the same period the sales of video players has dropped by about 50%. The drop in the price of DVDs has clearly influenced the demand for video players – an example of positive cross elasticity.

### Thinking point

Consider the following pairs of products and classify them as having either positive or negative cross elastic demand.

- Motor cars and tyres
- Butter and margarine
- CDs and CD players
- Tennis racquets and tennis balls

## Long-term competitive approaches

To stay competitive in a market takes planning. Here are some of the approaches firms may consider.

### Market entry

A business should always be considering whether the time is right to enter a new market. Technology and fashions are forever changing so a firm should continually review what it does to identify new market opportunities that could be exploited. Diversifying means spreading operations into a much wider range of products or services, and this is often a good way of both ensuring survival for the firm and maintaining a competitive advantage.

### Market exit

It is equally important to know when to get out of a market. Managers should not be complacent and assume that things will always be as good as they are today; changing technology, fashions and economic circumstances mean that they should be continually looking critically at what the business does, and if the signs are bad for a particular market the firm should consider withdrawing and entering new markets before damage is done.

### Increasing or decreasing involvement in a market

Market changes might also suggest that a firm should do more or less of a particular market activity, in order to use resources most effectively.

## Lowering costs

It may happen that a business finds itself at a competitive disadvantage in a market that is fundamental to its success. It could be that it is faced with cheap imports from foreign countries, or perhaps a competitor is simply able to produce more efficiently. Abandoning the market may not be a viable strategy – perhaps the company has too much capital equipment that can only be used for specific processes. In these circumstances the firm may need to lower costs in order to enable it to drop prices and make its products or services more competitive.

**Economies of scale** is a technical term used by economists to describe the benefits to a firm of producing on a larger scale. In principle it is cheaper to produce on a large scale than a small one. It is like the practice of buying in bulk, which is generally cheaper than buying a large number of individual items. Firms buying raw materials on a large scale can do so much more cheaply than those doing so on a smaller scale.

Production costs fall as the scale of the organisation increases, because the fixed costs per unit fall as production rises, and businesses are able to benefit from discounts for bulk purchase when buying raw materials or components. Since large-scale production is more efficient than small-scale production, this could be an option for a firm that finds itself at a competitive disadvantage.

Large businesses also find it more viable to employ specialist managers, raise cheap finance and employ the latest technology, so these are further good reasons for growth as an aid to productivity.

A just-in-time (JIT) system helps the firm keep stocks at a minimum level, thus reducing costs. You can find more detail on this method of cutting costs in Unit 10: Final Accounts.

## Moving 'up-market'

Many firms in the UK have had to cut costs in order to fight off fierce competition from abroad, but sometimes that is not possible. Perhaps the business has already cut costs as much as possible and further cuts would only damage service or undermine quality. Faced with this problem, many UK companies have had to move 'up-market'. Perhaps other firms can compete with the current products, but they would find it more difficult against a product with more innovative features or of a much higher quality. Many businesses in the UK have therefore increased the quality of their final product to tempt customers back to them. If you can't compete on price, you may be able to compete on quality.

## New product development

The best way to compete is often to keep ahead of the competition. Designing new ideas before the competition does or getting them on the market first can be crucial. Research and development (R&D) is often vital in keeping a firm competitive, but unfortunately it is very expensive and often only large businesses can afford to do enough R&D – this is another economy of scale.

The drive for developing new products and diversifying has led to a growth in firms known as **conglomerates**. A conglomerate operates in a wide variety of markets, many of which are totally unrelated to each other. Virgin Group is a good example of a conglomerate company, producing a wide variety of products and services, from music and mobile phones to rail services and cola. Diversifying to such an extent is often a good way of ensuring the survival of a firm in competitive environments. If the firm produces 10 widely differing products or services, when the market for one becomes difficult the other nine should keep the business afloat.

**Thinking point**

Consider a company you are familiar with that operates in a very competitive market. Outline a series of techniques that the company should consider in order to keep itself alive against the competition.

# Non-competitive behaviour

It is clear that competition in markets is very good news for consumers, as it leads to increased consumer choice, innovation, high quality and downward pressure on prices. However, companies are often less keen on competition than consumers. The problem with competitive behaviour, from a company's point of view, is that it costs money. Lowering prices, maintaining high quality, innovating and all of those other benefits of competition are expensive to a firm and reduce profits; consequently many firms would avoid competition if possible.

Being in a market where there is little competition, such as a monopoly, duopoly or oligopoly, allows a company to charge whatever price it wishes and keep costs low to maximise profits. Consequently it is not unusual for firms to try to avoid or even restrict competition if they can. The bigger a firm becomes, the more it is able to influence the market it operates in. Today we have many extremely large firms such as multinational corporations that are very wealthy and very influential; they hold considerable economic power, which some occasionally use to reduce competition and consequently boost their own profits. This is clearly bad news for consumers.

## Barriers to market entry and restrictive practices

There is, of course, nothing wrong with businesses trying to encourage us to buy from them, but some firms become over-vigorous in their tactics and may engage in activities that restrict customer freedom of choice to such an extent that consumers get a raw deal.

**Anti-competitive practices** are tactics that attempt to remove or prevent competition in order to benefit specific firms. These are bad news for consumers, and the government will punish businesses that engage in such behaviour.

**Restrictive practices** are tactics used by large, influential firms to strengthen their hold over the markets in which they operate, to increase their market share, to eradicate competition, or to restrict consumer choice and therefore allow the firm to charge prices well above those that would be established in a competitive market. Restrictive practices are anti-competitive and therefore illegal.

## Predatory pricing

Unfortunately, firms in monopolistic positions are often very large, and consequently when competition tries to move in they have the financial muscle to do something about it.

Predatory pricing involves the monopolist reducing its prices to such an extent that the new competitor cannot compete. This may involve the monopolist selling items at less than the cost of production, and while this will clearly lead to operating losses in the short term, the monopolist may consider it to be a price worth paying if it forces the competition out of the market.

When it launched its budget airline Go, British Airways was accused by EasyJet and Danair of engaging in predatory pricing by entering the budget flights market. While BA claimed that it was entering the market simply to promote competition and give customers a better deal, the small budget companies were concerned that it was simply trying to force the smaller firms out of the skies. Why else, they asked, would BA be prepared to launch a new company that would run at a loss for probably the first three years of operation? In the end, Go was not as successful as BA hoped, so the potential threat was never fully realised, and indeed Go has since been sold by BA.

## Vertical restraints

Another way the monopolist may seek to exclude new competitors from getting established in its market is by applying pressure on the retailers through which the products will be sold. There are a number of such methods, and they are known collectively as **vertical restraints**.

● **Retail price maintenance** is where the monopolist insists that its products are sold at specific prices, with the threat that a retailer who does not comply will not be allowed to stock the monopolist's products in future. Clearly if the line is one that makes significant profits for the retailer, he or she will have to comply or lose profits. A few years ago, the Office of Fair Trading investigated two sportswear manufacturers, Puma and Asics, who supplied replica Leeds United team strips. A retailer in Leeds was selling the strips at £25 instead of the usual £40. Puma and Asics had told the retailer that if he continued to do so they would not continue to supply him. Fortunately in this case, the OFT investigated and the firms were made to promise that they would not carry out such threats, allowing the retailer to continue to discount the shirts.

● **Exclusive dealing** is where the monopolist puts pressure on the retailer to only stock its brand of product and not those of rivals. Again the threat is that the monopolist will cease supplying if the retailer does not comply.

● **Exclusive supply arrangements** are where the supplier only delivers to one dealer in a specific geographical area, and in return the dealer agrees to stock its products exclusively. This has the effect of both restricting outlets to new firms and maintaining high prices.

● **Tie-in sales** is where the supplier requires the retailer to take all of its product range, thereby discouraging new market entrants. In October 1997 Microsoft was fined a record sum by the US Justice Department for requiring personal computer manufacturers who wanted to license its Windows 95 operating system to also license and distribute its Internet browser, Microsoft Internet Explorer.

● **Quantity discounts** are offered to the retailer which get progressively larger the more he or she buys. This encourages retailers to stock predominantly one brand, again discouraging competition by restricting the outlets they may sell through. In 1991 British Coal was employing a discount scheme that provided discounts only to those customers who bought exclusively from British Coal. The OFT decided that this was anti-competitive.

● **Long-term supply contracts** tie the retailer to one supplier and often carry hefty penalties for termination.

More details of examples of restrictive practices can be found on the Office of Fair Trading website at *www.oft.gov.uk*.

### Cartels and monopoly power

Sometimes price competition breaks out in oligopoly markets. While this is usually good news for customers, the same is not always true for the oligopoly companies themselves. When price wars begin, the company that starts the war will normally see initial increases in revenue, but this will not often last. The effect of a price war in an oligopoly market will always be to increase revenues for some firms in the short term, but they will lead to a long-term reduction in profits for all companies in the market, since at the end of the war generally market shares are similar to what they were at the start, but prices have fallen.

Oligopolists are well aware of these facts and consequently they will go to some lengths to avoid price wars breaking out. They are also well aware that if they all sell at similar prices, all the firms will benefit. This leads to oligopolists sometimes making informal agreements not to engage in price competition and to ensure that price rises are always timed together so that all firms benefit. These agreements are known as **cartels**.

Cartels are clearly bad news for consumers, as they prevent price competition, and if all the oligopolists raise their prices in unison, they can set prices that are unrealistically high and consumers still have to pay them as no cheap alternatives exist.

Cartels are therefore illegal, and the government takes a very dim view of firms that engage in cartel practices as they simply abuse customers by limiting choice and keeping prices high. If it can be proved that firms are operating a cartel, the

Office of Fair Trading will take rigorous steps to ensure that the practice is stopped. The problem, of course, is proving that a cartel exists. Firms wishing to engage in such behaviour are not foolish enough to write anything down – cartels will be verbal agreements, and this makes them very difficult to prove.

## Case study    Price fixing

In 1999 the OFT broke up a secret market-sharing and price-fixing agreement between bus operators providing home-to-school services to local authority schools in Kingston upon Hull. The bus operators met secretly and agreed on minimum prices at which they would tender to supply school bus services, and the routes that each operator would tender for.

1 Which groups of people or organisations do you consider would lose out as a result of this cartel?
2 Research some other examples of cartels in the UK or abroad.

## Contestable markets

American economist William Baumol suggests that the key to a competitive market is how easy it is to enter the market. His theory of 'contestable markets' suggests that even a monopolist will act as if it were part of a competitive market and offer keen prices if it would be easy for new competitors to get into the market. The mere threat of new entrants would be enough to prevent the monopolist from abusing its market position. Removal of barriers to entry, such as predatory pricing, should therefore create fairer and more contestable markets.

Some markets, however, are more difficult to make contestable, in particular those with high sunk costs. Sunk costs are costs of entry that cannot be recovered when the firm leaves the market, such as marketing and advertising costs. When these costs are high, it is harder for new firms to enter the market and consequently the market will be less contestable.

## Monopsony – Market power in buyer hands

When we looked at the perfectly competitive market we saw that one of the key features of a fair market is that there should be a large number of both buyers and sellers. So far we have looked at the unfairness of a situation where there are very few sellers in a market (a monopolistic position). But a market can also be very problematic if there are only a small number of buyers. Such a market is known as a **monopsony**.

## Case study    Large supermarkets

Farmers often have the problem of being unsure whether they will be able to sell all their produce at market. In recent years a number of farmers have been approached by big supermarkets wanting to buy all of their produce, which on the face of it has been a big weight off farmers' minds. However, there have been accusations that the supermarkets have abused this relationship by forcing those farmers to sell their produce at much lower prices, possibly to the extent that the farmer makes very little profit. The farmers have found themselves in difficult situations because they have no other customers to sell to, so they have been forced to accept the lower prices offered. We can see, therefore, that being the only buyer in a market also brings unreasonable influence over the price, and this can be unfair to the producer.

1 What are the problems faced by farmers who are in this situation?
2 Research other examples of a monopsony, either in the UK or abroad.

# Market regulation

## Government/EU regulation and deregulation

Both the UK government and the European Union are aware that the promotion of competition will lead to increasing consumer choice and downward pressure on prices. Consequently they are both active in encouraging competition. Between them they set up a range of measures to regulate competition issues, including both laws and organisations, and they are collectively known as UK Competition Policy.

The Competition Act 1998 was a very significant piece of legislation as it gave the Office of Fair Trading much increased powers for investigating and prosecuting anti-competitive behaviour, in particular cartel activities. The OFT now has the power to make unannounced visits to the premises of companies under investigation, to seize any documents there, to restrict correspondence in and out of the firm and to restrict the movements and activities of the staff and directors of the firm while the investigation continues. Ultimately firms can be fined up to 10% of turnover if the case against them is proved, which is a substantial deterrent to anti-competitive behaviour.

The Enterprise Act 2002 has taken the matter further and has now criminalised cartel behaviour. This means that individuals could be prosecuted, not just companies, and this could lead to jail sentences for those convicted.

### European Commission

The European Commission is the ultimate competition authority in the UK, although most competition matters will be resolved by the UK government.

Competition cases will be considered by the Commission if the firms or industries involved are sufficiently large and the case crosses national boundaries within the EU.

### Office of Fair Trading

The Office of Fair Trading is headed by the Director General of Fair Trading (DGFT). Its functions relating to competition law are as follows:

- investigating cases of unfair contract terms and misleading advertising

- investigating the fitness of consumer credit licence applicants

- investigating cases where the OFT has reasonable grounds to suspect a breach of the Competition Act

- with the Serious Fraud Office (and the Crown Office in Scotland) investigating potential criminal cartel cases

- considering public mergers and referring more complex cases to the Competition Commission

- a consumer education programme.

### Practice point

Visit the OFT website at *www.oft.gov.uk* and study the recent cases the OFT has been involved in. Prepare a short presentation to the rest of your group on the benefits of having the OFT in place.

### Competition Commission

The Competition Commission was established by the Competition Act 1998 and replaced the Monopolies and Mergers Commission in 1999. The Commission conducts in-depth inquiries into mergers, markets and the regulation of the major regulated industries. Every inquiry is undertaken in response to a reference made to it by another authority – usually by the Office of Fair Trading, but in certain circumstances by the Secretary of State or the regulators.

The Commission is responsible for making decisions on competition questions and for deciding on and implementing appropriate remedies. The Commission has to determine whether practices are against the public interest.

## Outcome activity 29.2

For this activity you should use the same market as you examined in Outcome Activity 29.1 earlier. Produce a further report to fulfil the following tasks.

### Pass
Describe the structure or relative competitive shares of the market.

1 How many major firms operate in the market and how you would define the market?

2 Name the major players and their relative market shares.

3 Assess how competitive you believe the market to be (you will need to give some evidence to support your judgement).

4 Describe what a new competitor would need to do to successfully enter the market.

### Merit
Analyse the key competitive strategies that are used in the market.

1 Describe the competitive strategies being used in the market.

2 Assess the effectiveness of the strategies.

### Distinction
Assess the extent to which your chosen market may be considered 'contestable'. This will require you to compare the market in detail with the perfectly competitive market model and reach a judgement.

# Impact of stakeholders on business decision-making

You have come across the concept of stakeholders before – a stakeholder is someone (or a group of people) likely to be affected by the success or failure of a business. The group of stakeholders in a business is quite a large one, ranging from the employees of the firm, through their business relations such as customers and suppliers, to the people who live locally, and right through to the UK government. All of these groups would either benefit from the firm doing well or lose out if the business failed.

In this unit, however, we look at stakeholders from a different perspective. Not only are stakeholders affected by a firm's actions, but they are also able to affect the firm by their actions. It is this effect that we will be examining in this section – the impact that stakeholders may have on the business.

## Stakeholders

Here is a reminder of a firm's stakeholder groups.

| Stakeholder | Concerns |
|---|---|
| Shareholders | As the owners of the business they are keen to see it expanding and developing in order that their shares may rise in value, and the business may earn additional profits which they can share. |
| Employees | Employees will be keen to have job security and to see improvements in their pay and conditions of employment. |
| Suppliers | The suppliers of the firm will be keen to see that the business is stable so that they will continue to be able to sell to it. |
| Competitors | The success of one firm may result in less success for another, so clearly competitors have a keen interest in each other's success. |

| Stakeholder | Concerns |
|---|---|
| Customers | Customers will hope that the firm continues to be successful because otherwise they will have to find an alternative business to buy from, which may be inconvenient. |
| Local community | People and businesses in the locality should benefit from the success of a firm through increased wealth, employment, local taxes and local investment, but they may also have concerns over levels of pollution created by some firms. |
| Government/ the nation | The nation has similar concerns to the local community but on a larger scale – concerns over employment, investment, growth and tax contributions. If a business fails, this can be a big drain on the public purse. |
| Creditors (including bankers) | Creditors will be keen to see the firm succeed as their repayments depend upon it. If the business fails, a creditor will also lose a valuable customer. |

## Impact of stakeholders

Each of the stakeholders mentioned above could take actions that would affect the performance of the firm. A number of them represent external influences over which the firm has only limited control, and even internal influences, such as from employees, could result in action that the management was unable to predict. Consequently the firm could find itself vulnerable to unexpected and unforeseen events. Strikes by employees, disputes with suppliers or pressure groups formed by the local community could all have a significant influence over a firm's actions, and a number of these might be totally unexpected.

Each of the stakeholders has different ways of putting pressure on a firm, and some of them are more influential than others.

| Stakeholder | Influences |
|---|---|
| Shareholders | As the owners of the firm, ordinary shareholders have a special influence over the firm. They are entitled to vote at general meetings, and if enough shareholders vote the same way it is possible to make major changes to the firm. In 2004 the shareholders of Eurotunnel (the owners of the Channel Tunnel) decided that the current directors were not running the company well. As a result they called for a vote of no confidence in the directors at the Annual General Meeting and the whole board of directors was voted out of the company. The shareholders then duly elected replacement directors in the hope that they would run the firm more effectively. |
| Employees | Employees may have grievances against their employers. Perhaps they feel that they are paid too little, or are unhappy over their working conditions. In such circumstances the employees could use a number of possible actions to put pressure on company management. <br><br> **Work to rule** – where the employees do no more than their contract requires them to do. Any actions that are normally done out of goodwill are stopped. Companies who ask their employees to 'help out' with a lot of activities that are outside their contracts could find that such action reduces productivity substantially. <br><br> **Go slow** – where workers deliberately slow down their work rate so productivity falls. <br><br> **Ban overtime** – refuse to work overtime when it is offered to them. Many firms rely on their employees to do overtime to get urgent jobs done, so a ban could result in a firm struggling to complete orders for customers on time. <br><br> **Strike** – if all else fails, the employees could refuse to report for work at all. Such action, if all employees join in, could result in the firm losing production completely. |

| Stakeholder | Influences |
|---|---|
| Suppliers | Suppliers have two ways to influence a firm, both of which could prove damaging to themselves. They could refuse to extend further credit to a customer, or stop supplying it altogether. Either of these actions would not be taken lightly, as they may result in the loss of a valuable customer. |
| Competitors | We have already considered the types of action that competitive firms engage in. To remind yourself, turn back to the section entitled 'Competitive behaviour' on pages 253–255. |
| Customers | Customers may be concerned for many reasons – possibly about the levels of service they have been receiving from a firm, perhaps because they have been sold faulty goods that have not been satisfactorily replaced, or possibly it has come to light that the firm is exploiting child labour in a developing country.<br><br>Unhappy customers have a number of options:<br><br>● stop buying from the firm<br>● protest outside the factory or store<br>● contact the media and give the firm negative publicity<br>● form a pressure group. This is a group of people who collectively protest over what a firm is doing. They will normally use a range of methods to publicise their cause, including the three methods listed above and also printing leaflets or setting up websites to let the public know their reasons for objecting to the activities of the firm. |
| Local community | The local community may have concerns similar to those of customers, but may also be concerned about the environmental impact of the firm's activities on the locality. The remedies that the local community can use are very similar to those of customers. |
| Government/ the nation | The government sometimes chooses to put deliberate pressure on firms, for example by taxing businesses that damage the environment. The government will also pass laws to regulate unwelcome activities, such as the Competition Act 1998 referred to earlier, which gives the OFT powers to investigate and prosecute firms forming cartels.<br><br>Government influence may also be unintentional, for example unfavourable international relations as a result of government action or inaction may have a knock-on effect on a business as the country concerned may be a key customer or supplier of a UK firm. The bad relations engendered by the government could result in a loss of custom or supplies for a firm. |
| Creditors (including bankers) | A bank approached for a loan may influence the company by obliging it to comply with certain requirements as a condition of granting the loan. If the bank is concerned about the possibility of getting its money back at any time, it may call for immediate repayment of a loan or overdraft in full. This could influence the firm by putting it under severe financial strain. Ordinarily, however, creditors are unlikely to do this, out of their own self-interest. |

## Practice point

Over the next week, watch TV news and/or read a good newspaper to look out for situations where different stakeholders have influenced companies. Pick out an interesting incident and prepare a short talk to be given to the class describing the events that took place and the possible impact on the company concerned.

## Porter's 'Five Forces'

In 1980, Michael Porter wrote a book called Competitive Strategy: Techniques for Analyzing Industries and Competitors. In it he described his Five Forces theory, which has since come to be regarded as a useful tool for analysing the competitive forces that influence a company. He identified five forces applicable to any company that shape the way it behaves. These are:

- the threat of new entrants
- the power of suppliers
- the power of buyers
- the availability of substitutes
- competitive rivalry within the industry.

These forces are often illustrated using this diagram:

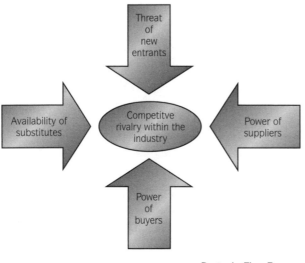

*Porter's Five Forces*

The five forces affect the company in the following ways.

- **Threat of new entrants –** this was discussed earlier in this unit in the section headed 'Contestable markets'. The easier it is for new firms to break into a market, the more difficult the level of competition becomes. Barriers to entry may limit the number of possible new entrants. Some of these may be put up deliberately by firms with monopolistic power in the market, and others may be natural barriers. Some examples include the required amount of sunk costs, brand loyalty, a scarcity of resources, legal

barriers, difficulty or cost involved with customers changing from one supplier to another, and predatory pricing.

- **Power of suppliers –** sometimes suppliers are able to influence a company, but only if certain conditions prevail. For example, if the supplier is a monopolistic one, it can dictate market conditions to a certain extent. This power is increased further if the product is a necessity to the buyer, there are few good substitutes available, or there is considerable difficulty or cost involved with customers changing from one supplier to another.

- **Power of buyers –** sometimes buyers can influence the company. A small number of buyers out of a large customer base will find it very difficult to bring influence to bear as their voice will be very small. However, if customers act in unison, or if a buyer is in a monopsony position, they can bring considerable pressure to bear on the firm. Other situations that increase buyer power are where a buyer buys a large proportion of the firm's output, or where there are many firms offering the same product and changing suppliers is easy.

- **Availability of substitutes –** in a market where few substitutes are available, the firm is in a more stable position. However, if there are many alternatives for customers and if switching to another is relatively easy, this threat will influence the firm significantly. The key factors here are the number and quality of the substitutes; the more there are and the more that are similar in quality, the greater the threat.

- **Competitive rivalry –** some markets are much more competitive than others. Markets containing many firms, none of which is dominant, tend to be competitive, as do those where different firms offer very similar standard products. The degree of rivalry will influence company behaviour considerably. The closer a market gets to the perfectly competitive model we saw earlier, the more the firm will be influenced by competitors.

Using the company that you researched from the news in the last activity (page 265), analyse the firm in the light of Porter's Five Forces model. Make notes on the extent to which each of the five forces are influencing your chosen company.

## Outcome activity 29.3

### Pass

1 Carry out secondary research to identify a case of significant stakeholder influence over a business. On-line newspapers such as www.telegraph.co.uk are a good source for this, as are business journals, TV and radio news.

Choose a case where a stakeholder has brought pressure to bear on a company, to the extent that the firm has had to change some aspect of its operations. This might be workers using industrial action to improve their working conditions, customers demonstrating outside a store in protest against certain products stocked, an environmental pressure group targeting a firm to force it to change its working practices, or any other such case. Have your list of stakeholders in front of you while doing your research to give it focus.

2 Write a newspaper article describing the events in this case.

### Merit

Conclude your article begun in the previous task by analysing the impact on the business concerned of the stakeholder influence.

To analyse it effectively, you will need to break down the case. One approach might be to examine each functional department of the firm and discuss how each might have been affected by the case. Explain how and why the effects you describe have arisen. Further secondary research into the case you have chosen should give you ideas about the impact of the events of the case.

### Distinction

Write a detailed evaluation of the potential effects of stakeholder influence on a selected business of your choice. Evaluate the extent to which stakeholders may shape major decisions on the part of a selected business.

Include all stakeholder groups in your analysis. It is essential that you also include theory in your response, including Porter's Five Forces. You should outline those aspects of the theory that are relevant to this topic and then relate the theory to the relevant stakeholder groups.

# The impact of e-business

Undoubtedly one of the biggest changes in the relationship between businesses and customers in recent years has been the increasing use of the Internet to both boost sales and to strengthen relationships with existing and potential customers. Cisco Systems Inc., a major supplier of networking equipment and network management for the Internet, describe e-business as 'the process of putting all business processes on Web-based networks and integrating them with all relevant information available globally', so you can see that this goes much further than simply selling things on-line. It means putting the whole business on a new Internet-based footing.

# Effects of e-business

E-business has helped to bring businesses and their markets closer to each other. The changes that the Internet has brought to businesses and their markets are many and various. Some of the key changes are described below.

## Boosting demand and encouraging supply

By selling over the Internet, firms can access a much wider customer base. A traditional business may sell only in its locality, but e-business allows firms to access customers worldwide, thus the target market is a lot larger. At the same time Internet trading conquers the problem of time differences. To sell across the world means that you might need sales staff available to serve customers around the clock, since night-time in the UK is day-time elsewhere in the world, but an e-commerce presence can be available 24 hours a day.

## Effects on pricing in global digital markets

E-business offers the opportunity to make significant cost savings. Such businesses are cheap to set up; in comparison to opening a High Street store, the premises costs are minimal, as are those for fixtures and fittings. Staff costs can also be reduced as the firm needs fewer sales staff and less administrative support. Such savings can allow the firm to offer cheaper prices, and this in turn should boost sales.

The Internet allows companies to quickly revise the pricing of products offered if circumstances change. Instead of having to reprint advertising and sales materials, a 'brochureware' site can be quickly and cheaply updated. Companies can therefore be very responsive to market changes.

A well-designed e-commerce site also offers a unique opportunity for firms to engage in 'dynamic pricing'. This technique is a method of charging different prices to different customers for the same item, based on factors such as where they live and their previous purchase history. Websites can easily track the buying habits of consumers and they will also have precise information about where the customer lives, so it is possible for sites to offer different prices to different visitors based on this information. Dynamic pricing could maximise sales income by offering attractively low prices to some customers and premium pricing to others who are likely to buy whatever the price.

Some websites are completely interactive between buyers and sellers and therefore dynamically produce a price directly relative to the levels of demand and supply for an item. The obvious example of this is eBay (www.ebay.com), where purchasers bid for items and the final selling price depends entirely upon how keen the bidders are to own the item.

### Thinking point

1 Search the Internet (using Google or another search engine) for 'dynamic pricing'. What examples can you find of firms engaging in such pricing methods?

2 What are the advantages and disadvantages of such a method?

3 As a customer, do you consider dynamic pricing to be a fair method for a firm to use? Give reasons to support your view.

## Effects upon provision of information

Providing information to customers is significantly easier today. In the past, organisations might have relied upon methods such as printed brochures, leaflets and catalogues being sent through the post, which took time and was relatively inefficient. Today, providing detailed information via a company website is a much better solution. E-business helps not only profit-making firms; it has also benefited many public organisations such as government and the health service. Sites such as www.direct.gov.uk and www.nhsdirect.com have made much more information readily available to UK citizens.

## Increasingly rapid adaptability of supply to demand

Because it is relatively easy to set up an e-commerce site, this breaks down some of the natural barriers to entry into markets, so firms can react quickly to new market opportunities. The 24-hours-a-day, seven-days-a-week nature of e-commerce also means that customers can shop at times that are convenient to them.

## Increasing individualisation of products in a mass market

Being able to offer a more personalised product can be a major advantage to a firm in a competitive market. A well-designed website can enable a firm to do just that. Many websites will now allow the customer to not only choose a product to buy but also choose extra features, colours and designs. Take a look at *www.evesham.com*, the website for Evesham Technology, which makes and sell PCs. If you choose a particular model to buy you can then choose from a wide range of additional hardware and software options to add to it, so you can design the product to meet your personal requirements exactly. The Audi site, *www.audi.co.uk*, contains the Audi Configurator, which allows you to select the interior and exterior colours for your new car, and you can see on screen exactly what your chosen combinations will look like. (To see this, go to 'New car', then click on one of the models featured, say the Audi 8, and click the option 'Configure your Audi'.)

### Practice point

1 Look on the Internet for other examples of firms offering individualised products to customers via their websites.

2 With a partner, decide on a product or service that could be offered over the Internet that would benefit from being sold on an individualised basis. Draw up a list of features that you could offer customers on this basis.

3 On flip-chart paper, sketch out the Web page that you would use to sell your product or service in this way.

## Precisely targeted direct marketing

The same tracking technology that is used to allow dynamic pricing on websites can also be used to make very precise direct marketing suggestions to customers when they visit the site. If you visit the Amazon site (*www.amazon.co.uk*) for example, it recognises you when you return (by means of a small piece of computer code called a cookie that it places on the hard drive of your machine) and calculates which products you might be interested in. It monitors all the pages you view and records all the purchases that you make, so it can select very precisely any new products you may be interested in. The site will then suggest the products to you as a series of recommendations. These will be different each time you visit. This is clearly much more likely to produce results than a system of randomly generated marketing suggestions.

## New or unique business opportunities

The Internet has allowed completely new business models to be developed, such as eBay. This method of worldwide auctioning of products could not be done in any other way – without the Internet this business model could not exist.

### Thinking point

Discuss with a partner some websites you have visited. Identify ones that represent unique business opportunities that have come from Web trading.

## Effects on provision of services

E-business provides companies and other organisations the chance to offer services to a much wider target market. This includes not only people who live in remote rural places and in other countries, but also those who have mobility problems such as elderly or housebound people. Via the Internet, such people can find out about the services that may help them much more easily and can also place orders without leaving their homes.

The Internet also makes it much easier for customers and companies to compare prices and specifications of products before they buy, which is clearly a better level of service. However, this could also prove disadvantageous to firms if they do not compare well with their competitors.

### Decision-making in response to market trends

Since websites are easy to set up and easy to amend, a company can be very responsive to changes in the market and can quickly be in a position to change what it offers to customers if necessary. In this way markets are coming closer to the perfectly competitive model that we saw earlier, as this makes a firm's factors of production much more mobile.

### Impact of on-line operations in gathering information

As we have already seen, a website offers a good opportunity for gathering information about customers' buying habits, which can inform promotions, but it also offers the opportunity for customers to give direct feedback about products and services through e-mail, chatrooms and message boards. These can prove to be valuable information sources, which is why so many firms include them on their sites.

Of course it is also a great way of keeping an eye on the competition. It is easy to find out which products and services competitors are offering, what prices they are charging and any deals they currently offer.

### Thinking point

It has been said that the Internet is making markets much closer to the perfectly competitive model that we examined earlier. Go back to that definition now, list the seven features and then make notes about how e-commerce is bringing us closer to this ideal.

## Developments in e-business

The rapid expansion of Internet usage has resulted in the emergence of an interconnected on-line global marketplace that has massive potential for firms worldwide. However, this is a dynamic market and firms need to keep abreast of developments in the market as changes can be very rapid.

### Global demographics of the Web-user profile

Webographics examines trends in the use of e-commerce and e-business, for example how many people are using the Internet to buy goods and services, and the trends in value of those transactions.

Things change very rapidly in the world of the Internet. For example in the 12 months to October 2004, the number of people actively surfing the Web from home each month in Europe grew by 12% to 100 million, according to figures published by Nielson Netratings (*www.nielsen-netratings.com*). At the same time the number of people in Europe using high-speed Internet connections from home increased from 34.1 million people to 54.5 million people, an increase of 60%. The largest increases occurred in Italy (120%), and in the UK (93%).

Among the big users of the Internet, young people are leading the way. About 2.2 million 12–17-year-olds used the Internet for entertainment in December 2004, which was 78% of all the 12–17-year-olds on-line in the UK. Almost half of these visited music-related sites during that month, with Yahoo!'s music channel 'Launch' being the most visited site.

In February 2005, 2.2 million more women visited multi-category travel sites compared to the previous year. At that time women accounted for 44% of visitors to those travel sites, compared to 36% at the same time the previous year.

Clearly this sort of statistical information is vital to businesses hoping to trade via the Internet, so that they have a good understanding of who uses what sort of site and how best to promote sites. This is fundamental to a successful e-commerce presence, so firms should keep a close eye on trends as they develop.

## Practice point

Research a detailed picture of webographic trends. Using the following websites, answer the questions below. If the exact page is unavailable, browse the site for alternatives. You may also be able to find some other relevant websites of your own by doing some searching.

*www.nielsen-netratings.com* – Look in the latest press releases section

*http://www.economist.com/surveys/showsurvey.cfm?issue=20040515* – There is a series of useful articles here on e-commerce

*http://www.actinic.co.uk/docs/2004_Actinic_Ecommerce_Report.pdf* – Actinic's 2004 E-commerce Market Report

*http://www.statistics.gov.uk* – Search for 'e-commerce'

*http://www.culture.gov.uk* – Search for 'UK Internet market trends'

1 What are the recent trends in customers placing orders over the Internet? Quote figures to support your answer.

2 What types of products and services are selling well over the Internet?

3 What are the recent trends in home Internet access?

4 What has happened to prices for Internet access in recent years?

5 To what extent have fast Internet access lines such as broadband increased in the UK?

6 Which members of society have least access to the Internet?

7 What percentage of businesses are now buying and selling on-line?

8 Give examples of government services that are now available on-line.

9 Identify possible trends for future use of the Internet.

10 Which search engines would you recommend a firm to advertise through? Which search engines get the best 'click-through' rates?

11 Which are the fastest-growing categories of goods sold over the Internet?

12 Which European countries have experienced the fastest growth in Internet usage?

13 To what extent do customers research on-line before buying from traditional stores?

14 What do on-line customers consider to be the most important features on a website when they are choosing where to buy?

15 What percentage of retail websites make a profit?

## *Factors shaping on-line business*

There are many factors that are influencing the shape and success of e-business. Some of the main ones are described below.

## *Popularity of Internet cafés/salons*

Internet cafés are one of the reasons why Web access has boomed in the UK over the past 10 years. They first started up in the early 1990s and soon became popular, and despite the fact that many homes now have Web access, their popularity continues. Internet use can seem to be a lonely occupation, but linking it with a social atmosphere and a comfortable environment still proves to be a draw, especially for travellers in unfamiliar places. The social side of Internet cafés has encouraged many people to try the Internet for the first time, and many of those people have become regular users. This has therefore opened up opportunities for e-business firms who provide services for people to use the Internet as a form of leisure pursuit.

## Cost barriers to computer ownership

The cost of buying a computer that was sufficiently advanced to make Internet surfing pleasurable used to be prohibitive, but that is no longer the case. It is now possible to buy a high-specification machine for significantly less than £500, and the cost of fast Internet lines has dropped significantly in recent years. Consequently more and more people have been in a position to give it a try. A much wider base of people with access to websites has made Web-based businesses much more viable.

## Opposition to computer use

Although a few years ago many people were worried by the prospect of using computers, so many people have to use them as part of their jobs today that the incidence of technophobia has reduced significantly. The UK government has also funded a range of part-time courses at local schools and colleges aimed at giving people the opportunity to build up their confidence in using computers, and this too has increased computer usage.

Many senior citizens also now see the benefits of buying and selling items on-line from their homes, as well as keeping in contact with distant friends and relatives by e-mail. The fact that so many more people are using the Internet regularly also encourages the development of e-businesses.

*Many senior citizens now see the benefits of buying and selling on-line from their homes*

## Censorship

There is still a lot of unpleasant material on the Internet and this does give cause for concern, but many people are less worried today that it will adversely affect their browsing experiences because of the wide availability of software that will prevent such sites intruding while we surf. Programs such as Norton Internet Security and McAfee Internet Security Suite prevent unwanted sites from being displayed, as well as protecting computers against harmful viruses and attacks from hackers. This increased confidence in using the Internet has also encouraged more people to use it.

## Variable business performance of on-line sales

Initially there may have been teething problems for some Internet sites and some received a bad press for not delivering promptly or allowing unauthorised access to their sites by hackers, but today the incidence of such events has declined and many established on-line retailers such as Amazon are recognised as being very reputable and efficient. Now the model for an e-business has had time to settle down, transactions are mostly dealt with efficiently and securely, and this too has encouraged more people to buy on-line.

## Customer-to-customer (c2c) websites

The desire people have to buy and sell their own items via the Internet has encouraged the emergence of c2c sites such as eBay and Amazon Marketplace. These are completely new business models that could not exist in a world without the Internet, and their popularity is huge. Consequently there are considerable business opportunities in this area. For example, net profits at eBay for the three months to December 2004 continued to climb at the rapid rate of 44% to $205 million!

## On-line discussion sites and consumer response sites

These on-line facilities give customers the opportunity to feed back to fellow customers and companies very rapidly. They have proved to be a very valuable source of primary information for

Internet-based firms, and this information has undoubtedly been used to shape their on-line businesses.

### Competitiveness of small on-line firms

It is often difficult for small companies to enter markets because of the sunk costs of setting up, but the Internet business model is so easy, quick and relatively cheap that many new small firms have been able to enter markets. This change encourages analysts to believe that markets are becoming much more 'perfect' as the barriers to entry are reduced.

### UK government support for enterprise

The UK government has been a big supporter of on-line businesses and it offers a great deal of advice and support for such new businesses. For more details visit the following sites:

www.ukonlineforbusiness.gov.uk
www.businesslink.gov.uk.

### Outcome activity 29.4

For the purposes of this task, assume that you are working for WebAlive, a Web-page design and Internet consultancy company based at 27 Goose Gate, Hockley, Nottingham, NG1 2NL. The company specialises in designing and maintaining websites on behalf of commercial clients.

**Pass**

1 Produce a brochure for the company to use in sales presentations to potential clients. This brochure should outline all of the potential ways by which a business might benefit from an on-line presence. Your brochure should include:

○ as many benefits as you can think of for companies having an on-line presence

○ the key webographic trends that show how essential an on-line presence is to a company today.

2 Choose a business local to where you live. This can be any business, but choose one that you think would benefit from Web trading (it may in fact have a site already). Produce a letter addressed to the manager of the business from WebAlive, explaining how that business would benefit from an on-line presence. The benefits that you discuss should be specific to that company, so think carefully about which benefits are most relevant to that type of business.

To make your answer clear you will also need to produce a separate short summary of the work that your selected business carries out.

### Key terms

**Anti-competitive practices**
tactics used by firms that attempt to remove or prevent competition in order to strengthen their market position

**Cartels**
informal agreements between companies not to engage in price competition and to ensure that price rises are always done together so that all the firms in the market make extra profits

**Competitor pricing**
monitoring closely the prices charged by competitors and reacting immediately when they change by matching them

**Complements**
products that we have to buy together, such as DVDs and DVD players – one is no good without the other and the demand for one affects the demand for the other

## Key terms

### Conglomerate
a firm that operates in a wide variety of markets, many of which are totally unrelated to each other, such as Virgin Group

### Cross elasticity of demand
measurement of how a change in price for one product can change demand for an alternative or complementary product

### Demand curve
a graph that illustrates the relationship between the price of a product and the demand for it

### Determinants of demand
factors other than price that influence levels of demand

### Determinants of supply
factors other than the price of the product that influence levels of supply

### Diversification
producing a wider range and variety of goods or services

### Duopoly
a market where there are only two suppliers of a particular good or service

### Economies of scale
the advantages of producing on a large scale; significant cost savings can be made by increasing the volume of products produced

### Equilibrium point
the point on a demand and supply diagram where the levels of demand and supply are equal

### Equilibrium price
the price at which the market will settle if we allow demand and supply to freely dictate the market; this is also known as the market clearing price

### Equilibrium quantity
the quantity of production at which the market will settle if we allow demand and supply to freely dictate the market

### Income elasticity of demand
measurement of how demand changes in response to changes in consumer incomes

### Market clearing price
the price at which the market will settle if we allow demand and supply to freely dictate the market; this is also known as the equilibrium price

### Monopoly
a market where there is only one supplier of a particular good or service

### Monopsony
a market where there are only a small number of buyers

### Oligopoly
a market where there are only a small number of suppliers of a particular good or service

### Penetration pricing
a launch strategy that involves setting a very low initial price to establish market share; the price is increased later to maximise profits

### Perfectly competitive market
an ideal market that is fair to both producers and customers

### Price elasticity of demand
a measurement of how responsive customers are to changes in price; where a change in price leads to a big change in the number of customers buying the product, it is said to be price elastic, and where a change in price leads to a small change in the number of customers buying the product, it is said to be price inelastic

### Product differentiation
a marketing activity that encourages customers to believe that one product is different from and better than that of a competitor

## Key terms

**Restrictive practices**
tactics used by large influential firms to strengthen their hold over the markets in which they operate, to increase their market share, to eradicate competition, to restrict consumer choice and therefore allow the firm to charge high prices

**Skimming pricing**
a launch strategy that involves setting a very high initial price to maximise profits in the short term; the price is dropped later to attract further custom from different market segments

**Supply curve**
a graph that illustrates the relationship between the price of a product and the supply for it

**Unique selling point (USP)**
something unique about a product or service that makes it stand out from the competition

**Vertical restraints**
pressures placed on retailers by large suppliers to stock limited ranges or sell at specific prices

# End-of-unit test

1 Which determinants of demand have been most influential in the mobile phone market in recent years?

2 To what extent can knowledge of the determinants of demand help us to predict changes in demand for a product?

3 Identify and describe three methods that a clothing firm could use to boost demand for its products.

4 Survey your class asking how many packets of crisps they would buy per week at different prices ranging from 5p to 75p per packet. Aim to interview at least 20 classmates. Use the information to calculate a demand schedule for crisps in your class and draw a demand curve to show the information.

5 Draw four simple sketch diagrams of the demand and supply curves for a leading brand of yogurt. Show what shifts of the curve would take place and how the equilibrium would change in each of the following scenarios.

- The company runs a successful advertising campaign for its yogurt.

- A new production method is designed that makes it significantly cheaper to produce the yogurt.

- There is a health scare about the content of the yogurt after a number of people fall ill after eating it.

- Yogurt becomes a more fashionable product among the public after a leading footballer is seen eating it before a big game. At the same time the manufacturer is having trouble obtaining raw material supplies as a supplier has just gone out of business.

6 What remedies are there for a consumer who feels he or she has been given poor service by a company?

7 Who are the utility regulators, and what is their role?

8 What are the differences between monopoly, duopoly and oligopoly markets?

9 Describe the differences between penetration pricing and skimming pricing. In what circumstances would each be useful?

10 Why do many companies consider price wars to be very bad news?

11 What are non-price competition strategies? Give three examples and say how they work.

12 Why is it important to consider the price elasticity of a product before the business decides on a price change?

13 Name three products/services that have been affected by income elastic demand in recent years. Name a further three that have been affected by negative income elastic demand in recent years.

14 What are economies of scale?

15 What are anti-competitive and restrictive practices? Give examples and explain the ways in which they disadvantage customers and/or competitors.

16 What is a cartel? Why are they illegal in the UK?

17 What is a monopsony? Who loses out as a result of a monopsony? Explain your answer.

18 Outline the ways by which dissatisfied employees might put pressure on their employers to improve their working conditions.

19 Why would the managers of a firm be well advised to start up an on-line presence for their company?

20 What are webographics? What do you consider to be the three most significant webographic changes in recent years? Explain your choices.

# Resources

## Texts

Allen, Kania and Yaeckel: *Internet World Guide to One-To-One Web Marketing*, John Wiley & Sons Inc, 1998

Anderton, A: *Economics 3rd Edition*, Causeway Press, 2001

Chaffey, Mayer, Johnston, and Ellis-Chadwick: *Internet Marketing*, Pearson Education Ltd./Financial Times-Prentice Hal, 2000

Goymer, J: *BTEC National E-Business Book 1*, Heinemann, 2004

Grant, Vidler and Ellams: *Heinemann Economics for Edexcel: AS Student Book*, Heinemann, 2003

Lewis and Trevitt: *Business Vocational A-Level, 3rd Edition*, Stanley Thornes, 2000

Palmer and Hartley: *The Business Environment, 4th Edition*, McGraw Hill Education, 2002

Stanlake and Grant: *Introductory Economics, 6th Edition*, Longman, 1995

## Journals

*Economics Today*

## Websites

*www.oft.gov.uk* The Office of Fair Trading

*www.tradingstandards.gov.uk/index.cfm* Trading Standards Department

*www.which.co.uk/index.jsp* On-line *Which?* magazine from the Consumers' Association

*www.ncc.org.uk/index.htm* The National Consumer Council

*www.citizensadvice.org.uk* The Citizens Advice Bureau

*www.ofcom.org.uk* Office of the Communications Regulator

*www.ofgem.gov.uk/ofgem/index.jsp* Office of the Gas and Electricity Markets Regulator

*www.ofwat.gov.uk* Office of the Water and Sewerage Operators Regulator

*www.rail-reg.gov.uk* Office of Rail Regulation

*www.bbc.co.uk/watchdog* BBC *Watchdog* programme

*www.statistics.gov.uk* Office for National Statistics

*www.telegraph.co.uk* The *Daily Telegraph*

*www.bized.ac.uk/glossary/econglos.htm* UK business and finance information source, economic glossary

*www.sosig.ac.uk/economics/* The Social Sciences Information Gateway to Economics

*www.boxesandarrows.com/archives/understanding_ organizational_stakeholders_for_design_success.php* Boxes and Arrows, an architectural website with details on stakeholder conflicts

*www.greenpeace.org.uk/* Greenpeace, environmental campaign group

*www.foe.co.uk/* Friends of the Earth, environmental campaign group

This unit starts by exploring the features of the very many retail sales environments that consumers can visit. It then discusses the factors that influence retail site choice such as closeness to 'honeypot' locations, for example Heathrow Airport. It continues by reviewing the merchandising methods, such as the aroma created in a store, to make products more attractive to consumers. In conclusion it considers the facilities demanded by shoppers. After all, the shopping experience is nowadays more than simply choosing and paying for the goods!

The second section investigates retail consumer buying behaviour, including developments such as the re-emergence of the convenience store, and the need for companies such as Arcadia to have seven different stores, including Topshop and Dorothy Perkins, all alongside each other in the High Street. Finally, it considers whether loyalty cards such as Tesco's Clubcard really do increase demand.

The unit next considers the principles and practices of effective retail selling. Will sales assistants really succeed if they always introduce themselves to a potential customer with the phrase 'Can I help you?'. Retailers in general do not produce anything, so how can they make the Sony television they are selling seem more attractive than the same product in another electrical store? Lastly, the section considers sales incentives and whether paying people based on the sales they make (commission payments) is the best method.

The final section examines the role of stock control as a retail sales support function. How can sales assistants, for example, ensure the oldest stock is sold first and reduce the number of out-of-stock products? In conclusion, it considers the 'technological revolution' taking place involving the movement of goods from supplier to retail store, such as satellite tracking of distribution trucks.

Unit 33 is therefore divided into four main areas:

- 33.1 Features of the retail sales environment
- 33.2 Retail consumer buying behaviour
- 33.3 Principles and practices of effective retail selling
- 33.4 The role of stock control as retail sales support.

## Features of the retail sales environment

Retailers exist to provide a service to customers at a profit. All the roles of retailing – operating from an appropriate location, offering attractive product assortments, ensuring enough stock is available to meet demand – add value to the products bought from suppliers and eventually sold to consumers. It is the retailer's role in adding value that creates profit for retail organisations.

## Points of sale

### Convenience stores

A feature of convenience stores is that customers can at short notice acquire the products they offer. These stores allow customers to buy products during and outside normal shopping hours seven days a week. Stores tend to be located in residential communities, and the catchment areas are generally quite small. Examples of such stores include Spar and Tesco Express.

## Niche outlets

**Niche outlets** offer specialist products such as clothes for tall men, or collectable toys. The staff, often enthusiasts, have specialist knowledge and can give consumers detailed information and advice. Customers will often travel miles for the information and products required. Locations frequented by enthusiasts, such as venues for their sport in the case of surfers, skiers or climbers, tend to attract stores catering for their requirements.

## Shopping malls

A modern alternative to the traditional High Street is an undercover shopping precinct or shopping mall in the centre of a town. These have several benefits for shoppers and retailers:

- shoppers are protected from traffic and bad weather

- all major outlets are in the same place, under one roof, together with service outlets such as coffee and sandwich shops

- the area is decorated attractively to reflect seasonal variations such as Christmas.

## Out-of-town retail parks

Huge shopping complexes have been built in several out-of-town sites in Britain. These have the same type of attractions as shopping malls, but on a larger scale. A wide range of facilities are

| Rank | Scheme | Location | Size sq ft (million) |
|------|--------|----------|---------------------|
| 1 | Bluewater | Dartford | 1.61 |
| 2 | MetroCentre | Gateshead | 1.58 |
| 3 | Merry Hill | Brierley Hill | 1.50 |
| 4 | Trafford | Manchester | 1.40 |
| 5 | Lakeside | Thurrock | 1.36 |
| 6 | Meadowhall | Sheffield | 1.35 |
| 7 | Arndale | Manchester | 1.30 |
| 8 | Milton Keynes Centre | Milton Keynes | 1.20 |

*Major out-of-town shopping parks in Britain*

provided – restaurants, cinemas, cash points – and they are near to main roads and/or motorways as well as train stations and provide large, secure parking areas.

Other out-of-town centres feature major stores such as Comet, Dixons, PC World, MFI and B&Q. The reason for their popularity with shoppers is that it is easy to park, prices are competitive and the size of the outlet means a variety of goods is on sale.

## High Street stores

The High Street has department stores (such as Debenhams), multiples (such as Dorothy Perkins) and other retailers such as building societies (for example, Nationwide) and banks (such as HSBC). Until the early 1990s there was massive growth in out-of-town centres, but these took business away from stores in town centres. This prompted the government to insist that companies proved there was no suitable site in or near the town centre before locating an outlet on the outskirts. Recently, supermarket retailers have been opening stores, such as Tesco Express, in city centres aimed at consumers who are working in these centres. These smaller supermarkets sell a limited range of goods and open for shorter hours, generally coinciding with office hours.

## Cash and carries

Cash-and-carry outlets are housed in large warehouses, generally on industrial estates. They offer low prices and a wide selection of products, including food. Customers must pay in cash and take the goods away with them. They tend to attract small business customers who are able to buy in quantities that suit their business and the space available to store products. An example is the national chain Makro.

## Independent outlets

Independent retailers are retail organisations with fewer than 10 branches. The market share and number of independent retailers has been declining for many years, particularly in the food sector as supermarkets gained in strength. This trend seems set to continue, especially as supermarket chains are now opening neighbourhood convenience outlets to complement their bigger stores.

Independent outlets tend to sell a specialist range of products (such as medicines) or are general convenience stores that sell a range of products including groceries, household goods, wines and spirits.

The key features of an independent retailer might include:

- personal service and a flexible approach to opening hours
- a specialist business such as a pharmacy
- pricing, discounts and other trading policies are at the discretion of the owner.

### Multiples

Multiple retailers are businesses with more than ten branches. Some multiples are classified as specialist stores, concentrating on a narrow range of items, such as Burtons for clothing. Others are multiple variety chains, such as Boots and Marks and Spencer.

Some features of a multiple chain are:

- centralised buying in bulk of fast-moving, branded products to obtain lower prices
- located in busy shopping areas, clustered together with other well-known multiples
- prices are usually relatively low, generating volume sales
- stores project a strong corporate identity, which makes them easily recognisable.

### Franchises

Franchising is the granting of sole selling rights in a geographical area. In return, the franchisee pays a fee based on sales, or perhaps agrees to buy supplies from the franchisor. It has become a popular method of trading in the UK. Well-known brands such as McDonalds and Kentucky Fried Chicken can be franchisee businesses.

The benefits for the franchisee can be:

- the trade name of the franchisor and all the goodwill associated with the name can be transferred to the new business
- the new business can be offered pre-opening assistance such as site selection, staff training programmes, operating manuals and assistance in finding suppliers
- once trading, the franchisor can help with advertising, bookkeeping, supplies and general advice.

### Shopping villages

**Shopping villages** offer permanent discounts on a wide range of top brands and designer labels. The goods on sale are surplus stock from the High Street or special buys, and are typically sold through stores run by the brands themselves.

*Shopping villages are home to top-brand stores offering surplus stock at a discount*

## Case study    McArthurGlen

McArthurGlen is careful to select the best possible locations for its designer outlets. When searching for a new site, visibility is key. The location must be no more than 10 km from a quality road or motorway. The location should have a minimum of 3.5 million people living within a 60-minute drive time, and 1 million within a 30-minute drive time.

At McArthurGlen it's not just about shopping. You find a whole host of activities taking place – from circus workshops to live jazz bands to home makeover days. Children can also enjoy a fun-packed school holiday thanks to a full calendar of events.

Each centre has a fully themed food court complete with a wide selection of cafés and food choices. They have everything from Pret-à-Manger to McDonalds to Pizza Express to Coffee Republic. Ample parking is provided right next to the centre. Younger visitors can enjoy themselves in a safety-approved play area. Regularly cleaned and checked toilets include baby-changing facilities. Centres are also wheelchair friendly with fully equipped disabled toilets. A free wheelchair loan service is also available.

1 What are the features that make shopping villages attractive retail sales environments for consumers?
2 What are the advantages of shopping villages for retailers?

## Concessions

**Concessions** are commonly called 'shops within shops'. They consist of the space that a host retailer lets to another retailer, wholesaler or manufacturer in order to sell goods under their own name.

An example is Freedom, the fashion jewellery brand. The Freedom range is available in 195 Topshop stores in the UK. Concessions are 100% owned and managed by the parent company. They attract their own loyal customers to the host business, increasing the numbers of store visitors, broadening the appeal of the main store and generally increasing sales. A successful partnership between host store and concession should provide a greater attraction than that achieved by the two companies operating separately.

## Factory shops

There is a difference between goods sold at shopping villages and the factory shops attached to a factory. A factory shop would normally be selling imperfect goods produced in the adjacent factory. Shopping villages are more likely to be selling last season's surplus stock, which had to be removed from in-store sales racks to make room for fresh goods.

## Market stalls

Although traditional markets account for a very small proportion of retail sales, they affect general retail sales wherever they are held because of their attraction. Many from market towns and even city-based ones have been successfully accommodated into new shopping centres. Perhaps the most famous market of all does not exist: the market in *Eastenders* provides a backdrop for many dramatic moments.

## Mail order/home delivery

Mail order retailing, which uses the mail to obtain orders and deliver them, takes several forms.

Some companies, such as Great Universal Stores, publish a catalogue that contains a large assortment of products. Orders have traditionally been gathered through a network of agents, who sell to their acquaintances, and are paid 10% commission on all the products they sell; however, increasing numbers of customers now shop directly through the Internet and/or telephone. Consumers benefit from free credit because they can normally pay over an extended time period, and from armchair shopping. Prices tend to be the above those charged elsewhere. In recent years catalogue shopping has been in decline, although it has been revitalised with the introduction of new catalogues such as the Next Directory.

Direct response mail order companies use newspapers and magazines to advertise products and encourage consumers to order. Firms such as Innovations have used this method successfully to sell a wide variety of products. Most national newspapers feature advertisements for mail order products, especially the colour magazines at weekends.

### Television sales channels

Cable or satellite television companies have dedicated shopping channels such as QVC (channel 630) and ExpressShop (channel 636), but usually require separate telephone ordering. Recent technological developments in interactive digital television sometimes allow the consumers to order immediately through their remote controls.

The advantages of television sales channels include:

- avoiding the drudgery of queuing at stores and carrying heavy bags
- relieving High Street congestion and transport or parking problems
- removing personal transport costs and increasing leisure time.

The disadvantages of television sales channels include:

- television is not available for normal viewing and the telephone not available for ordinary use while shopping
- there is a risk of error when ordering, and it is difficult to establish responsibility for errors.

### Direct selling

Direct mail is the use of advertising literature sent directly to the potential customer's home for the purpose of selling products. Books, CDs and wines have been successfully sold in this way by organisations such as Reader's Digest and the Wine Warehouse.

### Door-to-door

In door-to-door selling, a network of local agents distributes a catalogue to acquaintances and then collects any resulting orders. They consolidate the orders into one large order and on receipt of the goods distribute the products to customers. Betterware household products and Avon cosmetics are still sold in significant volumes using this method.

### Street vendors

The pedestrianisation of many of our city centres has allowed street vendors to trade effectively. They can be seen selling products such as flowers, fruit and even socks.

They can also be found in shopping mall concourses offering gifts, sweets and lottery tickets. Major sporting events attract street vendors selling programmes and team supporter merchandise.

### Vans

Vans are a common sight at outdoor events such as country fairs, concerts and sporting events. Perhaps the most familiar is the ice cream retailer, who signals the arrival of the van in a tuneful manner.

### Pyramid and party selling

Party selling has seen brands such as Tupperware plastic containers and Ann Summers lingerie become popular in the UK. It involves a person organising a party or demonstration in his or her home or at a friend's house.

**Pyramid selling**, sometimes called direct selling or multi-level selling, is similar to party selling except that organisers build distribution systems under their leadership. These people subsequently recruit further distributors until a distribution system structured like a pyramid develops.

The main distributor will buy goods from the parent company and sell them to distributors in his or her network. This process can occur several times as the goods pass through the distribution network. Each transaction generates a profit for the seller. This process can be of concern, as the final consumer may pay an inflated price to include the profits of everyone in the distribution network.

### E-tailing

Selling and buying products over the Internet continues to gain in popularity. The Internet has three main advantages: convenience, choice and cost. The convenience factor is shared with other forms of home shopping. Shopping via the Internet avoids the cost and time of making a journey, travelling along congested roads, sometimes paying for the privilege of parking and finally standing in a queue at the checkouts.

The second main advantage of the Internet is choice; in fact it is by far the biggest advantage. The Internet offers access to an enormous range of products from across the world. The advantage of choice also applies to the comparison with conventional shopping. No shopping centre can hope to match the range available on the Internet.

The third advantage is price. In general, goods sold on-line are cheaper than those sold in shops. This is because the e-tailer does not have the expense of maintaining shop premises or employing sales staff. The e-tailer does of course have costs, but they are generally lower than the conventional bricks-and-mortar retailers.

### Buying clubs

Consumers who join a **buying club** normally commit themselves to buying a certain number of products, such as books, each year over the length of their membership. These clubs advertise in national magazines such as *TV Times*. Clubs such as World Books (*www.worldbooks.co.uk*) offer plenty of product choice along with large discounts. Members generally receive a regular magazine about the products and offers available.

*Vending machines are always on duty and ready to serve*

### Vending machines

Selling from machines has for many years been associated with cigarettes, drinks and confectionery, but in recent years there has been a noticeable increase in the range of products available from vending machines (such as hot drinks). They are generally in vandal-proof areas such as sports centres and colleges. They provide consumers with 24-hour service seven days a week.

### Petrol stations

Petrol companies that have found it difficult to generate enough profit from simply retailing petrol have turned to providing convenience-style stores on the same site. Sometimes these developments have been in conjunction with supermarket chains, such as Tesco Express stores appearing on garage forecourts.

### Traffic light selling

Sellers of flowers, newspapers and windscreen-cleaning services nowadays approach traffic queuing at traffic lights. This is a method of retailing that most UK consumers see only in big cities such as London, or in films set in the US.

### Rail station kiosks

Main rail stations have self-contained units on their concourses selling, for example, fast food or newspapers, magazines, books and confectionery for travellers. A W.H. Smith retail kiosk is a common sight at many UK rail stations.

## Location choice

### Cost

Even a small outlet can cost over £250,000 to lease, equip and stock. As superstores are developed on more expensive land, especially in the south east of Britain, the development cost may be around £12 million for a superstore.

The location, site and building design of a store greatly influence running costs. A store requiring multi-level sales floors and/or car parking will have to cover the maintenance costs of escalators or lifts. A location with a high crime rate will inevitably have to bear the costs of increased security and theft.

### Clientele

The target market is the major determinant of the ideal store location. If the target market is composed of consumers whose primary concern is convenience, then the store must be located conveniently for those consumers. The definition of convenience may differ according to the customer and the merchandise being sold. A corner shop may be considered convenient for the purchase of a bag of sugar, but may be inconvenient for the purchase of a full week's shopping.

Similarly, an exclusive jewellery store will probably locate some considerable distance from its target market on the basis that convenience is not the major determinant of store choice for this type of merchandise. Quality and service may be considered of greater importance, along with the ambience only available in a top-class shopping area.

### Legality

Planning permission is the most important legal consideration in location choice. It has to be sought from the local planning authority. The Town and Country Planning Act 1990 directs local authorities to produce **local structure plans**, which show how shopping areas are likely to be developed over a 10-year period.

Nowadays retailers have to follow a particular sequence when seeking permission to build out-of-town centres. If a retailer puts forward a proposal it must consider certain options in strict

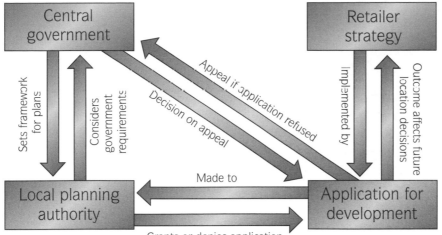

*The planning process*

order. These are whether the project can be accommodated:

1   in the town centre
2   on an established edge of town centre
3   in a local centre
4   in an out-of-town location that is, or can be made, readily accessible by a variety of transport options.

This makes it much more difficult for developers to gain planning permission for out-of-town developments. Local planners are particularly concerned that the development should not harm the vitality and viability of any nearby town centre, and that any proposals should not give rise to unacceptable vehicle or pedestrian traffic conditions.

### Investment costs

A retailer will constantly consider investment plans to enhance the appeal of its stores. Branches tend to be modernised every three to five years, depending on the products sold. Fashion stores tend to need a facelift more often. Strong local competition may speed up the process.

Sometimes a branch outgrows its size for the business it is doing and cannot be extended. Re-sites are considered very carefully because they occasionally produce a less than satisfactory return if the former branch benefited from cheap rents and other low charges. A new branch may open with expensive fittings and at a much higher rent.

### Future expansion possibilities

A favourite method of expanding is to open outlets in major cities and towns. Sainsbury's entry into Scotland is an example. Stores were opened in rapid succession in Glasgow, Edinburgh, Aberdeen and Dundee – Scotland's four largest cities. Smaller stores were opened in regional town centres, and local stores built to serve less populated areas.

It is often possible to extend branches that have become too small for their sales level. Sometimes it is possible to take over stockrooms or office space for extension of the sales area, but often the purchase of an adjacent shop is necessary. When Dixon's took over Curry's, the former was able to expand its branches in this way in several locations.

It is sometimes possible to buy existing shops owned by competing or even non-competing retailers. Tesco's expansion into Scotland was accelerated through the acquisition of Wm Low & Co, a regional grocery multiple and an established force in Scotland. Wal-Mart, the world's largest retailer, entered the British market by buying Asda.

### Road/rail/tram access

Many traditional centres are still dependent upon public transport for a high proportion of their customer traffic. Under such circumstances the types of transport currently available and their costs should be considered as part of any location decision. Centres such as Manchester are well served by rail services, but the long walk from the stations reduced the attractiveness of the city centre as a shopping destination. The solution was the construction of a new tram system.

Although public transport continues to fulfil an important role in many shopping centres, most new retail developments must pay attention to their accessibility to shoppers using cars. Access to these centres requires careful negotiation with local planners to avoid the creation of congestion points. Sometimes alterations have to be made to key junctions and feeder roads.

### Parking facilities and related facilities

The requirement for adequate car-parking places a heavy additional demand upon space required for a new shopping centre or free-standing store. Ground-level parking is usually preferred to multi-storey parking on cost and accessibility grounds, although an excessively large ground level car park may be inconvenient to shoppers in bad weather and may also at off-peak times give the impression that the store is not popular. Small businesses such as newsagents and sandwich shops also need some parking facilities to capture passing trade. Some have signs reminding motorists they can stop legally or park before 7.30 in the morning and after 6.00 at night.

Supermarkets generally have a petrol station on site and multiple rows of automatic teller machines (ATMs) so consumers can withdraw cash. Out-of-town retail parks tend to have the same facilities.

### Proximity to 'honeypot' locations

**Honeypot locations** are those that attract a great number of people and tend to become crowded at peak times. They can therefore be very attractive locations for some retailers. For example ports and airports are honeypot locations for shopping malls with multiple retailers as travellers arrive early and have time to shop.

# Sensory merchandising

### Purpose

The purpose of **sensory merchandising** is to make the merchandise more attractive to the consumer at the point of sale by appealing to the five senses – sight, smell, taste, hearing and touch.

- Sight – dramatic visual display to attract attention of customer
- Smell – consumer can try various fragrances
- Taste – shoppers able to taste latest products in store
- Hearing – customers informed and entertained by store radio station
- Touch – customers invited to touch a product

### Market research

The performance of the current products on sale must be reviewed to establish fast-moving, slow-moving, more popular and less popular items. The changing nature of the market must be noted in terms of identifying growth areas and products in decline.

Retailers must also take into account competitive developments in the market. Any change in competition may require some changes to the store's product range. If, for example, a new competitor is gaining many sales of smart casual clothing because women in the area are predominantly professionals, adjustments may need to be made to the products offered by the store.

Once the products to be offered to consumers have been established, a relevant sensory merchandising plan can be designed. A seemingly small change to give more space to women's clothes rather than men's will have an impact on any sensory merchandising plan.

### Merchandising approaches

The products and the nature of the consumer will require different approaches to be adopted to merchandising the product.

- Perfumes – brands clustered together create a pleasant smelling atmosphere
- Footwear – shoes displayed in racks along the walls and a central space with chairs for trying them on

- CDs – listening points adjacent to CD display

- Convenience foods – tasting opportunities next to product

- Clothing – racked in the centre of the store with fitting rooms to the side

## Management of display and sales space

A **planogram** is a diagram showing how products should be arranged on the store shelves and display fixtures. The aim is to maximise space, and therefore maximise profits. The most popular lines will be allocated the most space or facings. Producers will try to persuade stores to increase the number of facings for their own product. The more facings a product has the higher the level of sales. Some manufacturers will offer greater discounts on purchases to retailers to obtain more facings.

Special fittings will be installed so that goods can be displayed appropriately. The type of fittings will vary, from rails in a clothing store to high shelving in a DIY outlet. Most stores also display goods on gondolas – freestanding units with shelves of different depths. These can be joined together to form particular layouts.

| FORMAL PLAIN SOCKS | FORMAL PLAIN SOCKS | SPORTS SOCKS | SPORTS SOCKS |
|---|---|---|---|
| FORMAL PLAIN SOCKS | FORMAL PATTERN SOCKS | SPORTS SOCKS | SPORTS TWO PACK |
| | FORMAL PATTERN SOCKS | SPORTS SOCKS | SPORTS THREE PACK |
| SINGLE BRIEFS | MULTI PACK BRIEFS | MULTI PACK BRIEFS | SINGLE BRIEFS |
| BOXER SHORTS | BOXER SHORTS | BOXER SHORTS | |

*A planogram for a section of a menswear store*

Some display techniques used frequently by retailers include:

- placing popular products just below eye level

- placing high-demand items at the back of the store so customers are brought into contact with higher-priced impulse lines such as cosmetics and toiletries

- using the ends of aisles for special displays – goods here normally sell very quickly and these locations are called 'hotspots'

- placing some everyday products near the door to start customers buying early.

## Frequency of alteration

Where customers see shopping as a chore, products should be moved around in store as little as possible. Otherwise they become irritated if they cannot find the products they want.

Customers are less sensitive to changes in store layout where shopping is seen as pleasurable, such as in clothing stores.

Products can be moved about according to the seasons, with barbecue fuel being placed near the entrance in summer, for example. Window displays need to be refreshed every two weeks, otherwise the products on display start to deteriorate. Adjustments also need to be made for new products arriving in store; in some cases space is created by selling off unprofitable lines.

## Layout

There are several types of store layout. The grid layout steers consumers around a store in a particular way. Customers enter by a wall and continue to walk in the same direction until they meet a display, at which point they turn to move in another direction. This type of layout can be found in discount stores such as Toys R Us, supermarkets such as Morrison's and large DIY stores.

The flow-through layout creates a more relaxed atmosphere and encourages customers to browse.

Grid layout          Flow-through layout

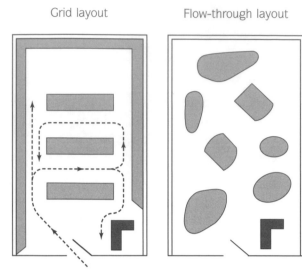

*Two different types of store layout*

You will find this layout used to sell clothes in stores such as Debenhams and Next. Products are grouped together to allow customers to circulate between particular displays. Cash tills are usually placed at strategic intervals among the displays.

## Siting

Retailers use a number of merchandising techniques to increase sales. Large and heavy goods are placed near the exit – so customers don't fill their trolleys too quickly. Frozen goods are also often placed there, so they don't defrost too quickly.

Displays are placed in 'hot spots', that is busy areas, unless there is a deliberate attempt to encourage people into areas they would not normally visit. Similar products and related products are grouped together for convenience and to encourage 'add-on' buying, such as pasta and pasta sauce.

Merchandise may be displayed differently to suit local and regional buying habits. Districts where many students live may feature convenience foods in the first aisles that consumers visit. Any goods being offered at a reduced price are put into special display bins or in a bargain basket.

## Shelving

A variety of shelving options are available. Their use is determined by the types of products to be merchandised. There are large and small floor-standing units, wall display units, and centre floor stands.

## Display and sale area risk assessment

Retailers are legally obliged to carry out a risk assessment of their premises. It is intended to protect both employees and shoppers. There are five steps to any risk assessment:

- identify hazards
- decide who might be harmed by them and how
- evaluate the risks and whether enough precautions are in place
- record the findings
- review the assessments on a regular basis.

Risk assessments must be 'suitable and sufficient'. If the risks are straightforward and easy to control, the risk assessment should also be simple.

### Practice point

Undertake a display and sales area risk assessment for a store you know. Follow the steps below, sharing your ideas with other class members as you proceed.

- Identify hazards you might encounter within the store selling area.
- Decide whether the risk of harm from the hazard should be classified as high, medium or low.
- Suggest ways in which all the identified risks could be controlled or reduced, but pay particular attention to high and medium risks.
- Produce a document recording the results of your risk assessment.
- Indicate when the next assessment should be carried out. Note any special circumstances when a new assessment might be needed – for example, after an accident.

## Consumer traffic analysis

Consumer traffic analysis allows store management to obtain a picture of consumer movements in and around a store. Cameras and electronic equipment help provide this information quickly, accurately and in an easily understood format. The information can be used for a variety of purposes:

- to show how many customers enter the store but fail to make a purchase

- to observe consumer circulation in the store as an aid to changing and improving store layout

- to assess the impact of sales promotions on such issues as customer flow through the store, car park usage and queue lengths

- to identify training requirements to convert browsers in key areas into purchasers.

## Celebrity association

Stores commonly use celebrities to bring excitement to their retail sales environments:

- Jamie Oliver has helped to raise the profile of Sainsbury's

- Sharon Osbourne was an unusual choice to remind consumers about Asda's 'Every Day Low Prices'

- Homebase have used the actors Neil Morrissey and Leslie Ash from *Men Behaving Badly* for some time.

Apart from featuring in their advertising, the celebrities often feature prominently in store on, for example, posters.

## Aesthetic sensory variety

The atmosphere or ambience in a store can be changed and influenced in many ways.

| Aesthetic | Merchandising points |
|---|---|
| Aroma | Scent can be used to create atmosphere. Fresh bakery smells circulated into appropriate areas of the store can stimulate purchase. |
| Music/mood | Pre-selected music likely to appeal to the shopper creates a relaxing shopping mood. The wrong choice of music can, however, damage the business. |
| Light | Lights are used to make stores look bright and welcoming from the outside. The light fittings themselves can enhance the appearance of the store. Lights can be used to create a different mood in certain parts of the store. |
| Warmth and use of colour | Colour is perhaps the most important display element. Warm colours such as yellow and orange should be used for windows and entrances as they are considered 'approach colours'. Red lettering is also appropriate for sale signs. Cool colours, such as blue and purple, are appropriate where customers need to think about the purchase. |

## Connections with catalogues

A number of retailers produce catalogues to support key selling seasons. For example Argos publishes two general catalogues annually alongside supplementary leaflets covering topics such as gardening.

The graphics, colour schemes and slogans used in the catalogues are reproduced in the design of posters, banners and bags. Large banners in the window of an Argos store look very much like the design theme of the current catalogue.

### Clarity of signage

The aim of merchandising is to make sure goods are easily available and easily found. This is achieved first by good displays and second by clear signposting. The type of signposting used will depend on the layout of the store and whether the store is self-service, or has personal sales staff. Self-service stores need the most signposting, to help customers find what they want.

Supermarkets, hypermarkets and mini-supermarkets have large signs hanging from the ceiling. These show the items sold at either side of each aisle.

Signs are also needed to identify customer facilities such as changing rooms, customer service desk and coffee shop.

Signs may also be used for promotional purposes. For instance, Tesco advertised its 'free computers for schools' campaigns with large promotional signs throughout the store.

### 'No frills'

Not all consumers respond to sensory merchandising, but instead favour stores that concentrate on low prices in a bland building which has the atmosphere of a warehouse. An example is Aldi.

## Facility considerations

The shopping experience is more than simply choosing and paying for the goods. Shoppers expect the stores they visit to have a range of facilities to enhance the shopping experience.

| Retail sales environment | Facilities requirement |
|---|---|
| Shopping village | Toilets – a necessity as consumers spend a considerable amount time at shopping villages |
| | Disabled entrances and exits – ramps and special parking areas are now a legal requirement |
| | Baby-changing rooms – so families with young children can spend the day at the centre |
| | Lifts – parents with buggies or people in wheelchairs cannot use escalators |
| | Supervised children's play areas – useful for parents who want to spend time shopping alone |
| | Refreshments – so consumers do not have to leave the centre for meals |
| Cash and carry | Customer loading bays – some customers will have a lot of heavy merchandise |
| | Special trolleys – customers will be buying bulk supplies of products such as soft drinks and confectionery |
| | Disabled access – ramp to entrance/exit, automatic doors, special parking areas, wide checkout with low checkout counter for wheelchair users |

### Thinking point

You are considering locating one of your stores to an out-of-town site on the outskirts of a major UK city. What facilities would you expect the site to have to make it an attractive proposition for your company?

## Outcome activity 33.1

**Pass**

Read the case study on Aldi below and describe the features of Aldi that enhance its suitability as a supermarket retailer. What makes this store better than similar competitors?

- Your description should cover three main sections – location, how the products are presented and the facilities offered to the shopper. Under location consider aspects such as access for all types of shopper, car-parking arrangements and related facilities such as banking and petrol stations.

- Next, look at how effectively the products are displayed. Are the product areas clearly signposted, is the store layout appropriate and does it have a welcoming atmosphere?

- Finally, review issues such as toilet provision, refreshment areas, availability of trolleys, baskets, bags, supervised play areas, customer loading bays and access for the disabled.

> Aldi provides a 'no frills' shopping experience, selling food, household items and alcohol. The building is new; the inside is bland and has the feel of a warehouse. The stock is all in the store and is displayed on pallets. Customers benefit from a limited range of quality products at value-for-money prices. Usually only one brand of each product is stocked.
>
> There are no in-store restaurants, toilets, fancy packaging or attractive shop décor. If brand names and the shopping experience are important to you, Aldi may not be for you!
>
> Aldi does not accept credit cards but does accept debit cards. Once the items have been put through the checkout, you pile it all back into the trolley and pack it into bags or boxes away from the till, freeing the till to serve the next customer. Empty boxes are available but if you require a carrier bag it costs 2p

# *Retail consumer buying behaviour*

## Changing shopping patterns

| Changing shopping patterns | Products | Comments |
|---|---|---|
| Out of hours – up to 24 hours a day | All products | Supermarkets and convenience stores offer long opening hours and in some cases stay open for 24 hours. More people are, for example, working flexible hours for call centres and telephone marketing companies, meaning that they leave work at unusual times. |
| Seven days a week | Most products | The Sunday Trading Act 1994 allows stores to open for six hours on Sundays. Some retailers were already opening on a Sunday before the alteration in the law as a response to changing consumer demands. |
| Rush-hour peaks | Products required at work (sandwiches) or evening (convenience meal) | Busy people who do not have the time to cook and prepare meals – breakfast, lunch and evening meal – resort to buying on the way to and from work. |
| Everyday | Products required for the evening and next morning | Supermarkets caused a decline in everyday shopping but it is returning as cash-rich and time-poor consumers, such as young professionals, buy what they need as they go along. |

| Changing shopping patterns | Products | Comments |
|---|---|---|
| Weekend | Considered purchases such as furniture Products requiring special trips such as cigarettes from European Union | Recreational and leisure activities are increasingly taking priority over shopping. Food shopping is seen as a chore to be done during the week. Nevertheless consumers visit shopping villages (such as MacArthurGlen) and out-of-town centres (such as Bluewater) at weekends as a leisure and recreational activity. Trips, especially to France, to buy cigarettes and alcoholic drinks at reduced prices have become popular in recent years. These trips become mini-weekend breaks for some people. |
| Bank holidays | DIY and garden products | Consumers often buy supplies for home improvements and gardening projects at bank holiday time. People take extra holiday to complete a project. |
| Distress purchases | Products people are forced to buy – insurance, road tax, television license | Consumers try to spend as little time as possible buying these products and have consequently started using the telephone and the Internet to research and buy them. |
| Impulse purchases | Products people decide to buy on the spur of the moment – small value products such as chocolates, drinks, ties or flowers | Rising disposable incomes allow consumers to indulge themselves, their family and close friends. Store cards, from retailers such as the House of Fraser, are instantly obtainable when a purchase is made and help to encourage this type of purchase. |
| Emergency purchases | Products that people unexpectedly run out of – toilet rolls, toothpaste, bread, tea bags, medicines | Convenience stores in neighbourhoods have enjoyed a resurgence in sales as households with two working adults find it difficult to undertake planned shopping on a regular basis. Consumers expect stores to be open and consequently feel confident that they can buy anything they need in a hurry fairly easily. |
| E-tailing | Music, books, DVDs – products where people know exactly what they will receive | Increasingly popular with consumers – its greatest potential is for products that can be bought using credit, debit, or charge cards and then delivered over the Internet as a download (such as music for MP3 players). However, supermarkets such as Tesco and Sainsbury's are also making a success of selling food over the Internet. |
| Window shopping | Increasing number of products | Consumers increasingly using the Internet to research products and compare prices. They do not always buy over the Internet, but visit stores to view and buy products. Other types of consumers visit High Street stores to look at products before buying from home over the Internet at lower prices. |

The Gateshead MetroCentre offers a unique shopping experience, and whether your choice is serious shopping or a family day out, there's always a treat in store for all the family.

MetroCentre offers the very best in 'retail therapy'. There are famous names such as Marks and Spencer, BhS, Littlewoods, House of Fraser, Gap and Next, plus many smaller special shops in unique themed areas. The Forum, Garden Court and The Village offer everything from Indian art to Victorian jewellery.

The centre opens seven days a week, staying open late every weekday, with many restaurants and leisure attractions open even later. More and more visitors come after work in the evening to enjoy some shopping and a meal in one of the restaurants and cafés. Longer opening hours also mean easy access during the weekend, making MetroCentre a relaxed shopping experience for everyone, every day.

But MetroCentre is more than just a shopping experience. Leisure attractions include the centre's unique theme park, Metroland, complete with rollercoaster, a UCI 11-screen cinema, crèche, Megabowl (offering 20 lanes of computerised ten-pin bowling) and Quasar, a state-of-the-art laser game.

1 Describe the special features of the MetroCentre.
2 How could the MetroCentre increase its appeal by understanding consumers better?
3 What emerging consumer behaviour is being catered for by the MetroCentre?

# Market segmentation

A segment is a group of consumers who share common characteristics, which make them different from other groups. Different segments require different retail experiences. Retailers therefore sometimes have to have different stores to appeal to different consumers (for example Topshop and Dorothy Perkins) or have noticeably different sections within their stores (such as a pre-school toy section and a computer games area in Toys R Us).

## Segmentation used by retailers

**Segmentation** is the process of dividing a potential market into distinct groups of consumers and selecting one or more segments as a target market to be reached with a distinct marketing mix. Retailers use a variety of segmentation approaches, such as gender, age or buying frequency. They use the approach that they believe will ensure they satisfy consumers' needs, provide them with a distinctive market image and deliver the level of profitability they are seeking.

Buying frequency is one method of segmentation. It influences, for example, the sales environments in which soft drinks can be bought.

Markets are also segmented by socio-economic group. Some sophisticated segmentation techniques combine research from many sources to identify types of neighbourhood. The assumption is that people who live in a particular neighbourhood will react to marketing activity in the same way.

ACORN (*www.caci.co.uk*) stands for A Classification Of Residential Neighbourhoods. It profiles customers based on social and economic data, dividing them into six categories so that marketers can understand more about consumer characteristics. Some retailers use this method of segmenting their market to design the retail experience appropriate for their customers. The example opposite shows the information available for the ACORN category called 'Expanding'. It provides quite a detailed picture of the consumer populating this category.

| Buying frequency | Product | Retail sales environment |
|---|---|---|
| Daily for lunch box or as a treat | Small size (250ml) | Supermarkets and convenience stores |
| Several in a day – need to quench thirst immediately | Aluminium can (330ml) | Vending machines in leisure centre, colleges and entertainment venues as well as convenience stores |
| Perhaps two daily – wanting to drink little and often | Screw top bottle (500ml) | Vending machines and convenience stores |
| Occasionally – with a friend watching a DVD at home | Share size bottle – 0.5litre | Convenience stores, DVD rental stores |
| Weekly – at home for family consumption | Multi-pack 6 or 12 | Hypermarkets and superstores |
| Occasionally – for a party or picnic | 2-litre bottle | Hypermarkets and superstores |

| ACORN category | ACORN groups | ACORN types | Statistics |
|---|---|---|---|
| Expanding (B) | Affluent executives living in family housing; well-off workers living in family housing | Affluent working families with mortgages<br><br>Affluent working couples with mortgages in new homes<br><br>Home owners with no children<br><br>Home owners with older children<br><br>Families with mortgage and young children | Number – 6.5 million or 11.8% of the population |

Another segmentation analysis technique called MOSAIC (*www.experian.com*) uses sources such as census data, credit history, share ownership and postcode data to identify household types. It identifies 12 groups. An example is 'High-income families'.

It is likely that no one market segment will contain just one ACORN category or MOSAIC group, but the profile of a segment can be constructed using these techniques. A MOSIAC profile for consumers who shop at Marks and Spencers shows their groups are clever capitalists, rising materialists, ageing professionals and small business owners. This represents 9.9% of the population.

Age and gender are often used in segmenting, but a single factor such as gender (that is, male or female) does not identify the groups in a market in sufficient detail to enable a company to truly provide a shopping concept that will have genuine appeal to its customers. A further segmentation factor such as age may be needed to highlight the groups of consumers for whom the shopping experience should be designed.

## Case study    The Marks and Spencer consumer

The profile of Marks and Spencer customers shows that prosperous pensioners, older couples in leafy suburbs, families living in semi-detached houses built between the wars and young families with mortgages shop at Marks and Spencer, but council tenants, singles and country dwellers tend to shop elsewhere.

1 How might this profile influence the managers of Marks and Spencer as they consider the shopping experience to offer their customers?
2 What shopping patterns might be followed by Marks and Spencer customers?

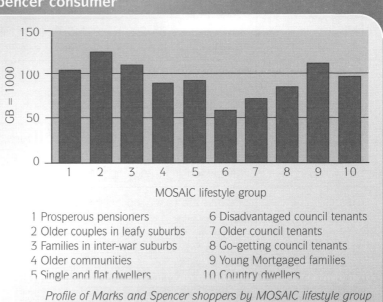

MOSAIC lifestyle group

1 Prosperous pensioners
2 Older couples in leafy suburbs
3 Families in inter-war suburbs
4 Older communities
5 Single and flat dwellers
6 Disadvantaged council tenants
7 Older council tenants
8 Go-getting council tenants
9 Young Mortgaged families
10 Country dwellers

*Profile of Marks and Spencer shoppers by MOSAIC lifestyle group*

An example of a major retailer that segments by gender and then by age is Arcadia, with its portfolio of High Street brands including Burton, Dorothy Perkins, Miss Selfridge, Outfit, Evans, Topshop and Topman.

It is not so difficult to understand why a High Street can feature all these stores in close proximity to each other.

Residential locations are another method of segmentation. The outstandingly successful retailer Tesco has a specialist team which recommends where new stores should be located and which type of store would suit that particular residential location. This is another example of a successful method of segmenting a market to design a shopping experience appealing to consumers.

Boots uses a segmentation approach that allows it to target certain consumer retail markets based on the purpose of the shopping trip. It consequently has a variety of store formats based on the categories fun and leisure shopping, essentials shopping, purposeful shopping, time-pressured and innovative shopping.

### Role of marketing information in training

Marketing information can provide a detailed profile of the consumers who populate a particular segment. Knowing more about the consumer can have a major impact on training. Staff need to be sensitised to the needs of the particular groups of customers they are likely to serve. Information taken from the ACORN category we have already looked at shows a company would need to prepare for customers looking to spend money on property improvements and possibly educational children's products. As many in this group have low disposable income, the store may need interest free credit or store charge cards.

| Brand | Gender | Age |
|---|---|---|
| Topshop | Female | 16–34 |
| Miss Selfridge | Female | 18–24 |
| Dorothy Perkins | Female | 20–50 |
| Outfit | Female | 25–45 |
| Evans | Female | 25–55 |
| Topman | Male | 16–34 |
| Burton | Male | 25–34 |

| Tesco store type | Description and residential location |
|---|---|
| Extra | Extra is Tesco's hypermarket format. These stores serve large, densely populated catchment areas such as city suburbs, selling a full range of food and non-food products. |
| Superstore | These are specialist food outlets, though the larger ones do carry clothing as well as non-food categories such as books, stationery and electrical goods. They serve smaller residential areas, such as towns. |
| Metro | Metro is the format developed for busy High Street locations. They sell a range of everyday products catering for the increasing number of city dwellers and professional people looking to do important shopping near to their workplace. |
| Express | Express is a convenience store format. These are focused on a local residential neighbourhood, selling fresh and convenience foods. Some are located on petrol forecourts. |

| Shopping intention | Store type description |
|---|---|
| Fun and leisure | Large stores in centres like Meadowhall in Sheffield stock the full range of products. Families enjoy a full day of shopping with the centre having everything – car parks, food halls, toilets, changing facilities – needed to enjoy the experience. |
| Purposeful | In substantial city centre stores, many shoppers enter with a purchase in mind. For example, they may be seeking a digital camera from Boots' reputable photographic department. |
| Essential | Smaller stores in suburban and small town locations stock the core Boots products (beauty, toiletry, perfumes) and in many instances incorporate a pharmacy. |
| Time-pressured and innovative shopping | Home-based shoppers can use the Internet – *www.boots.com* – or browse the Gift Guide catalogue before placing an Internet-based order. |

## Sales forecasting

Marketing information can provide the data required for forecasting sales – for example, to calculate the expected sales in a new store.

Store planners use the ratio method to calculate expected new store sales. They research the amount of selling space in a catchment area and calculate the share of selling space the new store will obtain. For example, if a new store will have 3,500 square feet of selling space in a catchment area that already has 62,550 square feet, its share of space would be 5.3% (3,500/66,050 × 100). The population figure for the area is then obtained and multiplied by the average consumer spend per week (such as 625,776 × £16.82 = £10,525,552). This is the total amount of money spent in supermarkets in the area in a week. The new store should capture 5.3% of this total – somewhere in the region of £557,854 per week.

### Practice point

What would the sales forecast be for a new store if it had a 4% share of space in a catchment area of 452,897 consumers spending on average £12.50 per week?

# Factors affecting demand
## Buying cycles and sales seasons

Some products are subject to buying following a particular pattern. For example with clothes autumn/winter and spring/summer ranges make up the yearly buying cycle.

The final three months of the year are particularly important for a great many retailers. Overall, nearly 30% of sales are made in this period, although its importance has been declining.

| Product type | Buying cycle |
|---|---|
| Toys | Over 70% of sales take place in November and December |
| Soft drinks | Sales in cans peak in summer, and in the Christmas holiday period the 2-litre bottle is most popular |
| Clothing | A large proportion of sales are made in the January sales |

## Payment types

The use of credit and charge cards has grown considerably in recent years. The number of outlets accepting credit cards has grown progressively as retailers have realised they are able to increase sales through this type of payment.

Charge cards can be used to make the same kinds of payments as credit cards, but offer short-term credit only. You are expected to pay the outstanding bill each month, and could face a large financial penalty if you fail to do so. Store cards are a type of charge card, but their use is restricted to an individual shop or store chain such as the House of Fraser.

Stores cards have an impact on demand in a number of ways.

- Customers' transaction values tend to be larger, with more unplanned purchasing.
- Loyalty to the store increases, generating further sales in the long term.
- Information gained about customers can be used to target special offers to interested consumers.

## Loyalty card points systems

Loyalty card schemes such as Tesco's Club Card affect demand in a variety of ways. Loyal customers buy more, pay premium prices and bring in new customers through referrals. They are appropriate in mature markets such as food and fashion. As price is no longer the major source of competitive advantage in these markets, retailers are forced to find other ways in which to differentiate themselves.

Major retailers such as Sainsbury's, Tesco and Boots operate high profile loyalty card schemes. Customers receive points for every pound spent in the store, which can be used to obtain free goods.

## Impact of external variables

Retailers are subjected to external events and developments over which they have no control, such as changes in consumer and business confidence, changes in the housing market and developments in employment levels. These are called **external variables**. The most successful retailers are the ones that react quickly to and in some cases anticipate these changes. They cannot be ignored without threatening the long-term survival of the organisation.

Different retailers are likely to be affected by a combination of factors. Some affect all retailers (such as falling consumer spending) and others apply to one sector only (such as toy retailers facing competition from computer games).

## Outcome activity 33.2

The following report examines the economic, demographic and other factors influencing demand for toys in the UK.

> **Incomes** Although disposable income might not have a direct bearing on the toys market, rising household incomes are having a positive indirect influence on the amount of money that parents are devoting to their children. This is both in terms of money set aside for presents and also money given on a regular basis as pocket money.
>
> **Fewer children to buy toys** The number of under-fives actually fell by over 7% between 1998 and 2003 and there will be a fairly significant fall in the number of 5–9-year-olds in the next few years, while the number of under-fives will rise slightly. Products such as fashion dolls, action figures and collectable cards are likely to be adversely affected.
>
> **Unemployment levels** Unemployment levels in 2003 stood at 1.5 million. The strong labour situation has had a major impact on consumer confidence during the past five years, encouraging spending in areas such as toys. Double-income households spend more on toys than other households.
>
> **Economic trends** The rise in consumer spending has been fuelled by rises in the property market. Rising house values have allowed consumers to borrow money against their properties as well as giving them a feeling of well-being because of the increase in value of the properties they own.
>
> **New technology** Traditional toys have come under threat from a number of external factors. Aside from the growing tendency to stop playing with toys at an earlier age, another threat has been competition from video and computer games. In addition the rising number of households with two or more TVs and the emergence of the Internet have had an effect in terms of opening up new leisure options for children.

**Pass**

Identify key features of retail consumer buying behaviour applicable to Toys R Us.

First, consider whether Toys R Us is subject to any changing shopping patterns such as rush-hour peak shopping. Then identify the way it segments its market – possibilities include buying frequency, gender, age, socio-economic group, residential location or target retail market. This can help reveal a great deal about the buying behaviour of the consumer. Finally, establish the factors that influence demand for Toys R Us, such as sales seasons and consumer confidence.

**Merit**

Explain ways in which Toys R Us could successfully increase its sales through a deeper understanding of retail consumer buying behaviour and the sales environment.

List suggestions concerning store layout, better product merchandising, a more welcoming atmosphere and more appropriate products. Think about the impact of changing shopping patterns on Toys R Us.

**Distinction**

Assess the extent to which the sales operations of Toys R Us reflect an understanding of retail consumer buying behaviour and suitable environment.

Look at the evidence available and form a view of how well Toys R Us understands the market it is trying to serve. If the suggestions you listed for the previous task were numerous this might indicate that Toys R Us is not reflecting consumer buying behaviour very well. Look at the evidence and draw your own conclusions.

# Principles and practices of effective retail selling

## Interpersonal sales skills

The sales skills available to a retailer are essential factors in securing efficient sales. The interpersonal skills needed in retail selling are described below.

### Identifying potential buyers

A variety of different buyers enter a selling environment. It is important for sales staff to recognise the type of buyer they are about to meet so that the right approach can be adopted. Examples of buyer categories are:

- just looking – they are probably browsing or comparing prices and qualities and should be left alone until some signs of interest are shown

- decisive buyer – they present few problems to sales staff because they have already made up their minds about what they want to buy; they should be served quickly while at the same time ensuring that the product will deliver what the customer requires

- silent buyer – they provide few clues about their views on the products available; sales staff should seek to demonstrate the product, allowing the customer to handle the merchandise so that his or her intentions can be gauged

- disagreeable buyer – they should be shown the stock available, but should otherwise be given the chance to do most of the talking

- opinionated buyer – they offer opinions that may not be correct, but should not be challenged; the correct information should merely be provided as part of the conversation.

## Meeting and greeting

The customer's first impression of the salesperson is important. A smile is vital. The most common approach question used by sales people is 'Can I help you?', and the most common answer is 'No, I'm just looking'. A better introduction would be something like 'That camera is the latest in the range and is on special introductory offer at present'.

It is important that sales staff maintain strong eye contact with their customers, or buyers may find it difficult to trust what is being said to them. Sales people who look friendly, personable and positive will be seen as approachable.

## Proactive accommodation of special needs

Good practice in dealing with buyers with special needs includes the following.

- Understand the capabilities of products for buyers with special needs – for example, whether a folding wheelchair would fit in a car boot.

- Know how products can be adapted for buyers with special needs – for example, extended handles on household appliances such as brushes.

- Know the location of disabled toilets and lifts and direct customers to checkouts with wide exits and lower counters.

- Provide, probably on request, assisted shopping for the disabled and the visually impaired.

- Ensure the special car parking regulations are enforced.

- Check on a regular basis that lifts for the disabled are in working order.

## Sensitivity to distinctive cultural attributes

Effective sales people understand the importance of being culturally sensitive. The following points are good practice.

- Ask consumers for their first or given name, not Christian name.

- Offer Muslims, whose religion condemns the payment or receipt of interest, different forms of buying goods other than interest-bearing arrangements.

- Avoid organising deliveries of goods on relevant festival days such as Divali.

- Understand how to react to differing attitudes to personal space – not everyone may have the same ideas as you about how close it is appropriate to get!

## Product-need identification and stimulation

It should go without saying, but sales people should help buyers select products that meet their needs. What suits one buyer may not suit another. Product selection tends to be influenced by the following factors:

- source – some sources have strong selling appeal, such as Swiss watches and Japanese cameras

- durability – many buyers are prepared to pay more for articles that are likely to last longer without replacement; this is important in the case of consumer durables but less so for clothing

- low running costs – something that may be cheap to buy may be expensive to use, so a consumer may be persuaded to choose a product that is economical to run, even if it costs a little more

- economy – price is invariably an important factor, and not just with the lower income groups. Customers balance price with the subjective idea of value.

## Persuasive presentation

Persuasive presentations are possible when skilled sales staff identify the buying motives of the customer and then discuss the benefits of a product that are important to that buyer. These should be communicated effectively in a manner that is pleasant and courteous, by sales staff who are appropriately dressed.

Having identified the buying motive, the skill is to select the product information that will appeal to the buyer. To do this successfully sales staff need to know:

- where particular goods are to be found in the store
- the price of individual items and the price ranges of particular products
- the variations that are available (such as colour, sizes)
- the key selling features of each product
- the different uses of each product
- the after-sales service available.

## Target consumer image

Sometimes it is important for the retailer to make connections between sales people and the image that the consumer is targeting.

## Industry-specific experience and training

Some retail staff need to know and understand the specialist language surrounding the products they sell. Failure to use such language would, in the eyes of the consumer, reduce the credibility of that store to sell such goods. The essential skill is to quickly identify the consumer who appreciates the technical side of the product or the use of specialist language, because not all customers enjoy such conversations.

Where specialist language is used, particular training is sometimes required. Sales staff also sometimes need technical expertise – staff selling computer software to businesses, for example, need to know how to use the software programmes in order to demonstrate the product's capabilities effectively.

### Thinking point

Write down a list of retailers where the sales staff have to use specialist language. For each retailer, highlight some specialist terms that might require the sales staff to undertake training. Now think of some stores where neither specialist language nor special training is required for sales staff to be effective.

| Buying motive | Implications for retail selling |
|---|---|
| Recreation and comfort | Greater discretionary income and increased leisure time have produced a boom in recreational goods and services. |
| Imitation | Consumers buy products to imitate those they admire. This is especially true of cosmetics and clothing. This is often referred to as 'aspirational marketing'. |
| Exclusiveness | Some buyers are seeking prestige and are willing to pay high prices for durables or clothing to underline their self-proclaimed leadership qualities. |
| Family affection | A great deal of money is spent on toys and clothes for children, and this is part of the general pleasure of giving. |
| Other motives | These can include health, habit, security, curiosity, novelty and pride. |

## Case study    Abercrombie and Fitch – living and wearing the brand

The retailer Abercrombie and Fitch is known across the US for its range of clothing for college students. The stores themselves are designed with a particular atmosphere in mind. On entering the store, customers are greeted by employees who welcome them. They all wear clothes that are currently on display in the store, and staff are attractive and of the same age as college students. Music is played and they use the specialist language of the generation they are serving. These marketing tactics all draw the consumers in, making them feel part of the brand and creating loyalty.

1 Can you think of any UK store that adopts this approach to retailing?
2 How could a retailer such as Toys R Us use this approach to increase its sales?
3 In contrast, identify a retailer where this approach might be inappropriate. Justify your choice.

### Demonstrations and use of visual aids

Demonstrations can be invaluable, especially to convey concepts such as quality or style. It is vital to present products in the most effective way, in order for the customer to appreciate their features properly. For example:

- curtain fabric should be gathered and draped to show how a pair of curtains might look

- graphic equaliser settings should be used to emphasise the best response from an amplifier when playing a CD

- an exclusive bottle of wine should be presented label first, with one hand cradling the neck of the bottle while the other supports the base.

### Reference to catalogues

There are a number of sales situations where reference to catalogues can be very useful. These include:

- when products cannot be effectively displayed in store – for example garden swings for children

- when a clearer picture of a product's capabilities is required – for example, a lawn mower working in a variety of situations

- when products or product options are not available in store but can be purchased by special order – for example, seat fabric options for a car.

Effective selling involves using catalogues in the best way to provide relevant information in cases such as these.

### Handling and pre-empting objections

When customers make objections, barriers to a sale are created, and these need to be overcome. For example, a customer might say; 'I wouldn't be able to assemble that barbecue successfully.'

It is best to anticipate common objections early in a presentation. Some sales people welcome objections because a successful solution to them can bring a sale. Methods of handling objections include:

- ignoring the objection for the time being and only addressing the issue if it re-appears later in the conversation

- asking questions to find out the concerns of the customer and then providing solutions

- countering objections by stating the product's key features and benefits

- using the testimony of a satisfied customer.

### Listening skills

Listening effectively is a key skill for successful selling.

Sales staff should attempt to pay full attention, remembering that listening requires self-discipline. Put effort into listening to the buyer and try not to interrupt while the buyer is speaking. If two people are speaking at the same time it is impossible for either party to listen properly.

Practise active listening by following these simple guidelines:

- give little nods to show the point has been heard, and maintain strong eye contact

- use brief comments to indicate you are listening and understanding, such as *right*, *yes* and *I see*.

Active listening helps sales people concentrate on the customer's interests and needs, so that they can then think about how these might be met.

## Negotiation

In many retail selling environments, sales staff do not enter into negotiation as the prices, delivery policy and payment terms are laid down in company policy. However, in some markets (such as car retailing or replacement window selling) negotiation is part of the process. There are three key aspects to any negotiation.

1   Sales staff must find out the limits to which they can negotiate, such as prices and changes to product features.

2   Sales staff should try to find out the precise needs of the buyer. This information can be used to identify the critical factors in the buyer's mind and to estimate the value to them of a concession. Many negotiations have been concluded successfully after agreeing to a minor concession such as the inclusion of coloured glass in a replacement UPVC front door.

3   Sales staff should keep as many concessions in reserve as possible. Concessions should be given only when necessary to achieve the order.

Proposals are written documents submitted to customers. They are used in retail selling when a kitchen or bedroom is to be refurbished, for example. They tend to contain the following sections:

- a summary of key points

- a list of all the important benefits of the product

- the ordering procedure and any endorsements from other satisfied customers

- the total cost to be paid and any other payment options that might be available.

A proposal can be a key element of a negotiation, although sometimes a customer requests a proposal as a polite way of telling a salesperson that he or she has not secured an order.

## Referring to supervisor

Sales staff should understand the limits to their job and know when they should refer matters to their supervisor. These limits will normally be laid down in company policy and will differ from organisation to organisation. However, the following guidelines are representative for a sales assistant working for a retailer. A supervisor should be consulted about:

- aggressive or troublesome customers

- complaints about products or other matters

- requests for discounts because a product is damaged

- refunds over the value of £25.

## Awareness of buying signals and closing techniques

Certain comments, remarks and questions can reveal that the buyer is beginning to take the product seriously and becoming increasingly interested in making a purchase. These are called **buying signals**. Sales people should be listening for buying signals because they should attempt to close the sale when the buyer indicates a readiness to buy.

Verbal buying signals include:

- 'How can I pay for it?'

- 'Do you accept credit cards?'

- 'Do you have my size in stock?'

Non-verbal buying signals include:

- touching the product, such as stroking the surface of a piece of cabinet furniture appreciatively, or flexing a shoe to judge the leather

- trying the item alongside something else, such as an accessory.

Closing is an attempt to conclude a selling conversation with a sale. A variety of **closing techniques** are available. A direct close is simply to ask for the order – 'Would you like to order one?' An indirect close is to use a question such as 'Would you like the red or blue model?'

Another approach is to summarise the key benefits and ask for the order: 'This car meets your requirements in terms of miles per litre and service charges. Shall we go ahead and order it?'

### Effective sales administration

While the majority of transactions in retailers' premises involve scanning the bar code, taking the money and giving change, some others require important administrative duties. These can include:

- processing an order for the customer if the goods are out of stock

- ordering replacement stock from the warehouse if levels are low

- organising delivery to a customer at the requested time on the right date

- recording the details of a customer complaint and the action taken

- processing a store card application.

### Post-sales follow up

Most organisations rely on repeat business, which means that customers must gain satisfaction from their purchases. Customers can feel anxiety after they have made a significant purchase. Sales staff need to reassure customers they have made the right decision.

Following up a sale can lead to extra sales in a number of ways. A complementary item can be suggested to the buyer. It is good practice to enquire, by telephone or by posting a card, about customer satisfaction after an expensive or complex purchase.

### Dealing with several interactions at once

There are a variety of methods of dealing with several buyers at the same time. This is an important skill in a busy store. Sales staff can:

- ask a colleague or supervisor who is available to assist

- try to conclude the sale quickly using a closing technique

- indicate to the customer what is happening – if leaving a buyer, staff should explain where they are going and how long they expect to be away

- make an appointment to see the customer at a mutually convenient time.

## Product features

Retailers in general do not produce any goods. They add value to the products they buy and subsequently sell to consumers by providing interesting shopping environments and adding product features such as guarantees, delivery and installation services.

*Sales staff can often have other administrative duties besides dealing with sales at the till*

## Product classification by type

At the beginning of this unit, retailers were classified by type, such as multiple retailers or factory shops. Another method is to classify retailers by the type of product they sell. This classification is summarised in the table below, with the role of sales staff explained.

## Price

Price for some retailers is very important. For others such as convenience stores, the main customer benefit is not low prices but convenience in terms of location and hours of trading. Price in retailing has traditionally been determined by adding a profit margin to costs, to ensure a profit.

The recommended method of setting retail prices is to take account of cost, demand and competition in a step-by-step approach.

1 Determine the basic price – this would usually be the cost of buying goods from suppliers, for example Heinz and Gillette. It would also include any relevant consumer features and benefits the retailer is offering.

2 Add the mark-up – mark-up is determined by the general approach to prices as dictated by the requirements of the market. If the need is for a best possible price, then a small mark-up to produce low prices would be offered. If exclusivity, service and status are required, a higher mark-up could be applied, producing higher prices.

3 Many retailers have a target mark-up to be achieved within a department or section, but some variation on individual items is allowed. As long as the overall target is reached, mark-up variations are permitted.

| Classification | Retailer's role | Sales staff role |
|---|---|---|
| FMCG: fast moving consumer goods – toiletries, clothing | Ensure stock always and widely available. | Keep product in stock and shelves well stocked. Not much personal selling involved. |
| Foods: groceries | Provide plenty of product choice on well-stocked shelves. Ensure products are easily obtainable through plenty of stores with long opening hours. | Keep wide variety of product in stock with shelves well stocked. Not much personal selling involved. |
| Fast food/retail catering: sit-down, drive-through and take-away meals | Serve a choice of meals quickly if required. Delivery throughout the day and evening. | Take order from menu, assemble meal and serve quickly. |
| Consumer durables: washing machines, televisions, DVD players | Provide plenty of product choice. Offer guarantees, after-sales and delivery service as well as sales advice. Arrange credit and loans if required. | Ensure consumer buys from the store. Explain product features and benefits, arrange credit if required and organise delivery. Use promotions to close order. |
| Home improvements: construction goods, garden products and decorative materials | Stock locally everything needed for building or garden projects. Arrange delivery as well as provide product and 'how to' advice. | Provide advice concerning products and skills needed to complete home improvements. Help load products, and organise delivery. Replenish stock when store is closed. |

**4** The variations on individual prices can be determined by competitors' prices as well as the pricing tactics being used by the retailer. Retailers look for consistency through **price lining**, odd/even pricing and complementary goods. These terms are explained below.

- **Price lining** – setting up a limited number of selling prices for product range with no other prices allowed. For example a range of ties may have the price points £9.99, £15.99 and £24.99.

- **Odd/even pricing** – it is believed that odd prices such as £2.99 or £49.99 give the impression of low prices. This type of pricing is widely used in retailing. Even pricing, such as £350, is said to give the impression that price does not matter.

- **Complementary goods** – sometimes the sale of one product is directly related to the demand of another. The sale of a regularly priced product can be boosted by a special promotion on another – for example special prices on shirts may well lead to greater demand for ties.

## Promotional offers

Promotional offers can originate from suppliers (such as Nestle) to retailers and from retailers themselves. Sales staff could find themselves dealing with both types of promotion.

Possible promotional offers from suppliers include:

- Price pack promotions – such as '10p off' on packaging.
- Premiums – small gifts attached, for example in cereal packets.
- Sampling – products given away free.
- Coupons – printed on packs or handed out in store, often allowing future discounts.
- Buy one, get one free (BOGOF) – consumers may have to send proof of purchase to claim free product.

Promotional offers devised by the retailer include:

- Loyalty cards – consumers acquire points as they buy goods, which can be used to acquire free goods later.
- Competitions – tend to be linked to a promotional theme.
- Free gifts – for example, retailers offer small electrical appliances as 'free gifts' to consumers buying high price electrical items.

A popular retailer promotional technique is to 'mark down' prices. This helps to sell out-of-date merchandise and creates space for new stock, as well as fostering customer goodwill. **Mark-downs** can be used to:

- sell remnants, slow-moving goods, damaged or shop-soiled products
- increase sales volume by offering lower prices
- sell surplus stock where too much has been bought or unpopular styles, sizes and fabrics have been purchased by the store
- bring prices into line with local competition
- make room for next season with an end-of-season clearance, for example winter goods sold to make way for summer fashions.

## Unique selling points

Unique selling points distinguish a product or a retailer from its rivals. Retailers sell many products from their suppliers which are designed with unique selling points (USPs). Retailers also need USPs to distinguish themselves from their competitors. Competition between retailers is so intense nowadays that they sometimes need a number of USPs to project a distinctive image. These USPs enable sales staff to convince consumers to buy from their store.

### Practice point

Identify some well-known retailers and consider their unique selling points. They must have some, otherwise they would not survive the tough competition they face every day!

| Retailer | Unique selling points |
|---|---|
| Toys R Us | Great product choice, plenty of car parking and helpful staff |
| Asda | Every Day Low Prices (EDLP), excellent locations, large car parks and helpful staff |
| Evans | Clothes for larger women (size 16+), High Street locations |
| Argos | Low prices, easy order process, quick service |
| Vision Express | Prescription glasses available that very day |
| Ikea | Innovative and stylish design coupled with low prices |

## Quality and reliability

Many sales people emphasise the quality of their product during the selling process. However quality seems to have a number of meanings and it is not always clear which meaning they are referring to during the selling process. Quality can mean one or more of the following for goods.

● **Performance** – what the product can do. A power drill with a variable speed of up to 3,000 rpm might be perceived as high quality because it has the ability to tackle any job. Sales staff need to explain the benefits of such features.

● **Durability** – the expected life of a product. Some consumers are prepared to pay more for a product that is likely to have a long useful life. Sales staff should offer advice on this topic.

● **Reliability and maintenance** – many consumers are concerned that a product could beak down or fail and that repairs could be costly and inconvenient. Retailers use guarantees and customer care support to reassure consumers about these aspects of the product.

It is worth noting that the quality of services is judged differently. A service should be reliable, responsive to needs of the customers, and undertaken competently while empathising with the consumer.

## Brand identity and status

A brand can be a name, a symbol or a design used to identify a specific retailer and make it appear different from its competitors.

A major development of retail marketing in recent years has been the development of the retailer's name as a brand, rather than simply a name over the shop. A situation has developed where the names of major retailers are better known to consumers than any but the biggest producer brand names. An important part of this change has been the evolution and growth of

| Characteristics of quality in services | Comments |
|---|---|
| Reliability | Staff should deliver the expected service as promised. Retailers should deliver the service 'right first time'. For example, processing a charge card application needs to be done properly. |
| Responsiveness | For sales staff, responsiveness means helping customers promptly and keeping promises – for example, sending out a leaflet when requested. |
| Competence | Sales staff should be able to identify customer needs and offer appropriate products. They should be able to use good product and company knowledge effectively. |
| Empathy | Consumers should be dealt with as individuals. This involves recognising regular customers, anticipating their needs and being attentive during any conversations. |

retailers' own-brand products. It is noticeable that some of the most successful companies have a strong commitment to their own brands.

The advantages of own brands for retailers are summarised below.

| Store image/customer loyalty | Competitive edge/extra turnover | Higher profit/better margins |
|---|---|---|
| Good value enhances store image | Own-brand products can be sold at lower prices | Margins tend to be 5–10% larger |
| Good value builds loyalty to the store | The offer can be different from and better than competitors | They can help break down a producer's hold over certain markets |
| Own brand may be perceived as equal to or better than producer brands | There is more control of product specification and quality | Increased store traffic leads to other purchases and higher profits |
| It is widely assumed that own brands are made by leading producers | More price variety is offered to the consumer | Sales can be promoted by placing own brands next to major brands |
| Own brands carry the retailer's name into the consumer's home | Own-brand products cannot be obtained elsewhere | The retailer's bargaining power increases as it becomes easier to switch suppliers |

## Reputation

If customers are uncertain about the quality of competing products and stores, they may fall back on their perceptions of the retailer. They may have bought from the store on another occasion and been happy with the experience.

Brand building in retailing means the development of the store's reputation. This is perhaps especially important in retailing because it is difficult for retailers to maintain an advantage based purely on the combination of products they sell. Retailers realise that quality in the marketplace is a matter of perception more than anything else.

## Related products in joint demand

Related selling involves inviting customers to purchase complementary items. There are four reasons to believe that related selling is in the interest of consumers.

- It offers enhancement of the primary purchase: suggesting a shirt to go with a new suit, or a tie to go with a new shirt, is an important service for the customer.

- It is convenient: if a consumer is buying a suite of furniture he or she may well want cushions, occasional tables and lamps to match. It is a great deal easier to buy from the same store than walk around other stores.

- It helps with maintenance: when a consumer has decided on a purchase, the motivation should be to protect and maintain the product. Any investment that helps maintain the appearance or extend the life of the product is likely to be welcomed by the consumer.

- It offers cost savings: consumers can be offered a second product at a discounted price. Some retailers remind sales staff about related products in joint demand by printing on the sales docket slogans such as 'sell second item'.

## Design

The design of a product can determine much of the content of sales staff's conversations with consumers. Design has a number of dimensions that are relevant to consumers. The skill of the salesperson is to identify the ones of most concern to the consumer.

| Design and the consumer | Implications for sales staff |
|---|---|
| Superior features | The product has some features that make it better than others on the market. Sales staff can emphasise these; for example an insurance policy that includes breakdown recovery in Europe at a small additional cost. |
| Excellent performance | The product is better than competitors' in key aspects. Sales staff can point this out, for example saying that their savings account pays a high rate of interest. |
| Reliability | The product keeps on working day after day, for example a watch. |
| Service levels | Service levels are beyond expectations. Sales staff can delight consumers with the level of service. |

## Packaging

A retailer must stock the correct packaging options. It is not simply a question of stocking the product, but of providing the appropriate shelf and store space for the various packaging options within a range. Malteser chocolates, for example, are sold in the following packs.

It can be seen from the Malteser example that retailers have a huge variety of pack shapes and sizes to display effectively. In some instances retailers will decide not to stock an item because it is difficult to display or stack.

| Type of packaging | Store location and reason for purchase |
|---|---|
| Regular bag | 37gms: lowest cost, pocket money option for a young child – generally displayed on the lowest shelf |
| Big bag | 60gms: low cost option for an older child – still displayed on lowest shelf |
| Easy open and re-closable bag | 175gms: adult purchase – placed at eye level in store |
| Fun size assortment | 280gms: contains numerous small packs to treat the family – also placed at eye level |
| Regular bag – multi pack | 4 × 37gms bags: normally displayed just below eye level in supermarkets |
| Small box | 146gms: positioned on top shelf |
| Large box | 312gms: positioned next to small box on top shelf |

### Thinking point

Recently, Corus announced it had developed a square can for packaging products such as baked beans and soup. Research this and find the advantages it suggested the design had over current packaging formats.

## Delivery

A delivery service is an important way of adding value to the product and for retailers to differentiate themselves from competition. The provision of a delivery service is essential for certain types of merchandise such as furniture or large electrical durables such as washing machines. For others, it can provide a competitive advantage and enhance the retail offering by providing convenience. Some fast-food operators, such as Domino Pizza, have chosen to offer a delivery service as one way of setting themselves apart from the competition.

## Clarity of instructions/assembly

A growing number of products require consumers to assemble the product (such as flat-packed furniture) or to complete some form of installation before use (such as computers). Sales staff need to ascertain whether customers require a fitting service or installation service.

These services are generally not provided free of charge. Sometimes they are a profit opportunity for the retailer or an associated company. Sales staff need to be able to recognise customers who might need to take advantage of the service.

## Competitor awareness

Not only do sales staff need product knowledge to compare the different products available in-store, but they also need to be fully aware of the products sold by competitors and the service support offered by them. The information sales staff should collect to raise their awareness of the competition includes:

- ranges
- product options available
- prices
- service provision
- other points, such as store charge card, opening hours and parking facilities.

## After-sales service

Sales staff are intimately involved in after-sales service. Most retailers recognise that customer service does not end when the customer leaves the store.

Customers can have a variety of after-purchase requirements. By responding to after-sales needs, retailers encourage further purchases and foster long-term customer relations.

Each retailer must decide which aspects of after-sales service are important to customers. Sales staff should be aware of what is available and use such support to secure sales. Examples include:

- fitting service for kitchens, bathrooms and bedrooms

- technical help line for products such as computers
- alteration service for products such as suits and bridal wear
- installation service for washing machines and computers
- removal service for products being replaced, such as cookers and refrigerators
- repair and servicing facility for products such as bikes and cars
- stock of commonly requested spare parts
- extended warranty or guarantee option for household appliances.

## Availability of spare parts

Some products need complementary items or spare parts, sometimes called consumables, such as bags for vacuum cleaners and print cartridges for printers. Sales staff need to reassure consumers that they are available within the store or from a credible alternative supplier. Sometimes the availability of spare parts will be one method a retailer can use to gain a competitive advantage.

### Changing specifications

In some retail sectors, sales staff have to keep up to date with rapidly changing technology. An example is the advances mobile phone technology has experienced in recent years.

# Legal awareness

Retailers must be aware of the legal obligations they have to their customers.

### Weights and Measures Act 1985

The Weights and Measures Act 1985 makes it an offence to give short weight, or inadequate quantity, or a wrong indication of amount. Pre-packed foodstuffs, whether in packets, bottles or tins, must be marked with the weight or quantity, otherwise an offence is committed.

### Sale of Goods Acts 1979, 1995

The Sale of Goods Act 1979 has been amended three times. It covers the fundamental requirements that goods must be:

- as described – this means that goods must conform to their description ('waterproof' indicates that the item does not leak, for example)
- of satisfactory quality – taking into account the price paid, the description and the age of the item
- fit for the purpose for which they are intended – a lawn mower must properly cut the grass, for example
- fit for any specific purpose that the seller has made clear to the buyer at the time of the sale. Therefore if the sales staff confirm to a buyer that a lawn mower can cut grass on a slope, it should perform to that standard.

A buyer of unsatisfactory goods is entitled to a refund within a reasonable time after purchase from the seller (not the manufacturer).

### Supply of Goods and Services Act 1982

Service standards are covered by this Act, for example buying the services of an electrician or of a garage to service a car. Buyers are protected against poor workmanship, delay and exorbitant charges. The Act states that all services should be carried out:

- for a reasonable charge
- within a reasonable time
- with reasonable care and skill
- using satisfactory materials.

### Food Labelling Regulations 1984

It is an offence to falsely describe food on labels. Ingredients must be listed in order of weight, and the name and address of the packer or labeller must be added. If a food retailer is accused of contravening the regulations it can plead 'due diligence' in defence – this means it can show that it has observed all reasonable precautions to safeguard products and customers.

### Consumer Protection Act 1987

This Act relates to price and safety. Under the Act it is an offence:

- to mislead consumers as to the price of goods, services, accommodation or facilities (such as by missing out the VAT when quoting the price)
- to mislead consumers over special offer prices and claim exaggerated price reductions
- to supply goods that are not safe.

The Consumer Protection Act is enforced by Trading Standards officers. It is also an offence not to co-operate with Trading Standards officers during any investigation.

# Sales incentives

Staff whose jobs involve selling goods are often given incentives to reward them for achieving good sales figures.

### Commission payments

Commission payments are amounts paid to staff in direct proportion to the amount of sales they achieve. Usually these payments are in addition to a basic salary. The commission-only method replaces salary completely, and offers retailers a highly cost-effective way of paying sales staff, since all payment is directly related to sales achieved. The method does, however, have some weaknesses.

It has a reputation for attracting lower-achieving sales staff who stay with a retailer for only a short period.

It is difficult to convince commission-only sales staff that they should do any task other than selling.

The pressure to sell at all costs may damage customer relationships. Selling inappropriate products to consumers because they generate the most pay for sales staff is a recipe for disaster.

The commission-only method does allow sales staff to earn unlimited income, although most retailers find that when a certain income level is reached the extra reward is found not to be worth the extra effort.

Most retailers prefer the approach where a fixed salary is paid and it is supplemented by commission payments. Income is not solely dependent on commission, and management gains more control over the sales staff, while sales costs will still vary with the level of sales achieved.

## Piece rates

**Piece rate** schemes pay sales staff according to the amount of work they complete. Sales staff could be paid piece rates on the following basis:

the number of customers agreeing to have a quotation, for example for a new kitchen

store card applications

customers taking out an extra guarantee or warranty

the number of new savings accounts opened.

## Incentive schemes

Incentives other than money can be used to motivate sales staff, such as winning holidays, tickets for a high-profile event, or gifts for all the family. Sales staff often enjoy the friendly competition that can be created by such schemes. It should always be remembered that non-financial incentives (such as paying for training) can also be very effective.

### Outcome activity 33.3

**Pass**

Identify and describe effective skills of personal selling in Toys R Us and the Car Phone Warehouse.

A good way to present the information may be in table format. The following points may be relevant – meeting/greeting buyers, identifying product needs, delivering persuasive presentations, using appropriate technical language, handing objections effectively, negotiating skilfully, spotting buying signals and employing effective closing techniques.

**Merit**

Analyse the relevance of personal sales skills in Toys R Us and the Car Phone Warehouse to their effective operation.

You might like to think about the view that greeting consumers effectively is important in the Car Phone Warehouse because to practise selling skills you have to engage the consumer in a worthwhile conversation. In Toys R Us the greeting may still be important, but only as an opportunity to take the consumer's money and wrap the product.

**Distinction**

Evaluate the extent to which personal sales skills may be transferred between Toys R Us and the Car Phone Warehouse.

Make a judgement as to whether selling skills used in Toys R Us could be effectively transferred to the Car Phone Warehouse. You could compile a table listing selling skills in Toys R Us at different stages in the selling process, and comment on whether they could be used in the Car Phone Warehouse. Do a similar analysis for the Car Phone Warehouse, and comment on whether you think the skills are genuinely transferable between the two organisations.

# The role of stock control as retail sales support

## Key procedures

Good stock control is vital to the effectiveness of any retail operation. If too much stock is held, money is tied up unnecessarily, but customers expect items to be available when needed.

### Re-ordering stock

It is useful for retail sales staff to have an awareness of the re-ordering procedure for a number of reasons.

- They can advise consumers whether further supplies are on order and when they are expected to arrive in store.

- They can check whether any buffer stock is in the stockroom waiting to be stacked on the store shelves.

- They will know if another stock order is likely to be placed shortly because the level of stock held is approaching the re-order levels.

Records of sales made and orders received give a picture of current stock availability. Stock will be divided into the individual items of the range according to size, style, and colour. This information is used for placing orders for replenishment stock. The 're-order level' is the stock level that generates a new order for the supplier.

The minimum stock level is known as the **buffer stock**. The store will want to keep a certain minimum level of stock for contingency reasons.

Retailers like to re-order in economic quantities. The **economic order quantity** (EOQ) calculates the optimum stock order level, given the delivery costs compared with the cost of holding stock. If the cost of delivery is high and stock-holding costs are low, the EOQ will be high. If the cost of delivery is low but the cost of holding stock is high, the EOQ will be a low number.

### Updating stock records

Unless retailers have an accurate knowledge of what they have in stock, stock management becomes very difficult. Updating stock records when deliveries arrive or when goods are returned to a supplier is very important. Current stock levels will match what is in the store only if deliveries have been recorded correctly, returns to suppliers noted properly and sales to customers accurately recorded.

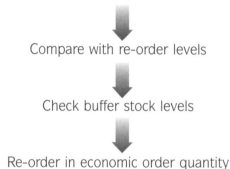

Record current stock levels

↓

Compare with re-order levels

↓

Check buffer stock levels

↓

Re-order in economic order quantity

↓

Update stock records for deliveries and returns

### Stock-takes

It is rarely possible to gain sufficient information on stocks without physical observation. Consequently, on a regular basis retailers count and value every item of stock in their stores, stockrooms and warehouses. Physical stocktaking is done for a number of purposes:

- finding out how long some products have been in stock and identifying fast and slow-moving lines

- finding out about stock losses and exactly what is in store – there is nothing worse than telling a consumer on the telephone that an item is in stock only to discover when he or she comes to collect the goods that the data held on the stock control system is inaccurate

- calculating the value of stock held.

Stock-taking has the added benefit of familiarising staff with the merchandise.

A stock check is a simplified or less comprehensive form of stock-taking that has as its object an assessment of the quantity of stock available for sale.

When the total amount of stock found during stock-taking is less than the records indicate, there is a stock shortage that needs to be reconciled.

| Reasons for shortages | Why they occur |
|---|---|
| Theft | Shoplifting by customers, pilfering by employees and sweet-hearting – employees selling products at reduced price to friends |
| Breakage | Accidental breakages or damage |
| Over-issue | Goods that are weighed or measured, and small articles that have to be counted, are subject to stock loss through carelessness |
| Under-supply | Faulty checking when goods are received – a smaller quantity is accepted than is paid for |
| Clerical error | Incorrectly counting at stock-taking, inaccurate recording, credits and returns not entered properly and simple calculation errors |

*New stock should be placed at the back so that the oldest stock is used first*

### Costs of stock-holding and stock-outs

Because the cost of holding stock is high, there is a strong motivation to reduce stock-holding as far as possible. Stock-holding costs can be estimated with reasonable accuracy.

The cost of running out of stock, on the other hand, is more difficult to determine. Research suggests that a typical retailer loses about 4% of sales through not having items on the shelves. **Out-of-stock situations** (OSSs) seem to occur because the retailer underestimates demand, does not order replacement stock soon enough, or has not managed to move it from the stockroom to the store shelf.

Worryingly for retailers, research suggests that 39% of consumers subsequently buy the out-of-stock product elsewhere. It is also important to remember that out-of-stock situations are likely to adversely affect the consumer's opinion of the retailer.

### Stock rotation

Wherever possible a retailer will organise **stock rotation** so it uses its oldest stock first. This principle is called first-in-first-out (FIFO). This helps to ensure that stock does not deteriorate, go past its sell-by date or become obsolete. Supermarkets, for example, should always put new stock at the back of the shelf to encourage shoppers to take the oldest stock first.

### Dealing with slow-moving goods

Ideally, a retailer should concentrate its efforts on those products that sell quickly at a good profit and remove the slow sellers from the range entirely. But in practice, every store will have some slow-selling lines.

Methods of dealing with slow-moving stock include the following:

- minimise the amount of stock held and delete it from the range
- mark down to a price that generates demand
- put out in a bargain bin near the store entrance or perhaps just outside the store

- offer it at a discount as a 'second purchase'
- consider redistribution though the store network
- incentivise the sales staff to sell the product.

## Stock-control equipment

New technology helps to improve the information available to retailers so they can improve their stock-control methods. Developments in technology mean that:

- the exact location of stock can be identified – sometimes even stock in transit from suppliers
- retailers know instantly how many of an item they have in stock, including different styles, sizes and colours
- goods can be re-ordered automatically when they are required
- the data available for management decision-making is accurate and up to date.

### In-store computers and universal product coding

The use of hand-held in-store computers and **universal product coding**, generally referred to as bar codes, is changing methods quickly.

## Warehouse/stockroom organisation

Many retail sales people are involved in handling and storing goods in the stockroom. Poor practices can lead to damaged and shop-soiled stock being stored, and also stock that is out of date. This would involve sales staff spending time returning goods to suppliers rather than serving consumers in the store.

### Location systems

The need for stockroom space varies from one retail trade to another, and between various methods of retailing. A stockroom should be used as efficiently and as infrequently as possible. The important factors determining stockroom organisation are:

- use of space – wall areas should be used to the maximum, and full use of floor-to-ceiling height should be attempted
- accessibility – all stock should be as accessible as possible, and the faster-selling items should be nearest to the sales area
- grouping – lines should be stacked so that they follow the same pattern and layout as the store

---

### Case study    The future is smart

Radio Frequency Identification (RFID) systems are made up of readers and 'smart tags' – tiny microchips with an attached antenna. The tags can be stuck on anything. When prompted by a reader – such as a hand-held in-store computer – the tag gives the information on the chip. Unlike the traditional bar code, which smart tags aim to replace, RFID chips give every tagged object a unique identification. A bar code describes only a class of product, such as cans of Tango.

Retailers expect to use RFID to track products on planes, lorries and ships through ports and warehouses, on to shop shelves, through tills and into homes and offices. Accurate tracking should eventually save millions of pounds as it improves distribution, reduces theft, cuts labour costs and reduces stock levels.

Marks and Spencer has started a trial in which tags are applied to suits, shirts and ties. The advantage of such item-level tagging is that it allows retailers to monitor stock levels with far more accuracy, and to order replacement goods at the end of each day to make sure that every size, style and colour remains in stock. Retailers hope that smart tags could help to drive sales. Imagine a customer taking a tagged suit to a kiosk, which then suggests a matching shirt and tie!

1 How might a retailer's stock control systems be improved using this technology?
2 What might be the benefits to sales staff of RFID tagging?
3 Can you suggest how this technology could be used to increase a retailer's sales?

● identification – as far as possible, lines should be kept in outer packs or cases, each properly marked with the contents.

### Training and skills

A wide variety of materials-handling equipment is in use in warehouses and distribution centres. However, the most common pieces of equipment are forklift trucks and pallets. Forklift trucks are used to transfer goods into and out of trailers, to transfer goods around the warehouse and to stack them at a variety of heights. Forklift-truck operators have to be well trained.

Pallets are an essential part of efficient materials handling as they provide a firm base on which to place individual items. Loaded pallets require materials handling equipment to move them safely, and this is one of the reasons why they are largely being replaced by roll cages. Roll cages are tall, metal, mesh-sided containers on wheels. They have made it possible to take a selection of products from the trailer to the sales area with minimal handling. Roll cages can be unloaded from the trailer in a matter of minutes, reducing the need for a stockroom, and there is no need to have trained forklift-truck staff.

### Storage conditions

The physical conditions in which items are stored have implications for the safety and security of stock.

## Security and theft

Security is an important issue for all retailers. Recently the Centre for Retail Research published the results of a survey of 'European Retail Theft', which revealed that average shrinkage (stock loss from crime or wastage) was equivalent to 1.42% of turnover. The study also revealed that nearly 30% of the shrinkage was attributable to employees.

In order to minimise theft by customers, the following measures can be taken:

● use secure glass display cabinets for expensive goods

● employ store detectives

● site expensive merchandise at the back of the store

● tag goods so that an alarm sounds if the tag passes through a photoelectric curtain at the exit, and chain expensive clothing such as leather coats

● install CCTV cameras and security alarms

● have a specific changing-room policy limiting and logging the number of items per customer.

To minimise theft by staff, it is advisable to:

● enforce a clear procedure for genuine staff purchases and storage of purchased items

● arrange for checkout operators to log on with their staff code when they start to use a cash

| Storage issues | Considerations |
|---|---|
| Storage on pallets | Must stack sensibly on a standard pallet – nothing can overhang. |
| Stacking products | If products are to be stacked on top of each other then outer packaging must not collapse when stacked. |
| Handling considerations | If a product has to be moved manually, it must be easy for a person to lift and move. Packaging must be able to withstand being moved on conveyors and chutes. |
| Packaging | Warehouse space is expensive, so products should be packed in boxes of appropriate size – not small products in large boxes. |
| Temperature | Chilled products need special warehouses. Sainsbury's have temperature-controlled warehouses. Consumer durables must be stored so they are not subjected to dampness or adverse weather conditions. |

register, and log off when they hand over to another operator

- ensure that all refunds are authorised by a supervisor and that 'cash backs' are signed or initialled by the customer

- use 'smart cards' to access stockrooms and install anti-tail-gating devices that re-lock the door immediately after opening to prevent unauthorised people entering the area.

Measures retail outlets have introduced to minimise break-ins and damage include:

- security alarms and CCTV operating 24 hours a day

- illuminated shop fronts and car parks, with metal grilles over the windows

- concrete blocks, concrete flower tubs or metal bollards in front of the store

- security lights inside the shop

- checking all rooms carefully at the end of the day to make sure no one is concealed on the premises.

If sales people disregard security and safety measures this can reduce the profit of the retailer while throwing suspicion on themselves unnecessarily.

## Stock distribution facilities and arrangements

A retailer may have an enticing store environment, well-trained staff and a distinctive brand reputation, but if the products are not available on the shelf when the consumer is shopping this will all count for nothing. Many retailers invest heavily to improve the methods used to obtain products from suppliers and have them on store shelves before any out-of-stock situations occur.

### *Delivery and associated logistics*

A modern distribution centre needs proximity to major transport routes, space for manoeuvring large vehicles and appropriate loading/unloading facilities. Such centres cannot be built without government approval and the support of the local community.

Sainsbury's Hams Hall **automated fulfilment factory** near Birmingham has all these characteristics.

---

**Case study** **Hams Hall**

Hams Hall is Sainsbury's 700,000-square-foot fulfilment factory. It can handle more than two million cases of products a week. The facility, situated at the centre of the motorway system in the West Midlands, has special unloading areas for fresh produce, slow-moving goods arriving from other Sainsbury's warehouses, bulky grocery goods and cans and bottles.

The site has space for manoeuvring Sainsbury's large vehicles, although one of the benefits of the fulfilment factory is that better organisation will mean the company needs 150 fewer vehicles at depots and on the road. The facility and its associated technology achieves fewer and more accurate deliveries to each store; stores will now receive all the products they need in one delivery. Previously, chilled products and standard produce were delivered separately.

Hams Hall is one centre in a distribution system that will see the number of Sainsbury's depots reduced from 21 to nine regional, two national and two frozen-food facilities, all located near major transport routes. Already two national centres have been opened near the M6 in Stoke-on-Trent and on the M25 at Rye Park, Essex, along with a regional centre at Waltham Point, also next to the M25 in North London.

**1** Why is it important that sales staff understand how stock is ordered and delivered to individual stores?
**2** What would be the impact for sales staff in store if Hams Hall was not working efficiently?
**3** Automated re-stocking procedures are replacing sales staff who re-order stock. Is this something sales staff and the consumer should welcome?

## Use of sub-contractors

**Third party logistics** (3PL) companies are enjoying rapid growth as retailers concentrate on their main business and leave distribution and warehousing functions to specialist firms.

Contracted-out distribution now accounts for about one-third of all distribution in the UK. The responsibility of finding a warehouse, agreeing a lease, setting it up and installing systems becomes the responsibility of the sub-contractor. The retailer obtains instant access to a national or international network of distribution centres. Additionally, 3PL systems allow retailers to obtain instant information about where and how much stock is in the distribution chain.

## Local authority planning restrictions

Local authority development plans weigh the importance of industrial and commercial development against that of maintaining and improving the environment. Government planning guidelines make special reference to modern distribution facilities:

'Some types of modern distribution facility have a low density of employment and are served by a very large number of lorries. Retail distributors depend on efficient distribution systems and require locations capable of serving regional, national and European markets. Sites for such developments are best located away from urban areas to minimise congestion. The sites should also be capable of access by rail and water transport.'

Organisations such as the North West Development Agency seek to find sites for freight terminals that can supply regional and national distribution centres and support the government's transport strategy. They use grants from government to make compulsory land purchases, reclaim land and market the sites. However, local communities do not always welcome such initiatives.

## Local objections

Large distribution centres can bring objections from local residents who fear traffic disruption, noise and environmental damage.

### Thinking point

A £260-million rail-freight terminal is planned at the former Parkside Colliery site, and promoted by the North West Development Agency. The public exhibition of the proposals was viewed by more than 1,000 visitors, and the proposed freight interchange would create 7,000 new jobs. Representatives from the developers answered questions from visitors. Local people, however, were nervous about how the development might impact on their property and the environment in which they live. People were concerned about traffic, the visual impact of the development and noise caused by the railway.

1 What would be your reaction if Asda decided to build a regional distribution centre behind your home?

2 How can the distribution needs of retailers be reconciled with local people's concerns?

## On-line logistics support

Many organisations improve their distribution through the use of satellite truck-tracking technology.

Organisations no longer need to call their drivers to find out their location. Managers can view the positions of all their vehicles, together with their speed and direction of travel, and even text drivers from the controlling computer. They can also design better routes by comparing alternative routes, using postcode route-planning tools, and identifying and eliminating the causes of delay.

## Outcome activity 33.4

### Pass
Explain the importance of an awareness of stock-control procedures for a retail salesperson in a Toys R Us outlet.

Consider why it is important that staff understand the re-ordering of stock. Comment on the benefits of undertaking stock takes, rotating stock and reconciling stock records with actual stock levels. Key terms that might appear in your answer include stock outs, cost of stock-holding and slow-moving goods.

Think about why it is important that sales people know the importance of storing goods properly in the stockroom, and how to use handling and storage equipment.

Finally, discuss the benefits of staff understanding the procedures that stores follow to improve security and identify theft.

### Merit
Analyse the implications for Toys R Us of poor stock-control management.

Discuss the implications in detail – key terms that might appear in your answer include stock-outs, slow-moving products, cost of holding stock, damaged products, shop-soiled and old products, management data, and consumer information.

### Distinction
Evaluate the importance for personal sales effectiveness of specific training in stock-control management.

Make a judgement about how important training in stock control is for personal sales effectiveness. Think about the benefits training in stock-control management might provide to someone required to undertake personal selling. Benefits might include the ability to identify for consumers whether new stock is on order, when it might arrive in store or even whether further supplies are already in the warehouse.

Training in stock-control management may also mean that sales people do not have to deal with damaged goods, out-of-date products and out-of-stock situations.

## Key terms

**Automated fulfilment factory**
a large retailer distribution centre, usually sited close to motorways

**Buffer stock**
the minimum stock a retailer decides to hold

**Buying club**
a club offering members plenty of product choice at low prices; in return, members commit to buying a certain number of products annually

**Buying signals**
comments or actions that suggest the consumer is interested in buying the product

**Closing techniques**
methods used to conclude a selling conversation with a sale

**Concessions**
shops within shops

**Distress purchase**
a purchase that a consumer is obliged to make, such as a television licence

**Economic order quantity (EOQ)**
the most economic size for a replacement stock order that a retailer would place

## Key terms

**External variables**
developments outside a business, over which it has no control, but to which it needs to respond

**Honeypot locations**
places that attract a lot of people and tend to become crowded at peak times

**Local structure plans**
plans showing how business is expected to develop in an area over a 10-year period

**Logistics**
in retailing, the process of distributing products from suppliers to the store shelf

**Mark-downs**
prices reduced by retailers on individual products, perhaps to sell out-of-date merchandise or create space for new products

**Niche outlets**
stores that sell specialist products, which perhaps have a limited consumer appeal, such as collectable toys

**Out-of-stock situations (OSSs)**
cases where consumers cannot find the product they want in store because stock has run out (also known as stock-outs)

**Piece rate**
a system of paying sales staff based on the amount of work they complete, for example the number of store card applications they obtain

**Planogram**
a diagram showing how products should be arranged on the store shelves and display fixtures

**Price lining**
the method of using a limited number of selling prices for a product range, such as £9.99, £15.99 and £24.99

**Pyramid selling**
a system where people buy goods from a parent company and resell them to distributors in a network; this process occurs several times before the final user is reached, so that goods pass through a distribution network that looks very much like a pyramid

**Segmentation**
dividing a market into groups that share the same characteristics; different segments require different retail experiences

**Sensory merchandising**
retailing methods that aim to make products more attractive to consumers by appealing to their five senses

**Shopping villages**
groups of retail outlets offering consumers permanent discounts on a wide range of top brands and designer labels

**Stock rotation**
arranging stock to ensure the oldest stock is sold first

**Third party logistics (3PL)**
the system whereby outside companies undertake the distribution of goods to stores for retailers

**Universal product coding**
the technical name for the bar code used by almost all retailers nowadays to record sales electronically, update stock records and generate replacement stock orders

# *End-of-unit test*

1 Describe the benefits to consumers of out-of-town shopping centres.

2 What is the difference between a shopping village and a factory shop?

3 Explain the term 'pyramid selling'.

4 What are the five steps of a sales area risk assessment?

5 Describe a 'no-frills' retail sales environment.

6 How are weekend shopping patterns changing?

7 What do consumers often do after they have used the Internet for window shopping?

8 Describe and explain the various store formats used by Tesco.

9 How could the potential weekly sales of a new supermarket be calculated?

10 List some external variables that could have an impact on the demand experienced by retailers.

11 Describe two buying motives that retail sales staff may encounter.

12 Explain two ways of handling buyers' objections.

13 Why might selling related products to consumers be in their best interests?

14 When might a retailer mark down goods?

15 What are the fundamental requirements of goods as detailed by the Sale of Goods Acts 1979 and 1995?

16 Describe the benefits of stock rotation for a retailer.

17 How could a retail store deal with slow-moving goods?

18 List some features you would associate with an effectively organised stockroom.

19 Explain the term 'out-of-stock situation' or OSS.

20 How can satellite truck tracking technology improve a retailer's distribution service?

# Resources

## Texts

Cox and Brittain: *Retail Management*, Prentice Hall, 2000

Fernie, J et al: *Principles of Retailing*, Heinemann, 2003

Gilbert, D: *Retail Marketing Management*, Prentice Hall, 1999

Omar, O: *Retail Marketing*, Prentice Hall, 1999

## Websites

*www.mcarthurglen.com* A shopping village information site

*www.dckconcessions.com* A concession commonly found in Debenhams

*www.gltc.co.uk* Great Little Trading Company – selling to parents of young children through catalogues and the Internet

*www.abercrombie.com* Abercrombie and Fitch, US retailer

*www.boots.com* Boots, the high street retailer

*www.tesco.com* Tesco, possibly the UK's most successful retailer

*www.asda.co.uk* Asda, part of the world's biggest retailer group Wal-Mart

*www.jadeshop.co.uk* Designers and installers of store interiors

*http://hams-hall.co.uk* Hams Hall site, offering virtual tours around potential regional distribution centres

# Glossary

**Acceptance**  A positive act by a person accepting an offer to create a contract

**Acceptance by specified means**  An acceptance of an offer in a particular way, as demanded in the offer

**Affiliate**  In Internet terms, a business that provides a link on its website to another site in return for a payment from any resulting sales

**Aims**  Long-term business goals

**Anti-competitive practices**  Tactics used by firms that attempt to remove or prevent competition in order to strengthen their market position

**Assets**  Items of value held by an organisation including money owed to the firm (debtors)

**Authentication**  Methods by which parties to a transaction can prove who they are

**Authority**  Power given to bodies by Parliament through the law; or to individuals either by virtue of job position, expertise, qualifications or ability

**Automated fulfilment factory**  A large retailer distribution centre, usually sited close to motorways

**Balance sheet**  An overview of a company's financial position on a particular date, showing its total assets and liabilities

**Banner advertisement**  Typically a rectangular graphic, often animated, at the top of a Web page, designed to promote a brand or a business service

**Bias**  The difference between the answer obtained from respondents and the truth

**Breach of contract**  Where a person fails to fulfil his or her side of the contract

**Broadband**  A fast method of transferring data across the Internet

**Buffer stock**  The minimum stock a retailer decides to hold

**Buy-side**  Transactions in which a business makes purchases

**Buying club**  A club offering members plenty of product choice at low prices; in return, members commit to buying a certain number of products annually

**Buying signals**  Comments or actions that suggest the consumer is interested in buying the product

**B2B**  Business to business – transactions between organisations

**B2C**  Business to consumer – transactions between businesses and individual consumers

**Capacity**  The ability of a person to enter into legal relationships

**Capital**  Money put into the business by the owner(s) to get it started or to buy equipment

**Capital-intensive**  Making more use of technology and machinery than humans during production

**Capitalism**  The economic system based on private enterprise

**Cartels**  Informal agreements between companies not to engage in price competition and to ensure that price rises are always done together so that all the firms in the market make extra profits

**CATI**  Computer-Assisted Telephone Interviewing, where interviewers key answers directly into the computer. Answers automatically route respondents to the next appropriate question

**CATS** Completely Automated Telephone Surveys, where interactive voice technology is used to ask questions, with participants using touch-tone telephones to respond

**Channel conflict** Where an Internet method of direct selling threatens existing business partnerships

**Civil litigation** The collective name for court action when civil law matters need to be resolved

**Clicks and mortar** A business combining an on-line and an off-line presence

**Click-through** Where a website visitor clicks on a banner that takes them through to another Web page

**Closing stock** The value of stocks of finished products held in the business at the end of the year

**Closing techniques** Methods used to conclude a selling conversation with a sale

**Commercial espionage** One firm spying on another

**Company reports and accounts** Documents produced annually by each public company giving details of its financial position and a summary of the past year's trading

**Competitor pricing** Monitoring closely the prices charged by competitors and reacting immediately when they change by matching them

**Complements** Products that we have to buy together, such as DVDs and DVD players – one is no good without the other and the demand for one affects the demand for the other

**Concessions** Shops within shops

**Conglomerate** A firm that operates in a wide variety of markets, many of which are totally unrelated to each other, such as Virgin Group

**Consideration** The value given to the promises on a contract

**Contract** An agreement that the law will enforce

**Corporate culture** The way people usually behave within a particular business; the formal or informal set of rules that influence employees' behaviour

**Corporate manslaughter** The offence of a corporation causing death

**Corporation tax** Tax on business profits

**Counter-offer** A new offer that will cancel out an earlier offer

**Creative accounting** Organising and presenting company accounts in a way that might benefit the company concerned, but relies on unethical or dishonest accounting practices

**Creditors** The total of sums owed to suppliers who have offered the company credit

**Cross elasticity of demand** Measurement of how a change in price for one product can change demand for an alternative or complementary product

**Current assets** Money that is readily available in the company for paying debts

**Current liabilities** Amounts that are owed to suppliers or lenders that are due to be repaid fairly shortly (normally within one year)

**Data controllers** The persons responsible in a business for looking after data

**Debenture** A method for a company to borrow money; a bond that pays a fixed rate of interest and is usually secured on the assets of the company

**Debtors** The total of all monies owed to the company

**Defamation** Damaging a person's good reputation by use of untrue comment

**Deferred shares** Similar to ordinary shares except that dividends are only paid in certain circumstances, such as at a certain level of profit; they appear in the 'Capital and reserves' or 'Financed by' section of the balance sheet

**Deforestation** Clearance of large areas of rainforest to allow other forms of development

**Demand curve** A graph that illustrates the relationship between the price of a product and the demand for it

**Depreciation** The loss in value of the assets of the firm over time, due mainly to wear and tear

**Determinants of demand** Factors other than price that influence levels of demand

**Determinants of supply** Factors other than the price of the product that influence levels of supply

**Discrimination** Treating an individual or group differently based on race, nationality, sex, age or religion

**Disintermediation** Removing intermediaries and cutting out the middle man

**Distress purchase** A purchase that a consumer is obliged to make, such as a television licence

**Diversification** Producing a wider range and variety of goods or services

**Dividend** A share of company profits received by shareholders every six months or annually; they appear in the appropriations section of the profit and loss account

**Domain name** A Web address

**Drawings** Money taken from the business by the owner or a partner for his or her own use

**Duopoly** A market where there are only two suppliers of a particular good or service

**Dynamic pricing** Updating prices in real time according to market conditions

**E-business** Where all exchanges between business processes and with external business stakeholders and partners are digitally (electronically) based

**Economic order quantity (EOQ)** The most economic size for a replacement stock order that a retailer would place

**Economies of scale** The advantages of producing on a large scale; significant cost savings can be made by increasing the volume of products produced

**Empowerment** Giving responsibility and decision-making powers to employees

**Equilibrium point** The point on a demand and supply diagram where the levels of demand and supply are equal

**Equilibrium price** The price at which the market will settle if we allow demand and supply to freely dictate the market; this is also known as the market clearing price

**Equilibrium quantity** The quantity of production at which the market will settle if we allow demand and supply to freely dictate the market

**Equity** Fairness in the law

**Ethics** Questions to do with right and wrong

**European Union** The political and economic union of 25 nation states that is subject to governance from Brussels and Strasbourg

**Exemption clause** A term in a contract that attempts to limit the liability of a party who is in breach of the agreement

**Exit interviews** Interviews that take place when employees leave a business, to find out why individuals are leaving and whether improvements can be made

**External data** Secondary research information that is available outside the organisation, such as government statistics

**External variables** Developments outside a business, over which it has no control, but to which it needs to respond

**First instance courts** Courts that hear cases for the first time

**Fixed assets** Capital items of value that the firm has bought and will use for an extended period of time, such as buildings, machinery, equipment and vehicles

**Fixed capital** Money or value contributed by the owner(s) of a business; often used to buy fixed assets for the business

**Fixed-term contract** A contract that is set for a specific amount of time

**Flexible working practices** The ability to make work fit in with an employee's needs, e.g. flexi-time when employees can choose starting and finishing times as long as they work the agreed number of hours in a week (or over a longer period)

**Gearing** How much borrowing the business has in comparison to the amount of capital invested by the owners

**GIF** Graphics Interchange Format, used for images

**Glass ceiling** A concealed limit to the amount of advancement an individual can achieve because of racial, age or sex discrimination

**Gross profit** The profit figure at the end of the trading account; the difference between a company's total revenue and how much it cost to make the product or buy products in – not including the general expenses of the firm

**Harassment** Unwanted behaviour towards a person based on his or her race, nationality, sex, religion or some other factor

**Home and work life balance** Making sure that work and home lives have equal status so that employees can, for example, control the number of hours they work and work doesn't have a negative effect on their families

**Honeypot locations** Places that attract a lot of people and tend to become crowded at peak times

**Hyperlink** The means by which a visitor can move from one Web page to another by clicking on a link, usually underlined on the page

**Income elasticity of demand** Measurement of how demand changes in response to changes in consumer incomes

**Inequality** Unfair treatment; treating an employee differently because of age, race or gender

**Inertia selling** Sending out goods to people who have not asked for them (unsolicited goods) in the hope of gaining payment for them

**Infomediary** A business that captures consumer information, profiles it and sells it on to third parties

**Intention to create legal relations** The necessary intention to form an enforceable contract

**Interim dividends** Dividends that are paid part way through a company's financial year before final profits are calculated

**Intermediary** In Internet terms, an on-line site bringing together buyers and sellers

**Internal data** Secondary research information held inside the organisation, such as sales records and customer complaint reports

**Internet** The physical network of computer networks across the globe

**Job enlargement** Giving employees additional tasks at the same level

**Job enrichment** Redesigning employees' jobs to give them more challenging tasks to do and/or increased responsibility

**Job security** The feeling that your job is safe

**Job share** An arrangement where two or more employees share the hours of one full-time job

**Just-in-time (JIT)**  A stock control system where an order is generated for new supplies when stocks are about to run out and is timed so that the new stock arrives just as supplies run out

**Labour**  The physical and mental effort given by employees

**Labour-intensive**  Needing a lot of labour as part of business production, as opposed to technology or machinery

**Liabilities**  Monies that the firm owes

**Liquid assets/liquidity**  Monies immediately available to a company for business use

**Litigation**  Legal action – referring a matter to a court of law

**Lobbying**  Asking questions of and making demands from politicians

**Local structure plans**  Plans showing how business is expected to develop in an area over a 10-year period

**Logistics**  In retailing, the process of distributing products from suppliers to the store shelf

**Long-term liabilities**  Sums that have to be paid for in more than one year's time, such as a mortgage on company property or a long-term bank loan

**Mark-downs**  Prices reduced by retailers on individual products, perhaps to sell out-of-date merchandise or create space for new products

**Market clearing price**  The price at which the market will settle if we allow demand and supply to freely dictate the market; this is also known as the equilibrium price

**Marketing mix**  The combination of product, price, place (sometimes called distribution), promotion and packaging offered by an organisation to potential customers

**Marketing research**  The collection and evaluation of data in order to assist organisations to better understand their consumers, competitors and market

**Mass customisation**  The capacity offered by Internet technology to create individually tailored on-line products or marketing messages

**Maternity leave and pay**  The time off and money paid to a female employee when she has a baby

**Minors**  Persons aged under 18 – they normally cannot form contracts

**Monopoly**  A market where there is only one supplier of a particular good or service

**Monopsony**  A market where there are only a small number of buyers

**Multinational**  A company with operational activities in several nations, often world-wide

**Multi-tasking**  Doing more than one task at the same time

**Niche outlets**  Stores that sell specialist products, which perhaps have a limited consumer appeal, such as collectable toys

**Non-probability sampling**  Using a subjective procedure to select participants, such as people who are considered typical consumers

**Objectives**  Short to medium-term, measurable business targets (such as to achieve 2.5% growth next year)

**Offer**  A statement of the terms on which a person or business is willing to be contractually bound

**Oligopoly**  A market where there are only a small number of suppliers of a particular good or service

**On-line value proposition (OVP)**  Something of value offered by a specific on-line service that makes it distinct from other offerings

**Opening stock** The value of stocks of finished products held in the business at the start of the year

**Opportunity cost** The cost to the business of investing money in one area of a business rather than elsewhere

**Ordinary shares** The most common form of share ownership – holders become part owners of the company and may vote at general meetings of the firm; ordinary shares appear in the 'Capital and reserves' or 'Financed by' section of the balance sheet

**Organisational culture** The collective attitudes within a business, led by management, that determine the way the organisation works

**Out-of-stock situations (OSSs)** Cases where consumers cannot find the product they want in store because stock has run out (also known as stock-outs)

**Outsourcing** The arrangement whereby a business pays another to do work for it that has previously been performed by employees

**Ozone depletion** The thinning of the Earth's protective ozone layer

**Paternity leave and pay** The time off work and pay given to a male employee when his partner has had a baby

**Pay scales** The list of different salary levels that an employee can receive in a workplace

**Penetration pricing** A launch strategy that involves setting a very low initial price to establish market share; the price is increased later to maximise profits

**Perfectly competitive market** An ideal market that is fair to both producers and customers

**Personalisation** Where Web page content is made personal to the individual user

**Piece rate** A system of paying sales staff based on the amount of work they complete, for example the number of store card applications they obtain

**Planogram** A diagram showing how products should be arranged on the store shelves and display fixtures

**Portal** A gateway website to other Web services

**Postal rules** The rules of acceptance whereby an offer is deemed to be accepted as soon as the acceptance is placed in the post box

**Power** The capacity to cause someone, or a group, to take actions they would not otherwise have done

**Preference shares** Shares that offer the holder a fixed percentage dividend; they appear in the 'Capital and reserves' or 'Financed by' section of the balance sheet

**Pressure group** An organised body existing to put pressure on government or business to follow certain courses of action

**Price elasticity of demand** A measurement of how responsive customers are to changes in price; where a change in price leads to a big change in the number of customers buying the product, it is said to be price elastic, and where a change in price leads to a small change in the number of customers buying the product, it is said to be price inelastic

**Price lining** The method of using a limited number of selling prices for a product range, such as £9.99, £15.99 and £24.99

**Primary research** Research carried out to find new information required for a marketing research project, which has never previously been collected

**Private sector** That part of an economy that is privately owned and controlled, usually profit-seeking businesses

**Probability sampling** The systematic selection of participants, for example every tenth person in the telephone directory

**Product differentiation** A marketing activity that encourages customers to believe that one product is different from and better than that of a competitor

**Product liability** The liability of a manufacturer for any faulty product that could cause harm

**Productivity** The output of either individual workers or whole groups of workers; how efficiently a company uses its factors of production to produce products/services and profit

**Promisee** A person who receives a promise

**Promisor** A person who makes an offer

**Proposed dividends** Dividends paid by the company at the end of the financial year, after profits have been calculated

**Prosumer** A pro-active consumer – the tendency is for on-line customers to be closely involved in specifying their requirements

**Purchases** For a manufacturing company, the value of raw materials purchased; for a service business, the cost of items bought to sell to customers or used to provide a service to customers

**Purchase returns** Money paid back to the company by a supplier when it returns items, for whatever reason

**Pyramid selling** A system where people buy goods from a parent company and resell them to distributors in a network; this process occurs several times before the final user is reached, so that goods pass through a distribution network that looks very much like a pyramid

**Qualitative research** Research that provides information of a qualitative nature, such as why people buy, what motivates them to buy or their impressions of, for example, products and advertisements

**Quantitative research** Research that produces numbers and figures, such as the number and percentage of consumers who are aware of a brand

**Ratio analysis** Mathematical tools used to judge the financial condition and performance of a company

**Research brief** Written by the organisation that has an information need, to show the objectives of the research, possible research methods, a timetable and reporting requirements

**Research proposal** Written by the organisation that will conduct the research, to respond to the research brief, and include research methods to be used, costs and reporting details

**Reserves** Profit that is not distributed to shareholders but is put on one side and may be used for replacement of capital assets in the future

**Respondent** A person who is asked and agrees to participate in a marketing research project

**Response rate** The number of people who participated in a research project compared with the total number of people approached

**Restrictive practices** Tactics used by large influential firms to strengthen their hold over the markets in which they operate, to increase their market share, to eradicate competition, to restrict consumer choice and therefore allow the firm to charge high prices

**Retained profit** Profits that have not been distributed to the shareholders but are saved to finance future expansion of the business; they appear in the appropriations section of the profit and loss account

**Sales (or turnover)** The total amount of money received in sales for the year

**Sales returns** Money paid back to customers when they return items, for whatever reason

**Search engine**  Specialised websites used to search out key words from indexes of registered Web pages

**Secondary research**  Research that makes use of work already carried out by someone else for some other marketing research project or other purpose

**Segmentation**  Dividing a market into groups that share the same characteristics; different segments require different retail experiences

**Sell-side**  Transactions between a supplier and a consumer

**Sensory merchandising**  Retailing methods that aim to make products more attractive to consumers by appealing to their five senses

**Sequencing**  The careful ordering of questions to reduce the impact of bias as well as putting questions into a logical order to encourage completion

**Shareholders**  People who have a financial share in the value of a business and are therefore often entitled to a share of the profits

**Shopping villages**  Groups of retail outlets offering consumers permanent discounts on a wide range of top brands and designer labels

**Site stickiness**  The factor that determines how long visitors stay on a website

**Skimming pricing**  A launch strategy that involves setting a very high initial price to maximise profits in the short term; the price is dropped later to attract further custom from different market segments

**Skip questions**  Technique to ensure respondents only have to answer the questions relevant to them by asking them to skip certain questions on the basis of previous answers

**Solvency**  How easily a firm can pay its debts

**Spam**  E-mail messages that are not wanted

**Staff turnover**  The measurement of how many staff are leaving an organisation, expressed as a percentage of the average size of the workforce

**Stakeholders**  Groups or individuals with any kind of vested interest in what an organisation does

**Standard form contracts**  Pre-written contracts used by individual companies

**Stock**  The total value of raw materials that will be made into goods for sale, partly manufactured items, and also items that have been completely made or bought in by the firm and are available for sale to customers

**Stock control**  Ensuring that there is always enough stock to meet demand from customers but never too much, as that ties up money that could be used for other purposes in the business

**Stock rotation**  Arranging stock to ensure the oldest stock is sold first

**Subjectivity**  The feature of qualitative data analysis that means the research findings and conclusions are only the opinions that the researchers formed from the research

**Supply curve**  A graph that illustrates the relationship between the price of a product and the supply for it

**Sustainability**  The general question of whether the Earth's natural resources can continue to keep up with economic development

**Targeting**  Aiming a marketing message at a specific segment of a market

**Tax avoidance**  Lawfully taking steps to avoid taxation by, for example, moving a firm's location

**Tax evasion**  Illegally taking measures to avoid taxation, such as deception and false accounting

**Teleworking**  Working from home using computer and/or telephone technology for communication

**Third party logistics (3PL)** The system whereby outside companies undertake the distribution of goods to stores for retailers

**Track system** The three types of track or court that civil cases are allocated to: the small claims track, the fast track and the multi-track

**Trade union** A group of workers who join together to negotiate pay and working conditions, for example the National Union of Teachers

**Trading account** The first of the set of final accounts, showing how profitably the firm makes goods or processes them for sale to customers; it calculates the gross profit earned

**Transaction** An exchange between two parties, such as exchanging a product for cash

**Trial balance** The act of totalling all the debit balances and all the credit balances to confirm that total debits equal total credits

**Unfair dismissal** When an employee is dismissed from an organisation because of race, gender, religion or other unfair reason

**Unique selling point (USP)** Something unique about a product or service that makes it stand out from the competition

**United Nations** New York-based body representing the collective views of world nations

**Universal product coding** The technical name for the bar code used by almost all retailers nowadays to record sales electronically, update stock records and generate replacement stock orders

**Values** Things a person or organisation holds to be important

**Vertical restraints** Pressures placed on retailers by large suppliers to stock limited ranges or sell at specific prices

**Viral marketing** Rapid transfer of marketing messages to potential customers via e-mail

**Voidable term** A valid term of a contract but one that can be declared void at the request of the parties

**Whistleblowers** Workers who disclose unsafe practices to their employers or the authorities

**Working capital** Money needed for the day-to-day running of the business, calculated by current assets minus current liabilities

**Working capital cycle** The movement of cash within the business from when it is paid out to buy raw materials to the time it comes back in when goods are sold

**Working time directive** An EU instruction to introduce a maximum 48-hour working week and rules for rest breaks

**World Wide Web** The worldwide body of software designed to operate across the Internet that enables access to and communication of data

# Index

acceptance 203, 204, 235
  by specified means 205, 235
acid test ratio 36, 40
ACORN market segmentation 293–4
affiliates 109, 122, 131
after-sales service 309
agreements, and contracts 209–10
aims 169, 199
Amazon 111, 115–16
anti-competitive practices 259, 273
appraisal system 158–9
appropriation accounts 9–11
arbitration 212
asset turnover 33, 39
assets 14, 24, 41
authentication 119, 129, 131
authority 174, 199
automated fulfilment factories 316, 318

B&Q Direct 105, 111
b2b (business to business) marketing 112–13,
  115, 131
  buy-side 100
  Internet marketing 95
  relationship marketing 113–14
  reverse auctions 104
b2c (business to consumer) marketing 112–13,
  115, 131
  comparison shopping 118–19
  Internet marketing 95
  sell-side 100
balance sheets 14–15, 41
banner advertisements 106, 131
bar charts 82, 84
benchmarking 160–1
bias 75, 86, 90
Body Shop 171–2
brand identity 306–7
brand names, e-marketing 110
breach of contract 213–14, 235
broadband Internet connection 99, 131
buffer stock 312, 318
business to business marketing *see* b2b marketing
business to consumer marketing *see* b2c
  marketing
businesses, profiling 123
buy-side 100, 131

buying clubs 283, 318
buying signals 302–3

capacity 207–9, 235
capital 3, 21–7, 41
capital-intensive businesses 136, 164
capitalism 177, 199
cartels 260–1, 262, 273
channel conflict 126, 131
child labour 178–9
Citizens Advice Bureaux 251
civil litigation 211–12, 235
  alternatives to 211–13
click-throughs 106, 131
clicks and mortar 105, 131, 189
closing stock 4, 41
closing techniques 303, 318
commercial espionage 196, 199
communities
  corporate culture and 142–3
  and ethics 191–2
  as stakeholders 176, 264–5
comparison shopping 118–19
competition
  long-term 257–8
  markets 253–4
Competition Act 1998 262
Competition Commission 262
competitor pricing 254, 273
competitors, as stakeholders 263, 265
complements 243, 273
completely automated telephone interviews
  (CATS) 63, 90
computer-assisted telephone interviewing (CATI)
  63, 90
computers, misuse of 234–5
concessions 281, 318
conciliation 212–13
conglomerates 258, 274
consideration 203, 206–7, 235
Consumer Protection Act 1987 219–20, 310
consumers
  defective goods 219–20
  exemption clauses 217–18, 236
  protection 215–17
  shopping patterns 291–2
Consumers' Association 250